INSIDE THE ENIGMA

Inside the Enigma

British Officials in Russia, 1900–1939

Michael Hughes

THE HAMBLEDON PRESS
LONDON AND RIO GRANDE

Published by The Hambledon Press, 1997

102 Gloucester Avenue, London NW1 8HX (UK)
PO Box 162, Rio Grande, Ohio 45674 (USA)

ISBN 1 85285 160 0

A description of this book is available from
the British Library and from the Library of Congress

Typeset by Carnegie Publishing, 18 Maynard St, Preston

Printed on acid-free paper and bound in
Great Britain by Cambridge University Press

Contents

For My Parents
Anne and John Hughes

Preface

A few days before the final draft of this book was completed, the Russian government announced it had obtained evidence that nine British diplomats were involved in activities incompatible with their official status; four of them were eventually instructed to leave the country. Whether or not the luckless officials in question really had been spying will probably never be known. In any case, the role of the diplomat – the 'honest spy' – has always been an ambiguous one. When relations between two governments are good, foreign representatives are usually able to go about their work confident that their hosts will not look askance at their activities. When relations are bad, even the most innocent contact or activity can easily be construed as evidence of hostility. During the past century, relations between Britain and Russia have seldom been harmonious. At the same time, the destinies of the two countries have been bound together in the roller-coaster of international politics. Successive British and Russian governments have therefore always been eager to obtain as much information about each other as possible – while at the same time seeking to ensure that they do not give away sensitive material that could prove harmful to national security. The game has not, though, been a symmetrical one. Russian governments, in both their Soviet and Tsarist guises, have always been far more secretive than their British counterparts. For this reason, the job of British officials posted to Russia has invariably been a difficult one.

This book does *not* pretend to provide a history of Anglo-Russian relations. It focuses instead on the way that British diplomats, consular officials and military men posted to Russia between 1900 and 1939 reported on the economic and political changes which transformed the country in the course of just two generations. As my research progressed, it became clear that examining the way in which officials carried out their 'reporting role' also required some study of their personalities and beliefs. The men who represented Britain in Russia during these years were not simply impersonal 'cameras', recording a changing panorama for their superiors back in London. Their own opinions and experiences shaped the way they went about their work. It is for this reason that I have not confined my research to the official records, voluminous and illuminating though these are. The publication of much of the Foreign Office's 'Confidential Print' on Russia a few years ago has provided the historian with ready access to information that was once only to be found buried in files at the Public Record Office in London and a few other specialist collections. However, while such documents provide useful insights into the attitudes of generations of British representatives posted to Russia, they do not have much to say about the way in which their authors actually went about the task of keeping London informed of the huge changes taking place around them. Nor do the official records give much insight into the character and outlook of the men writing the reports. It is for this reason that I have chosen to make considerable use of private papers and other materials that help to provide the colour missing from official dispatches and telegrams.

Anyone who has worked with the primary sources on British foreign policy will know something about the scale of the problems involved, particularly when dealing with a topic like the one addressed here. Many of the relevant Embassy and Consulate archives were destroyed during the two World Wars. The surviving records (not to mention the published records) do not always show the precise authorship of official documents, which naturally makes it hard to discuss with precision the attitudes and views of particular individuals. Although Ambassadors (or, in their absence, the Chargé d'Affaires) signed written dispatches, they were in some cases just summarising or approving reports presented to them by their junior officials. The same was true of telegrams sent to London, which were recorded under the name of the permanent or acting Head of Mission. As a result, a signed document could reflect the views of more than one person. The difficulties are not, though, insurmountable. The British Embassy in Russia was, before 1939, a very small institution. All Ambassadors took a detailed interest in the process of political reporting. The more important political dispatches and telegrams sent back to London were usually 'all their own work', in the sense that they either drafted them or read and amended drafts submitted by their staff. Even the least 'interventionist' Ambassador, Lord Chilston, who served in Moscow from 1933–38, diligently reviewed the correspondence sent to London over his name. In addition, thousands of signed reports and memoranda written by officials other than the

Ambassador were sent to the Foreign Office. These provide the historian with valuable insights into the views of more junior officials. The existence of early drafts of documents, along with a host of private correspondence, also helps to illuminate the views of particular individuals, giving a useful clue as to who authored a particular document. Although there is certainly a danger of conflating the opinions of the Ambassador with those of 'the Embassy', a sensitive handling of the documents can overcome the worst of the problems. There was, in any case, usually a high level of agreement among British diplomats in Russia about the nature and significance of the upheavals that transformed the country during the first few decades of the twentieth century (a situation that was certainly not always true at other foreign Missions). The most significant divisions occurred between diplomats and consular officials or, more frequently, between civilian officials and the military men who flocked to Russia during the years of war and revolution.

A further problem which inevitably arises in any discussion of Russia during the first two decades of the century concerns the problem of dates, since the Russian calendar did not correspond with its western counterpart until 1918. The dates in the text are given in the western calendar. As a result, the collapse of the Tsarist regime is described as taking place in March and the Bolshevik revolution as occurring in November. Although this may seem a little strange to readers who are used to thinking in terms of the February and October Revolutions, the use of the western calendar reflects the practice at the British Embassy and Consulates, where most officials dated their reports according to the conventions of their own country rather than the one in which they lived.

What follows, then, is a chronicle of Russian history as seen through the eyes of British representatives based in the country over forty years. I have tried, whenever possible, to illustrate the strengths and weaknesses of these reports by highlighting cases in which they were particularly acute or (much less frequently) horribly wide of the mark. I have naturally chosen to concentrate as far as possible on the great and enduring questions that concern any student of Russian history: the causes of the disintegration of the Tsarist regime; the 'inevitability' of the Russian Revolutions of 1917; the desperate attempts by Lenin and the early Bolshevik leaders to stay in power in the face of overwhelming odds; the reasons for the horrors that ripped Soviet society apart during the 1930s. Examining the past through the prism of diplomatic reports does not necessarily provide much new substantial knowledge, but it can provide fresh perspectives that sometime escape the historian bound down by the weight of hindsight. The reports filed by British officials sometimes fell into the trap of missing the wood for the trees. At the same time, though, they remind later generations that nothing was inevitable in the sad course of Russian history – even if the weight of culture and tradition always meant that certain outcomes were more likely than others.

I have incurred numerous debts while carrying out the research for this book, which has taken place in the spare moments left during a hectic period of teaching and administration. My first thanks are due to the large number of libraries and archives which have supplied me with material: the British Library (Manuscripts Reading Room); the British Library (Oriental and Indian Collections); the British Library of Political and Economic Science (London School of Economics); the Brotherton Library (Leeds University); the Cambridge University Library; the Churchill Archives Centre (Cambridge University); the Guildford Muniment Room; the House of Lords Library; the Imperial War Museum (Department of Documents); the Leeds Russian Archive (Leeds University); the London Library; the Public Record Office (Kew); and the Royal Archives (Windsor Castle). No individual can be an expert on all the vast number of subjects covered in this book. Since I am by background a student of Russian history rather than a student of British diplomacy, I have had to rely a good deal on other people for advice. The late Sir Fitzroy Maclean was kind enough to share with me his memories of his time in Russia, while Lady Mary Keswick provided me with fascinating details about the life of her father (Sir Francis Lindley). Mr Peter Bosanquet allowed me to look at the letters which his father sent home from Russia during the early years of the century. Richard Davies has been most helpful in providing me with material from the Leeds Russian Archive. Dr Anthony Glees was instrumental in stimulating my interest in diplomatic history, while Professor Dominic Lieven of the London School of Economics has given valuable advice about many aspects of my research. My sister Dr Kathryn Hughes has been generous enough to discuss at length the problems involved in writing any kind of history – even one so far removed from her own area of interest. Martin Sheppard of the Hambledon Press provided advice and support throughout the project, as well as invaluable help with editing the final manuscript. My colleagues and students in the Department of Government at Brunel University also deserve thanks for putting up with the bad temper of an increasingly overworked Senior Tutor during the final stages of this project. I owe a particular debt to those who have given me permission to use material of which they are the copyright holders, or who were kind enough to go through family papers in order to see if there was any material there of value for my research. I would also like to thank the editors of *Diplomacy and Statecraft*, the *European History Quarterly* and the *Journal of Contemporary History* for allowing me to use material that I have previously published in these journals. Material in the Royal Archives is reproduced by the gracious permission of Her Majesty Queen Elizabeth II. Crown copyright material in the Public Record Office is reproduced by permission of the Controller of Her Majesty's Stationery Office.

My greatest debt is to my parents. The three years that I have spent writing this book have been happy ones. Too many of the preceding ones were not. This manuscript would never have seen the light without their support during that time. It is dedicated to them with love and affection.

London   Michael Hughes

1

Diplomats and Russia

The role of professional diplomats posted abroad by their governments has remained curiously stable over the past few centuries, despite the enormous economic and political changes that have taken place across the globe[1].[1] Although the organisation and relative power of the various national diplomatic corps have varied from time to time and country to country, authors of modern diplomatic manuals are still happy to refer their readers for inspiration and advice to the works of seventeenth-century writers like Samuel von Pufendorf and François de Callières. The belief that effective diplomacy rests on the possession of a set of personal qualities rather than formal technical knowledge has been a hallmark of the European diplomatic mind since at least 1648, and it endures despite the technological and political revolutions that have taken place in the twentieth century.[2] The diplomatic 'art' practised by an envoy at the Court of Louis XIV is, on this interpretation, not so very different from the one practised today by a delegate at the United Nations in New York. In both cases, an effective diplomat requires the intelligence and presence, the shrewdness and *nous*, to advance his own government's interests while at the same time making sure that he avoids so antagonising the representatives of other countries that agreement of any kind proves impossible. Only those who possess these elusive human qualities can hope to succeed in the intricate world of professional diplomacy, which has changed so greatly, and yet stayed so much the same, during the past 300 years.

Many writers have since the seventeenth century attempted to define the qualities that make a good diplomat. De Callières believed that the ideal foreign representative should be 'quick, resourceful, a good listener, courteous and agreeable'.[3] The German Ambassador in London before the First World War, Prince Lichnowsky, stressed the importance of 'tact, social culture, a natural instinct for men and things'.[4] More recently, the diplomatic *littérateur* Harold Nicolson suggested that a first-rate diplomat needed to display the qualities of 'truth, accuracy, calm, patience, good temper, modesty and loyalty'.[5] Although some twentieth-century politicians and writers have looked askance at the 'diplomatic mystique', fearing that an emphasis on intangible human qualities can too easily be used to justify keeping the diplomatic corps as the preserve of a small privileged elite, even the most cynical of observers has generally acknowledged that questions of personal character play an important role in diplomatic life. Despite the fact that the management of international relations has been transformed since 1918, as politicians have come to play an increasingly high-profile role in conducting foreign policy, the occasional 'frenzies' of summit diplomacy are merely the tip of a much larger diplomatic iceberg.[6] While many important treaties have, since the time of the Versailles Treaty in 1919, been negotiated face to face between political leaders, days and weeks of detailed discussion among their officials are almost always necessary before any major international agreement can be reached. There is therefore still, as there has been for centuries, a widespread agreement among students of diplomacy that the art of negotiation is the most important part of the diplomatic craft – which in turn requires an ability to combine tenacity and determination with a readiness to understand the interests and concerns of others. However, although there is no doubt that the effective conduct of international negotiations demands its own particular skills, it is by no means the only task that has traditionally been performed by diplomats. The most effective foreign representative has always been the one with the greatest insight into the attitudes and mores of the people he lives among. Ever since diplomats were, in the words of Sir Henry Wotton, first 'sent to lie abroad for the good of the state', monitoring the political and economic affairs of their hosts has been among the most important tasks performed by the resident envoy. Indeed, during the early years of the Renaissance, when the states of western Europe began to exchange permanent representatives with one another on a regular basis, the collection of sensitive political information was often considered to be the single most important function of the diplomat.[7] In the centuries that followed, right down to the present day, the reports sent home by Missions abroad have played an important role in influencing the way that governments around the world conduct their relations with one another. The collection of 'political intelligence' about the domestic affairs of other countries – a concept which in its widest form covers everything from the intricacies of high politics through to mundane details about the state of the harvest – has helped governments both to understand each other's motives and to make informed judgements about their relative strength and power. It is these reports, or at least a small fraction of them, which form the subject of this book.

Russia has always occupied a distinctive place in the British imagination, providing a particular challenge for officials sent there to represent their government and keep it informed about the country's turbulent social and political life. When Winston Churchill famously observed that the country was a 'riddle wrapped in a mystery inside an enigma', he was simply giving voice to a sentiment that had been expressed by his compatriots over many centuries. For 300 years after the explorer Richard Chancellor arrived at the Court of Ivan the Terrible in 1553, following the wreck of his ship in an ill-fated expedition to find the fabled North-East Passage to India, British diplomats and other official representatives were one of the most important sources of information about Russia. Their letters and reports played a significant role in shaping the image of Russia in the minds of their fellow countrymen. Until the middle of the nineteenth century, few Britons travelled to Russia, while the number of Russians appearing in the towns and cities of western Europe only rose to a significant level in the 1830s and 1840s. Although the great 'westernising' reforms of Peter the Great in the early eighteenth century were intended to overcome the economic and cultural backwardness of the country, it was still seen by most Europeans in the decades that followed as an alien and barbaric land. Russia's rise to Great Power status in the eighteenth and nineteenth centuries might have given the country a more significant presence than before in the European political consciousness, but the sentiment remained strong in the west of the continent that the Tsarist Empire was politically and culturally quite distinct from its neighbours. Although the conservative rulers of the Prussian and Austrian Empires were keen to ally themselves with a regime that was an unashamed bulwark of traditionalism in a changing world, they would have been shocked by the idea that there was any fundamental affinity between their own lands and those of their semi-oriental neighbour to the east. In more liberal countries like Britain, the Russian Empire was viewed by the politically literate public with even greater distaste, as a spiritual home for the kind of repressive authoritarian rule that had disappeared from their own country at least 200 years before.

A diplomatic posting to Russia in the centuries that followed Chancellor's journey to Moscow was never easy, setting a pattern that has continued down to the present day. Foreign visitors were seldom made welcome unless, like the carpenters and shipwrights who travelled to the new city of St Petersburg in the early eighteenth century, they had skills and talents that could be used by the Tsarist regime to enhance the country's economic and technical prowess. The seventeenth-century writer Samuel Purchas noted correctly that 'Such is the disposition of the Russes that they will not indure to have the secrets of their state bee made known'.[8] English Ambassadors sent to the country by Tudor and Stuart monarchs were only too well aware of this painful truth. One Ambassador who visited Muscovy in the late sixteenth century wrote indignantly that members of his party were 'beaten in with clots and such things as lay in the streets' when they dared to appear in public.[9] Another diplomat sent to the country a few decades later bitterly complained that he, like many other foreign representatives, was kept waiting for weeks outside Moscow in filthy roadside hovels whose owners 'seem more like beasts than men'. Even Guy de Miège, who represented the Court of Charles II in the 1660s, was forced to temper the admiration he felt for his hosts when he and his colleagues found their 'freedom was so regulated and restrained that for the first days we were shut up close in our House, and not permitted to stir abroad'.[10]

Not surprisingly, few British representatives posted to Russia before the nineteenth century had very much good to say about the country, either in their official dispatches or their published memoirs. Their reports played a significant part in bolstering the general impression back home that Russia was an alien land whose people had nothing in common with their neighbours in western Europe. Antony Jenkinson, who visited the country soon after Chancellor, dismissed the Russians as 'great talkers and liars, flatterers and dissemblers'.[11] Giles Fletcher, sent to Moscow as English Ambassador in 1588, was equally repelled by the coarseness of Russian society, where drunkenness was commonplace and women were regularly beaten in public by their husbands. He was appalled by the despotic system of rule which struck him as 'plaine tyranicall', and condemned the government for preventing the development of 'any learning or litteral kinds of knowledge' in order to ensure that the people remained 'fitter for the servile condition wherein they are now in'.[12] Few of Fletcher's successors were quite so outspoken, but almost all of them endorsed his belief that the Muscovite government was little more than an oriental despotism 'after the Turkish fashion', whose rulers were more interested in increasing their own power and wealth rather than promoting the welfare of their subjects.[13] The Petrine reforms of the early eighteenth century made little impact on this view. Although British representatives in Russia were impressed by the heroic nature of Peter's attempt to drag his country into the modern age, they were sceptical about its likely success. Sir Charles Whitworth, appointed British representative around the time Peter was setting his reforms in motion, did not believe that a single man could 'by the strength of his own genius' overcome centuries of sloth and indolence.[14] One of his successors, who served in Petersburg a decade or so after Peter's death, observed that despite 'the pains which have been taken these last forty years to bring the country out of its ancient state, it is only violence and superior force which prevents it falling back immediately, as it will do one day or other'.[15] Catherine the Great's attempt to sponsor a cultural revolution in the second half of the eighteenth century, by encouraging celebrated foreign artists and writers to come to the country, was treated with similar scepticism by British officials in Petersburg. Sir George Macartney, who served as Envoy Extraordinary in the country during the 1760s, was convinced that the Russian nobility had no real interest in culture or learning, but simply 'devour all that is set before them without selection, and lose their delicacy of taste in enormity of appetite'.[16] James Harris, who served as Ambassador in the 1780s, agreed, writing in one of his early letters home that 'A slight though brilliant varnish' could not conceal 'illiterate and unformed minds'.[17] He was particularly scathing about the Empress herself, whom he believed combined a masculine obstinacy with 'the weaknesses vulgarly attributed to her sex, – love of flattery, and its inseparable companion, vanity; an inattention to unpleasant but salutary advice; a propensity to voluptuousness, which leads her to excesses that would debase a female character in any sphere of life'.[18] While Russia changed greatly in the two and a half centuries after Chancellor first arrived in the country, the reactions of British officials posted there proved to be surprisingly consistent. They were both intrigued and appalled by the backwardness of Russian society and the despotic power of the Tsars over their subjects, features which they believed set the country apart from the mainstream of European civilisation.

Although the relationship between Britain and Russia deteriorated sharply in the course of the eighteenth century, the clash of national interests was seldom serious enough to lead to direct conflict between the two countries.[19] This started to change rapidly in the nineteenth century, when the global struggle for empire created new tensions between London and Petersburg. Russia's borders had since the eighteenth century been advancing towards the Caucasus and Afghanistan, incorporating many of the lands of central Asia, along with exotic towns like Samarkand and Tashkent that had exercised a hold on the

European imagination since the days of the Silk Road many centuries before. At the same time, India was being integrated ever more closely into the British Empire, in which it occupied a place of enormous practical and symbolic importance. The destinies of the two countries were therefore inextricably bound together in a vast arc ranging from the Balkans through to India and beyond. Any move by either country in this sensitive area was immediately pounced on and dissected by the other in a search for secret motives that might have implications for its own security. The hidden drama of the 'Great Game' – the battle between British and Russian agents for power and influence in the mysterious mountainous lands north west of India – was of course a natural child of this struggle for empire.[20] So too were the more open conflicts over the fate of the crumbling Turkish Empire, since the British were reluctant to allow the Russians to expand their power and influence in a region that lay directly between Europe and India. The rise of the Anglo-Russian antagonism had a pronounced impact on public opinion in Britain, or at least on that section of the educated public which followed foreign affairs and sought to influence the behaviour of govern- ments. The development of strong russophobic instincts among the British public was fed by newspapers like the *Morning Post* and *The Times*, which bitterly attacked Russian foreign policy and condemned the repressive behaviour of the Tsarist regime at home.[21] Travel books written by the growing number of private visitors to Russia were usually equally scathing. One typical account condemned Russia as 'the lowest in the scale of those nations that have any claim or pretension to be called civilized',[22] while another published in the 1840s described the Russians as 'a whole people, suffering and debased, without any end in its suffering and abasement, beyond ministering to the morbid appetite for power of a single family'.[23] In the second half of the century, hundreds of books and pamphlets appeared attacking the Tsarist Empire as the main threat to British interests in India, and demanding a more vigilant policy to prevent Russian expansion across Asia.[24] Although publications calling for a more moderate policy were also printed,[25] russophobia developed deeper and deeper roots in British political culture as the nineteenth century progressed. The immediate threat posed by Russia to Britain's imperial interests, when combined with older disquiet about the challenge of oriental despotism, combined to create the fear of the 'Russian bogey' that has been a familiar feature of the British political landscape from the early 1800s through to the present day.

Ironically, while British public and political opinion was growing more russophobic in character, the views of the country's diplomats posted to Petersburg were becoming a little more positive, which in part reflected a growing professional determination to provide detailed and accurate political reports that did not simply echo the crudities of ill-informed national stereotypes. When Sir Edward Disbrowe was posted to Russia in 1825, both he and his family found members of the Royal Family to be extremely approachable and sympathetic, in marked contrast to the seventeenth and eighteenth centuries when foreign representatives were usually treated with disdain and even contempt by members of the Court. Lady Disbrowe suggested that the Petersburg *beau monde* was similar to its counterpart in western Europe, writing in a letter home that 'Society folks are much the same in all countries'.[26] Both Sir Edward and his wife were convinced that the civilised ethos of the wealthy nobility living in the capital was genuine and not, as Macartney had suggested sixty years earlier, simply a thin crust concealing a deep-seated parochial insularity and ignorance. The decision of Tsar Alexander II to launch a series of major reforms in the 1860s, including the emancipation of the serfs in 1861, further encouraged British diplomats to take a more positive view than their predecessors of the Russian state and its rulers. Lord Napier, who served as Ambassador in Petersburg at this time, praised the courage of Alexander II in promoting the cause of emancipation against the instinctive conservatism of the landed gentry, and observed that his action 'had earned the Russian Sovereign the good will of all reasonable friends of progress'.[27] However, the Ambassador was clear-sighted enough to recognise that the decision did not signify a fundamental change in the autocratic character of the Tsarist regime. He bitterly attacked the government's use of force to crush the Polish rebellion in 1863, even though he had little instinctive sympathy with the nationalist aspirations of the Catholic Poles.

Napier also criticised the government's failure to address properly the question of administrative reform, which was vital given the legendary venality and incompetence displayed by the Tsarist bureaucracy. Thomas Michell, a prescient and intelligent consular official who served in Russia for more than twenty five years during the second half of the century, reflected the views of his colleagues when he wrote in 1863 that real political and social reform could never be successful as long as absolute power was maintained in the hands of a single person.[28] In reality, though, no Tsar was willing to accept reforms that might impose limits on a power supposedly given to them by God, a stubbornness that eventually played a considerable part in bringing about the disintegration of Imperial Russia. Following the assassination of Alexander

II by revolutionaries from the Narodnaya Volya organisation in 1881, the murdered Tsar's successors became more committed than ever to defending a traditional interpretation of the autocratic constitution. This lurch towards conservatism at home, when combined with the continued growth of Anglo-Russian tension abroad, led British officials to adopt once again a more jaundiced attitude towards the Tsarist regime. Even those like Sir Frank Lascelles, who arrived in Petersburg in 1894 determined to establish a close rapport with his hosts, soon found that it was difficult to report positively on a government that seemed quite insensitive to the sentiments and concerns of its own people. The rise of the revolutionary movement and the increase in popular discontent, which were both given fresh impetus by rural famine and rapid urbanisation in the 1890s, persuaded officials who worked at the British Embassy that chaos was lurking just beneath the surface of Russian life. By the beginning of the twentieth century, most of them were convinced that the government was facing a political crisis of threatening proportions, particularly since the new Tsar, Nicholas II, showed himself to lack any of the talents and aptitudes required by a man in his position. It was not, though, until the new century was underway that they began to realise that the survival of the regime itself could be in question.

British diplomats and other officials who served in Russia after 1900 faced problems and difficulties that were as great as any encountered by their predecessors. The first four decades of the twentieth century were among the most turbulent in the entire history of Russia. The revolution that took place in the spring of 1917 swept away the Romanov dynasty, which had been a feature of the European landscape for more than 300 years. The seizure of power just eight months later by a small band of revolutionaries, committed to the construction of an entirely new form of human society, signalled the beginning of a dramatic experiment in social engineering which had consequences that resonate down to the present day. Joseph Stalin's subsequent rise to power in the late 1920s, following the defeat of his rivals in the Bolshevik leadership, paved the way for the hideous events of the 1930s, in which millions of ordinary Soviet citizens lost their lives in the *gulag* or as a result of the famine brought about by the dictator's enforced collectivisation of agriculture. In the course of just forty years, Russia was transformed from a backward peasant country into a modern industrial state, ruled over by a government that never tired of claiming it represented the vanguard of a huge wave of social and political change that would soon sweep across the entire globe. Although other countries have followed a similar path in the past fifty years, in few of them have the changes been so abrupt or bloody.

The chapters that follow look at the way in which British officials in Russia struggled to make sense of the changes that took place around them in the years after 1900. Diplomatic historians have not on the whole given enough attention to the role played by staff at Missions abroad in analysing and interpreting the economic and political development of their host countries. These reports, even when not accompanied by specific recommendations about policy, inevitably play a part in shaping the perceptions and actions of those who read them. This was especially true in the case of Russia, in both its Tsarist and Soviet guises, since there were so few alternative sources of information about the country. At the beginning of the twentieth century, newspapers from countries like France and Germany regularly arrived in Britain just a few hours after they first came off the press, while thousands of visitors of one kind or another streamed between London and the continent. Although British Embassies in the capitals of western Europe could use their expertise to provide more authoritative reports than could be culled from newspapers and the accounts of casual travellers alone, there were always significant alternative sources of information available to those responsible for making foreign policy in London. Russian newspapers, by contrast, seldom arrived promptly in Britain either before or after 1917. The number of travellers who visited Russia was very small – and became smaller still after the Revolution – while the proportion of policy-makers who could speak the language was minuscule. Since a knowledge of the domestic context was necessary to understand the foreign policy pursued by *both* Tsarist and Soviet governments, the reports filed by the British Embassy and Consulates were of great importance throughout the years between 1900 and 1939. British representatives posted to Russia were required to cultivate many of the skills characteristic of a first-class political journalist, ranging from a diligent verification of sources through to an imaginative and lucid interpretation of material that was often contradictory and obscure.

This book is mainly concerned with the dispatches filed by professional diplomats, though a certain amount of space also has to be given to the reports of other officials based in Russia after 1900. Members of the accredited diplomatic corps usually only formed a minority of British representatives posted to the country at any one time. They were generally outnumbered by consular staff who, until 1943, belonged to a separate organisation charged with carrying out a miscellaneous set of tasks, ranging from the promotion of trade through to the protection of British travellers.[29] In practice, though, consular officials also submitted reports about important political and economic developments, which were sent back to London where they provided Foreign Office staff with valuable insights into provincial life of a kind that were sometimes lacking in the dispatches sent home by the Ambassador and his colleagues. Nor were consular staff the only set of officials other than professional diplomats who kept the British government informed about affairs in Russia. After 1914, various military men of one kind or another flooded into Russia following the outbreak of war; some of them stayed there until 1921, when they were finally withdrawn following the failure of allied intervention in the Russian Civil War. British army officers posted to Russia during these troubled years were almost invariably bitterly hostile to the revolution set in motion by Lenin and the other Bolshevik leaders, and actively supported policies designed to undermine the new regime. Although civilian representatives were equally appalled by the behaviour of the men who came to power after the November Revolution, they were consistently more sceptical about the wisdom of interfering in the country's domestic agonies. The difference was echoed back in London, where the War Office and Foreign Office frequently came to blows over the whole issue. Although the development of British policy towards Russia during the critical years of war and revolution is beyond the scope of this book, a study of the political battles and bureaucratic fragmentation associated with it could certainly benefit from exploring how these were exacerbated by the conflicting recommendations put forward by civilian officials and army officers based in the country between 1917 and 1921.

Diplomats and their kind have of course seldom received a good public press at any time or in any country. When one of Goethe's characters condemned the typical Ambassador as a 'punctilious fool', devoted only to eradicating the trivial grammatical errors of his juniors, he was expressing sentiments that were already widespread in eighteenth-century Europe. John Bright's celebrated jibe that the British Diplomatic Service was 'neither more nor less than a gigantic system of outdoor relief for the aristocracy' showed that opinion had not become any more favourable by the middle of the following century. In the years after 1900, the chorus of criticism reached a crescendo, as deputies and parliamentarians across the world launched increasingly fierce attacks on the incompetence and privileges of the 'cookie pushers' who inhabited the Foreign Ministries and Embassies of the world. The hideous series of blunders and miscalculations that led to the cataclysm of the First World War brought about the final collapse of Old Diplomacy, as public opinion desperately sought scapegoats to blame for the carnage that ripped apart Europe. Historians have long since acknowledged that many of the attacks launched on the institutions of Old Diplomacy were both inaccurate and unfair. Much of the blame for the outbreak of the First World War should more correctly be placed on the politicians of the combatant nations, who signally failed to manage the tensions that exploded in the summer of 1914. In any case, the privileged world of the salon diplomat, concerned only with 'Court gossip, invitations, and the order of seats at table',[30] was already fading from the scene by the beginning of the twentieth century. However, such images die slowly. They certainly persisted in the years between 1918 and 1939, when professional diplomats once again took much of the blame for allowing Europe to descend into war for a second time in quarter of a century. Indeed, as even the briefest glance at some of the more lurid tabloid headlines will show during times of international tension, popular suspicion of diplomacy and its works continues today. Diplomats around the world remain tempting targets for any journalist or politician seeking to rally public sentiment against the often imaginary worlds of bureaucratic sloth and incompetence.

It is difficult to make a simple judgement about something so complex as the quality of a country's overseas representation. Diplomacy remains an essentially human business, even in a century which has witnessed the dramatic transformation of the global community. The role of professional diplomats posted abroad has always been an extraordinarily complex and multi-faceted one. The skills required for the effective performance of some diplomatic functions, such as the conduct of face to face negotiations, are not necessarily the same as those required for other tasks including the management of the day to day work of an Embassy. However, by concentrating on one aspect of the diplomatic craft – political reporting – and focusing in particular on the reports sent from Russia during the first four decades of the century, it is possible to acquire a new perspective on the ability of the men who represented Britain abroad during a critical period in European history. Britain's representatives in Russia responded remarkably effectively to the challenges they faced during these years, particularly given the difficulties under which they laboured. The Tsarist and Soviet regimes were both obssessively secret and unwilling to allow foreign representatives to collect information about the country. Successive British Ambassadors and their staff therefore had to devote an enormous amount of time and energy to developing new strategies allowing them to provide the Foreign Office in London with accurate and perceptive reports, despite the problems involved in gathering material on sensitive political and economic matters. Their diligence and industry reflected a commitment to the ethic of public service that compared well with their colleagues in other branches of the Civil Service. It is of course no easy matter to compare their reports with 'the historical record', not least because historians can still not agree today about such vexed questions as the origins of the Russian Revolution or the nature of Stalinism. Nevertheless, the dispatches sent to London between 1900 and 1939 stand the test of time surprisingly well. The picture they paint of a country going through the agonies of war and revolution can still provide new insights into some of the most important and dramatic events of the twentieth century.

2

There Will Be a Catastrophe

The British Embassy in Petersburg was housed at the beginning of the twentieth century in an imposing palace overlooking the Troitsky Bridge across the River Neva.[1] The distinctive blood-red building had been built in the 1780s by Catherine the Great, for one of her lovers, and was leased by the British government from the wealthy Saltykov family who continued to occupy part of it as their private residence. As visitors to the building passed through the elaborate entrance porch, they immediately entered a grand red-carpeted hall from which an imposing split marble staircase swept up to an ante-room lined with huge portraits of various British monarchs. On the first floor, fronting the river, was a large ballroom more than forty feet square, from where it was possible to look out across to the golden spire of the Peter and Paul fortress, in which were imprisoned some of the most dangerous enemies of the Tsarist government. Next door to the ballroom were two beautifully furnished drawing rooms where guests would be received by the Ambassador and his wife. Running down the left-hand side of the building stretched a large dining room and an enormous supper room more than eighty feet long, ideal for formal dinners and receptions. The Embassy was widely acknowledged to be one of the finest in the city, and appeared to the casual visitor as a suitable emblem of the power and prestige of the British Empire. And yet, for those who had to live and work in the building, the reality was surprisingly different.

Like most Russian palaces, the building that housed the British Embassy was originally designed to impress guests rather than to ensure the comfort of its inhabitants. Although the formal reception areas were extremely ornate and elaborate, the back portion was 'of wretchedly poor construction'. The Embassy stables were close to the rear entrance to the building and the stench of horses on warm summer days could be overpowering. The sanitation system was so badly designed that a visiting architect who inspected the building for the Foreign Office noted in his report that he was 'not surprised to hear that throats of

a diphtheric tendency are very common in the Establishment'. Another
visitor was so horrified by the atrocious condition of the plumbing that
he could not understand how 'any of the inhabitants of this ... Palazzo
should have survived'. Indeed, so serious were the problems that
throughout the early years of the twentieth century the Foreign Office
was always on the look out for a new building to house its representatives
in Petersburg, though in the event it was decided to avoid the cost of
a move and spend the money instead on improving the existing Embassy. The rotting grandeur of the Embassy building, which was typical
of the large palaces that lined the more fashionable boulevards of
Petersburg, was in its own way curiously reminiscent of the condition
of the Tsarist Empire in the decades before 1917. The imposing façade of the autocratic government similarly concealed a deep-seated
decay, which in time caused the whole edifice to fall apart. However,
the crumbling Embassy was also in a less obvious way a symbol of the
problems confronting the *British* Empire at the beginning of the twentieth century. While Britain's power was in some respects at its height
in 1900, close observers both in London and abroad knew that changes
were taking place across the globe that would soon destroy the effortless
dominance of the Victorian era. Although the difficulties facing the
British Empire were as nothing compared with the ones faced by its
Russian counterpart, they proved in time to be almost equally fatal.

During the first few years of the twentieth century, Britain's relationship with the rest of the world went through a sea-change.[2] In previous
decades, successive governments in London had instinctively promoted
a policy of 'Splendid Isolation', and carefully avoided signing any treaties
or accords that might entangle the country in international conflicts
where its vital interests were not at stake.[3] In 1902, however, the Conservative government led by the elderly Marquess of Salisbury signed a
treaty with Japan in which each side pledged to provide military support
should the other be attacked by its rivals in a conflict in the Far East.[4]
Two years later, the Entente Cordiale was put in place between Britain
and France, following months of intense negotiation between the two
governments. Finally, in 1907, the most dramatic change of all took
place when the Liberal government headed by Sir Henry Campbell-
Bannermann established a Convention with the Russian government,
designed to reduce tension and eliminate the risk of war between the
two countries. Although the retreat from Splendid Isolation was not
quite so swift or abrupt as sometimes imagined, the change in British
foreign policy during the first decade of the twentieth century still
represented a veritable revolution for a country that had traditionally

avoided international entanglements. The fact that both Liberal and Conservative administrations felt impelled to seek closer relations with other countries, often braving significant opposition from their own back-benchers and public opinion in order to do so, reflected a growing concern that Britain was no longer able to rely on its economic power and naval strength to secure its position in the world.

The sense of unease which informed British foreign policy making in the early years of the twentieth century had a number of roots. The defeats in the Boer War graphically illustrated the weakness of Britain's defences and, as Rudyard Kipling noted, provided 'no end of a lesson' for politicians in London who were not accustomed to such indignities.[5] The other major powers all took a frank enjoyment in Britain's discomfort and quickly moved to turn it to their own advantage, highlighting the fact that at times of difficulty the country's international isolation could be distinctly more threatening than splendid. The British government's decision to seek an entente with France was largely driven by a hope that it would provide a bulwark against rising German power in Europe, while simultaneously reducing the scale of costly imperial rivalry in Africa. Although the policy faced a good deal of criticism in some quarters, it was nothing like as controversial as the Anglo-Russian Convention established three years later. Diehard Conservative politicans had for decades believed that the Tsarist Empire represented the principal threat to British interests in Asia,[6] while radical Liberals were appalled by the autocratic Russian government's authoritarianism and brutal treatment of political prisoners.[7] Popular hostility towards Russia became even more powerful during the Russo-Japanese War of 1904–5, when the Russian fleet accidentally sunk two British trawlers in the North Sea under the bizarre impression that they were Japanese warships.[8]

In spite of these tensions, the Liberal government that came to office at the end of 1905 was determined to renew the search for an understanding with Petersburg that had begun under its Conservative predecessor two years earlier, before being interrupted by the outbreak of hostilities in the Far East.[9] The new Foreign Secretary, Sir Edward Grey, and his Ambassador in Petersburg, Sir Arthur Nicolson, were both convinced that Russia had the ability to pose a powerful challenge to the British position in India and central Asia. Their fear was on the face of it rather curious. During the years before the outbreak of war in 1914, Tsarist Russia was racked by a social and political upheaval of such enormous proportions that diplomats at the British Embassy feared for a time that the regime was on the point of collapse. Even when the immediate crisis had passed, they continued to speculate freely in their dispatches about the prospects for its long-term survival. British diplomats and politicians had for so long been used to dealing with the threat of Russian power that they found it difficult to accept the reality of Russian weakness.

The British officials who worked at the Petersburg Embassy during the years before the First World War were typical practitioners of the Old Diplomacy.[10] The overwhelming majority were from aristocratic or professional backgrounds, and had been educated either by private tutor or at one of a small handful of prestigious public schools. Since all new entrants to the Diplomatic Service were required to possess a private income of £400 *per annum*, and to receive a personal endorsement from the Foreign Secretary, it was almost impossible for any young man from outside the confines of 'the Establishment' to aspire to a career as a professional diplomat. Senior members of the Diplomatic Service firmly argued that 'the net is thrown very wide for candidates',[11] but were seldom able to convince the growing number of critics who believed that the organisation was 'effectually closed to all His Majesty's subjects ... who are not possessed of private means'.[12] Nor was the social elitism of the Diplomatic Service the only concern of its antagonists. Parliamentary critics feared that the men responsible for managing Britain's foreign relations lacked the expertise and training to promote their country's interests in a rapidly changing world, while radical publicists like Norman Angell and E. D. Morel were concerned that the culture of secrecy whch surrounded the whole conduct of international affairs helped to create a climate of mistrust and uncertainty that could easily lead to war.[13] On the eve of the First World War, the notion was rapidly gaining strength in British society that the country's diplomats formed a tiny privileged elite that was operating outside the normal mechanisms of democratic control.[14]

This image of Old Diplomacy was in large part mistaken. By the early years of the twentieth century, the Foreign Office and Diplomatic Service were both going through something of a revolution.[15] Although new recruits were still largely drawn from privileged backgrounds, gaining entry to one of the two organisations depended on success in competitive examinations that covered a large number of subjects ranging from languages and history to arithmetic.[16] Almost all aspiring young diplomats and Foreign Office officials were sent by their families to Scoone's Academy in the Strand in London, where they were 'crammed' for many months in the various subjects that formed part of the entrance requirements. Success in these exams and the subsequent interviews was invariably a cause for celebration both for the candidate and his family, anxious to see their son established in one of the most prestigious careers available to a young Englishman of the Edwardian era. However, by the early years of the twentieth century, passing the entrance examination for the Diplomatic Service was no longer a passport to a leisurely career in the salons and drawing rooms of European capitals. The culture of the Diplomatic Service itself was undergoing a rapid change. Although the outward form of diplomatic life remained similar to previous decades, Britain's diplomats abroad were increasingly expected to combine the ceremonial and social aspect of their job with a high degree of professional competence and dedication. The formal rituals of the salon and diplomatic reception were only the public face of a profession that was becoming increasingly complex and demanding.

The four men who served as British Ambassador in Russia during the first decade of the twentieth century could hardly have been more different in character and aptitude. Sir Charles Scott, who presided at the Petersburg Embassy from 1898 to 1904, was an unusual choice for such an important position, since most of his previous experience had been gained in minor posts like Copenhagen. Several of his colleagues in the Diplomatic Service openly expressed their belief that he lacked sufficient understanding of 'the larger political questions of Europe' to justify the appointment,[17] and Scott himself seemed somewhat taken aback when asked by Salisbury whether he wanted the Petersburg Embassy.[18] Scott's talents were in many ways best-suited to the vanishing world of nineteenth-century diplomacy. During his six years in Petersburg, the good-natured Ambassador and his 'charming and pretty wife' were very popular in society, attending numerous private dinners and receptions given in their honour across the capital.[19] Scott was also well-liked and respected by his own officials.[20] The younger staff at the Embassy lunched with the Ambassador and his wife virtually every day. They also dined there several evenings a week, after which the assembled company settled down to play cards or bridge for hours on end. However, while Scott excelled at dealing with the social and ceremonial aspect of his job, he lacked the qualities that a really successful Ambassador required to carry out his duties effectively. One member of his staff recalled that because Scott himself was so 'straightforward and extremely honest', he was too 'inclined to judge others by his own high standards',[21] with the result that he was easily hoodwinked by Russian officials such as the wily and experienced Foreign Minister Count V. N. Lamsdorff.[22] Scott also tended to be rather garrulous, sometimes

to the point of indiscretion, and when interviewing people who 'might
have valuable information to impart' he was inclined 'to do most of the
talking himself instead of encouraging the person interviewed to become expansive'.[23] Nor did he have a particularly good knowledge of
Russian, a considerable handicap even in a city like Petersburg where
French was the *langue de preference* among diplomats and high society
alike. Despite his shortcomings, Scott's virtues outweighed his weaknesses. Although he lacked the intellectual stature of his successors, and
was regarded as rather 'lightweight' at the Foreign Office in London,
he proved himself to be a diligent and hard-working Ambassador who
encouraged his talented staff to work to their full capacity.

Scott was replaced as Ambassador by a man who was in many ways
his mirror-image, the formidable Sir Charles Hardinge, a consummate
Foreign Office 'insider' who went on to serve as Permanent Secretary
on two separate occasions.[24] Hardinge was well-connected with the Royal
Family, a fact which undoubtedly helped the progress of his career
since King Edward VII acted for many years as an unofficial 'patron'.
However, the real secret of his success lay in his driving ambition, which
was combined with considerable ability and occasional ruthlessness
towards his colleagues. Unlike Scott, Hardinge was already well-versed
in Russian affairs when appointed as Ambassador to Petersburg in 1904,
having previously served there as Secretary of the Embassy from 1898
to 1903. During his time as Scott's deputy, Hardinge mastered the
complexities of the Russian language, which gave him an opportunity
to read a wide range of official documents and journals. This in turn
allowed him to produce a series of detailed reports about economic
conditions in the Tsarist Empire, which were of particular value at a
time when the Russian government was pursuing a programme of rapid
industrialisation that transformed many of Russia's major cities in the
two decades before 1917.[25]

Hardinge's successor as Ambassador was Sir Arthur Nicolson, who
served in Petersburg between 1906 and 1910, and played a pivotal role
in the negotiations that led to the Anglo-Russian Convention of 1907.
Like Hardinge, he was a diplomatic 'heavyweight' who later went on
to serve for many years as Permanent Secretary at the Foreign Office,
though perhaps with rather less success than his illustrious predecessor.
Nicolson's own son, the diplomat and *litterateur* Harold Nicolson, acknowledged that his father was 'neither imaginative nor intellectual'.
He was, though, 'intelligent, honest, sensible, high-minded and fair' –
qualities that won him a good deal of respect during his long career
in the Foreign Office and Diplomatic Service.[26] Some of those who met

Nicolson while he was in Petersburg from 1906 to 1910 found him rather inscrutable. One academic visitor recalled that although the Ambassador was among 'the brainiest that we had',[27] he never actually seemed to say very much of real substance, though this undoubtedly reflected an instinctive caution and reserve rather than a lack of any firm ideas. Unlike Hardinge, Nicolson did not have any personal knowledge of Russia when he was appointed to the Petersburg Embassy. He had, though, been posted earlier in his career to a number of countries on the periphery of the Tsarist Empire, and was reasonably well-versed in the nuances of Russian foreign and domestic policy. Nicolson's instinctive russophilism – which was sometimes a source of controversy with those who did not share his views – was in large part a product of his assessment of the potential of Tsarist power in central Asia. His enthusiastic support for the Anglo-Russian Convention did not reflect any great liking for Russia itself, but rather a realpolitik recognition of the need to avoid conflict with a country capable of challenging vital British interests in Asia. Although Nicolson had no particular interest in Russian culture or society per sc, he encouraged his staff to devote a large amount of energy to monitoring the social and political changes that occurred in the wake of the 1905 Revolution. The Ambassador himself spent a good deal of time reporting to London on the experiment in 'semi-constitutional' politics that took place in the years before 1914. During his four years in Petersburg, Nicolson's diligence and steady nerve played an important role in helping to place Anglo-Russian relations on a new footing, as well as providing the Foreign Office with the reports needed to help officials there understand the massive social and political changes that pulled Russia apart in the wake of the 1905 Revolution.

The most controversial man to serve as British Ambassador during the final years of the Tsarist Empire was without doubt Sir George Buchanan, who arrived in Petersburg in 1910 following Nicolson's return to London. He remained there until the beginning of 1918, when he finally left the country, broken physically and mentally by the strain placed on him and his staff during the traumas of war and revolution. In the years after 1917, Buchanan was blamed by many Russian monarchists for failing to act with sufficient vigour to prevent the slide into chaos which culminated in the Bolshevik Revolution. A few individuals even bizarrely suggested that the Ambassador had himself been in league with the revolutionaries. Buchanan's distant manner often made a bad impression on those with whom he came into contact. In a barely fictionalised account of a meeting with 'His Excellency' that took place in 1917, the novelist Somerset Maugham described how he was received 'with a politeness to which no exception could be taken, but with a frigidity that would have sent a shiver down the spine of a polar bear'.[28] In reality, the Ambassador's formal bearing was more the hallmark of a typical career diplomat, complete with 'monocle', 'finely-chiselled features' and 'silver-grey hair'.[29]

Although Buchanan certainly did not enjoy the same kind of informal relationship with his staff that Scott had encouraged a decade earlier, most of those who served under him spoke with respect about their chief, praising his ability to retain an appearance of 'imperturbable serenity' even during times of great crisis.[30] Sympathetic observers recognised that his detached manner was at least in part simply a product of chronic absent-mindedness and shyness. The distinguished academic Bernard Pares, who spent many years in Russia and had extensive dealings with the British Embassy there, praised Buchanan for representing 'all that the best of England stood for – honour, frankness, a deeply-understanding sympathy'.[31] Nothing, though, had prepared Buchanan for the role he was eventually forced to play in Russia. He knew little about the country at the time he was appointed and never developed even a rudimentary knowledge of the language. During his eight years in Petersburg he proved himself to be a competent administrator, displaying considerable political skill in the years after 1914 when the Tsarist government finally disintegrated as a cohesive body. Nevertheless, Buchanan lacked the instinctive understanding of the Russian mind that Charles Hardinge and Arthur Nicolson both possessed in abundance. It is impossible to say with any certainty whether either of these men could have coped more effectively with the collapse of Imperial Russia. They might perhaps have brought a greater degree of insight to the job, but there was in truth very little that any British Ambassador could have done to influence the way events unfolded in Russia after 1910. In spite of his critics' claims to the contrary, Buchanan's ability to influence developments for good or ill was really very limited.

Although the personality and ability of individual Ambassadors played a vital role in determining the atmosphere at the Embassy, other senior officials also influenced both the course of day to day work and the texture of everyday life. One of the most colourful characters to work in Petersburg in the years before the First World War was Cecil Spring Rice ('Springy'), Secretary at the Embassy from 1903 to 1906, an 'altogether delightful personality, impulsive, humorous, unconventional and imaginative'.[32] Like most of those posted to Russia, Spring Rice did not have much knowledge of the country at the time of his arrival, when he looked forward to filling in 'the missing link in my experience of the world'.[33] He learnt his lessons quickly. Within a few weeks, Spring Rice had come to loathe both the country and its people, though his naturally ebullient and engaging personality masked the depth of his russophobia from all but the most careful observer. Other officials, by contrast, took a more sanguine view of their surroundings. H. J. ('Benjy') Bruce, who arrived in Petersburg shortly before the beginning of the war, quickly fell in love with the 'grandeur of the town, and the fairylike quality of its vastness, its atmosphere'.[34] He also fell in love with – and married – the celebrated ballerina Tamara Karsavina, which doubtless helped to strengthen his admiration for all things Russian, and particularly 'the world of the stage, the world of poets, of musicians and, more especially, of painters'. Other senior staff posted to Russia reacted more soberly to their surroundings, sharing neither Bruce's sense of enchantment nor Spring Rice's feelings of distaste. Typical of such officials was the 'quiet and wise' Counsellor of the Embassy, Hugh O'Beirne, whose diligence and knowledge made him a vital source of help to George Buchanan, following the Ambassador's arrival in Russia in 1910.[35] At a time when the Ambassador lacked the knowledge and linguistic skills to fulfil his duties properly, his deputy's experience proved invaluable in allowing the work of the Embassy to continue uninterrupted. O'Beirne left Russia in 1913 following his appointment as British Minister in Sofia. He died tragically three years later when a German U-boat torpedoed the *Hampshire* on which he was travelling back to Russia from Britain, as part of the ill-fated mission headed by Lord Kitchener.

The more junior staff who worked at the Embassy between 1900 and 1914 did not always relish a posting to Petersburg since it was a notoriously expensive city where the cost of living soon consumed their meagre pay and allowances, a concern that was also expressed by senior diplomats like Charles Hardinge.[36] Officials in the Consular Service were able to turn to journalism and writing to augment their income,[37] but this strategy was ruled out for members of the Diplomatic Service proper. Nevile Henderson, who went on to become Ambassador in Nazi Berlin during the 1930s, found that the £600 annual allowance sent to him by his mother was soon exhausted. Although he supplemented his allowance from winnings at bridge, this expedient could not suffice forever and he was eventually forced to ask for a transfer to a cheaper post.[38] Accommodation was particularly expensive in the Russian capital, so officials newly arrived from London usually tried to get rooms at the Embassy or in a flat with a diplomat already *en poste* in order to save money. In spite of these problems, the Petersburg Embassy was fortunate enough to have a number of outstanding young officials posted to it during the first years of the twentieth century, including Henderson, Ronald Graham and Viscount Cranley (later Lord Onslow), all of whom went on to have successful careers in diplomacy or politics.[39] As was the case with senior officials at the Embassy, their reactions to Russia and the Russians varied enormously. Some, like Henderson, relished the challenge of finding themselves in a new country that was so different from anywhere they had lived before. Others, like Cranley, were frank about their dislike of Russia and its inhabitants.[40] Both men, though, recognised that a posting to Petersburg was quite unlike a tour of duty in other major European capitals such as Paris or Berlin. Although the diplomatic and social milieu in which they spent most of their time was not on the surface very different from its counterparts elsewhere, Russia possessed a distinctive character that set it firmly apart from the other Great Powers of Europe.

The British Diplomatic Service was woefully underfunded at the beginning of the twentieth century, despite the widespread belief among contemporaries that its members led a life of comfortable leisure paid for by the unfortunate taxpayer. The Treasury exercised strict control over all aspects of expenditure relating to the organisation of Britain's overseas representation, which meant that the number of diplomatic posts was limited to 125. The pay was scarcely munificent either. When Sir Charles Hardinge was Ambassador in Petersburg in 1905 he received a salary and allowances of £7800 per annum, which was very generous in comparison with senior posts in the Home Civil Service. However, his deputy received a salary of just £1050, while junior officials were not paid at all for the first two years of their service. Few recruits were therefore attracted to the Diplomatic Service by the financial prospects, unless they were confident enough to be certain of one day being appointed to an ambassadorial post where they could reap their reward for twenty-five years of low pay. The appeal of life in the diplomatic corps rested instead on more nebulous considerations, ranging from a desire to live abroad through to a conviction that a diplomatic career was one of the few professions that did not compromise the social status of its practitioners.

The shortage of resources inevitably affected the ability of overseas Missions to carry out their work properly, a problem from which the Petersburg Embassy was not immune. There were on average just seven

British diplomats in Russia during the early years of the twentieth century, between them responsible for managing the day-to-day business of diplomatic relations, as well as reporting on the changes taking place in Russia itself. Since the Anglo-Russian relationship was a stormy one during this period, and because Russian society went through a series of dramatic convulsions in the decade before 1914, Embassy staff had to struggle hard to meet the demands that were placed on them. To make matters worse, they had no secretarial or clerical assistance to help them in the more mundane aspects of their work, including typing dispatches and deciphering telegrams. The Foreign Office in London was even reluctant to authorise expenditure on such basic facilities as new typewriters, in spite of the fact that the lack of modern machines slowed down the business of the entire Embassy while officials bickered over who should have access to one of the two working models.[41] When Robert Bruce Lockhart first visited the Embassy in 1912, following his appointment as a junior consular official in Moscow, he was stunned to find there 'a typing and telegraph bureau conducted by old Etonians'.[42] He neglected to add that old Etonians were perhaps not the people best suited to carrying out such humdrum work efficiently.

The only way that officials in Petersburg could meet the demands placed on them was by hard work. At the beginning of the twentieth century, when Sir Charles Scott was still in charge of the Embassy, Petersburg had a reputation in the Diplomatic Service for being a comparatively easy post. In reality, the leisured ethos of an earlier age had already faded away there, as it had in other major posts like Paris and Berlin. Although the daughter of Sir George Buchanan recalled in her memoirs that the Chancery usually only operated for six or seven hours a day,[43] her perception seems to have been warped by her detachment from the daily work of the Embassy. While some officials did deliberately cultivate an ambience of nonchalance and indolence, far more typical was a man like Herbert Norman who, as Head of Chancery, 'for two or three years ... never missed coming to office for a single day, Sundays included'.[44] Nevile Henderson recalled that even as a junior official his work was 'hard and incessant. I had to be in Chancery at 9.30 a.m., and often worked till 8 p.m.'[45] Successive Ambassadors were well aware of the stress under which their staff operated. When Hardinge left the Embassy at the beginning of 1906, he wrote to Sir Edward Grey in London praising his officials for their willingness to spend long hours in the Chancery, 'often lasting the whole day and till the early hours of the morning'.[46] The Embassy archives for the period contain numerous tributes to the skill and dedication of individual members of staff.[47] Even though some individual diplomats did spend a good deal of time mixing with the Petersburg *beau monde* and enjoying the social life of the city, the daily grind of Embassy business demanded most of their energy and attention. Ironically, this workaholic ethos was in sharp contrast with the one prevailing at the Russian Foreign Office, where a 'working diplomat' was considered to be a very 'rare bird' indeed.[48]

Diligence alone could not solve all the problems faced by British diplomats at the Petersburg Embassy before 1914. The lack of staff and resources made it difficult for them to keep abreast of the social and political changes that took place across Russia during the early years of the twentieth century. Since they had to devote so much of their time to routine clerical business, it was hard for them to 'keep [their] eyes open and notice anything which may be of interest to the authorities at home'. Ever since Sir Robert Morier had been Ambassador in the 1880s, staff at the Petersburg Embassy spent a good deal of time monitoring the Russian press and translating key articles and official pronouncements for onward transmission to London, where few officials had any knowledge of the Russian language.[49] While such 'desk-bound' reports were useful, they could not yield all the information required by diplomatic staff to carry out their reporting role properly. As the Russian press was heavily censored, it seldom gave a full account of the problems facing the country or the way in which the government intended to respond to them. Nor, of course, did it provide many real insights into the government's views on foreign affairs, though staff at the Embassy knew that certain newspapers such as *Novoe Vremya* had close links with Ministers and usually echoed the latest official thinking. During the years before the First World War, British officials therefore had to develop a range of formal and informal contacts to help them acquire the knowledge necessary to carry out their work effectively. It was not an easy task.

Successive British Ambassadors and their staff identified the Russian Court as the most important centre of political power throughout the years 1900 to 1914, even after the constitutional reforms announced in the Imperial Manifesto of October 1905 brought about considerable changes in the autocratic structure of the Tsarist state. This created a particular problem for the Embassy, since the diplomats based there found it difficult to make many lasting contacts among the secretive world of Nicholas II's immediate entourage of relatives and advisers. Every Ambassador attended formal audiences with the Tsar, as well as more frequent informal meetings at various receptions and ceremonies, but only Charles Hardinge managed to establish anything like a personal rapport with Nicholas (though George Buchanan became more successful in this regard after the outbreak of war in 1914).[50] When Arthur Nicolson arrived as Ambassador in 1906, he invited his old friend, the former *Times* journalist Sir Donald Mackenzie Wallace, to spend time at the Embassy acting as a kind of 'unofficial diplomatist'. Wallace obtained regular audiences with the Tsar, who spoke to him surprisingly openly about the problems facing Russia; as a result, he was able to provide Nicolson and his staff with valuable insights into Court politics at a crucial time in Russia's constitutional development.[51] However, even Wallace's best endeavours could not break down altogether the wall of secrecy that surrounded the Tsar.

British diplomats were certainly not alone in finding the Court largely closed to them during the years leading up to the outbreak of war in 1914. Their experience was shared by other representatives of the diplomatic corps in Petersburg, as well as by many members of the city's *beau monde*. Neither Nicholas nor his wife Alexandra were ever very comfortable among the denizens of Petersburg's high society, where the lax moral tone offended their delicate sensibilities.[52] After the outbreak of the Russo-Japanese War in 1904, there were no more of the great Court balls and receptions that had once been the highlight of the social calendar in the Russian capital.[53] During the era of semi-constitutional politics that began in 1906, the Emperor and Empress preferred to 'live in comparative retirement' at Tsarskoe Selo, their ornate summer palace a few miles outside the Russian capital, while a sort of *ersatz* Court developed in the city around the Grand Duchess Maria Pavlovna (widow of the Grand Duke Vladimir Alexandrovich). This retreat into a private world of domesticity caused considerable concern at the British Embassy, since the staff there feared it might deepen the gulf that developed after 1900 between the Court and Russian society.[54] In the years leading up to 1917, the seclusion of the Royal Family was instrumental in giving rise to the fantastic rumours about the 'mad monk' Rasputin and his supposedly malign influence upon the Empress – rumours which played a considerable role in destabilising Russian political life. Both Nicolson and Buchanan worried that the Tsar and his wife were too ready to put their trust in conservative Ministers and half-crazed mystics, who encouraged the adoption of policies that were quite unsuitable for dealing with the complex problems facing Russian society.

Embassy staff were normally circumspect when discussing the character of the Tsar himself. In spite of the traditional animosity between

Britain and Russia, the two royal families were intimately related
by ties of blood and marriage. Nicholas was the nephew by marriage
of King Edward VII, and the two men corresponded with some frequency both on questions of state and personal matters.[55] Since the
more important dispatches sent from Petersburg to the Foreign Office
were copied to the King, Ambassadors and their staff usually observed
a discreet silence on the question of the Tsar's opinions and abilities.
They preferred to endorse the polite fiction that the problems inflicting
Russia were not the responsibility of Nicholas himself, but rather a
consequence of the poor judgement of his Ministers. Even so, their
doubts about his intellectual calibre and political skill inevitably
cropped up from time to time in dispatches and telegrams, receiving
far more vehement expression in private correspondence and memoirs.[56] When Hardinge was in charge of the Embassy, he was very
concerned by the Tsar's refusal to acknowledge the scale of the social
and political problems facing his country, particularly after the disorders of 1905 when Nicholas indulged his instinctive desire to retreat
to Tsarskoe Selo behind a network of barbed wire, in order to live in
a secluded world where 'Every gardener and haymaker has a sentry
over him to shoot him if he does anything suspicious'.[57] Spring Rice
was also a vehement critic of the Tsar, attacking him for doing nothing
but sit in the palace garden at Tsarskoe Selo where he 'plays with his
baby [the young Tsarevich] and will hear nothing but baby talk'.[58]
Viscount Cranley was blunter still, writing in the unpublished version
of his memoirs that Nicholas was 'weak' and 'obstinate' and had 'the
brains of a sheep'.[59] British officials were perturbed above all by the
Tsar's instinctive conservatism and reluctance to accept any changes
that might threaten the autocratic nature of the regime. At the same
time, paradoxically, they were frustrated by his failure to act with the
authority needed to give his Ministers a clear sense of direction and
purpose. Even Arthur Nicolson, who was usually quite generous in his
comments about Nicholas, could not help but acknowledge that the
Tsar did 'not always act with the required firmness and decision',[60] a
weakness which the Ambassador feared would lead to an increase in
the influence of the conservative and pro-German milieu that surrounded him at Court. Nicolson was especially critical of Nicholas's
failure to support the handful of Ministers who had the energy and
vision to promote new policies to deal with the various problems
facing the country. While British representatives who had personal
dealings with the Emperor were always struck by his kindness and
generosity, none of them believed that he had the skill required to

help his country overcome the crisis that threatened to rip it apart in the years after 1900.

Even though it was difficult for members of the Embassy to penetrate the secretive milieu of relatives and friends that surrounded the Tsar at Court, they made valiant efforts to develop good relations with the men who occupied formal ministerial posts, particularly after the constitutional changes announced in 1905–6 allowed the more vigorous Ministers greater independence than before.[61] Before the Anglo-Russian Convention was signed in 1907, British diplomats in Petersburg were usually treated in a distant manner by Tsarist officials. The closest links were with officials at the Ministry of Foreign Affairs, though even here relations were never particularly warm as long as the reclusive and unapproachable Count V. N. Lamsdorff remained as Minister.[62] However, the appointment of the more ebullient A. P. Izvolsky as Foreign Minister in 1906 helped to improve the atmosphere between the Embassy and the Ministry, which in turn smoothed the path during the negotiations that led to the signing of the Convention. The 'very able and adroit'[63] Izvolsky was never entirely trusted by the British diplomatic corps,[64] but his commitment to the cause of Anglo-Russian rapprochement was not generally doubted, though there were fears that he might prove unable to resist pressure from those who wanted Russia to develop closer ties with Germany.[65] His successor, S. D. Sazonov, was even more warmly regarded at the Embassy, particularly after the outbreak of war in 1914 forged closer ties between the British and Russian diplomatic establishments. Buchanan described Sazonov in his memoirs as a statesman endowed 'with the gifts of tact, patience and forbearance',[66] and was desperately alarmed by the rumours that circulated periodically indicating that the Foreign Minister was about to resign. It is difficult to say with any certainty whether the good relationship between the Embassy and the Russian Foreign Ministry was a cause or a consequence of the 1907 Convention. However, the Ministry certainly had a large number of anglophiles among its staff, who between them played a significant role in countering the powerful Court faction that sought to encourage Nicholas to adopt a more pro-German foreign policy during the critical years leading up to the First World War.

It was harder for Embassy staff to cultivate close contacts with Tsarist officials who worked outside the Foreign Ministry, since there were fewer opportunities for regular meetings. They did, however, establish good links with Peter Stolypin, Prime Minister (Chairman of the Council of Ministers) in the critical years between 1906 and his assassination in 1911, during which time this most able and energetic of Ministers fought to put in place policies capable of providing a sound basis for Russia's future development.[67] He also actively involved himself in the management of his country's foreign policy, which on occasion brought him into conflict both with Izvolsky and the Tsar himself. Stolypin was perhaps the only one of Nicholas II's Ministers who ever managed to command the complete respect and trust of the Embassy. Although officials there recognised the ability and dedication of Count Sergei Witte, who as Minister of Finance was the architect of Russia's programme of industrialisation during the 1890s, they suspected him of holding strong pro-German sympathies; they also believed that his driving ambition and ruthlessness made him an untrustworthy individual with whom to have dealings.[68] The Embassy was therefore perturbed when Witte briefly became Prime Minister in 1905, before losing favour with the Tsar who took the first opportunity to get rid of a man whose views and personality he despised. By contrast, Stolypin was described by Arthur Nicolson as 'a great man ... the most notable figure in Europe',[69] while even the normally grudging Charles Hardinge described him during a visit to Petersburg in 1908 as 'a very straightforward, strong and courageous man'.[70] Wallace was still more impressed, praising Stolypin in an audience with the Tsar as 'a fine, courageous honest man, intelligent and singularly sympathetic'.[71]

Both Wallace and Nicolson established a good personal relationship with Stolypin. During their frequent meetings the Prime Minister spoke with remarkable frankness about the crisis facing Russia and his proposals for resolving it. He even provided Wallace with secret documents about various revolutionary groups that had been seized by the Secret Police, in order to help his visitor gain an insight into the goals and psychology of the extremists.[72] The high regard in which Stolypin was held at the British Embassy was not simply a reflection of his manifest personal integrity and readiness to talk with foreign representatives about the problems facing his country. The Prime Minister was a controversial figure in Russia, earning the undying hatred of both radicals and conservatives at a time when public opinion was becoming increasingly polarised. The supporters of radical constitutional reform bitterly criticised Stolypin for his high-handed and authoritarian attitude towards the newly-convened Duma (Parliament), which first met in 1906, while conservatives at Court attacked him for promoting innovative policies designed to resolve the social and political tensions that were ripping the country apart. However, Stolypin's desire to restore order in Russia, while simultaneously overhauling the traditional fabric of government, endeared him to British officials who believed that his policies alone could save the country from catastrophe. As the Prime Minister displayed many of the qualities which the Tsar so clearly lacked, the Embassy hoped that he could give the government a sense of direction and leadership that Nicholas was so manifestly unable to provide.

While British diplomats found it difficult to obtain an *entrée* to the secretive world of the Russian Court and bureaucracy, they found it a little easier to gain access to Petersburg high society. Even so, at times of tension between Britain and Russia, the doors of houses belonging to the capital's wealthy families were often abruptly slammed shut. This was particularly true during the Russo-Japanese War of 1904–5, when there took place 'something like a boycott of the Embassy',[73] since many Russians believed that the British were providing tacit support to their Japanese allies. During these years, members of the British diplomatic corps in Russia were largely forced back on their own devices when seeking entertainment, though the formal receptions hosted by the network of foreign Missions and Embassies in Petersburg naturally remained open to them. Hunting was popular with almost all officials posted to the Embassy, several of whom tried their hand at bear-shooting in the forests outside the city, before finding to their disgust that the sport lacked any real challenge since the quarry proved to be 'such pathetically good-natured beasts that to kill [them] seems almost a crime'.[74] A few of them hired country cottages in nearby Finland, in order to fish for trout in the streams and rivers there. Several officials were also involved in the establishment of a polo team that drew its members from the foreign diplomatic corps in the Russian capital, polo being almost unknown in the country at this time. Even the somewhat portly Charles Hardinge joined in, though on one occasion he had a nasty fall when riding a pony that was 'perhaps not quite up to his weight'.[75] During times when Anglo-Russian relations were more harmonious – which of course applied to most of the years that followed the Convention of 1907 – officials were invited with some frequency to receptions and dinners at the houses of wealthy representatives of the Petersburg nobility. The Grand Duke Vladimir asked members of the Embassy to attend the informal shooting parties which he hosted at Tsarskoe Selo,[76] while grandees like Prince Orlov invited Embassy staff to receptions at his home. Embassy staff were also befriended by members of the Belosel'sky-Belozersky family, in spite of their pronounced panslav sympathies.

Junior officials often relished the feverish pace of the social life enjoyed by the younger set in the Tsarist capital, at least when they still had sufficient energy following long hours spent in the Chancery coding telegrams and preparing reports for transmission to London. Henry Beaumont, who served as Second Secretary at the beginning of the century, would often accompany parties of young well-to-do Russians to lavish restaurants, after which the party would board horse-drawn sleighs to visit the outskirts of the town where they were entertained until the early morning by gypsy musicians and dancers. Nevile Henderson recalled how he spent many nights in the clubs and restaurants of Petersburg, enjoying a hectic life in which one met 'everybody in one's particular crowd every night'.[77] Patrick de Bathe, a young Honorary Attaché at the Embassy, was also very adroit at making his way through 'the social whirlpool of what was then one of the gayest capitals in Europe'.[78] Ambassadors and other senior officials, by contrast, usually preferred the more dignified and sedate atmosphere of the snobbish Yacht Club, where they were able to mix with some of the wealthiest and most influential people in Petersburg society – though moving in such exclusive circles invariably proved a costly drain on their salaries and expenses.

Participation in the social life of Petersburg not only provided a form of entertainment and relaxation for British diplomats in the Russian capital, it also gave them access to possible sources of information that could be of use in their work. Arthur Nicolson placed great emphasis on the snippets of information he received while dining out: his dispatches to the Foreign Office in London were full of news picked up in casual conversation with the Russians he met at dinner parties and receptions.[79] Charles Hardinge also kept the Foreign Office apprised of the sentiments expressed by people he met when mixing in Petersburg high society. Nevertheless, the value of such information was limited, though the British Embassy was by no means alone among foreign Missions in encouraging its staff to frequent the drawing rooms of the capital.[80] Although supporters of Old Diplomacy habitually argued that cultivating informal contacts was a vital part of the warp and woof of diplomacy, since it provided insights into the *mentalité* of the ruling class,[81] most Russians met by British officials knew little of what was going on in the political world. There had existed since at least the middle of the nineteenth century a marked division in Russian society between members of the wealthy nobility and the state bureaucracy. Although the individuals who occupied the top ministerial posts were usually drawn from long-established noble families, their immediate subordinates were often professional bureaucrats dependent on their jobs for income and status. By contrast, the houses to which members of the British Embassy were most frequently invited belonged to wealthy aristocrats who seldom held any political or administrative posts of much consequence. In addition, as the Court itself became increasingly remote and detached from the mainstream of Russian society, even the best-informed host was unlikely to be able to offer his guests much in the way of accurate political gossip, unless he happened to be one of the small number of intimates of the Royal Family. Most of the information which staff at the British Embassy picked up in the course of their social round therefore consisted of little more than unreliable rumours and speculation.

The value of information gleaned by Embassy staff from their contacts among the bureaucracy or the Petersburg *beau monde* was also lessened by the fact that it reflected the perspectives and prejudices of an urban elite largely divorced from the rest of Russian society, a serious problem in such a vast and heterogeneous country. Ambassadors and their staff found it difficult to make contacts with individuals who did not belong to the metropolitan establishment of the capital. On average, only two members of the British diplomatic corps posted to Petersburg had a good enough command of the Russian language to qualify for the special allowance of £100 *per annum* paid by the Foreign Office. This was not necessarily a serious handicap when dealing with government officials and 'polite society', since most members of the social and political elite had a knowledge of either English, French or German. However, even in the Russian capital ignorance of the local language could sometimes pose a problem, since it made British diplomats too dependent on the 'Young Russian officials with fluent English' who were charged with chaperoning the representatives of foreign governments.[82] The absence of appropriate linguistic skills certainly reduced the value of the 'fact-finding' visits which Embassy staff occasionally made outside the capital, to see at first hand the state of agriculture in the Ukraine or the conditions of the Jewish population in the Polish provinces.[83] In any case, since these visits were usually quite short, they could only yield vague impressions formed after cursory inspection rather than through detailed observation and discussion with local officials and residents. Provincial Russia always remained *terra incognita* to the Embassy in the years before 1914, a shadowy and anarchic world in which an ill-educated and ignorant peasantry constantly threatened to rise up in a fearful jacquerie. Although they knew that a powerful instinctive loyalty to the Tsar ran deep in the political culture of peasant Russia, British diplomats based in Petersburg feared that it could never tame an even deeper desire for land and for freedom from exploitation by local landlords and officials.

It was not only shortage of time and the vastness of Russia which made it difficult for the Embassy to build contacts outside the established metropolitan elites. Successive Ambassadors and their staff had to be cautious when dealing with individuals and groups overtly critical of the Tsarist regime. Some senior members of the British Diplomatic Service were convinced that such contacts should always be avoided, in case they undermined 'friendly relations between Governments'.[84] It was partly for this reason that Arthur Nicolson first encouraged Wallace and Pares to spend time at the Embassy, so that they could provide officials there with information derived from 'sources normally closed to diplomatists'.[85] Both men had contacts with underground organisations in the capital, and the information they obtained helped British diplomats to build up a general picture of the activities and ideology of the various groups committed to the destruction of the Tsarist regime. These 'unofficial diplomatists' also helped to keep the Embassy informed about the activities of the constitutional parties that emerged after 1905, including the liberal-radical Cadets and the moderate-conservative Octobrists, whose members exercised considerable influence in the various Dumas that met in the years before 1917. Although regular diplomatic staff watched the progress of the 'Constitutional Experiment' which took place after 1905 with considerable attention, they were still wary of developing close personal links with politicians whose views and activities were despised by Tsar Nicholas and his immediate entourage. Pares and Wallace, by contrast, were under no such constraints. They talked at length with many members of successive Dumas, gathering material and insights that were fed back to the Embassy and the Foreign Office. As 'semi-official' observers, the two men enjoyed the freedom of the journalist and the authority of the diplomat. The reports of Wallace, in particular, played an important role in keeping the Embassy and Foreign Office informed of the political changes that took place in Russia in the aftermath of the 1905 Revolution.

There was one source of information which the Embassy neglected to a surprising degree: namely, the reports filed by the network of British Consuls dotted around the major cities of the Tsarist Empire.[86] Members of the Consular Service in Russia, like their colleagues posted to other countries, laboured under enormous difficulties when carrying out their work during the years before the First World War. They were expected to carry out a large number of duties, ranging from the compilation of reports on local political developments through to advising British firms about export opportunities and markets in their particular region. The resources made available to them were, by contrast, very meagre. Lockhart ruefully observed that a career in the Consular Service was 'the worst-paid service in the world', and recalled in his memoirs that the Moscow Consulate where he worked was 'housed in surroundings of which a Malayan Sanitary Board inspector would have been ashamed'.[87] The Consul-General in Warsaw, Alexander Murray, periodically ran out of money and had to ask London for an advance on his salary so that he would not face the indignity of having to 'borrow from the Jews'. In spite of these problems, consular officials in Russia worked tirelessly to perform their duties effectively, even if they received scant respect for their efforts. Lockhart recalled in his memoirs that the Embassy took little interest in the reports which he and his chief, Montgomery Grove, regularly sent to Petersburg about political developments in the Moscow region.[88] Although this was not altogether true, diplomats at the Petersburg Embassy were certainly inclined to dismiss reports compiled by men who belonged to a 'Cinderella Service' that lacked the social prestige and cachet of their own profession.[89] This was undoubtedly a mistake, since many consular officials were intelligent and shrewd observers who were well placed to report on social and political changes taking place in the provinces. At times of crisis, most notably during the disturbances of 1905–6, staff at the Embassy and Foreign Office did read their dispatches with attention, since they were the best source of information available about the breakdown of order outside Petersburg. In more peaceful times, however, the consular network was not used to its full potential, with the result that a valuable opportunity to overcome the metropolitan bias of diplomatic reporting from Russia was lost.

The Military and Naval Attachés at the Embassy also represented a useful source of information about life in the Russian provinces, since they regularly toured the country in order to observe manoeuvres of 'the navies and armies to which they are accredited'.[90] Captain Aubrey Smith, who was Naval Attaché from 1908 to 1912, travelled frequently to the Caucasus to report on Russian naval and military activity in an area that was of great strategic concern to the British. As well as meeting Tsarist naval officers and officials, he also had the opportunity to acquaint himself and his colleagues with life in some of the remoter provinces of the Empire, particularly as his family owned property in the region.[91] The role of an Attaché could, though, be a difficult one, since the boundary between legitimate observation and illegal espionage was a very fine one. One British Military Attaché who served in Petersburg at the start of the twentieth century noted that he always refused to be 'in any way associated with the individuals employed in spy service in Russia ... or to be informed even of their names'.[92] The Russian authorities were not convinced that all his colleagues were so scrupulous. In 1911 an employee of the Admiralty was put on trial accused of selling secret documents to Smith, a charge indignantly denied both by the Naval Attaché himself and by George Buchanan, who was anxious to assert the traditional principle that British Embassies were never involved in any form of spying.[93] Some British officials in Russia were in reality involved extensively in espionage in Russia during the early years of the twentieth century, particularly before the Anglo-Russian Convention reduced tension between the two countries. Charles Hardinge paid an official at the Russian Foreign Ministry to provide him with sensitive information on a regular basis.[94] At least two British Consuls based in southern Russia were given Secret Service money to bribe informants to provide details of military activities in the area. One of these officials, Patrick Stevens, who served as Consul in the town of Batum on the eastern shore of the Black Sea, built up an elaborate network of agents which provided him with a mass of information that was sent back to the Foreign Office and Military Intelligence in London. One of his agents was even responsible for setting up a printing press used by the Russian military authorities in the central Asian city of Tashkent, which gave the British access to copies of vital maps of military installations in the region.[95] The authorities in London were well aware of the importance of Stevens as a source of information, and funded his activities comparatively generously out of the small Secret Service budget. It seems certain, though, that most members of the British diplomatic corps in Petersburg were not aware of the whole business, since the material he obtained through clandestine means was usually sent direct to London by courier.

The British were not of course the only ones to engage in the complicated game of espionage and counter-espionage. The Petersburg Embassy was itself the target of repeated attempts by the Tsarist authorities to obtain copies of confidential documents and dispatches.[96] The Russian intelligence service had at this time a formidable reputation for its skill in code-breaking, which meant that the normal cyphers used by the Embassy did not provide much security.[97] As well as regularly intercepting mail and telegrams, the Russians bribed one of the servants at the Embassy to obtain copies of secret documents from the Chancery. Although he was caught and dismissed from his post, the problem did not go away and vital papers continued to go missing. Embassy staff went to great lengths to catch the culprit, bribing a

Russian employee of the Secret Police to give them information and spending long nights crouched in the dark waiting for the spy to appear. Their efforts were unsuccessful. On one occasion Arthur Nicolson was almost shot by a member of his own staff after appearing unexpectedly at dead of night in the Chancery. On another occasion, the 'intruder' turned out to be one of the Embassy maids returning from a date. When the problems were particularly bad, Spring Rice was reduced to suggesting that the Embassy should be sent a policeman or detective from London who could sleep in the Chancery. He also sought advice about security from Scotland Yard and the American Embassy, as well as approaching a member of the Swedish Legation who 'ran a very efficient Secret Service and for a consideration gave us all very useful information'. In the event, however, the improved relations that followed the signing of the Anglo-Russian accord in 1907 largely eliminated the problem, since the reduction in tension meant that neither side was as concerned as previously to obtain information about the other's military capacity and intentions. By the time war broke out in 1914, the two governments were even able to begin cooperating with one another on intelligence matters.

Despite the problems they faced when trying to find out information about the social and political problems besetting Russia, British diplomats and consular officials still proved surprisingly successful at reporting on the disintegration of the Tsarist Empire. The reports they sent to the Foreign Office in London during 1900–14 showed that they were sensitive to the depth of the crisis facing Russia – more sensitive, perhaps, than the Tsar and many of his Ministers. Their reports of the 1905 Revolution, and the constitutional changes that took place in its wake, were both accurate and perceptive. The Embassy recognised that the government faced a fundamental challenge not only from the various revolutionary groups whose activities threatened the lives of leading officials, but also from a public that was becoming increasingly discontented with the economic and political status quo. The tiny band of revolutionaries that assassinated Alexander II in 1881 never enjoyed much significant popular support either in the town or the countryside, with the result that the autocratic regime was easily strong enough to survive the loss of its most potent symbol: the Tsar himself. Twenty years later the situation had changed dramatically. The programme of industrialisation set in place by Sergei Witte in the 1890s had led to a big increase in the urban population, much of it comprised of first-generation workers drawn from the countryside to the alien and barbaric world of town and factory.[98] The shortage of land in the countryside, combined with severe famine in the early 1890s, created a growing malaise in the villages.[99] In both town and countryside, there emerged the nucleus of an educated professional middle class that was not willing to endorse the autocratic political values zealously defended by Nicholas II and his closest advisers.[100] While the small groups of revolutionaries who carried out systematic campaigns of terrorism against senior officials in the early years of the twentieth century did not enjoy much popular sympathy, they were challenging a regime that was less and less able to identify with confidence the sources of its own legitimacy and support.

The figure of the Russian revolutionary had intrigued and terrified many Britons from the middle of the nineteenth century onwards. The first generation of exiles who sought refuge from the Tsarist regime, in the 1840s and 1850s, was largely composed of intelligent and prosperous liberals assured of a welcome in the progressive circles of at least some west European countries, including Britain. The next wave of emigrés exhibited a very different character, including among its numbers such figures as the infamous Sergei Nechaev, whose cunning and violence made him a legend even in Russian revolutionary circles that were not known for the delicacy of their moral sensitivities.[101] By 1914 the sinister image of the Russian 'anarchist' in exile had become a stock part of the British imagination, promoted in such literary works as Joseph Conrad's *Under Western Eyes* as well as through reports in newspapers and journals. Staff at the British Embassy in Petersburg naturally found it hard to obtain much information about the revolutionary groups active in the country before the events of 1905, though even the briefest look at the local newspapers showed the bloody fruits of their activities. In 1901 Ronald Graham wrote a detailed report about a recent upsurge in violent protests at universities across Russia, arguing that the students' penchant for direct action was gradually attracting increasing support which in turn reflected a rise in public disenchantment with the political status quo.[102] Sir Charles Scott complimented the report for its thoroughness, but his own dispatches made it clear that he was less concerned than Graham about the activities of the radicals. In a breath takingly naive report to the Foreign Office, he suggested that the government could solve the problem by offering 'safety valves for the exuberance of youthful energy',[103] particularly by supplying more sporting facilities at universities to allow them to work off their angst. Although the reports compiled by his staff showed that the bout of labour unrest which spread across the country a few months later was made worse by 'the instigation of labour agitators',[104] the Ambassador remained optimistic about the future. Despite the fact that senior Tsarist officials spoke to him regularly in the following years about the danger posed by revolutionary cells skilled at exploiting 'every local labour dispute to further their revolutionary propaganda',[105] Scott was still confident that the regime was secure enough to survive the challenge.

By the time Scott left Russia in 1904 the situation was becoming more fraught, and it was difficult for even the most sanguine observer to ignore the repeated assassinations of senior officials carried out by members of clandestine organisations such as the Socialist Revolutionaries. Charles Hardinge viewed the prospect of widespread public disorder in Russia far more seriously than Scott when he returned to Petersburg as Ambassador early in 1904, perhaps because he had a better knowledge of the damaging social consequences of the industrialisation programme promoted by the government during the previous ten years or so. Spring Rice was also concerned about the dangers posed by the terrorists and assassins, particularly after the 'strong man' of the government, the Minister of the Interior V. K. Plehve, was assassinated in the summer of 1904. Plehve had earned the bitter hatred of critics of the government as a result of the harsh measures he introduced to restore order.[106] Spring Rice rightly observed soon after the assassination that 'Plehve has no successor. If the successor walks in his footsteps he will be killed like Plehve. If he doesn't the Emperor will disgrace him. There is no strong man left about this Government – only a number of weather-cocks: and the wind blows all ways at once'.[107] Nevertheless, Spring Rice remained confident during his first year in Russia that widespread violent upheavals were unlikely in the near future, believing that the handful of revolutionaries lacked any substantial popular support. In December 1903, when Scott was still in charge of the Embassy, he wrote to a friend that 'I don't think there will be a revolution because the people are too stupid and the army too faithful'.[108]

Exactly one year later, on the eve of the Bloody Sunday massacre that marked the beginning of the 1905 crisis, Spring Rice told his sister that 'the people seem to accept the Government as it does the climate – something that comes from God or the Devil but in any case cannot be changed by cursing'.[109] Charles Hardinge, by contrast, was more prescient, perhaps because he did not share his deputy's instinctive belief that the Russian character was by nature inert and passive. Whereas Spring Rice believed that the war which broke out with Japan in February 1904 would bind the Russian government and people more closely together, Hardinge sensed that a serious military setback would quickly arouse a strong reaction among a volatile public. The Ambassador wrote during the early stages of the conflict that the mass of ordinary Russians were at best indifferent to the war,[110] with the result that they were likely to turn against it once it began to affect their lives in the form of conscription or the loss of friends and relatives. The events of the next few months seemed to confirm his belief, as defeat after defeat created public disquiet over the organisation of Russia's military effort. By December 1904 Hardinge was convinced that the recent upsurge of popular clamour for 'the most liberal and far-reaching demands for constitutional change',[111] particularly among the urban middle classes, was creating a challenge to which the government was unlikely to respond effectively. He was certain that 'there will be a good many internal troubles during this winter',[112] and feared a 'recrudescence of nihilism which may become a serious danger to the Emperor's personal safety'.[113]

Even the Ambassador was not prepared for the scale of the crisis that befell Russia the following month. Hardinge vehemently condemned the Bloody Sunday slaughter of January 1905, in which troops from the Petersburg garrison mowed down hundreds of 'peaceful and harmless' unarmed peasants and workers who were marching to the Winter Palace with a petition seeking radical political and economic reforms.[114] His colleagues were also appalled by the killings, which they believed were entirely unjustified given the orderly nature of the protests.[115] Although the incident was not alone responsible for destroying the image of Tsar Nicholas as the Little Father of his people, it served as a spark that set off numerous riots and disorders across the country. In the eighteen months that followed, peasants went on the rampage in the countryside, labour unrest crippled industry, while large sections of the urban professional classes voiced calls for more and more radical constitutional reform. Hardinge believed that the Bloody Sunday killings were evidence of the weakness and vulnerability of the Tsarist government in the face of rising popular opposition. He wrote to the Foreign Office in London soon after the slaughter, condemning the government for its 'absence of any direction' in the days following the tragedy, which the Ambassador believed was largely due to the lack of any effective coordination between the various ministries.[116] A few days later, he told Lord Knollys, the King's Private Secretary and a long-time confidant of Hardinge, that 'the Emperor missed the chance of his lifetime', since if he had been prepared to receive the petition and make minor concessions 'he would have obtained the undying loyalty and admiration of the lower classes of his subjects'. Instead of this, news had now 'gone abroad that when his subjects came to present their grievances to the "Little Father" they were mown down by his troops and a gulf has been created between the Emperor and his people which will not be easily forgotten'.[117] Neither Hardinge nor his staff believed that the tragedy of Bloody Sunday was the direct responsibility of Nicholas, blaming instead the 'blunderings' of the police and troops who were charged with keeping order.[118] The Ambassador was even 'convinced that a few London policemen could easily have managed that crowd'.[119] Nevertheless, while it was recognised at the Embassy that the Emperor had not ordered the killings himself, officals there could not exonerate him from at least some responsibility for the government's short-sighted and negative response to the demands for social and political change that were bubbling up across the country.

The scale of the disorders that followed Bloody Sunday quickly became obvious at the Embassy, where a good deal of time and energy was devoted to following the drama as it unfolded. Even in the middle of 1906, when the immediate crisis had passed, British diplomats in Petersburg still found it difficult to get away from the Chancery, while the Ambassador was sending more than one hundred dispatches and two hundred telegrams a month to London.[120] During the first few months of the disturbances, the Embassy found it hard to build up a coherent picture of the upheavals spreading across Russia. Hardinge was still reasonably confident at the beginning of February that a full-scale revolution could be avoided, since the killings in Petersburg had so scarred the popular consciousness that the 'people have been too severely punished not to remember it for some time'.[121] Just two weeks later, however, the Ambassador had begun to 'dread to think of the future [since] the position seems to be growing worse every day'. Embassy officials were at first convinced that the disturbances in both town and countryside were spontaneous reflections of poverty and popular resentment against the government. Their opinion began to change during April and May, once it became clear that the disorders were not going to come to a rapid end. The government's loss of authority in Petersburg itself was particularly striking, as groups of workers and middle-class professionals launched demonstrations and protests demanding an end to autocratic rule. In May Spring Rice told London that the reports arriving at the Embassy suggested 'that the strikes are in most cases fomented by political agitators'.[122]

The Embassy's best source of information came from consular officials spread across the country, whose reports were for once read with considerable avidity by diplomatic staff eager to gain an insight into the scale of disorder in the provinces. British Consuls in Russia were themselves divided as to whether the upheavals were primarily an expression of 'natural discontent with the existing conditions of life' or a direct consequence of agitation carried out by revolutionary groups like the Socialist Revolutionaries and Social Democrats.[123] As the year progressed, there was an increasing consensus among them that many of the disorders had been 'carefully planned beforehand'.[124] Consul-General Murray in Warsaw indignantly blamed 'Jewish socialists' in his district for creating a situation in which 'the whole of the lower classes have got completely out of hand'.[125] Montgomery Grove in Moscow also believed that political agitators had infiltrated all the factory and strike committees in the city, though he acknowledged that it was only the poverty of the working class in the city which made them susceptible to radical propaganda, a point echoed by Patrick Stevens in Batum.[126] The break-down in law and order sometimes posed a threat to the life of consular officials, even though they tried hard to avoid becoming involved in political controversy. A number of them applied to the Foreign Office for grants to improve the security of their Consulates,[127] while one unfortunate individual was even shot when walking in the street near his home. Diplomatic staff based at the Embassy in Petersburg faced less direct danger, since the government worked hard to keep order in the capital's streets despite the formation of numerous factory committees and, later in the year, a Soviet of Workers Deputies headed by Leon Trotsky. Even so, Nevile Henderson recalled that it was common throughout 1905 for his colleagues to hear 'a bomb explosion at any time in the day'.[128]

Senior British representatives in Russia strongly criticised the Tsarist government's response to the crisis that erupted following the Bloody Sunday tragedy. Charles Hardinge wrote shortly after the killings that 'upon a soil prepared by misgovernment and corruption the seed of revolution has fallen and borne fruit'. He went on to condemn the Ministers surrounding the Tsar as a 'hopelessly weak and invertebrate body ... drifting with the tide and quarrelling amongst themselves'. The Ambassador was certain that the autocracy so beloved by Nicholas was doomed and '*must* be modified – it is an anachronism, and reforms are now absolutely necessary'.[129] In the early spring of 1905, however, Hardinge was still sceptical as to whether the government would steel itself to make any real changes, despite the introduction of minor reforms intended as a sop to public opinion. He feared that as the public became increasingly 'dissatisfied with the procrastination of the Government',[130] popular anger would undermine the entire fabric of government, leading to even greater chaos. The Ambassador remained hopeful that the struggles taking place across the country could in time lead to a new phase in Russia's political development, writing to the Foreign Secretary in July that 'a very remarkable change is passing over this country ... The disorders and outbreaks which have occurred are characteristic of the efforts of a down-trodden race to acquire greater liberty'.[131] He believed that if the government could be persuaded to respond to public pressure for real political reform, then the autocratic system of rule could be transformed into a constitutional model similar to ones found in western Europe.

Hardinge's sanguine views were not shared by his deputy, who as ever took a much bleaker view of the Russian character. Spring Rice believed that the vast majority of the Russian population – the peasantry – 'were entirely indifferent to politics unless politics can bring them food or land'.[132] The radical urban professionals who called for change were not in his opinion 'an element which can organise or act',[133] with the result that even in the middle of 1905 he remained certain that there would be no successful revolution against the government, though he conceded the possibility of 'general disorganisation and a sort of peaceful anarchy'.[134] In a private letter written around the same time, he observed laconically to his correspondent that 'The elephant is dead – the hide is tough, the jackals pull at it in vain, but it is rotting inside'.[135] Although Spring Rice recognised that the structures of the autocratic state had virtually disintegrated, he saw little prospect of any new form of government rising from the ashes to take its place.

The government's uncertain response to the 1905 Revolution was in large part the fault of Nicholas himself, though the Tsar was more inclined to blame his Ministers whom he impatiently condemned as 'a lot of frightened hens' clucking impotently in the face of impending disaster. Even Charles Hardinge, who hoped that the upheavals might lead in time to the adoption of a more constitutional form of government, could not help wishing at times for a strong leader of 'initiative and courage' – precisely the qualities which Nicholas lacked.[136] The Ambassador was afraid that the only really 'strong and able' individual who might be able to cope with the chaos engulfing Russia was Sergei Witte. The Tsar himself firmly denied that his unwillingness to introduce real constitutional reform was simply a consequence of his desire to hold on to power. A few weeks before Bloody Sunday, he told one of his Ministers that 'I don't hold to autocracy for my own pleasure. I act in this sense only because I am convinced that it is necessary for Russia.

If it was simply a question of myself I would happily get rid of all this'.[137] Nicholas was doubtless honest in saying that he believed his autocratic powers were part of a sacred inheritance that he felt duty-bound to pass on intact to his invalid son, but it had a catastrophic impact on the government's ability to respond to the crisis of 1905. All his Ministers could do was search in vain for policies that would meet popular demands for political reform while preserving intact the fabric of the traditional autocratic constitution. The public mood was far too radical to accept the minimal compromises that Nicholas was willing to offer. Spring Rice's belief that the government could maintain its position by mobilising the support of the 'ignorant masses' against the middle-class radicals and revolutionary organisations was almost certainly wrong.[138] Charles Hardinge was, by contrast, correct in arguing that the events of 1905 signified a deep-seated change in popular attitudes which would make it impossible for the archaic autocratic system to remain unchanged.

When real constitutional reform was finally announced by the Tsar in October 1905, it was ironically the ministerial 'wet hens' who succeeded in persuading Nicholas that he had no choice but to proclaim the establishment of a new Duma equipped with real powers. An upsurge of strikes on the railways and in the factories graphically demonstrated that the government could not contain the anarchy that had overtaken Russia, unless it made a dramatic gesture responding to the public mood. Nicholas reluctantly agreed to appoint Sergei Witte as Prime Minister, recognising that his former Minister of Finance was the only person who had the talent and ability to cope with the crisis facing the government. The strategy set in motion by Nicholas and his advisers was in time successful. The political concessions announced in the October Manifesto proved after a few weeks to be enough to win back the support of at least a section of the wealthier urban classes, appalled by the anarchy that threatened to destroy not only the autocracy but also their own lives and property. In the immediate aftermath of the proclamation of the Manifesto, however, it was by no means clear that the concessions would be sufficient to calm the public mood. A series of half-hearted reforms earlier in the year had proved to be still-born and ineffectual, with the result that there was a good deal of popular mistrust of the Tsar and a corresponding reluctance to accept his good faith. Jubilant marches and demonstrations took place through the streets of Petersburg celebrating the announcement of the Manifesto, but strikes in the factories and disorder in the countryside continued almost unabated. Perhaps for this reason, the potential significance of the reforms announced in October was not properly understood at the Embassy. Charles Hardinge had returned temporarily to Britain at the beginning of the month. While he would almost certainly have recognised the decision to convene a new elected assembly as a step on the road to constitutional reform, the irrepressibly cynical Spring Rice watched developments through more jaundiced eyes. Although he had excellent contacts providing him with details about the heated discussions which took place among Ministers during this critical period,[139] his dispatches to the Foreign Office attached little significance to the importance of Nicholas's decision to concede, at least *in principle*, the end of autocratic government in Russia.

In spite of Spring Rice's dismissive treatment of the October Manifesto, some of his colleagues realised that it could help the government to begin the long process of restoring public order. Montgomery Grove in Moscow played an important role throughout 1905 in keeping the Embassy informed of developments in a city where the inhabitants considered themselves to be closer to traditional Russian sentiments and values than the bureaucrats in the new capital on the banks of the Neva. During the final weeks of the year, Grove reported that many middle-class liberals who had previously been active in protests against the government were increasingly disturbed by the continuation of the disorders, and therefore more willing than before to help 'strengthen the hands of the Government, and assist Mr Witte in his task'.[140] Grove also believed that the concessions announced in the October Manifesto had at least some soothing effect on working-class opinion in the city. He was certain that the mass of ordinary workers did not share the extreme views of the professional revolutionaries, who attempted without much success to harness popular anger in order to create a direct challenge to the regime. The Consul even suggested that the outside world greatly overestimated the significance of the bloody events which took place in Moscow during the final weeks of the year, when an abortive uprising was crushed with considerable brutality by troops loyal to the government.[141] Unlike Spring Rice, Grove recognised that the Russian workers were not simply an inarticulate mass easily susceptible to manipulation by revolutionaries and government officials alike.

The Embassy was forced to devote a good deal of attention during 1905–6 to the atrocities committed against the Jewish population,[142] since the whole issue was a source of considerable controversy back in London. British newspapers had carried reports of pogroms in Russia since the 1880s, and the Foreign Office was frequently bombarded with demands that it register a formal protest against such outrages.

Successive Foreign Secretaries worked hard to avoid responding to this pressure, however, fearing that it might be seen as interference in the internal affairs of another country. When the first reports of anti-Jewish atrocities reached Lord Lansdowne in the spring of 1905, he too resisted calls from the Anglo-Jewish community for formal representations to be made to the Tsarist government. This attitude was endorsed by British representatives in Russia itself, even though they were under no illusions about the scale of the terror directed against the Jewish population. Senior staff at the Embassy were determined that the issue should not be allowed to complicate Anglo-Russian relations, which had already been placed under great strain as a result of the Dogger Bank incident. Spring Rice did speak to the Assistant Minister of the Interior in November, though he privately doubted whether Ministers were in a position to call a halt to the violence. Like most of his colleagues, he was convinced that the new government headed by Witte was genuinely opposed to the pogroms, but did not believe it had the authority to challenge the antisemitic sentiment that was so deep-rooted in Russian political culture. In any case, while it would be quite unfair to indict British officials in Russia of a latent antisemitism, many of them made little attempt to conceal their belief that the involvement of many Jews in the revolutionary movement made the Jewish population as a whole a natural target for reprisals and counter-attacks. Indeed, this argument closely mirrored the one put forward by Witte and his colleagues, who repeatedly claimed that the pogroms reflected deep public frustration against the various revolutionary groups that had come to prominence over the previous few years. Although Spring Rice and his colleagues usually treated the claims of Tsarist Ministers with suspicion, they were quite willing to endorse the notion that the government could not be held responsible for the sufferings of Russia's Jews during the disorders of 1905.

The defeat of the Moscow rising in December marked the end of the most acute phase of the 1905 Revolution, though uproar continued in the countryside for many months afterwards. Even in the middle of 1906 Viscount Cranley still recorded numerous cases of 'lawlessness and anarchy' in his fortnightly reports,[143] ranging from the sabotage of railway lines through to the murder of policemen and landlords. The gradual return of a comparative peace to the towns was naturally welcomed by staff at the Embassy, who recognised that the government's victory over disorder was in large part due to the loyalty of the army and the refusal of most soldiers to side with the protesters. Although British officials recorded numerous cases of mutiny and desertion during 1905,[144] they were struck by the failure of these episodes to escalate into a full-bloodied collapse of military discipline of the kind that was to take place in 1917. Even the mutiny of the battleship *Potemkin* in Odessa, so lovingly mythologised in Eisenstein's later film, was recognised by Hardinge as little more than a minor affair that 'fizzled out ingloriously'.[145] By the beginning of 1906, just before he left Russia to take up his new duties at the Foreign Office, the Ambassador told London that the worst of the crisis was over since,

> The workmen are weary and want to earn some money for themselves, the revolutionaries are disheartened, the regular troops have proved themselves loyal, and the waverers are rallying to the party of order.[146]

While Hardinge was right to suggest that the immediate threat to the survival of the Tsarist regime was fading, the return of comparative tranquillity to the major cities did not mean that the deep-seated social and political tensions facing the country had been resolved. Long-term political stability depended on the success of the 'Constitutional Experiment' announced in the October Manifesto, and above all on the ability of the proposed new Duma to bridge the gap between the Russian state and Russian society. The new constitution was itself profoundly ambiguous, since it still contained references to Nicholas's autocratic powers while simultaneously laying down the powers of the new assembly.[147] The political omens were therefore not particularly promising when Arthur Nicolson arrived in Russia in May 1906. The Tsar was clearly regretting his decision to part, however tentatively, with any portion of his autocratic inheritance. The more radical elements among the workers and the urban professionals, by contrast, were still deeply suspicious of a government that had only been impelled to make political concessions in the face of the most dire challenge to its existence. The atmosphere was not conducive to the development of the trust and good faith required to establish an effective relationship between the restructured government and the new Duma.

During his first months in Russia, Nicolson could not decide whether the country was about to collapse into anarchy or embark on the road to lasting constitutional reform. Soon after his arrival, he wrote to Lord Knollys that although it was difficult for 'so recent an arrival as myself, to form an opinion as to the future development of this complicated situation ... I may state my impressions and they are that matters are not so critical as they appear to be'.[148] On other occasions, he was more pessimistic, telling the Foreign Office that he feared 'there will be a catastrophe' should the peasantry and working class respond to the calls of revolutionary agitators who sought to direct their fury against the government. Nicolson's views about the prospects for Russia continued to oscillate sharply more or less throughout his four years in the country. At times he believed that a new constitutional order was successfully being established similar to the ones that existed in western Europe; at other times, he doubted whether the government or its critics had the determination and far-sightedness to make constitutional politics work properly. Harold Nicolson suggested many years later that his father had been torn between an instinctive liberalism and an intellectual conviction that effective reform could only be introduced by a strong and secure government.[149] In reality, the ambassador's ambivalence about the Constitutional Experiment probably reflected a deeply-held belief that political reform always needed to be gradual and appropriate to local conditions.

While it is impossible to generalise about the political views held by senior members of the British Diplomatic Service in the early years of the twentieth century, a large proportion of them were by instinct committed to a sort of 'whiggish constitutionalism' that combined a defence of social and political order with a recognition of the rights of different sections of the population to some form of political representation.[150] They believed that the gradual inclusion of wider groups in the population into the confines of the political nation inculcated a respect for the principles of property and order, which in turn discouraged the recently enfranchised from using their new-found voice to mount a fundamental challenge to the position of the existing social and political elites. Any attempt to prevent reform altogether would lead to the kind of social and political explosion that took place in Russia in 1905. By contrast, any attempt to incorporate the entire population into the political process at a single stroke would create chaos, since fragile representative institutions could not cope with the passions of an ill-educated populace lacking an intuitive understanding of the subtle foundations of social and political order.

The commitment of Nicolson and his colleagues to the cause of gradualist reform helps to explain their reaction to the furore surrounding the activities of the first two Dumas which met in 1906–7.[151] Both assemblies were elected on a comparatively democratic franchise, with the inevitable result that many of the new deputies were bitterly critical of the government. At the same time, neither the Tsar nor his Ministers showed any real desire to forge an effective relationship with the new legislature, reflecting Nicholas's perennial ambivalence about engaging in any kind of constitutional politics that limited the scope of his autocratic powers. Nicolson steadfastly refused to blame either side for the 'strained and intolerable' relations that existed between the government and the first Duma during its brief life, which ended when the Tsar used his constitutional power to dissolve the assembly and disperse its radical majority. Both he and Wallace were, however, strongly critical of the deputies' millennial illusions and their persistent demand for radical reforms, which included land reform and an amnesty for all political prisoners.[152] In spite of the dissolution of the first Duma, the Ambassador remained hopeful that the experience obtained by deputies during the weeks it was in session might help to develop a sense of political realism that would in time promote the cause of constitutional development. In the following months, however, Nicolson became more pessimistic, suggesting in his reports to London that there was little real support among the population for the cause of moderate constitutional reform. As a result, he feared that 'two great opposing forces, the extreme parties and the Government, will have to fight out the future of Russia between themselves'.[153] The Ambassador was particularly perturbed by the lack of popular support for the reform-minded Octobrist Party and its policy of responsible opposition, designed to build a political dialogue between the government and its more moderate critics.[154] Since the members of the second Duma which met in spring 1907 were once more elected by a mass franchise, radical deputies again formed a majority – much to the dismay of staff at the Embassy. Wallace was present at each of its sessions, and quickly became disenchanted by its members 'incapacity for serious legislative work'.[155] The Ambassador himself was also frustrated by the deputies' penchant for engaging in political rhetoric and gesture politics, rather than concentrating on the introduction of effective legislation to deal with the problems facing Russia. When the Tsar predictably dissolved the Duma in June, after it had been in session for just a few weeks, the Embassy supported the move. Wallace believed that 'a large section of its members were conspiring to overthrow the monarchy and establish in its place a socialist republic by means of an armed insurrection' (the precise reason which Stolypin gave for the dissolution).[156] Nicolson also blamed the Duma for the breakdown, criticising its members' intransigence and lack of political realism. However, the Ambassador remained surprisingly optimistic about the long-term future for constitutional reform in Russia, despite the bitterness surrounding this second dissolution, arguing in one of his dispatches that the relations between the government and the deputies had in reality been 'far better than was the case during the first essay of Constitutional Government'. He continued to hope that 'gradually Russia will move onward on her constitutional path'.[157]

The appointment of Peter Stolypin as Prime Minister in 1906, before the second Duma opened, was undoubtedly a critical factor in encouraging the Embassy to adopt the *étatiste* perspective of the government. The staff there shared the new Prime Minister's view that constitutional reform needed to be carefully controlled in order to prevent 'irresponsible' opposition by radical critics of the regime, who would use every opportunity to promote political instability and disorder. Once Stolypin started to assert his authority both against his fellow Ministers and the Tsar, Nicolson and his colleagues began to hope that he really could be successful at promoting genuine political reform while simultaneously restoring public order. When a third Duma was elected in the second half of 1907, on a limited franchise designed to ensure the return of a stronger landed element among the deputies, British diplomats showed little inclination to complain about Stolypin's 'constitutional coup'. The results of the election were predictable. The number of deputies representing the radical Cadet Party fell when compared with the second Duma, while the number of moderate-conservative Octobrist deputies rose. The proportion of deputies from the right of the political spectrum increased even more sharply. Not surprisingly, therefore, the deputies who arrived in Petersburg at the end of 1907 were very different from their predecessors. Wallace observed approvingly that 'this Third Duma is very different in outward appearance from its predecessors. The members are better dressed and look more civilized. There are no unkempt Bohemians and very few peasants'.[158] The behaviour of the new deputies reflected their more sober appearance. Nicolson's hope that they would act in a way that would prove to the government that 'a Duma is not an institution to be feared and viewed with distrust' was largely borne out. The quieter tone of the proceedings was far more acceptable to Ministers. Although there were some major disputes between Ministers and deputies, usually reflecting uncertainty about the constitutional division of powers between them,[159] there was no repeat of the radical rhetoric and behaviour evident in the first and second Dumas. By the summer of 1908, Hugh O'Beirne commented hopefully that the Duma had 'definitely taken root among the national institutions', and praised its members' 'moderation and political sense'.[160]

The optimism of Embassy officials over the prospects for establishing a new constitutional form of government was not even shaken by the harsh measures that Stolypin took to restore order in the countryside from the moment he first became Prime Minister. Embassy staff were for the most part trenchant critics of the judicial executions and martial law that were used extensively throughout the time Stolypin was in office.[161] Their distaste was, however, outweighed both by their desire to see strong leadership in Russia and by their enthusiastic support for Stolypin's agrarian policies, which were designed to build up a stratum of wealthy peasantry in the countryside capable of providing a natural bulwark for the defence of order and property.[162] Hugh O'Beirne echoed the views of his colleagues when he wrote in 1908 that although 'it is of course impossible to defend a system under which a man can be deported by decision of the administrative authorities', such measures had undoubtedly 'proved efficacious in crushing the recent revolutionary movement and in restoring order'.[163] Nicolson was a particularly strong supporter of the Prime Minister's attempts to build up support among the prosperous 'mercantile and industrial classes' in order to enlist their help in the battle against 'immorality' and 'morbid degeneracy'.[164] By the end of 1908, the Ambassador was convinced that Stolypin's policy of combining strong government with economic and social reform was beginning to bear fruit. He wrote in his Annual Report for the year that it was 'extremely unlikely' that the events of 1905–6 would recur, since the government was both stronger and more responsive to public opinion than had been the case three years earlier. The Ambassador in fact became rather more pessimistic during his last twelve months in the country, as Stolypin showed himself increasingly willing to by-pass the Duma altogether when its members refused to pass legislation that the Prime Minister believed was vital for the good of the country. Nevertheless, when he left the country in 1910, Nicolson was still hopeful that the country would continue on its path towards economic and political modernity without any return to the anarchy of the past.

Nicolson was too optimistic in believing that the Constitutional Experiment might be able to provide a suitable foundation for Russia's long-term political development. Although the dialogue that developed between Ministers and deputies during the five years the third Duma was in session proved to be far more constructive than had been the case with its predecessors, the ambiguous allocation of constitutional powers always threatened to create unmanageable tensions and rivalries. Above all, too much depended on the personality and political skills of Stolypin. When George Buchanan arrived in Petersburg in 1910 to take up his duties as Ambassador, he was at first more hostile towards the Prime Minister than his predecessor, criticising him for adopting 'unwarranted and unconstitutional' powers.[165] He also distanced himself from Nicolson's optimistic assessment about the stability of the country, warning Sir Edward Grey in London that it was 'impossible to say ... what the future may have in store'.[166] Nevertheless, the logic of circumstances soon forced Buchanan to change his views, and he began to acknowledge that Stolypin's authoritarian style of rule might be the only means of keeping control over an increasingly anarchic and fractious population. After the Prime Minister was assassinated in a Kiev theatre, in September 1911, following a number of previous unsuccessful attempts, the Ambassador wrote to the Foreign Office that Stolypin's 'mistakes were largely outweighed by the services he conferred', even though his policies had not been entirely successful in destroying 'the seeds of unrest that still germinate under-ground'.[167] Buchanan was even more complimentary in a personal letter to King George V, in which he suggested that 'Monsieur Stolypine's death is an irreparable loss' for Russia,[168] as well as a blow to Britain since it removed a strong anglophile from the heart of government. The new Prime Minister, V. N. Kokovtsov,[169] was by no means an incompetent or unimaginative man, but the Ambassador could not hide the fact that he did not have 'quite the same feeling of absolute confidence and sympathy for him' as he had for his predecessor. Buchanan hoped that Kokovtsov would be able to perform the same delicate balancing act that Stolypin had appeared to manage for five years, 'maintaining order with a firm hand' while simultaneously attacking 'the causes which engender unrest and discontent in this country'. His hope was not to be realised. The new Prime Minister lacked Stolypin's ability and vision. He also lacked the strength of personality to establish his authority and independence, which inevitably made him vulnerable to the machinations of Court politics that did so much to destabilise the Empire during its final years. Stolypin's death probably robbed Russia of the last opportunity to pursue the kind of economic and social reforms that might have given the regime some prospect of long-term survival.

The immediate pre-war years were a time of drift and uncertainty in Russia. Although the British Embassy continued to monitor the domestic situation with a good deal of care, the attention of its staff was increasingly taken up by the threatening international situation. The periodic crises in the Balkans, which at times threatened to place an unbearable strain on Anglo-Russian relations, became the main focus of discussion in the meetings that took place between Buchanan and senior Tsarist officials. While there was no repeat of the chaos of 1905, the Ambassador and his staff were convinced that the apparent tranquillity of Russian society was deceptive. Embassy officials became more and more critical of Kokovstsov's performance as Prime Minister, particularly when it became clear that he would not introduce any significant reforms. The appointment of the reactionary N. A. Maklakov as Minister of the Interior compounded the problem.[170] Government Ministers found it increasingly difficult to come to any kind of terms with members of the new fourth Duma, first elected in the autumn of 1912, even though most of the deputies again represented political parties from the centre or the right of the political spectrum. In November 1913 O'Beirne informed Sir Edward Grey in London that 'It must, I think, be admitted that things in Russia are moving slowly in a direction not very favourable to the successful development of a constitutional system of Government'.[171] Although reports filtered through to the Embassy of various attempts to assassinate the Russian Imperial Family, the diplomats there still believed at the end of 1913 that the main threat to the country's embryonic constitution did not come from the radicals and revolutionary groups but from the reaction and intransigence of the Tsar and his more conservative Ministers. Their views changed rapidly in the first few weeks of 1914, however, as the Embassy began to receive a growing number of reports that widespread disorders were threatening to erupt once again.

In January, Consul Woodhouse in Riga described how large-scale strikes had been staged by workers across the city in memory of the victims of Bloody Sunday.[172] By March, Buchanan was writing to the Foreign Office of 'very considerable strikes of a political nature among the working classes in this city ... the demonstrators going so far as to assault and disarm the police – a step which marks a distinct advance in the daring of the Petersburg mob'.[173] The appointment of the elderly and incompetent I. L. Goremykin as Prime Minister in place of Kokovtsov, at the beginning of 1914, did not ease the worries of Embassy officials, since they knew he lacked the imagination and determination to deal with the crisis facing the country. Arthur Nicolson, who had by now become Permanent Secretary at the Foreign Office, used some extremely undiplomatic language when he heard rumours of the change.[174] By the early summer of 1914, strikes were breaking out across all the major cities of the Empire and it seemed that the government might soon be faced with a repetition of the 1905 crisis. In the event, the Russian government's declaration of war on Austria-Hungary and Germany in July 1914 provided a degree of relief. The upsurge of patriotic sentiment helped to dilute the radical mood for a time, as large sections of the population put aside their economic and political grievances against the government in order to concentrate on the conflict with Russia's enemies abroad. Even so, the respite proved temporary. While no European country came out of the First World War with its social and political system unchanged, Russia was transformed for ever.

3

Drawing Near the End

The outbreak of the First World War in the summer of 1914 brought enormous changes for all British officials based in the Tsarist Empire. At the beginning of the conflict, most politicians and military men in London assumed that Britain's direct involvement in hostilities would be limited to 'blockading the coasts and offering financial support to her allies',[1] while the country's two main continental partners, the Russians and the French, would bear the brunt of the actual fighting.[2] Since a good deal of importance was placed on the contribution which the Russian armies could make to the defeat of the Central Powers, a considerable number of British civilian officials and soldiers were sent to Russia during the early months of the war to help coordinate the military policies of London and Petersburg. The Conservative MP Samuel Hoare (the future Viscount Templewood), who headed the British Intelligence Mission in Russia during 1916–17, recalled in his memoirs that by the time he came to the capital the Embassy was full to bursting with 'a staff that had grown ten-fold during the war'.[3] Although Hoare exaggerated the rise in the number of people working in the building, the arrival of a whole new cohort of officials in the years after 1914 certainly transformed the character and *modus operandi* of the British presence in Russia. So too did the growing domestic political crisis that confronted the Tsarist government, as it struggled unsuccessfully to cope with the economic and political strains created by the war. As time went by, British diplomats and military men alike found themselves sucked into the vortex created by the country's slow drift towards revolution.

One of the first new arrivals in the country was General Sir John Hanbury-Williams, who was appointed Head of the British Military Mission to Russia in autumn 1914. During the years between October 1914 and April 1917 he spent most of his time at Russian military headquarters (the *Stavka*), and 'did not often come to Petersburg' (a name that was changed to the more patriotically resonant Petrograd soon after the outbreak of hostilities).[4] Hanbury-Williams was a man of undoubted charm who boasted excellent social connections, but the decision to post him to Russia was on the face of it a curious one. One prominent historian has suggested that the only distinguishing feature of the General's dispatches to London during his two and a half years at the *Stavka* was their 'weakness in spelling [and] a very shaky knowledge of eastern-European geography'.[5] Although this judgement is too severe, it would certainly have been endorsed by the regular Military Attaché at the Embassy in Petrograd, the able if abrasive Ulsterman Alfred Knox, who bitterly resented the appointment of Hanbury-Williams as Head of the Military Mission. Knox had worked at the Embassy since 1911, during which time he built up excellent contacts with senior Tsarist officers, as well as developing a good knowledge of the Russian language. He therefore believed he was better placed than any newcomer to coordinate Anglo-Russian military relations, and was convinced that he had only been passed over as head of the Military Mission because of his comparatively humble social origins. The War Office claimed, with some reason, that Knox's rank was too junior to justify giving him such an important post, and argued that it was necessary to appoint a more senior officer to represent Britain at the *Stavka*.[6] Nevertheless, the Military Attaché was probably right in believing that the decision to send Hanbury-Williams to Russia was dictated at least in part by social considerations. A man of the General's considerable social standing was more likely to command respect in the snobbish world of the senior Tsarist officer corps than an individual from a less elevated background.

In spite of these tensions, relations between the Military Mission and the Embassy were generally good. During his time in Russia, Hanbury-Williams was in some ways better placed to report on 'high politics' than George Buchanan. All the senior foreign officers at the *Stavka* met the Emperor regularly, particularly after Nicholas appointed himself Commander-in-Chief in September 1915 in order to exercise greater control over the day-to-day operations of his armies. The atmosphere at military headquarters was very informal, and Hanbury-Williams enjoyed a degree of intimacy with the Emperor and his family that was denied to regular diplomats.[7] Perhaps for this reason, he was consistently more com-plimentary about both the Emperor and Empress than any British civilian official in Russia. The energetic Admiral Sir Richard Phillimore, who headed the British Naval Mission to Russia, also spent a good deal of time at the *Stavka*, though he was more inclined than Hanbury-Williams to travel around Russia to see at first hand the condition of the country's

armed forces. Like the General, Phillimore found Nicholas to be surprisingly open and frank in his manner.[8] However, while both men had
regular access to the Emperor, their dispatches seldom contained many
real insights into the intricate world of Tsarist politics. Some British
officers in Russia, including Alfred Knox, developed an acute political
sense that allowed them to comment with great shrewdness on
events that were outside their immediate area of military competence.
Hanbury-Williams and Phillimore were not among those who possessed
this talent.

The British Intelligence Mission also stuttered into life in Petrograd
during the first months of the war.[9] In the years that followed, it led
a somewhat checkered existence and was frequently the cause of bad-
tempered controversy among British officials. George Buchanan firmly
opposed the decision to establish the Intelligence Mission, which was
in effect part of the British Secret Service, in spite of the fact that its
members were instructed by London to work closely with the Russians
to collect details about the movement of enemy troops. Although the
primary role of the Mission was *not* to gather information about
the Tsarist Empire itself, the Ambassador feared that its operations
might jeopardise Anglo-Russian relations and make life difficult for his
staff, particularly as some of its members were formally attached to the
Embassy. There is little doubt that the Intelligence Mission did on
occasion provide London with material about developments taking
place inside Russia, even though the collection of such information was
outside its formal remit. When Samuel Hoare was in charge of the
Mission during 1916–17, his dispatches to London contained vital
information and insights into the administrative chaos and political
stagnation which dogged the final years of the Tsarist regime.[10] The
Russian authorities themselves took a rather wary attitude towards the
Intelligence Mission, which was hardly surprising since they knew perfectly well that just a few years earlier one of the main goals of Britain's
Secret Service had been to obtain confidential information about the
Tsarist military. Nevertheless, relations between British intelligence
officers and their Russian counterparts were usually good throughout
1914–17, though the Russians always rather suspected that they provided their opposite numbers with more substantial information than
they received from them.[11]

In addition to the military and civilian representatives based permanently in Russia, many other British officials visited the country for
short periods of time during 1914–17 in order to liaise with the authorities there about one aspect or another of Anglo-Russian relations. Staff

from the Ministry of Munitions and the War Office regularly came to Petrograd to discuss military and supply questions with their opposite numbers, while Treasury officials arrived to offer help and advice about the financing of the Russian war effort. Embassy staff had to spend a good deal of their scarce time organising these trips and chaperoning visitors around the city, a part of their job which they bitterly resented. They did, however, receive a good deal of help during the war years from various fellow-nationals living in Russia who, though nominally independent of either the military or the Diplomatic Service, were able to contribute in some way to the war effort. The journalist Harold Williams, who had lived in Russia for many years and possessed a tremendous range of political contacts, was frequently asked by the British Embassy for help and advice. In the final year or so before the March Revolution, he 'became the chief source of political information on Russian internal politics for the British Embassy',[12] and was instrumental in developing links between diplomatic staff and members of the burgeoning liberal opposition.[13] Williams's role as an 'unofficial diplomatist' was in many ways similar to the one played by Donald Mackenzie Wallace and Bernard Pares during the pre-war years. After 1914 Pares himself continued to spend a good deal of time in Russia, firstly as an 'official correspondent' for the Foreign Office and latterly as correspondent for the *Daily Telegraph*. However, his influence on Embassy officials and Foreign Office staff in London was no longer very great, since it was believed by members of both institutions that his reports were no longer as astute or well-informed as before.[14] Although Pares knew a vast amount about Russian history and culture, he simply could not match Williams's impressive range of contacts and detailed knowledge of contemporary politics.

Partly as a result of Pares' shortcomings, considerable efforts were made in the second half of 1915 to improve British propaganda in Russia, in an attempt to counter the widespread impression that Britain was not providing enough support for its ally. This led in time to the establishment of the Anglo-Russian Bureau, headed by the prolific novelist Hugh Walpole, which was set up to encourage the Tsarist press to report more favourably on Britain's efforts to provide material and strategic assistance to the Russian military.[15] Walpole was greatly admired by Buchanan, and worked in close consultation with regular diplomats at the Embassy, though the Bureau's activities in practice made little impact on public opinion in Petrograd or elsewhere. Nevertheless, Walpole's stay in Russia did at least allow him time to continue his literary work, and provided the inspiration for his novels *The Dark*

Forest and *The Secret City*. Nor was he the only British writer to gain personal experience of Russia during these stormy years. William Gerhardie, the future author of *Futility* and *On Mortal Love*, served as assistant to Alfred Knox at the Embassy in Petrograd.[16] Somerset Maugham spent a brief period in the Tsarist capital during 1917, while on a mission for the British Secret Service, and made use of his experiences when writing the celebrated Ashenden stories. Arthur Ransome worked as a foreign correspondent in Russia throughout the years of revolution, though his radical sympathies meant that he never established particularly close personal or working relations with staff at the British Embassy. The dramatic breakdown of Russian society under the strains of war had the unexpected side-effect of providing excellent material for literary men seeking a theme likely to capture the imagination of their readers.

By the end of the first year of the war, then, a considerable number of British civilian and military officials in Russia were sending dispatches to London containing information about the country's political development. Between 1914 and 1917 George Buchanan was forced to fight a vigorous bureaucratic 'turf-war' to establish the Embassy's role as the principal source of authoritative information on Tsarist Russia. This was particularly difficult given the small size of the regular diplomatic staff, who lacked the resources to coordinate the British presence effectively. When Frank Lindley arrived at the Embassy as acting Counsellor in the summer of 1915, the officials there still lacked sufficient secretarial and clerical help, even though the demands on their time had increased enormously.[17] The activities of the Intelligence Mission were a source of particular controversy. During the first few few months of its existence, the Ambassador wrote to London warning the Foreign Secretary, Sir Edward Grey, of the difficulties that would result if the Mission's members sent incorrect 'political gossip' back to the War Office. Buchanan was particularly concerned that the need to correct false information would add 'to my already heavy work by rendering it necessary for me to contradict it'.[18] The whole question continued to fester throughout 1915, as Buchanan struggled between his desire to bring the Mission more firmly under the control of the Embassy and his fear that its links with the British Secret Service might in some way compromise normal diplomatic activities. At the beginning of 1916, a partial compromise was reached when the War Office finally agreed that the Mission's members should be placed under Knox 'as regards military discipline'.[19] In practice, this seems to have been little more than a sop to the sensitivities of Buchanan and his Military Attaché,

since British intelligence officers continued to send their reports direct
to the War Office as before. As a result, the status of the Intelligence
Mission continued to be a cause of tension throughout the following
year.

During the years after 1914 Buchanan also came into repeated conflict
with British military men in Russia. He was particularly scathing about
the Armoured Car Squadron headed by the colourful Commander
Oliver Locker-Lampson, who drifted about Russia without apparently
taking orders from anyone (though he was nominally under the command of the naval authorities in London).[20] The Ambassador also
criticised Admiral Phillimore at the *Stavka* for neglecting to keep the
Embassy properly informed about his activities.[21] The authorities in
London were well aware of Buchanan's sensitivities, and British representatives in Russia who were not formally under his authority were
advised to keep the Ambassador informed of any matters 'which have
a political bearing'. In practice, this did not always happen. Many of
Buchanan's reports to the Foreign Office complained bitterly of being
'kept entirely in the dark' by officials in both London and Russia, which
he believed made his work far more difficult and less effective than was
necessary.[22]

Buchanan's concern about his loss of authority over other British
representatives in Russia was not just an expression of personal paranoia.
The formal position of the Ambassador vis à vis individuals from departments other than the Foreign Office was indeed unclear, although as
the King's representative he could certainly claim some kind of prece-
dence over his fellow countrymen. In reality, Buchanan's struggle for
authority reflected a wider shift in the status of the Foreign Office and
Diplomatic Service that took place during the Great War. The outbreak
of hostilities in 1914 severely damaged the prestige both of diplomats
and the system of Old Diplomacy which had failed to avert the conflict.
In any case, politicians inevitably took a detailed interest in foreign
policy during times of war, and their intervention diminished the
autonomy and independence of professional diplomats.[23] The appointment of Lloyd George as Prime Minister half way through the conflict
accelerated this trend, since he was generally contemptuous of the
abilities of diplomats (though he had a certain amount of respect for
Buchanan himself).[24] At the same time, as the war progressed, representatives from departments like the War Office and the Admiralty
became more influential and assertive. Many senior British military and
naval officers in Russia were quite open about their contempt for civilians
in general and diplomats in particular. The British Vice-Consul at the

port of Archangel, which served as an important point of entry for war
material sent from Britain to Russia, recalled that diplomats were the
'pet aversion' of the Senior Naval Officer in the port, who made little
effort to keep British civilian representatives in the town informed of
his activities. Lieutenant J. R. Parsons, a Royal Naval reservist who served
as an aide to Admiral Phillimore, commented bitterly in a letter to his
wife that British naval officers in Russia shared 'an impossible belief in
the general and universal superiority of the Naval officer over all other
people'.[25] The problem even cropped up among service Attachés at the
Embassy, though they were quite clearly formally subordinate to the
Ambassador. The Naval Attaché, Captain Harold Grenfell, was taken to
task on more than one occasion for expressing views about the conduct
of the war that would have embarrassed both the Ambassador and the
British government should they have become public knowledge.[26] Nevertheless, while the position of British diplomats in Petrograd was a
difficult one throughout the war years, they still had a vital part to play.
Since Buchanan and his staff possessed a more substantial knowledge
of Russia than any of the 'new men' who arrived in the country during
the early months of the war, their reports continued to provide the most
reliable source of information about developments in the Tsarist Empire
available back in London.

When war broke out in the summer of 1914, the attention of staff at
the British Embassy turned away from the internal social and political
crisis that had absorbed so much of their time in the weeks leading up
to August. This was hardly surprising. The declaration of war proved
in the short term to be a wonderful catalyst for reducing political tension
and rebuilding a degree of sympathy between the government and
people of Tsarist Russia. Although some of the Tsar's most influential
Ministers feared that involvement in a European war could create
economic and social problems that might destroy the regime,[27] in the
first few days after the beginning of hostilities patriotic demonstrations
quickly took the place of angry protests on the streets of Moscow and
Petrograd. When Britain entered the struggle against Germany and
Austria on 4 August, cheering crowds appeared in front of the Embassy
and George Buchanan was forced to go out on to the balcony and play
the unwelcome role of public orator. It was an experience that was to
become more familiar to him over the years that followed, as the
Ambassador became an increasingly significant figure in the turbulent
world of Russian politics.

During the first few months of the war, officials at the Embassy did receive a number of reports suggesting that the new-found trust between the Russian government and people was comparatively fragile. Although some British consular officials sent in dispatches reporting on patriotic demonstrations in their own cities and regions,[28] those based in areas where ethnic groups other than the Russians formed a large proportion of the population often told a different story. At the end of August, Patrick Stevens wrote from Batum – where a large section of the population was of Turkish origin – that there was only limited support for the war in the city and its immediate hinterland.[29] During the following months, consular staff in Odessa also told of the 'discontent' which followed the imposition of higher taxes to pay for the war.[30] British Consuls based in the western provinces of the Empire wrote at some length on the damage done by the government's renewed policy of Russification, which they believed earned the hatred both of the Jews and of the indigenous German population, who were treated 'both harshly and unjustly' by the authorities.[31] For the most part, these signs of possible trouble ahead were ignored by staff at the Petrograd Embassy. They were instead more inclined to trust the evidence of their own eyes, which seemed to indicate that the Russian population enthusiastically supported the government's determination to bring the war to a satisfactory conclusion. This in turn partly blinded them, in the short term at least, to the unpleasant fact that the country still faced serious social and political problems that could easily undermine its value as an ally in the war against the Central Powers.

The defeats suffered by the Russian armies during the first months of the war naturally created great concern among British representatives in the country, as well as their political masters in London. It was clear from the beginning of the conflict that the chaotic nature of the Tsarist administration would weaken the country's military performance on the battlefield. The dreadful defeat which took place in the last week of August at the battle of Tannenberg, at the hands of the Germans, was an ominous sign of the difficulties ahead. During the weeks that followed, communication between the British and Russian military authorities was not always as smooth as it might have been. Hanbury-Williams noted a few days after his arrival at the *Stavka* that although he was shown 'all possible kindness and civility' by the Russians, they still treated him 'more as the Military Attaché of a *Foreign* Army in peace time than as the Representative of an Allied Army in War time'.[32] Six weeks later, the General was already expressing a fear that public opinion in Britain took too optimistic a view of the military potential of the Russian army. While he recognised that it was a better-trained force than its predecessor in the Russo-Japanese war of 1904–5, it was still '*not* the same highly trained machine that the German army is'.[33] In December Hanbury-Williams' dispatches also began to contain references to the problems faced by the Russian military as a result of its lack of munitions, particularly rifles and shells,[34] a theme that was echoed by Alfred Knox in his reports from the Front.[35] By the beginning of 1915, the munitions crisis was rapidly becoming the most important and controversial issue in Anglo-Russian relations. It remained so for the rest of the war.

In spite of the failure of Russia's invasion of East Prussia, and the awful human and material losses that accompanied it, Britain's diplomatic and military representatives based in the Tsarist Empire continued to have faith that the Russian 'steamroller' would soon prove itself on the battlefield and advance westwards once again.[36] It was an assumption that was endorsed even more strongly by officials and politicians in London. Their reluctance to abandon this belief was understandable. British strategy during the first year of the war was, as seen earlier, based on the assumption that the Russian and French armies would carry out most of the actual fighting while Britain provided financial and logistical support. As a result, Russian success on the Eastern Front against the Austrians and the Germans was crucial to ensure that the Central Powers did not divert manpower and armaments to the Western Front, which would inevitably create a need for the British to expand the size of the Expeditionary Force sent to France during the first weeks of the war. Although this strategy came under increasing pressure as 1915 wore on, the belief that Russian military success was vital for Britain's national interests remained largely intact. Since neither politicians nor generals were adept at changing their strategic beliefs during the 1914–18 war, the early Russian defeats and the burgeoning munitions crisis failed to have an immediate impact on their thinking.

The reluctance of British officials to allow the early defeats on the Eastern Front to affect their basic assumptions about the course of the war had other roots as well. The centuries old belief that the Russian soldier was a naturally hardy and ferocious warrior died hard: indeed, it was an integral part of the 'steamroller' image that continued to dominate so much British thinking about the war throughout 1915. Hanbury-Williams noted in a dispatch sent to Buchanan in January 1915 that, although there had been some desertions in the face of enemy fire, 'The Russian soldier seems a patient unexcitable being who accepts the order of his commander as Kismet and does not worry to

ask questions'.[37] Bernard Pares echoed these sentiments in his reports
from the Front, speaking of the bravery of the Russian soldiers in the
face of terrible injuries and disease.[38] Even Alfred Knox, who was more
sceptical about the calibre of the Tsarist troops, wrote admiringly of
their willingness to fight when they had almost no ammunition or
weapons with which to do so. In part, of course, these positive assess-
ments of the Russian forces' potential simply reflected a desire to think
the best of an ally. At the same time, they also concealed a reluctance
to think seriously about the significance of the crisis which faced the
Russian military.

Professor Norman Stone has shown in great detail how the Russian
authorities used the 'shells crisis' as an excuse to explain military defeats
that were in reality the consequence of poor tactical thinking and
downright incompetence.[39] The war plan prepared by the Russian
General Staff was deeply flawed and overly simplistic, since it failed to
take into account the need for mobility in modern warfare. The reliance
on cavalry also proved to be a disaster, since its use was not integrated
effectively with the deployment of the infantry. However, many British
civilian and military officials both in London and Russia were only too
willing to accept the official Russian explanation for these defeats. By
endorsing the notion that a shortage of munitions was the principal
factor preventing the Russian steamroller from rolling, they were able to
convince themselves that the introduction of new measures to improve
the supply of war material would soon allow the Tsarist armies to
advance once again. This, in turn, meant that they were not forced to
rethink basic questions of political and military strategy. Of course,
some officials in London were aware that the failure of the Russian
military during the first months of the war might demand some fundamental reappraisal of the role of the British army in the years that
followed. The rise of the 'Westerners' grouped around General Sir
William Robertson, who favoured an increased British involvement on
the Western Front in France, was at least in part a result of growing
disenchantment with the performance of the Tsarist military. Nevertheless, throughout most of 1915, hopes remained high in London
that, given enough time and supplies, the Russian armies would still
be able to play the role which had originally been envisaged for them
at the beginning of the conflict in 1914.[40]

British diplomats at the Petrograd Embassy were better placed than
most to understand that the munitions crisis was not just the result of
a time-lag resulting from the difficulties involved in converting a
peace-time economy to war-time production, but rather a reflection of

deep-seated administrative failings that had been the hallmark of the Tsarist state for centuries. George Buchanan reported at length on the Russian authorities' failure to act in an 'expeditious and businesslike' way when trying to organise the purchase of guns and ammunition in foreign countries (where Russian purchasing agents sometimes found themselves in the absurd position of bidding against one another for the same supplies).[41] The Embassy also made strenuous efforts to liaise with the military authorities in Petrograd so as to obtain details about their exact munitions requirements, but a combination of ignorance and secrecy meant that the information was seldom forthcoming. Britain's diplomats had of course known for decades that bureaucratic corruption and incompetence were endemic in the Tsarist Empire, and instrumental in preventing the adoption of the kind of social and economic policies that could have alleviated the strains of modernisation during the decades before 1914. As was seen in the previous chapter, most British representatives did not believe that any significant reform of the administrative system could take place unless accompanied by wider changes in the autocratic structure of power. Even so, during the first half of 1915, Buchanan and his staff were surprisingly willing to endorse the prevailing belief that technical measures to increase the flow of munitions could alone resolve the supply crisis and improve the appalling performance of the Russian armies. They were closely involved in the attempts made by the British government to help the Russians obtain military supplies abroad via the provision of advice and financial support. One of Buchanan's most important roles during 1915 was to manage the tension caused by the breakdowns in communication which often accompanied this time-consuming and complex process. His support for the establishment of the Anglo-Russian Bureau was in large part a reaction to the collapse of Britain's prestige in Russia during 1915, which came about as the population started to blame the British for failing to provide enough material support to its ally. However, the Ambassador and his colleagues were far more worried by the rapid growth in popular discontent with the *Russian* government, which began to reach a crescendo in the middle of the year. By the early summer of 1915, Embassy staff were increasingly anxious that political instability in the Tsarist Empire could affect the country's ability to wage war far more seriously than a simple shortage of munitions. The lull in political unrest which had started with the outbreak of war in July 1914 lasted in practice for just a single year.

By the late spring of 1915 the Tsarist military machine still showed few signs of improving its dismal performance. Russian armies retreated in the face of a determined German offensive, suffering a disastrous defeat at Gorlice in early May. A few weeks later the town of Lvov was lost to the Austrians. These catastrophes pushed the patience of the Russian population to its limits. In June serious rioting broke out in Moscow. Although the fury of the rioters was directed against German-owned businesses and houses, the difficulties encountered in quelling the unrest provided an ominous symbol of the widening gulf between the population and the authorities. At the same time liberal opinion began to take an increasingly critical view of the government's activities, following the comparative quiescence of the previous few months when most moderate critics of the regime had generally favoured a policy of cooperation with the authorities. In June 1915 a conference of the Cadet Party called for the appointment of a government whose members commanded public support, a demand which was to be heard on many occasions over the following eighteen months. British officials were quick to realise the significance of this change in the public mood. At the end of June, Buchanan told the Foreign Office that the loss of Lvov had provoked 'increasing public discontent with the management of the war'.[42] Consul-General Roberts in Odessa went further, informing London of the gloomy mood in the city and predicting the possibility of 'internal troubles'.[43] Reports that came to the Embassy from other cities around the Empire, including Moscow, confirmed that public disquiet was on the increase and was threatening to destabilise the political situation. The summer of 1915 marked an important stage in Russia's political development, as wider and wider sections of the population began to realise that recent military failures were in large measure brought about by the administrative ineptitude of the Tsarist regime. The more vocal critics of the government started to attack the Emperor and his Ministers not only for failing to live up to the constitutional promises which had been contained in the October Manifesto of 1905, but also for their chronic incompetence and inefficiency. British officials were quick to recognise the explosive potential of this dual challenge to the legitimacy of the regime, which harnessed patriotic sentiment to the cause of political reform.

The Tsar and his Ministers recognised the danger posed by the chorus of criticism that became increasingly audible in the early summer of 1915, and in July Nicholas made a number of gestures designed to ameliorate public concern about the conduct of the war. He appointed General A. A. Polivanov as Minister of War in place of the unpopular

V. A. Sukhomlinov, who was widely (if unfairly) held responsible for the disasters that had overtaken the army in the previous year. At the same time, the irreproachably honest A. D. Samarin was made Procurator of the Holy Synod. Perhaps most important of all, Nicholas announced his intention to recall the Duma. These gestures were enthusiastically welcomed by Buchanan and his staff, who were convinced that political calm could only be restored in Russia if the government showed itself willing to listen to public opinion and respond to popular disquiet about the conduct of the war. However, the changes announced by the Tsar had much less impact on the sentiments of the general population. Instead of serving to reduce political tension, they simply acted as a catalyst for even more radical demands. The first session of the Duma, which met on 1 August, showed the depth of the gulf which had developed between the Russian government and its critics. The French Ambassador and novelist manqué, Maurice Paléologue, who was admittedly never slow to place a melodramatic interpretation on the world around him, wrote in his diary that the atmosphere during these days was 'heated, heavy and full of the promise of storm'.[44] George Buchanan agreed, writing to London a few days later that the speeches made by several of the deputies were 'far more outspoken than has ever been the case previously'. The Ambassador reported at length on the attacks which had been made by speakers on the 'system of intrigue and corruption', and went on to note that 'It can hardly be doubted that this debate will have a profound effect on public opinion in Russia'. His conclusion was particularly stark:

> It is true that the forces of the bureaucracy are entrenched behind defences which have shown themselves proof against many an attack, and it is not likely that they will succumb during the confusion and side-issues of a great war. But the misfortunes through which it is passing have stirred the country to its depths, and it is hard to believe, when the settlement arrives, it will ever again tolerate the old order of things.[45]

Buchanan's earlier optimism that the recall of the Duma could reduce political tension had virtually disappeared by the middle of August, as the Ambassador realised that the chorus of criticism was unlikely to be assuaged by anything less than a complete reform of the political system.

Some of the most detailed accounts of the growth of opposition to the regime in 1915 came from Lockhart in Moscow, who had been made acting Consul-General following the departure of his superior to England on sick-leave. The importance of Lockhart's dispatches was in part a consequence of their author's skilful powers of observation and vivid writing style, which meant that they were eagerly read both at the Embassy and back at the Foreign Office in London. The value of his reports was enhanced by the breadth of his contacts with leading members of the Russian liberal movement. Lockhart was a close friend of M. V. Chelnokov, Head of the Union of Cities, and Prince G. E. Lvov, Chairman of the Union of Zemstvos. Both these organisations, which were together usually referred to by their combined acronym as the Zemgor, were based in Moscow, a city that had since the eighteenth century served as the spiritual home for all those who viewed with distaste the activities and *mores* of the bureaucrats who dominated political life in the new capital on the banks of the Neva. The Zemgor had from the early months of the war fulfilled a number of important tasks, including the provision of hospital care for the wounded, which the regular administration seemed to be utterly incapable of carrying out.[46] Although the government looked with suspicion at the Zemgor, fearing that they might serve as a challenge to its authority, their pragmatic and efficient working-style endeared them to large sections of the population. Officials at the British Embassy also looked with favour on the Zemgor, which seemed to them to symbolise the ideals of efficiency and civic initative that were close to the heart of most members of the Diplomatic Service.[47]

Lockhart's friendship with many leading figures in the Zemgor meant that he was continually exposed to the ideas and opinions of a section of the population that was deeply critical of the Tsarist government, a fact which inevitably coloured his reports. By the beginning of August 1915, he told Buchanan that the population's 'general disgust at the failure of the bureaucracy' could in time develop into 'active political trouble'. He also noted that 'probably 90 per cent of the population of the towns is in favour of a proper constitution and a responsible Ministry', and informed the Ambassador that the Royal Family was becoming more and more unpopular with every passing day.[48] Nor did Lockhart believe that such critical sentiments were limited to the comparatively small cabal of middle-class liberals who dominated the leadership of the Zemgor. In a second dispatch, written around the same time, he described the growth of the labour movement around Moscow and predicted that 'Were a situation to arise which would give the workmen a favourable opportunity of achieving success by force, I do not believe they would hesitate to employ it'. The only bright spot on the horizon, he suggested, was that popular support for the war continued unabated among both middle-class liberals and workers. As long as the conflict continued, there was unlikely to be a sustained challenge to 'law and order'.[49]

Given the 'whiggish' instincts expressed by so many of those who served in the Diplomatic and Consular Services, it is not surprising that British officials in Russia reacted with despair at the events of autumn 1915, when the Emperor reversed almost all the concessions he had made in the previous two months. The Duma was prorogued in the middle of September and, a few days later, Samarin was dismissed as Procurator of the Synod after just a few months in the post. At the same time, the conservative A. N. Khvostov was made Minister of the Interior in place of the more moderate Prince N. B. Shcherbatov. A few days before these changes occurred, Nicholas also announced his intention of taking over as Commander-in-Chief of Russian forces at the *Stavka*. Although this decision was opposed by several of his Ministers, who feared that the Emperor's personal authority would be tainted by association with any further military defeats, Buchanan at first treated the prospect with equanimity,[50] even though he had been asked by the Grand Duke Dmitry to dissuade Nicholas from taking such a drastic step.[51] Before long, the Ambassador came to realise the enormity of the move, which effectively reduced the Emperor's authority over the conduct of day to day affairs in Petrograd while simultaneously enhancing the power of Ministers such as the elderly and incompetent Prime Minister I. L. Goremykin. More damaging still, the absence of Nicholas from the capital increased the influence of both the Empress and Rasputin on the conduct of state affairs. Although historians have sometimes overestimated the power of Alexandra and her cabal during the period before the March Revolution, the vitriol which both she and her enigmatic holy man attracted was undoubtedly a significant factor in undermining popular support for the government during the fatal period leading up to March 1917. While Rasputin's ability to influence minsterial appointments and important state decisions was in reality quite limited, his celebrated hypnotic ability to relieve the pain caused by the young Tsarevich's haemophilia undoubtedly gave him considerable influence over the boy's mother. Nicholas generally had the good sense to ignore the advice given to him by his neurotic wife and her spiritual adviser, but his desire to preserve the tranquillity and serenity of his domestic life meant that he usually at least went through the motions of listening to their counsel.[52] This not only enraged his Ministers, it also helped to encourage the spread of rumours that the Tsar was dictated to by his part-German wife and her circle of intimates. As a result, Alexandra and Rasputin quickly began to serve as a focus for the popular discontent and frustration which eventually destroyed the Russian *ancien régime*.

Lockhart's dispatches from Moscow described in detail the popular fury that erupted in the city following the government's change in policy. The liberal leaders of the Zemgor were appalled by the decision to prorogue the Duma, which they interpreted as a high-handed defiance of public opinion. The work-force in the city's factories was also infuriated by the move, which led to an outbreak of strikes and protests throughout the second half of September. Lockhart was himself convinced that only 'Mr Goremykin's dismissal would ... greatly relieve the tension, and ... until he resigns, the unrest and discontent are bound to continue'.[53] Even though he acknowledged that it was possible to overestimate the extent of public dismay, he was struck by the widespread popular belief that 'there are traitors in high places', observing laconically to Buchanan that 'in Russia a cry of this sort is difficult to stop'.[54] The Ambassador did not need to read the reports from Moscow in order to gauge the depth of anger amongst all classes of Russian society, since it was equally widespread in Petrograd itself. He wrote to Sir Edward Grey in September describing a series of strikes which had broken out in the city, including one at the huge Putilov works which supplied large quantities of war material to the Russian military.[55] The Ambassador was particularly concerned by the growth of popular feeling against the Royal Family. Even in August, when the Duma was still in session, he had written to London describing the 'growing unpopularity' of the Emperor amongst the officer corps, which had traditionally been one of the strongest bastions of support for the regime.[56] Six weeks later, he sent a 'Personal and Secret' telegram to Sir Edward Grey telling him that 'The Empress, Rasputin and Goremykin are regarded as three malignant councillors of the Emperor's present policy and hatred is the only word that can describe [the] feeling against the Empress'.[57] While Buchanan had been worried for some time about the influence of Alexandra and Rasputin on Nicholas, which he feared might propel the Tsar towards more conservative and pro-German policies, it was only with the drift to reaction in the autumn of 1915 that he believed the situation was beginning to reach a critical point. Since the Ambassador realised that continued political instability would damage Russia's value as a military ally, in October he made, in consultation with the Foreign Office, the fateful decision to become involved more actively in the country's domestic politics. From this moment onwards, it was increasingly accepted both in the Embassy and at the Foreign Office in London that the internal affairs of the Tsarist Empire were a matter of vital concern and legitimate comment for its allies. Buchanan spent much of his time in the eighteen months before the March Revolution vainly trying 'to persuade the Emperor to appoint a Prime Minister who inspired confidence in Duma and patriotic circles'.[58]

By the early autumn of 1915, Buchanan had already become accustomed to expressing his concerns about the political situation in Russia to the handful of liberal Ministers in the government, though only in private conversation. At the end of September he told the Minister of Agriculture, A. V. Krivoshein, that he was concerned about the government's instinctive tendency to resort to repressive measures in the face of popular protest and unrest.[59] It was, though, one matter to speak of such concerns to Ministers whose discretion could be relied upon. By contrast, diplomatic protocol required that foreign representatives should be very careful before becoming more openly involved in the domestic politics of the country to which they were accredited. Although Buchanan was by instinct a cautious individual who had no wish to break with the conventions that had bound his professional life for more than thirty years, by the beginning of October 1915 his fears about Russia's future outweighed his natural prudence. On 16 October he bluntly told the Foreign Office in London that 'the country is almost ripe for revolution',[60] and asked whether he should seek an audience with the Emperor to warn him of the impending crisis. On the following day, he also sounded out the Russian Foreign Minister about the wisdom of taking such a drastic course of action. Sazonov approved the idea.[61] The Foreign Office also approved the Ambassador's proposal, particularly since, as the Permanent Secretary Sir Arthur Nicolson noted, 'We can trust to Sir George Buchanan handling the matter with tact and circumspection'.[62] Even though Grey recognised that Buchanan would be breaking with normal diplomatic protocol by speaking openly about Russia's internal politics, he was confident that 'the Emperor will allow you to speak frankly to him, and will understand that it is a friendly and confidential exposition of views'.[63] The Ambassador therefore decided to press ahead with his plan. While he claimed in his memoirs that he did not talk to Nicholas about internal affairs until 1916,[64] it was in reality the crisis of autumn 1915 that first led him to break with the traditions of the past and intervene in the internal politics of the Tsarist Empire.

Buchanan's scheme in fact seemed to be in danger of falling apart on the day after the Foreign Office gave its blessing. It became clear during a second meeting with Sazonov that the Foreign Minister had become alarmed at the prospect of the audience and was reluctant to let it go ahead.[65] The reason for his change of heart is not clear. He told Buchanan that the pretext they had agreed upon for the Ambassador's visit to the *Stavka* – to introduce a visiting British General to Nicholas – was too transparent. The Foreign Minister was also afraid that if the Ambassador spoke too frankly it would offend the Emperor and 'might even affect [his] feeling towards His Majesty's [George V's] Government'. Buchanan proposed to circumvent this problem by employing the same diplomatic fiction he used during subsequent audiences when conveying sentiments that he knew were likely to offend the Emperor: to claim that he was speaking on his own authority and not that of his government.[66] Sazonov remained reluctant to give his blessing to the project, insisting that if the audience were to go ahead the Ambassador should not think of saying anything against Rasputin 'as that was far too dangerous a question for us to tread on'. The Foreign Minister was still in a cautious mood on the following day, so Buchanan more or less decided to shelve the scheme.[67] However, a few days later the Emperor paid an unexpected visit to Petrograd from the *Stavka*, providing the Ambassador with an opportunity to press ahead with the original plan.

Buchanan's report to London after the audience suggested that he was very frank indeed during his meeting with Nicholas. He told the Emperor that although 'patriotic people would prevent the outbreak of any serious disturbances so long as the war lasted, there was much combustible material which a spark might set alight at any moment'. The Ambassador went on to say that he was 'afraid of what might happen when the war was over'. He also told Nicholas that while the Russian people did not question 'His Majesty's determination to do all in his power to bring the war to a successful issue ... they had lost all faith in the instruments whose duty it was to give effect to His Majesty's orders and issues. They wanted in fact a thorough reform of what they considered [a] corrupt and incompetent bureaucracy'. Buchanan found it difficult to judge Nicholas's reaction to his words, though the Tsar can hardly have taken kindly to being lectured by a foreigner about the state of his own country. The Ambassador believed that he had handled the situation with sufficient tact, particularly by playing on the centuries-old myth that the evils affecting Russia were due to the corruption and incompetence of the Emperor's advisers rather than any failings in the ruler himself. Even so, he was still not optimistic about the efficacy of his remarks, since he doubted whether they could 'bear fruit' as long as the Empress continued to exercise influence over her husband's political decisions.[68]

During the final weeks of 1915 the political situation in the Tsarist Empire became somewhat calmer, though British officials had no illusions that the underlying tensions had disappeared. In November Lockhart suggested that the continuing strikes in Moscow need not be taken too seriously, since they had 'no support from public opinion', which he believed had 'become more or less indifferent to questions of political reform'.[69] At the same time, he did not believe that the general sullenness and resentment exhibited by large sections of the population boded well for the future. Buchanan's new deputy at the Embassy in Petrograd, Frank Lindley, agreed with this assessment of the political situation, warning that public quiescence should not be taken as evidence of 'general satisfaction ... in the present Government and their methods'.[70] Similar views were heard from British officials in the provinces. The consular representative in Odessa wrote to Buchanan in December 1915 that 'It is extremely difficult to discover the opinion of people as to what may happen after the War'. He noted, however, the existence of constant 'murmuring' against the 'appointments of certain Ministers', and suggested that the public were unlikely to remain passive for long in the face of government reaction.[71] At the beginning of 1916 British officials across Russia were still watching the domestic political situation with considerable anxiety, fearful that a single spark could set in motion a chain of revolutionary events that would have momentous consequences both for the country and its allies.

It is perhaps too easy for historians of Russia to see the events of 1916 simply as a slow but sure drift towards revolution. The contours of the looming crisis had been clear since the summer of 1915, when support for the principle of wholesale political change began to spread rapidly among a population that was increasingly concerned about the course of the war. However, a close look at the views of those who lived in the Tsarist Empire during the fateful months leading up to the March Revolution helps to provide a rather different perspective. When they eventually came to write their memoirs, Tsarist officials and foreign diplomats alike generally treated 1916 simply as a prelude to the collapse of the Russian *ancien régime*. In reality, they found it much harder to make sense of developments when they were living through them. British representatives in Petrograd and the provinces were no exception. Although many of them had a powerful sense that the society around them was sliding into chaos, their attention was usually focused on more specific and localised events. In their dispatches dire warnings about the future were often interspersed with speculation as to whether the appointment of some new ministerial non-entity could succeed in halting the descent into anarchy. The perspective of Buchanan and other British officials in the Russian capital was clouded by the need to interpret and report on short-term and essentially trivial developments.

Almost all British representatives based in Russia during this period, whether civilian or military, found themselves submerged by the sheer scale of their duties. If the staff at the Petersburg Embassy had shown themselves to be diligent workers in the years before 1914, their workload became still greater once the war began. Although the calibre of staff was extraordinarily high, their abilities and stamina were sorely tested by the demands placed upon them every day of the week.[72] The stress was even greater on senior officials. George Buchanan often fell ill during 1916, his health undermined by periodic bouts of exhaustion. His absence made life particularly difficult for Frank Lindley, who had to deputise for the Ambassador even though his own time was already fully occupied with monitoring the local economic and political situation.[73] Lockhart in Moscow also fell victim to the stress of his job, despite the fact that he was only half the age of the Ambassador. In the spring of 1916 he was struck down by a severe throat infection and a deep bout of depression, triggered at least in part by his growing doubts as to whether Russia could continue to be an effective ally in the battle against the Central Powers. During Easter 1916 he was able to take a few days rest in order to recuperate from the stress of his official duties, visiting the ancient monastery at Sergievo to the south of Moscow, where he was able to relax in a countryside that was 'a mass of primroses and cowslips'.[74] Yet, as Lockhart soon discovered on his return to the city, while such brief sojourns could lead in the short term to a recovery of 'energy and fresh hope', there was no real respite for the representatives of Russia's allies from the 'chronicle of almost unrelieved pessimism'.[75]

It was no easier for staff based in Petrograd to escape the pressure of work. George Buchanan still insisted on taking his regular morning walk through the streets of the capital, but found it increasingly difficult to find time to play golf, the pastime which had always served as his main form of relaxation. Although the Ambassador was occasionally able to take short holidays in Finland or the Caucasus, they were not long enough to provide him with the physical and mental relaxation he needed. Frank Lindley was physically much stronger than Buchanan, as well as many years younger, and was therefore able to find a little more time and energy to pursue his sporting interests. During the winter he skied to the Embassy across the frozen Neva from his flat on Vassily Ostrov. In the summertime he travelled to Finland to fish in the River Voksa, famous for its trout and grayling.[76] 'Benjy' Bruce naturally had an entreé to the capital's cultural and artistic elite through his wife, the ballerina Kasavina, but was seldom able to take advantage of it since his position as Head of Chancery kept him fully occupied. Even the indefatigable Hugh Walpole found it more and more difficult to find the energy to keep up his writing. Officials in both Moscow and Petrograd continued to have a social life of sorts, but it became almost indistinguishable from their offical duties. Buchanan hosted receptions of various kinds at the Embassy in Petrograd, while Lockhart was continually required to act as tour guide and master of ceremonies for British military and civilian officials visiting Moscow. Ironically, the most relaxed style of life was probably the one enjoyed by senior British military and naval officers at the *Stavka*. Since military headquarters was remote from the bustle of Petrograd, life was far more ordered than in the city. Although General Hanbury-Williams did occasionally visit the various theatres of war, he was less active than the Military Attachés at the Embassy who travelled regularly to the Front in order to report on the situation there. A good deal of his time was spent in conversation with the Emperor, or attending the cinema shows and displays of gypsy dancing that were regularly put on for the entertainment of the Royal Family.[77] Life could also be fairly pleasant for junior army officers attached to the *Stavka* or the Embassy. Lieutenant John Parsons developed a strong dislike for his chief, Admiral Phillimore, but he could at least spend much of his time reading or sending letters back to his wife in England.[78] Back in Petrograd, William Gerhardie even found that he had enough spare time from his duties as Knox's assistant to devote long hours to the cultivation of a nonchalant style of dress and manner carefully designed to appeal to the young women of the city.[79]

Gerhardie was of course merely a junior officer and therefore not really expected to carry out many important duties. For those in more responsible positions, there was no time to spare for the trivial occupations which absorbed the future author of *Futility*. At the very beginning of 1916, the Emperor's decision to replace the incompetent Goremykin as Prime Minister raised hopes amongst liberal Russians and allied diplomats alike that real political change might lie ahead. Such hopes were short-lived. Goremykin's replacement was B.V. Stürmer, a man who quickly earned the hatred of almost everyone at the British Embassy. In his memoirs, Buchanan remembered him as 'a second-rate intelligence, without any experience of affairs, a sycophant, bent solely on the advancement of his own interests, and extremely ambitious'.[80] In October 1916, after the Prime Minister had been in post for a few months, the Ambassador's view of Stürmer was even more vitriolic. In a letter to Charles Hardinge at the Foreign Office, he described the Prime Minister as 'corrupt, cynical, incompetent and lying'.[81] The Ambassador was deeply concerned that Stürmer was by instinct more sympathetic to the Germans than the allies, and feared that he might try to exert pressure on the Emperor to make a separate peace with Berlin, a subject that exercised Embassy staff almost constantly throughout 1916. He was also convinced that the Prime Minister owed his advancement 'to the fact that he was a friend of Rasputin and that he was backed by the Empress's camarilla'.[82] The truth of such an accusation is unclear. The correspondence between Nicholas and Alexandra during this period certainly shows that Rasputin had considerable influence on the Empress, and that she in turn was listened to carefully by her husband. However, whether Buchanan and his staff were right in suggesting that the two exercised a decisive influence over the Emperor's choice of Ministers during the months leading up to the March Revolution is less certain. Nevertheless, staff at the Embassy assumed throughout 1916 that the rapid turnover of Ministers could only be explained by reference to the influence of the 'dark forces' at Tsarskoe Selo. In March Lindley argued in his fortnightly Summary of Events that the recent dismissal of A. N. Khvostov as Minister of Interior only came about because he was attempting to persuade Nicholas of the danger posed by Rasputin.[83] Other ministerial resignations were usually explained by the Embassy in similar terms. Although there was never much firm evidence for these accusations, Buchanan and his staff were convinced that the Emperor could 'never hope to regain his popularity' as long as he 'allows himself to be influenced by Rasputin and other persons in the Empress's entourage'.[84]

Throughout 1916 Buchanan actively tried to persuade Nicholas to appoint Ministers who commanded a degree of public support in the hope that such a move would reduce political tension, though he was always careful to avoid attacking Rasputin by name. His first attempt of the year came in February, during an audience with the Emperor at Tsarskoe Selo. In the telegraphic account of the meeting that was sent to London, the Ambassador reported that:

As the Emperor told me I might be perfectly frank with him I kept nothing back. I told him how a few months ago one heard revolutionary

talk in nearly every Drawing Room, how officers had openly declared
the impossibility to tolerate continuance of present regime under the
war, how though things now were quieter there was widespread discontent, and how the best elements in the country were being alienated
and discouraged.[85]

In spite of his injunction to the Ambassador to be 'perfectly frank',
Nicholas reacted less favourably than in the previous November. By
the end of the audience he 'looked pale and worried'. Buchanan was
convinced that his outspokenness aroused the anger of the 'dark forces'
grouped around Rasputin, and complained bitterly in his memoirs how,
during a visit which he made to the *Stavka* a few months later, he was
deliberately prevented from speaking to the Emperor. Whether or not
this is true – and at least one British military representative later
questioned the accuracy of the Ambassador's account – Nicholas's reaction at the February audience showed the sensitivity of any attempt
by British representatives to intervene in Russian affairs.[86] Throughout
the war, Tsarist military and civilian officials alike reacted with hostility
whenever they believed that their position was being usurped by their
British counterparts.[87] Nor was their reaction simply evidence of
oversensitivity. The attitude of British army and naval officers was all
too often patronising and arrogant. Many of them made little secret
that they considered 'people of other nations ... as dirt alongside the
Englishman', a sentiment that was hardly calculated to smooth the path
of Anglo-Russian cooperation.[88]

Buchanan's most dramatic attempt to influence the Emperor came
in the summer of 1916, when rumours began to circulate that the
Foreign Minister was about to be dismissed. Diplomats at the Embassy
were appalled at such a prospect, both because Sazonov had always
been a staunch supporter of the Anglo-Russian alliance and because
he was seen as a force for moderation in domestic politics. The Ambassador decided to send a telegram to Nicholas, begging him to retain
the Foreign Minister on the grounds that he commanded the trust of
all the allied governments.[89] The appeal met with little success, even
though Buchanan sought the help of Hanbury-Williams at the *Stavka*
to bolster his case. Sazonov soon resigned, ostensibly on health grounds,
though opinion among the diplomatic community in Petrograd assumed that his support for a more liberal policy towards Poland was
the real source of tension with the Emperor. In fact, Hanbury-Williams's
temporary replacement at the *Stavka* during the summer of 1916,
General W. H. H. Walters, was told by Nicholas that the real reason
for Sazonov's dismissal was more predictable: that 'he was going too

fast and too far, and raising hopes which, with an illiterate people like mine, could not be realised for generations'.[90] Whatever the true circumstances behind the Foreign Minister's resignation, Buchanan was still not daunted by yet another failure to influence the course of Tsarist politics. In November 1916 he used a further audience to warn the Emperor once more about 'the profound discontent prevailing all over the country'.[91] His attempt was, as always, triggered by fear that the government's consistent refusal to respond to public opinion would create political instability that might damage Russia's war effort and even challenge the survival of the regime itself. During the first part of the year, the concern of British representatives about the public mood had been assuaged by the comparative tranquillity of the population: sullen indifference to political questions was felt to be marginally preferable to outright rebellion. By the final months of 1916, however, they were increasingly concerned about the growth of anti-war sentiment among the population, fearing that it might undermine Russia's war effort and encourage Nicholas and his Ministers to seek a separate peace with Germany. Nevertheless, Buchanan's attempts to encourage the Tsar to sack unpopular Ministers like Stürmer proved to be hopeless. Although the Ambassador had no doubt that Nicholas himself was well-disposed towards Britain, he feared that a large section of 'The governing clique is our enemy, and takes little pains to conceal it'.[92]

Lockhart in Moscow maintained his close contacts with the leaders of the Zemgor throughout 1916, all of whom continued to support the vigorous prosecution of the war against the Central Powers. He was, however, warned by a number of them that the rise in anti-war sentiment among the population would make it difficult to guarantee the future supply of men and material required to keep the Russian army in the field, particularly if further defeats served to undermine morale still further. The Embassy in Petrograd also began to develop more direct contact with the liberals of the Zemgor and the Progressive Block in the Duma. Harold Williams proved adept at setting up meetings between British officials and prominent 'opposition' politicians, taking advantage of the connections he had through his wife, who was a leading member of the Cadet Party. Buchanan himself was seldom at ease when in the company of such people, fearing that association with them might compromise the Embassy in the eyes of the Tsarist authorities.[93] Nevertheless, as the Ambassador became increasingly sceptical about the government's ability to introduce effective reforms, he recognised that it made sense for his staff to build discreet bridges to some of the more moderate groups calling for constitutional change.

The consular reports which arrived in Petrograd from around the country during the second half of 1916 echoed the growing mood of alarm felt by diplomats at the Embassy, although there was usually a degree of confidence that 'disorders are unlikely in the coming winter'.[94] Some consular dispatches contained information about riots in the provinces,[95] but they were the exception rather than the rule. Three months before the March Revolution, the Vice-Consul in Kiev noted the rise of a 'rebellious spirit' among workers in the city and 'the middle class who hold no official occupation under government'.[96] Consular staff in other major cities in southern Russia, however, although acknowledging that high prices and food shortages were creating 'a large undercurrent of discontent', still considered that serious trouble was unlikely in the months ahead. They hoped instead that a combination of high wages and firm action by the authorities would combine to keep any uprising in check.[97] By contrast, during the last weeks of 1916, staff at the Embassy became more and more worried by the radical shift in the public mood. Frank Lindley wrote at the end of October that the Embassy had recently been told that there was among the peasantry a 'determination ... to have the land after the war as their own, without payment or conditions of any kind'.[98] In the cities, the number of strikes rose sharply towards the end of the year, and although Buchanan noted at the beginning of November that he was still hopeful that 'the trouble will blow over',[99] he was afraid that a shortage of food would lead to even greater unrest in the months ahead. Several days earlier he had already confided to the Foreign Office that 'never since the war began have I felt so depressed about the situation here'.[100] In his daily walks through the streets of the city, the Ambassador was appalled by the long queues for food, and feared 'that when the hard winter weather sets in these lines will become inflammable material'.[101] In November one of the leading members of the Cadet Party, Paul Milyukov, added to the sense of crisis by making a dramatic speech in the Duma savagely attacking the 'dark forces' surrounding the Tsar, and calling for the appointment of Ministers who commanded public support. By the beginning of 1917 the Ambassador had no doubt that 'Revolution was in the air'. In his memoirs, he recalled that the only question left was 'whether it would come from above or below'.[102] Lockhart held the same opinion, reporting to Buchanan at the end of December that Prince Lvov had told him privately that 'we [are] drawing near the end and drifting into anarchy and revolution'.[103]

During the first weeks of 1917, the political question that most occupied Buchanan and his staff in Petrograd was of course the nature of the 'great political change' predicted by Lvov. Reports reaching the Embassy suggested that the sentiments of the army towards the Emperor and Empress were becoming 'very critical'.[104] In January a British officer based in Russia wrote to the War Office that 'there is no doubt that today the army is on the side of the people. If 1905 repeats itself, and it will, the Army will be one with the people, and who then can stop the movement'.[105] Some of the rumours percolating through Russian society were even more menacing. British officials in Petrograd were amazed to hear frank discussion among 'persons in responsible positions' about the possible assassination of the Emperor and Empress.[106]

The Ambassador and his subordinates naturally wanted the impending upheaval to take a form that would impose the least possible disruption on Russia's war effort. This was particularly true following the appointment of Lloyd George as Prime Minister in December 1916, after which greater emphasis was once again placed by the British government on the role of the Tsarist armies in achieving a final allied victory over the Germans and Austrians. The arrival of a delegation of British officials in Petrograd in February 1917, under the leadership of Lord Milner, was intended to devise ways of improving the material help given by Britain to Russia. There seems in retrospect to be something pathetic and slightly absurd about this misplaced jamboree of a visit that for several weeks absorbed the time and energy of officials at the Embassy, much to the disgust of Frank Lindley and a number of his younger colleagues.[107] Nicholas made it clear from the beginning that no discussion of Russia's internal affairs would be permitted.[108] As a result, the delegates spent most of their time talking about dry technical questions when the only real issue of substance was clearly the approaching political crisis. By night, the visitors were ushered around the nightspots of the capital, where they were plied by their hosts with vodka, caviar and a slightly bemused goodwill. By day, they held negotiations with Russian officials on the vexed question of supplies, planning elaborate schemes that they knew would probably never be implemented.

The leaders of the Milner Mission have sometimes been criticised for failing to understand the depth of the political crisis facing Russia. Samuel Hoare wrote in frustration that Lord Milner himself seemed unable to realise that 'The world of Russia was so different from the world of Whitehall' that it made no sense even to think about devising new plans for supplying the country's military;[109] the deep-seated administrative incompetence of the Tsarist authorities meant that such schemes would be no more successful than in the past. However, the reports submitted to the War Cabinet by leaders of the delegation on their return to London showed that they were in reality well aware of the political problems facing Russia. If anything, it was those who sent the Mission to Petrograd who were at fault. As in 1915, politicians in London were still too inclined to see the problems facing Russia as technical ones that could be resolved by purely administrative measures, rather than as symbols of a deep-seated social and political malaise. Lloyd George in his memoirs accused Lord Milner of being blind to the impending revolution,[110] but the Prime Minister was himself at the time equally convinced that Russia could still be counted upon as an effective and powerful ally, despite the domestic unrest. More than anything else, the saga of the ill-fated Milner Mission showed how senior politicians in London simply refused to believe the reports which their own representatives in Russia had sent them throughout the previous eighteen months predicting catastrophe.

In January 1917, shortly before the arrival of Lord Milner and his delegation, Buchanan had already decided to make one last attempt to persuade Nicholas to introduce reforms before it was too late. The dramatic murder of Rasputin by Prince Felix Yusupov at the beginning of the year raised brief hopes at the Embassy and Intelligence Mission of possible changes ahead. Samuel Hoare, in particular, believed that the death of Alexandra's holy man might signal the beginning of a new political era, in which the influence of the 'dark forces' attacked by Milyukov would be weaker than before. In practice, nothing altered in the weeks following the killing – proof, perhaps, that Rasputin's influence at Court had in reality always been quite limited. Reactionaries like Alexander Protopopov, the Minister of the Interior, remained in office,[111] while the Emperor showed no greater inclination than before to listen to the chorus of voices telling him that only by granting political concessions could he hope to survive. On 4 January 1917 Buchanan telegraphed to the Foreign Office saying that:

> I am ready, if you think it advisable, to make one more attempt to bring home to the Emperor the gravity of the situation, as well as the danger to which the Dynasty may be exposed if the present tension is allowed to continue.[112]

He went on to ask for a letter from King George V to be sent to the Embassy expressing anxiety about the situation in Russia, which he could use as a pretext for seeking an audience. On this occasion, the new Foreign Secretary Sir Arthur Balfour was reluctant to approve a course of action that might not be 'well received' or 'lead to any practical result'.[113] Following the resignation of Sir Edward Grey from the Foreign Office a few months earlier, the Ambassador had begun to feel that his judgement about Russian affairs was no longer given as much weight in London as before.[114] Even so, Buchanan was not to be put off, and on 7 January he sent a second telegram to London arguing that the 'Situation is becoming so serious that it is in my opinion a duty we owe to the Emperor himself, to Russia, and to ourselves as Russia's ally, to speak plainly'.[115] On receipt of this telegram, Balfour reluctantly agreed to allow the audience to go ahead given the 'very strong views' of the Ambassador, though he made no attempt to hide his misgivings about the whole enterprise.[116]

The audience eventually took place on 12 January and proved to be the last occasion on which Buchanan ever saw Nicholas. He said little that was new during the meeting, but simply reiterated his fear that 'in the event of a revolution only a small portion of the army can be counted on to defend the dynasty'. The Ambassador concluded by making one desperate last plea for the political concessions which he believed were the only way to avert disaster:

> You have, sir, come to the parting of the ways, and you will now have to choose between two paths. The one will lead you to victory and a glorious peace – the other to revolution and disaster. Let me implore Your Majesty to choose the former.[117]

Nicholas was clearly shaken by these stark words, but they had no discernible effect on his behaviour or that of his Ministers. Over the next few weeks, the Embassy received confidential information about a possible coup d'état against the Emperor, as well as the usual reports about the growth of labour unrest and popular anger against the government. And yet, although all the British representatives in Russia sensed that the crisis was close, they were still not certain what form it would take nor when it would occur. Indeed, in the second half of February, there was even a renewed burst of optimism among Britain's military and civilian representatives in Petrograd, apparently situmulated by a brief revival in the fortunes of Russia's armies on the battlefield. The session of the Duma which took place at this time was rather less confrontational and controversial than some of its predecessors, which also helped to brighten the mood of staff at the British Embassy. On 18 February Buchanan telegraphed to the Foreign Office that, although Russia faced serious economic and political problems, he was cheered by the fact that it was 'a country that has a happy knack of muddling through'.[118] At the end of the month, the Ambassador even felt that the situation was quiet enough to allow him to travel to Finland for a short holiday. Buchanan's judgement was for once seriously at fault. Soon after he had left the capital, widespread riots broke out on the streets of Petrograd. Just ten days later, Imperial Russia was no more.

4

A Scene of Extraordinary Disorder

George Buchanan returned to Petrograd from the peace of his Finnish vacation on 11 March to find that the revolution was already well and truly underway. Two days earlier, staff at the Embassy had informed the Foreign Office about the outbreak of a 'certain amount of disorder' on the streets of the capital, but were for the most part sanguine that it was 'nothing serious'.[1] Their mood began to change the following day, as news arrived that 'great numbers of workmen from [the] suburbs are marching on [the] town'.[2] On the same day, Knox informed the Director of Military Intelligence in London that the 'men are getting out of hand', but still hoped that 'things may quiet down if bread is obtained'.[3] By the time the Ambassador arrived back, however, the trams and cabs were on strike and serious bread riots had taken place across the city. The centre of the capital was full of workers who had flocked in from the suburban factories and swarmed along Nevsky Prospect and other major streets of the town. When the Ambassador's daughter returned to Petrograd from Finland a few hours later, in the early morning of 12 March, the revolution had progressed even further and the streets were littered with overturned cars and trams.[4] Soldiers from the various Guards regiments stationed in the city had begun to mutiny and refused to follow orders to fire at the crowd. Although the government still did not accept the inevitable, its fall could not be long delayed once it became clear that it had lost any hold over the army.

On the first morning after his return to Petrograd, Buchanan went with his French counterpart to see the Minister of Foreign Affairs, N. N. Pokrovsky, who had been appointed in December and was regarded as a 'most capable man' by staff at the Embassy.[5] Although the streets were relatively peaceful, there was a certain amount of small arms fire as demonstrators exchanged shots with policemen who had taken up position on top of buildings across the city. Upon arrival at the Ministry, the Ambassador not surprisingly found that Pokrovsky 'took a gloomy view of the situation', a sentiment which deepened when

Buchanan told him that the British Embassy had just received information that rebel troops were now in control of a large part of the city
centre. The Foreign Minister told his visitor that the government had
decided to prorogue the Duma for a number of weeks, a move which
the Ambassador incredulously condemned as 'an act of madness' that
would infuriate the public and encourage the spread of the 'insurrectionary movement'. Pokrovsky was unmoved by this reaction, arguing
that the government could not possibly come to terms with soldiers
who had broken their oath of loyalty to the Emperor. All Buchanan
could do was warn the Foreign Minister that 'a policy of unqualified
repression would alienate British sympathy altogether', and return to
the Embassy in order to telegraph to London about the continued
spread of disorder across the town.[6]

The government's decision to suppress the uprising by declaring
martial law was quite futile, since it no longer had the resources to
carry out such a plan. The troops in Petrograd refused to follow orders,
while the number of policemen who were prepared to continue the
fight grew fewer with every passing hour. When the extent of the
government's loss of authority became clear, staff at the Embassy quickly
became worried that the situation in Petrograd might soon 'get out of
hand' and descend into anarchy. This fear grew still further when news
arrived that the arsenal had been captured and 'arms distributed to
[the] public', a development that threatened to bring about a huge
increase in violence on the streets.[7] The Ambassador and his colleagues
soon learnt, however, that certain members of the Duma, who had
refused to obey the ukaz proroguing their current session, were trying
to establish their own authority amidst the chaos. On 13 March General
Knox visited the Duma building where he found a 'scene of extraordinary disorder' and confusion, as soldiers and passers-by thronged
through all the passages and staircases.[8] Buchanan, took a more positive
view, informing London the same day that the legislature had formed
a twelve member Executive Committee which was already 'gradually
assuming [the] functions of a Provisional Government'.[9] He also told
the British Foreign Office that he had held a further meeting with
Pokrovsky during the morning, who was still talking vainly of the need
to crush the uprising by force – a move which Buchanan attacked as a
certain prelude to Civil War. Even though it was less than thirty-six
hours since the Ambassador had returned to the capital from Finland,
he had already concluded that the regime and the monarchy could
only be saved by offering immediate far-reaching political and constitutional reforms. He told the Foreign Minister that any attempt to use

force against the revolution would simply create 'scenes of carnage' and suggested that:

> if driven to despair [the] insurgents might sack and burn the town ...
> A policy of concessions and conciliations was the only one to follow and
> I believed that if only the Emperor would come to Petrograd and speak
> to his people all would yet go well.[10]

The Emperor was in no position to follow Buchanan's advice. On 11 March M. V. Rodzyanko, the President of the Duma, had already sent a telegram to the *Stavka* demanding the appointment of a government that commanded the confidence of the country. Nicholas indignantly refused to reply to the telegram, since he believed that the crisis in the capital could still be contained. When it became clear on the following day that the situation was out of control, the Emperor did decide to leave for Petrograd, though it is not clear what course of action he intended to follow on arrival there. The Grand Duke Michael telegraphed to his brother proposing the appointment of Prince G. E. Lvov, Chairman of the Union of Zemstvos, as the new Prime Minister, but by the time the message arrived at the *Stavka* the Emperor had already left. Nicholas never in fact reached the capital, since striking railway workers refused to allow him to complete his journey. His train was diverted instead to the town of Pskov where General N. V. Ruszky, Commander on the Northern Front, had his headquarters. Like most senior army officers, the General had already come to the conclusion that it would be impossible to crush the uprising in Petrograd by force. During the evening of 14 March, he therefore desperately tried to convince the Emperor that peace could only be restored by acceding to Rodzianko's call for the appointment of a new government directly responsible to the Duma. Stubborn to the last, Nicholas continued to insist that as an autocratic ruler he was 'responsible before God and Russia for everything that has happened and is happening'.[11] Eventually, after hours of lengthy and painful argument, he was finally persuaded by Ruszky to concede to the demands for radical constitutional reform.

Staff at the Embassy found it difficult to follow these developments, though the information they relayed to London actually proved to be remarkably accurate. On 14 March the Ambassador told the Foreign Office that the Duma was insisting that Nicholas should abdicate in favour of his son, and that Grand Duke Michael should act as Regent until the boy reached his majority. However, in another telegram sent later on the same day, following a meeting with the Grand Duke himself,

Buchanan thoroughly confused officials in London by suggesting that abdication was no longer one of the conditions being imposed by the Duma.[12] Staff at the Embassy were not of course in any position to influence events, since they had no direct contact with the Emperor; nor did they have much access to Rodzyanko and his colleagues, whose time and energy were taken up by their attempts to establish their authority across Petrograd. The same was true of General Hanbury-Williams, who lost direct contact with Nicholas following his departure from the *Stavka* on 12 March. Two days later, the General decided to write to the Emperor urging him to bow to the inevitable and accept the end of autocratic rule by appealing 'to the peoples of Russia to assist you in the heavy task that lies on your shoulders'.[13] This well-intentioned advice proved to be redundant, since Nicholas was already reluctantly arriving at the same conclusion under the intense prompting of General Ruszky at Pskov. In any case, the Emperor never actually received the letter, which was later returned to its author unopened with the seal intact. By the time Hanbury-Williams saw him again, Nicholas had abdicated and was referred to by the new rulers of Russia simply as Colonel Romanov.

At 5 o'clock on the afternoon of 15 March, Buchanan telegraphed to the Foreign Office saying that the Embassy had just received a telephone call 'to the effect that Emperor has signed Act of Abdication and that Grand Duke Mikhail Alexandrovitch has been appointed Regent [to the Tsarevich]'.[14] Earlier that day, the Ambassador had met with Pokrovsky who told him that that most of the old Ministers had now been arrested and that he himself would shortly resign. The collapse of the government raised an immediate problem about the legal status of relations between Britain and Russia. Buchanan was naturally concerned that there should be no hiatus that might damage cooperation over matters relating to the war, and suggested to London that he should be 'authorized to enter into official relations' with the government that was slowly taking shape. In the meantime, the Ambassador agreed with Pokrovsky that he should meet Paul Milyukov, who was to be Foreign Minister in the new government, in order to discuss 'any questions of immediate importance affecting international situation and conduct of war'.[15] The events of the next twenty-four hours caused still further confusion, as the Embassy received news that Nicholas had not only abdicated in his own right, but was also refusing to allow his son to be appointed in his place. At the same time, opinion among the Duma leaders was shifting as they began to comprehend the full extent of the anti-monarchical sentiment expressed by the demonstrators on the streets of the capital. By the evening of 16 March, the telegrams sent from the Embassy to London made it clear that the rule of the Romanov dynasty was coming to an end. Even so, while the collapse of the Tsarist *ancien régime* was more far-reaching than a simple change in ruler, the Foreign Office was still willing to allow Buchanan to recognise de facto the new government. On 17 March he received a telegram from the Foreign Office noting that:

> Doubtless your action in this matter will largely depend upon the attitude of the new Government towards the War. All your influence should be thrown into the scale against any Administration which is not resolved to fight to a finish.[16]

Two days later, the War Cabinet approved the Foreign Secretary's decision to allow the Ambassador in Petrograd full discretion in deciding whether to extend recognition to the Provisional Government.[17] In the course of just one week, British diplomats in Russia, along with officials and politicians in London, had been forced to come to terms with the collapse of a regime that had played a pivotal role in European politics for more than three centuries.

The reaction of British officials in Russia to the end of the Romanov dynasty was influenced by a number of considerations. The traditional distaste felt by members of the Diplomatic Service for the Tsarist autocracy meant that any shift towards a more constitutional form of government was likely to be welcomed, at least in principle, by representatives from Europe's leading liberal power. In addition, the Tsarist government's repeated failure to respond effectively to the administrative and organisational challenges posed by the war had undermined British officials' lingering respect for the regime, which increasingly seemed to them to combine venality and incompetence in more or less equal measure. Buchanan's strong support for the rapid introduction of constitutional reform, following the outbreak of the March Revolution, was a natural reaction from a man who was by instinct a believer in the principle of representative government. During the first few days of the revolution, when the Duma leaders refused to obey the Emperor's ukaz calling for them to disperse, Buchanan was quick to praise the Provisional Committee as a responsible body whose members possessed 'great organising powers' and were committed to the 'vigorous continuation of the war'. The Ambassador also praised the behaviour of the crowds of demonstrators during the revolution, telling London that 'the most striking consideration has been shown to British subjects' by troops and public alike.[18] Even Lady Buchanan, whose dislike of Russians was rivalled only by her fear of anarchy and mob rule, admitted in a letter to her sister that 'It is wonderful how much order there was considering that all the biggest criminals were let out of prison'.[19] Soon after the Tsar abdicated, her husband sent a telegram to the Foreign Office stressing the need to make sure that the British public knew the revolution was a genuinely popular one, and that 'throughout Russia [the] entire army and public has welcomed [the] new order of things'.[20]

While most British representatives in Russia had little instinctive sympathy for the old Tsarist regime, few of them responded with much real eagerness to the events of March 1917. In his memoirs, Lockhart wrote scathingly of the 'feigned enthusiasm' with which official Britain responded to the revolution,[21] suggesting that the messages of goodwill and support sent to the Provisional Government lacked any real warmth. His judgement may have been too harsh. In London, a large number of politicians from various political parties on the left and centre welcomed the news from Petrograd, rejoicing at the collapse of the autocratic *ancien régime*. Some Foreign Office officials believed that a political revolution might presage the introduction of the kind of administrative reforms needed to improve Russia's military performance, while simultaneously helping to mobilise the population more effectively behind the country's war effort. These hopes were echoed for a short time by a few British representatives and soldiers in Russia, including Alfred Knox and Samuel Hoare, but their enthusiasm did not last for very long. Most British representatives in the country were acutely conscious that the collapse of the Romanov dynasty was likely to create as many problems as it solved, since the monarchy was the glue which had for centuries held the vast and ramshackle Tsarist Empire in one piece. For all its flaws, it had acted as a focus for disparate ethnic and social groups whose members had almost nothing in common with one another other than the fact that they were subjects of a single ruler. Just three days after the abdication of Nicholas, George Buchanan himself expressed a hope that there might at some point be a 'chance of return to some form of monarchical Government which is in my opinion the only one possible [way] to hold this vast Empire together'.[22] Although deeply critical of the old regime, he was shrewd enough to realise that many of its shortcomings were the product of difficulties and stresses which would have to be faced by *any* Russian government. The Ambassador believed that a constitutional monarchy could provide a far more suitable form of government for Russia than a republic – provided, of course, that the monarch possessed the talents required to make such a system work properly.

While British officials had a low opinion of Nicholas's abilities, and believed that the Tsar was at least in part responsible for the demise of his dynasty, his fate was inevitably a question which greatly occupied them in the days and weeks following his abdication. The Provisional Government, which was officially recognised by Buchanan on 22 March, was itself at first very keen to see the Emperor and his family move abroad. Milyukov told the Ambassador that his colleagues were perturbed by the attempts being made by various 'extremists' to exploit popular resentment against Nicholas and his family in order to destabilise the political situation. He therefore hoped that 'The departure of the Emperor would ... strengthen the Russian Government and help matters to settle down'.[23] It did not at first seem that this request would pose any problems, particularly since Buchanan was himself instructed by the Foreign Office to ensure that the Provisional Government gave the Royal Family permission to move to England as soon as possible.[24] This policy, however, was already under urgent review in London, where the King and senior politicians began to question whether it was 'advisable that the Imperial Family should take up residence in this country'.[25] After a good deal of debate and confusion, Lord Stamfordham, the Private Secretary of George V, wrote to Balfour in the first week of April asking that the invitation be withdrawn, since the presence of the Emperor and Empress in Britain would 'be strongly resented by the public'.[26] Several days later, the Foreign Office informed Buchanan accordingly.[27]

Over the next few months, the Ambassador found himself in the unenviable position of interceding with the authorities to demand good treatment for the Russian Royal Family, while simultaneously representing a country that was unwilling to offer its members asylum. Buchanan subsequently faced a good deal of criticism in some quarters for failing to act with sufficient vigour to prevent the tragic chain of circumstances that led to the death of Nicholas and his family at the hands of the Bolsheviks in the summer of 1918. In reality, his ability to influence the situation was always very limited once the British government had decided that the Tsar should not be offered asylum in Britain. The Ambassador intervened constantly with the authorities throughout 1917 in an attempt to defend the interests and welfare of the Royal Family, but he had little leverage either with members of the Provisional Government or with the Bolsheviks who succeeded them. Although it is far from certain that Nicholas would have wanted to leave Russia, even if he had been given the opportunity to do so, the whole incident proved to be one of the less edifying episodes in the history of British foreign policy. Members of the government in London, along with others who were close to the throne, were frightened by the rise of republican and socialist sentiment in Britain during the course of the war, which they feared could in time come to challenge the constitutional status quo. Their desperate suggestion that Nicholas and his family might find refuge in 'Denmark or Switzerland' owed everything to political expediency; it owed nothing to political principle.

The fears which British diplomats felt about the future of Russia following the collapse of the monarchy did not only centre on the fate of the Emperor and his family. From the moment the Provisional Committee of the Duma came into existence, staff at the Embassy desperately sought to understand its political composition in order to gauge its members' likely attitude towards the continuation of the war. The Embassy had for some eighteen months before the March Revolution been developing discreet links with a number of those who came to power following Nicholas's abdication. The sober and cautious Prince Lvov, who became the new Prime Minister in the Provisional Government, was already well known and well liked by Lockhart in Moscow; he had also met diplomats from the Embassy itself on a number of occasions. The appointment of Paul Milyukov as the first Foreign Minister of the Provisional Government was also welcomed by staff at the Petrograd Embassy, since they knew that he was a political moderate firmly committed to continuing the war. There was, though, some concern at the appointment of Alexander Kerensky as Minister of Justice. In the months that followed, Kerensky became a familiar figure to staff at the Embassy, particularly after he replaced Prince Lvov as Prime Minister in July, but at the time of the March Revolution they knew little about him other than the fact that he was a staunch socialist who possessed formidable oratorical skills. Most Ministers in the first Provisional Government, including Kerensky, were in reality committed to a set of liberal constitutionalist values that should hardly have caused alarm to Buchanan and his colleagues, but the Ambassador in particular was always inclined to overestimate the radical instincts of its members. Samuel Hoare recalled with some justice in his memoirs that Buchanan himself 'had lived so continuously in conservative and official circles that all parties of the Left, whether Cadets or Social Revolutionaries, seemed to him to be equally dangerous'.[28] In fairness to the Ambassador, the radical rhetoric employed by many Russian liberals during the heady days of the March Revolution made it difficult for most foreigners

to distinguish between the liberals and moderate socialists, who dominated the first Provisional Government, and the more extreme socialist
parties whose influence in the capital grew steadily during the weeks
following the abdication of the Tsar.

Whatever the private views of British officials towards the March
Revolution, the issue that governed their reaction more than any other
was of course that of the war. Buchanan's quick recognition of the
Provisional Government was, as seen earlier, predicated on the belief
that its members were committed to endorsing the war aims adopted
by its predecessor over the previous two and a half years.[29] As Britain
was pursuing a military strategy based on the assumption that a considerable part of the Central Powers' manpower and munitions was
committed to the Eastern Front, the first priority of the country's
representatives in Petrograd was to encourage the new government to
restore domestic order and military discipline which had broken down
during the chaotic days following the Tsar's abdication. The success
or failure of the March Revolution in British eyes rested, at least in
the short term, on whether the new regime was more effective than
the old one in promoting the effective conduct of the war. Since many
members of the Provisional Government had been actively involved in
the Zemgor before the Revolution, Buchanan and his staff at first
hoped that the confusion and disorder which had existed before March
would give way to a more orderly and efficient style of public administration. Such hopes were short-lived. They quickly realised that the
collapse of the Tsarist regime had unleashed new social and political
forces that could not be easily accommodated by the new government.
Alfred Knox wrote in his memoirs that 'What was wanted in the interests
of Russia was an orderly transition to constitutional government', a
sentiment that would have been echoed by just about every other British
official in Petrograd.[30] In reality, the Provisional Government was never
able to establish sufficient authority to guide the country along such
a path.

The signs of impending social and political disintegration were present from the beginning, as the soldiers and workers who had come
onto the streets during the heady days leading up to Nicholas's abdication showed little inclination to return to the tedium of life in the
barracks and factories. On 15 March, General Frederick Poole, who
was in charge of a unit set up to ensure that munitions sent to Russia
from Britain were utilised effectively, told Kerensky that he was perturbed by the failure to reopen the capital's factories. The General
feared that the closure would damage Russia's war effort and make the

country more dependent than ever on supplies of armaments from overseas. Kerensky agreed that the decline in production was a serious problem, but warned that any attempt to 'coerce the people' back to work could lead to further disorders since they were 'now within a measurable distance of Anarchy'.[31] Hanbury-Williams at the *Stavka* was also horrified by the breakdown of order among the civilian population, writing in his diary on the day following the Emperor's abdication that 'the mischievious head of Anarchy is beginning to protrude its ugly face on the scene'.[32] Alfred Knox was particularly concerned by the collapse of military discipline, which began with the mutinies in the barracks of Petrograd. On 17 March, he noted angrily that 'Socialist orators are so far allowed free run of [the] barracks', where they attempted to capitalise on the chaotic situation in order to encourage the troops to greater radicalism.[33] On the same day, George Buchanan warned the Foreign Office that although there were some signs of a return to order on the streets, the 'extreme Socialists still present danger'.[34]

From the very first days of its existence, the Provisional Government faced opposition from the Petrograd Soviet of Soldiers and Workers Deputies, which was modelled on the organisation that sprang to life in the city during the 1905 Revolution. The relationship between the government and the Soviet was an extraordinarily complicated one throughout the months following the March Revolution. The delegates to the Soviet represented a constituency of workers and soldiers, and were therefore usually far more radical than members of the Provisional Government; at the same time, there was often a considerable degree of cooperation between the two bodies, which was helped by the fact that certain individuals (including Kerensky) belonged to both of them. The activities of the Soviet were regarded with grave suspicion by staff at the British Embassy who feared, with some justification, that the delegates there would respond to the pacifist mood among the troops by trying to force the government to seek peace with the Germans and Austrians. British officials were particularly infuriated at the attempt made by delegates to establish their authority over the army by means of the infamous 'Order Number One', which laid down that troops should only obey orders that were approved by the Soviet. This action inevitably undermined the authority of the officer corps over their men, an issue that quickly became a matter of grave concern to Britain's military representatives in Russia. Hanbury-Williams noted on 20 March that numerous reports were arriving at the *Stavka* detailing the breakdown of order throughout the army, adding sadly that 'This is all madness, but they are mad and have started a fire which will be mightily hard to put out'.[35] On the same day, Frank Lindley wrote to George Clerk at the Foreign Office that:

> The real difficulty here is that we have two Governments: the real one under Prince Lvow, and a Committee of workmen's and soldiers' delegates without whose orders none of the men will do anything ... The result is that it is absolutely impossible to enforce anything.[36]

Three days earlier, the Foreign Office had already been told by the Embassy that 'many people think that a trial of strength between [the Soviet] and the government is inevitable and that [the] outcome of such a struggle is doubtful'. Over the following months, the Petrograd Soviet became a symbol to British representatives of the forces of anarchy and chaos that were engulfing Russia. Nevertheless, while many of the demands put forward by delegates were extremely distasteful to officials at the Embassy, they could not ignore the fact that the Soviet enjoyed a good deal of support among the population. Buchanan and his staff quickly recognised that the Provisional Government would find it very difficult to establish its control over Russia. Just ten days after the Emperor's abdication, the Ambassador wrote to London that his early optimism had been unfounded and the 'hopes which I at one time entertained of [the] War being prosecuted with greater energy and efficiency are gradually dwindling'.[37] As long as the Soviet continued to attract the support of the workers and soldiers in the capital, the situation in Russia would inevitably be a 'precarious one'.

During the months that followed Buchanan's gloomy message to the Foreign Office, little happened to make the Ambassador and other British officials take a more optimistic view of the situation. The Provisional Government failed to restore order in the barracks, while the factories continued to be hotbeds of disorder and chaos. In early April, Hanbury-Williams recorded in his diary that in Petrograd:

> The streets are full of loafing soldiers smoking cigarettes and talking; no more halting, facing a general, and saluting when one passes ... The people are like naughty children who have run away from school, but the situation grows worse and worse every day ... If the armies don't pull themselves together, I see nothing but anarchy left.[38]

Knox was even more horrified at the collapse of military discipline. He indignantly condemned the Soviet Order Number One as a 'charter of licence for cowardice and anarchy', which gave solders an excuse not to obey any orders which they disliked.[39] A few weeks later his assistant,

Colonel Thornhill, wrote in a memorandum on the 'Effects of the Russian Revolution' that:

> The Army has now largely become a series of armed debating societies in which questions of internal politics and army reform have very largely eclipsed the question of the prosecution of the war and the common interests of the allies ... All along the front the men are crossing to the enemy's trenches to discuss conditions of peace under the delusion that the Germans are prepared to overthrow the Monarchy and institute a republic.[40]

The British Military Attaché and his staff tried to counter the collapse in morale by touring the barracks in a forlorn attempt to instil in the Russian troops an eagerness for the war. Their efforts were quite hopeless. By the beginning of May, most army officers in the capital had given up any pretence of being able to control their units, being content instead to play cards and smoke while Knox and his assistants tried desperately to fire the enthusiasm of their men. Although the troops usually gave the Attaché a reasonable hearing, he sadly noted that they were equally responsive to the 'pasty-faced' and 'fanatical' agitators who arrived from the naval base at Kronstadt calling for the overthrow of the Provisional Government.[41] The situation was even more desperate on the Eastern Front itself, where millions of Russian soldiers deserted from their regiments and returned home to avoid the horrors of the battlefield. However, while Knox's diary vividly chronicled the collapse of military discipline both in the Russian capital and at the Front, its author was unable to come up with any viable proposals about the best way of restoring order and ensuring that the army remained an effective fighting force capable of resisting German and Austrian advances. At times he showed a streak of astonishing naivety, suggesting that 'a little common sense' and a game of football could 'bring all ranks together'.[42] On other occasions, he condemned both the Provisional Government and the officer corps for lacking the character and resolve to assert their authority.

There was in truth little that the authorities could do to prevent the drift to anarchy, either in the army or among the population as a whole. The collapse of the Tsarist regime had destroyed long-established patterns of loyalty, and its disintegration left a vacuum of authority that could not easily be filled. Although the Lvov government desperately attempted to assert itself amidst the chaos, it was quite unable to establish its legitimacy in the eyes of large sections of the population. Its members' determination to continue the war alienated the troops both in Petrograd and at the Front, while their reluctance to implement far-reaching social and economic reforms cost them support among workers and peasants. The commitment of the Prime Minister and his colleagues to convene a special Constituent Assembly to determine the future political and administrative structure of Russia might well have appealed to middle class liberals, but it was hardly the sort of policy calculated to win the support of an increasingly radicalised population.

George Buchanan had more dealings with the Provisional Government than any other British official. Even when he recognised the new administration, the Ambassador found that its members were 'not such as to inspire me with great confidence for the future. Most of them already showed signs of strain and struck me as having undertaken a task beyond their strength'.[43] On 10 April he told Lord Milner that he doubted whether any group or party would be able to extend its authority across Russia over the coming months, with the result that 'we shall probably see a series of revolutions and counter-revolutions'.[44] Throughout April and May, the Ambassador was infuriated by the government's failure to act decisively to restore order on the streets and in the barracks, a reaction that was shared by almost all his staff. Like his political masters in London, Buchanan believed that unless the Provisonal Government could contain the wave of anarchy engulfing the country, Russia could not serve as a reliable ally in the war against the Central Powers. The whole subject recurred endlessly in the numerous conversations which he held with the Foreign Minister. Paul Milyukov was sympathetic to the complaints of the Ambassador, not least because he was himself firmly committed to the war and intensely concerned about the effect of domestic chaos on Russia's ability to continue the fight. The British Ambassador suspected that the government's weakness and confusion was at least in part a consequence of its members' temperamental reluctance to adopt any strong measures that ran contrary to their liberal instincts. There was some truth in this, but the main reason was more prosaic. The Minister of War told Knox in early April that the Provisional Government simply lacked the 'physical power' to confront the extremists in the Soviet and the army, and did not dare risk provoking an uprising by seeking to reimpose military discipline in the barracks. He begged the Military Attaché to keep this information 'very secret', for fear that it might encourage attempts to overthrow the government should it become public knowledge.[45] This assessment of the weakness of the government was undoubtedly correct, and its position became even more fragile in the months that followed. However, while the Minister of War was quite open about the perilous situation in which he and his colleagues found themselves, many British diplomats and soldiers clung to the erroneous belief that the situation could be resolved in favour of 'the forces of order' if only Lvov and his fellow Ministers were willing to take tough measures to assert their authority.

Milyukov's vigorous support for the war may well have endeared him to Buchanan and his colleagues, but it also made him one of the most controversial Ministers in the Provisional Government. In the end, his vigorous pro-war stance cost the Foreign Minister his job. At the end of March the Soviet issued a proclamation calling for the start of peace negotiations between the various combatant nations in Europe based on the principle of 'no indemnities and no annexations'.[46] Milyukov bitterly criticised this move, arguing that Russia had been through almost three years of war, suffering millions of casualties in the process, in order to unite Austria's Ukrainian provinces with Russia and to gain control over Constantinople; to abandon these war aims would nullify the heroic efforts that had been made since 1914. The Foreign Minister's views were increasingly unrealistic given the collapse of discipline in the army and the general war-weariness of the Russian population. There was little evidence that the flagging spirit of troops at the Front could be raised by the prospect of still more fighting in order to extend Russian territory. As a result, the Provisional Government was eventually forced to endorse the Soviet's position, issuing a declaration that Russia had no wish to gain more territory but instead sought a peace based on the principle of national self-determination. However, when a draft of this declaration was first sent to the allied powers, Milyukov included an ambiguous covering note suggesting that Russia would in reality continue to seek a 'decisive victory'. Although many members of the Provisional Government tacitly agreed with the Foreign Minister, his position was becoming more and more untenable.

On 14 May the Minister of Finance privately sounded out Buchanan about the British government's likely reaction should Miliukov be dismissed – a move which reflected the Provisional Government's sensitivity to the concerns of its allies. The Ambassador firmly, and untruthfully, replied that 'such purely internal matters' were no concern of London, and added that the British would support any Minister who wanted 'to prosecute the war energetically to a victorious finish'.[47] A few days after this conversation, the membership of the Provisional Government was overhauled in an effort to win greater popular support. Prince Lvov remained as Prime Minister, but a number of new socialist Ministers were appointed, including the radical socialist V. M. Chernov who was a long-standing critic of the expansionist war aims adopted by the old Tsarist regime. The place of Miliukov at the Foreign Ministry was taken by the staunchly pro-war M. I. Tereshchenko. Milyukov's failure to defend his position caused a good deal of anxiety at the British Embassy, in spite of Buchanan's claim that the composition of the Provisional Government was not a matter of legitimate concern for Russia's allies. However, Lvov and his colleagues had little real choice but to retreat over the question of Russia's war aims, given popular sentiment in the Russian capital and other major cities across the country. Both soldiers and civilians were increasingly unwilling to accept the sacrifices involved in fighting a war that seemed remote from their everyday concerns and interests.

Although the Provisional Government's gradual shift to the left caused anxiety both at the Embassy and the Foreign Office in London, politicians and officials alike recognised that they had no choice but to accept the situation. Soon after the appointment of the first Provisional Government in March, the British Cabinet had arranged for a message of support to be sent to its members by a number of prominent figures in the Labour Party, in the hope that it would persuade the more radical Ministers that Britain was willing to cooperate fully with them.[48] A few weeks later, several representatives from the British Labour Movement, including Will Thorne and James O'Grady, arrived in Petrograd to examine the situation for themselves. In the second half of May the British War Cabinet decided, however, that a further gesture was still needed to prove Britain's good faith towards its Russian ally. At its meeting on 23 May the Conservative Minister Lord Robert Cecil, who was standing in for the Foreign Secretary, suggested to his colleagues that Buchanan might 'no longer [be] the ideal British representative in Petrograd', even though his hard work and dedication over the previous few years had been exemplary. The meeting accepted this verdict, and concluded that a new representative should be sent to Petrograd who was more likely to influence 'the democratic elements which now predominate in Russia to pursue the war with energy'.[49] Rightly or wrongly, it was felt that Buchanan was too closely associated with the old Tsarist government to command sufficient authority over those who had come to power in the wake of Nicholas's abdication. The growing penchant of Lloyd George and his colleagues for by-passing the normal channels of professional diplomacy threatened to bring to a premature end the career of one of Britain's most senior Ambassadors.

The new representative chosen by the War Cabinet was the Labour MP and Minister Arthur Henderson, believed by his colleagues to have the kind of background and political profile likely to command respect among the 'democratic elements' in Petrograd. It was hoped that he would be able to persuade the more radical socialists in the Russian capital to endorse allied war aims and to support the continuation of hostilities until the German and Austrian armies had been completely defeated. The choice was in many respects a curious one. Henderson had no experience of diplomacy, spoke no Russian and had little knowledge of Russian affairs.[50] Not surprisingly, the decision to send him to Petrograd horrified staff at the Embassy, who not unreasonably interpreted the move as an attack on their professional competence. On 26 May, shortly after the Embassy had first been informed of the decision, the appalled Head of the Chancery, 'Benjy' Bruce, sent a 'strictly private and confidential' telegram to a senior official at the Foreign Office asking him to intervene in the situation. Bruce suggested that if Buchanan were to be recalled, the new 'Minister for Foreign Affairs [Tereshchenko] will regret his departure enormously ... I am absolutely convinced that ... nobody could permanently replace the Ambassador here'. The Head of Chancery noted that he was aware of the 'enormity of my action' in sending such a presumptious telegram, but believed that the situation was desperate enough to warrant his intervention.[51] On the same day, Alfred Knox sent a similar confidential telegram to London, this time to the Director of Military Intelligence at the War Office. Like Bruce, Knox believed that 'No British Ambassador at Petrograd has ever to an equal degree enjoyed the confidence of the Russians', and suggested that the recall of Buchanan would have extremely damaging consequences for Britain. He therefore asked the DMI to contact those who were responsible for the decision, in order to convince them that their action 'arises from a complete misreading of the situation here'.[52]

The situation did in fact resolve itself, though not as a result of pressure applied by staff at the Embassy. The War Cabinet eventually decided that Henderson's departure for Petrograd did not necessitate the immediate withdrawal of Buchanan as had originally been planned, and the Ambassador was informed that he no longer need return to London for 'consultations'.[53] When Henderson finally arrived in Russia in June, he soon realised that he lacked the skill and expertise required to make any significant impact on the local situation, and quickly acknowledged that the traditional institutions of 'Old Diplomacy' could not be so easily circumvented as he had once believed. Lockhart recalled in his memoirs that the Labour MP had little in common with the more extreme socialists in Petrograd, whose language and values were quite

alien to him;[54] there was therefore little prospect of building a meaningful dialogue between 'left and left', as members of the War Cabinet
had originally hoped. Lindley recalled that 'Henderson never liked
Russia' from the moment he arrived in the country, and was appalled
by the sight of 'agitators and soldiers hob-nobbing on the station
platform'.[55] The Labour Minister was also outraged by the chaos and
anarchy that existed in Petrograd, a phenomenon that was brought
home to him in a particularly personal way when intruders ransacked
his hotel room during his first evening in Petrograd. After a short time
in the city, he informed London that 'he had come to the conclusion
that no good purpose would be served by the removal of a man
[Buchanan] who understood Russia' so well and had 'shown himself
remarkably free from all party bias'.[56] Henderson can certainly have
been in no doubt about the attitude of his prospective colleagues at
the Embassy, which may well have coloured his view of the whole
situation. Buchanan did not even bother to meet the Minister on his
arrival in Petrograd, and ostentatiously refused to provide accommodation for him at the Embassy. When Henderson did dine with the
Ambassador and his staff, Lady Buchanan spent her time 'poking fun
at him behind his back'.[57]

The War Cabinet's decision to follow Henderson's advice and retain
Buchanan in Petrograd was naturally welcomed by staff at the Embassy,
where Bruce gleefully observed that it had been 'very hard to contem-
plate throwing the Ambassador to the wolves to make a Socialist
holiday'.[58] While the whole episode had little long-term significance,
beyond creating mistrust between Buchanan and Lindley, whom the
Ambassador wrongly believed had been involved in the decision to
remove him,[59] it did illustrate the naivity and confusion prevailing
among policy-makers in London. The idea that any single British
socialist could have made a real impact in such a confused and chaotic
situation as the one which existed in Petrograd was simply a fantasy.
Although other attempts were made during 1917 by both the British
and French governments to build bridges to the Russian left, none of
them met with any real success.

The situation in Russia continued to deteriorate during the early
summer of 1917, at least in the eyes of British representatives whose
main concern was to see the restoration of social order and military
discipline. The reformed Provisional Government was no more successful than its predecessor at establishing its authority across the country.
Staff at the Embassy were generally complimentary about the new
Foreign Minister, whom they acknowledged was committed to the

vigorous prosecution of the war, but they still did not believe that Tereshchenko and his colleagues were determined enough to crush the various revolutionary groups whose members operated quite openly across Russia. On 1 June Knox informed the War Office that the 'Struggle between labour and capital is very rapidly coming to a head ... Force is [the] only thing that will bring workmen to their senses'.[60] Other officials at the Embassy were less forthright, but their views were not far removed from those of the Military Attaché. They believed that some kind of show-down between the Provisional Government and the more radical elements in the Soviet and the army could not be long delayed.

By June the reports arriving in Petrograd from British Consulates across Russia were also beginning to reflect a rise in the level of unrest. During the first few weeks following the March Revolution, the dispatches sent by consular staff from the provinces indicated that the transition in most areas had been surprisingly smooth, although there was of course a certain degree of disorder and confusion.[61] The consular reports which arrived from the end of April onwards started to tell a different story, and on 12 May Buchanan informed the Foreign Office that 'the epidemic of lawlessness which started at Petrograd is spreading to the various provincial centres'.[62] The Ambassador's telegram was apparently prompted by a report from Consul-General Picton Bagge in Odessa, received at the Embassy a few days earlier, which noted that little work was being carried out in the town's factories where 'much time is wasted in talking and meetings. Production has gone down. Economic demands of men pass all measure and they interfere in administration'.[63] Similar dispatches arrived from other major cities across Russia. In early June Lockhart wrote to Buchanan from Moscow that 'I regret that at the present moment the situation here must be described in rather black colours. The town is quiet, but little work is being done. Strikes are assuming threatening proportions, and the country seems to be drifting helplessly towards complete financial and economic ruin'.[64] The picture was no brighter elsewhere. The consular representative in Nicolayev, Henry Brown, condemned the growth of labour unrest in the town, indignantly attacking the workers' attempts to interfere in 'administrative matters' by setting up factory committees to oversee production.[65] A few days earlier, he had sent a report describing how the town's appearance of normality was largely illusory:

> during the day there is no noticeable difference between the old and
> the new regimes. In certain parts of the city, however, there is a marked

difference at night. During the evening large numbers of soldiers and sailors gather on the main street, and in the public squares and gardens in the vicinity of the barracks and the camp, and there is a freedom of manner, often accompanied by indecent behaviour, which under the old police rule and military discipline would not have been tolerated. These gatherings attract a class of women which were conspicuous by their absence in such places under the old conditions.[66]

Curiously enough, while Brown and his colleagues were adept at reporting the breakdown of order in the towns, neither consular nor diplomatic staff seem to have been particularly aware of the great upheavals taking place in the Russian countryside, where the peasantry was seizing large amounts of land from its erstwhile owners. In April Buchanan informed the Foreign Office that, although there was a good deal of disorder in rural areas, there did not seem to be anything 'in the shape of an organized *Jacquerie*'.[67] Over the next six months, there were only sporadic references in reports by British officials to unrest in the Russian countryside. This was doubtless in large part because their attention was concentrated on the dramatic events taking place in Petrograd and other large cities. As was the case before 1917, this metropolitan bias limited the perspective of Embassy staff and reduced the quality of their reports on the upheavals taking place across Russia.

The private lives of British representatives, whether in Petrograd or the provinces, were inevitably dominated by the drama taking place around them. The breakdown of the old political and social structures meant that they were less and less insulated from the events on which they reported. One of the worst problems faced by many of them was a rapid descent into an unaccustomed and unwelcome poverty. The salaries paid to members of the Consular and Diplomatic Services were seldom munificent, and the rapid rise in prices which took place in Russia after 1914 created great hardships for all those based in the country. Even before the March Revolution, the Consul in Petrograd had approached Buchanan on behalf of his colleagues, pointing out to the Ambassador that inflation meant that postings to Russia were now only 'suitable for people with plenty of means to live on' (a category to which few members of the Consular Service belonged).[68] A few weeks after the March Revolution, members of the regular diplomatic corps also complained to the Ambassador that they were facing an intolerable level of financial hardship. Buchanan wrote to the Foreign Office in April describing how one senior Chancery official had been unable to afford a new apartment when the lease on his old one ran out, and was as a consequence 'forced to take a room at the hotel Europe. He and his wife, nurse and baby all lived in one room for 3 months and his bare living expenses have amounted to 1200 rubles a month'.[69] The official's salary was, by contrast, just 400 rubles a month. Buchanan asked the Foreign Office to intercede with the Treasury in order to obtain higher allowances for civilian officials in Russia, a move that was eventually successful (perhaps surprisingly, given the Treasury's notorious parsimony where the funding of the Diplomatic Service was concerned). Even so, throughout 1917 the high cost of living made life very difficult for most British diplomats and consular officials – an indignity that was compounded by the contrast between their own situation and that of British military men posted to Russia, since army and naval officers were paid up to twice as much as their civilian colleagues.[70]

While a lack of money was distressing, the brooding atmosphere of violence which hung over many Russian cities during these months was of even greater concern. Although most British officials avoided falling victim to it, few foreign representatives could escape altogether the consequences of a general breakdown in order. On one occasion, the unfortunate Consul at Kronstadt faced a 'visit' from sailors at the nearby naval base who departed with a selection of his personal belongings.[71] On another occasion, the Head of the Chancery returned home to find that thieves had broken into his apartment and ransacked his wine store.[72] The Commercial Attaché at the Embassy, Henry Cooke, had an even more alarming experience when he was forced to take shelter from flying bullets in the courtyard of a mansion block, only to have his possessions stolen from him by the porter on duty there.[73] A simple walk or drive through the streets ran the risk of an encounter with one of the groups of ill-disciplined soldiers who regularly commandeered cars and accosted passers-by with demands for money. Buchanan's daughter, Meriel, who worked in the British Red Cross hospital, recalled in her memoirs how the collapse of military discipline among the wounded troops created chaos in the institution and eventually led to its closure.[74] The Ambassador himself continued to take his daily walk through the streets and parks of Petrograd, but the capital was no longer the well-ordered city that it had been in previous times. The same pattern was repeated in other towns across Russia, where British consular officials had to take care not to fall victim to one of the incidents of random violence that became a regular occurrence across the country during 1917.

The strain of daily life inevitably took its toll on British representatives and their families. The Ambassador and his wife attracted resentment from some of their staff for refusing to make more accommodation available at the Embassy, forcing officials who worked there to journey through the streets even during the dangerous hours after nightfall. Lady Buchanan was particularly disliked by a number of her husband's colleagues, who resented her high-handed and distant manner, while the small number of diplomatic wives who remained in the country did not always believe that she gave them enough help to cope with the material privations of their daily lives.[75] The Embassy laid in a large stock of canned food to serve as an emergency store in case provisions disappeared entirely from the shops, but there was still constant anxiety about the food situation. There was also general alarm at the rumours which circulated periodically suggesting that the building was about to be stormed and its inhabitants killed or taken prisoner. Tempers became frayed in this atmosphere of tension and uncertainty, leading to minor squabbles between officials exhausted from working twelve or fourteen hours a day. Nevertheless, in spite of all the problems, soldiers and civilians alike tried to ignore the potential danger of their situation. Lindley recalled how his family's nanny 'showed true English contempt for foreigners and for danger' during the weeks following the Tsar's abdication, insisting that the daily routine of the family should remain unchanged. Extra guards were posted at the Embassy and a number of private residences, in order to protect British officials against possible attack. Even in the latter half of the summer of 1917, when the Provisional Government was close to complete disintegration, Britain's military and civilian representatives continued to display a dogged determination to carry on despite all the problems they faced. A certain 'Empire Spirit' seemed to instil a confidence that British citizens would somehow manage to overcome the appalling difficulties and dangers surrounding them.

By the beginning of July the situation was showing no signs of improving; indeed, the chaos was if anything growing worse, and the Provisional Government seemed to British representatives to have become more powerless than ever. During the second half of June, they began to send telegrams to the Foreign Office in London recounting rumours of an impending Bolshevik coup designed to overthrow the Provisonal Government and take Russia out of the war.[76] The Embassy had taken considerable pains to monitor the activities of the Bolshevik Party from the time of the March Revolution, although as in previous years they found it difficult to obtain much detailed information about its members' activities. Lindley, who was assigned particular responsibility for keeping abreast of political developments in Russia, had not even heard of Lenin until the Bolshevik leader completed his famous journey by sealed train across Germany and arrived in triumph at the Finland Station in Petrograd during April.[77]

The return of revolutionary emigrés to Russia was followed with some care both at the Embassy and in London, not least because of a fear that German agents intent on undermining the Russian war effort might be included among their number. British officials in Petrograd, both civilian and military, were from the beginning of the war convinced that the Bolsheviks received money and assistance from the German government. Documents released after 1945 certainly show that the government in Berlin made strenuous efforts to provide the Bolsheviks with funds, in the hope that their anti-war propaganda would sap morale.[78] It is less clear how much of this money was ever received by leaders of the Bolshevik Party, who naturally took great care to avoid being associated with the Kaiser's government for fear that it would damage their revolutionary credentials. During the spring and early summer of 1917 the reports compiled by British diplomats and consular officials contained comparatively few direct references to the Bolsheviks, although Lindley did accuse them in one memorable phrase of being 'drunk with the idea of the brotherhoods of the proletariat of the world'.[79]

The Embassy knew that Bolshevik agitators played an important role in organising the periodic demonstrations that took place in Petrograd against the Provisional Government, but staff there had little detailed knowledge of their activities in the army or the various factory committees which sprang to life following the Tsar's abdication. This was due in part to a straightforward failure of political intelligence. It also reflected the fact that, during the months immediately after the March Revolution, the Bolsheviks themselves commanded comparatively little public support when compared with other radical parties such as the Mensheviks and Socialist Revolutionaries. Lockhart rightly recalled many years later that the Bolsheviks' 'trump card' was their unrelenting hostility to the war, which in time strengthened their appeal to a war-weary population that grew increasingly sceptical of the Provisional Government's willingness to bring hostilities to an end. Nevertheless, even when combined with Lenin's rhetorical commitment to redistribute land and transfer 'all power to the Soviets', during the early summer of 1917 the Party could still not count on the support of a majority of workers in the capital. The Bolshevik leader himself remained an enigma to British officials in Petrograd, despite the fact that a number of them regularly passed the house where he had taken up residence and heard the speeches he made from the balcony there setting out his Party's programme. William Gerhardie, who admittedly was not always the most perceptive of observers, later recalled that when he heard these speeches he saw 'nothing in the man's speech or looks to give an inkling of his future career'.[80] Although civilian officials at the Embassy held a rather higher view of Lenin's abilities, it was not until the end of June that they suspected that the Bolshevik Party could mount a really effective challenge to the government.

During the weeks before the so-called July Rising, in which a Bolshevik inspired revolt posed the Provisional Government with its sternest test to date, there had been so many rumours of an impending coup that when it actually happened it took almost everyone in the city by surprise. Embassy staff were so used to hearing that their building was about to be burnt down that they had become almost insouciant about the prospect, though Lady Buchanan continually fretted about the danger faced by her husband.[81] Ironically, Lenin was among those unprepared for the events which came to a head in the middle of the month,[82] even though members of his own Party played a key role in the drama. Although the Bolsheviks had been planning an uprising for some weeks, their leader's hand was forced by the action of a crowd of workers and sailors who tried to storm the Tauride Palace, which housed the Petrograd Soviet, in an attempt to force its members to take power. The uprising coincided with a crisis in the Provisional Government that had begun following the resignation of several Cadet Ministers over the vexed question of Ukrainian independence, which made its position even more fragile than usual. On the first day of the uprising, street battles broke out all around the British Embassy, which was particularly vulnerable since it was in the direct line of fire between the Peter and Paul fortress – where the insurgents had seized control – and the Winter Palace. A good deal of fighting between rebels and troops loyal to the government took place at the end of the Troitsky Bridge, just in front of the Embassy, and those inside the building were able to watch the drama unfold directly in front of them.[83] Meriel Buchanan recalled in her memoirs how 'ruffians with unshaven faces' took control of the streets and created an 'atmosphere of dread that seemed to brood over the town'.[84] However, while the Ambassador's daughter was understandably terrified by the collapse of order which took place during the July Days, the uprising was in reality badly planned and the 'ruffians' were unable to decide what action to take. Although the rebels were at one stage in a position to arrest several members of the government, they lacked the confidence to push home their advantage. Since Lenin and the other leading Bolsheviks had not anticipated the uprising, which was driven by rank and file Party members and sailors from the Kronstadt naval base, they were unable to provide effective leadership. The Provisional Government was therefore able to take advantage of the confusion to restore order, using loyal Cossack troops to disperse the mob and regain control of the Peter and Paul fortress.

British officials in Petrograd were without doubt in greater personal danger during the July Rising than at any previous time. Buchanan declined the Foreign Minister's offer of accommodation elsewhere in the city, even when informed that the Embassy was likely to come under fire from the rebels in the Peter and Paul fortress, telling Tereshchenko that he did not want his departure to 'cause panic in the [British] colony'.[85] The staff inside simply moved to the back of the building and remained there until the fighting had finished. The conditions were not pleasant, since they were forced to shut the windows and 'sit in closed rooms, dying of heat'.[86] While it was difficult for Buchanan and his colleagues to follow the events taking place on the streets, they recognised that the trial of strength between the Provisional Government and its most vocal opponents in the factories and garrisons of Petrograd was a key moment in the development of revolutionary Russia. As soon as the uprising was over and the rebels were defeated, the Ambassador immediately contacted the Foreign Minister to ask that the government should take advantage of the situation to crush the Bolsheviks once and for all, in the hope that such action would weaken opposition to the war and reduce the number of agitators in the army.[87] Even while the fighting was still in progress, Buchanan had already told the Foreign Office in London that 'normal conditions cannot be restored without bloodshed and the sooner we get it over the better'.[88] However, as had happened so often before, the Provisional Government found it difficult to take the kind of resolute action called for by the representatives of Russia's allies. The political crisis created by the resignation of the Cadet Ministers led, within a few days of the end of the July Rising, to the formation of a third Provisional Government, politically to the left of its predecessor, in which Alexander Kerensky replaced Prince Lvov as Prime Minister. Because the new government was desperate to attract as much support from the Petrograd Soviet as possible, so as to marginalise the extreme socialists in the Bolshevik Party, it was constrained from pursuing any policies that might appear as a return to the autocratic ways of the past. Although Lenin was forced to flee for a time to Finland, other senior Bolsheviks remained in the capital where the organisational structure of the Party remained largely intact.

British civilian officials and military representatives could only look on in frustration as their demands for stern action against the Bolsheviks, along with a vigorous restoration of military discipline, were largely ignored. Knox was particularly aghast at the government's failure to crush its opponents, and concluded a few days after the uprising had collapsed that 'It is difficult to hope that it is not already too late to save the army'.[89] Unlike the Military Attaché, civilian officials at the Embassy were at least in part aware that Kerensky was not a free agent when deciding whether to adopt strong measures. Lindley observed in one of his fortnightly reports that the government's need to attract support from the Soviet meant that it would inevitably face great problems in winning support for 'the execution of the concrete measures which the situation imperatively demands'. He also noted in early August that 'there has been more talk than action in pursuit of the "strong" policy which was to mark government disapproval of the riot of 16th and 17th July', but conceded that 'a certain amount has been done to discourage its repetition'.[90] Even so, the new Prime Minister was a controversial figure among British officials in Russia. More often than not, they held him personally responsible for the Provisional Government's failure to assert its authority and prevent the further disintegration of the Russian army.

The most bitter critic of Kerensky among British officials was Alfred Knox, who commented acidly in his memoirs that the Russian Prime Minister 'had all the theatrical qualities of a Napoleon, but none of his moral courage or useful ruthlessness'.[91] At one stage during the summer of 1917, Buchanan had to ensure that the two men did not meet face-to-face for fear that the Attaché might 'go for Kerenski'.[92] Needless to say, Knox's dislike was heartily reciprocated. The Ambassador's own feelings about Kerensky were less vitriolic, though he too believed that the Prime Minister lacked the courage and determination required by someone in his position.[93] Yet Buchanan never doubted, however, that the Russian leader was genuinely committed to continuing the fight against the Germans and Austrians, which helped to smooth relations between the two men. Most British officials who came into contact with the Prime Minister paid tribute to his undoubted oratorical skills and his ability to win over a crowd. Buchanan and Knox both hoped that these talents would be decisive in keeping Russia in the war, since Kerensky showed himself tireless in touring the Front in an attempt to raise the morale of the troops who still remained at their posts there. Kerensky's strenuous efforts to keep Russia's armies in the field also explains why at least some senior members of the British Intelligence

Service were anxious to offer support to the Prime Minister, sending
the novelist Somerset Maugham on a secret mission to offer help to
his government and all the 'patriotic socialists' who wanted to continue
the war against Germany.[94] In reality, these hopes lacked any firm
foundation. By the time Kerensky became Prime Minister in July 1917,
it was probably too late for any government to establish its authority
and prevent the spread of anarchy across Russia.

Even though there was a good deal of agreement among all British
civilian and military representatives about the need for stronger and
more assertive government in Petrograd, they disagreed among themselves over the best way of bringing it about. As was seen in the previous
chapter, George Buchanan never fully established his authority over
British representatives in Russia who did not belong to the Diplomatic
and Consular Services. There was a sharp contrast between Buchanan's
opinions about the Russian domestic political situation in 1917 and the
views expressed by at least some representatives from the War Office
and Admiralty. Buchanan was a professional diplomat, trained to be
aware of the sensitivities of the government to which he was accredited.
Although committed to keeping Russia in the war, he recognised that
the domestic political context placed powerful constraints on the Provisional Government which its members could ignore only at their peril.
By contrast, Britain's military representatives in Russia viewed the country's domestic problems through a rather different prism, as many of
them never really understood how the social and political turmoil that
had erupted after the March Revolution placed limits on the Provisional
Government's freedom of action. Most of them believed that strong
leadership alone could resolve the crisis. Buchanan also wanted the
government to show greater boldness, but he understood that strong
leadership could only be effective when a large part of the population
was willing to follow it.

The desire for a more assertive government in Petrograd was not of
course limited to foreign officials wanting to prevent the final disintegration of the Russian army and the collapse of opposition to Germany
and Austria on the Eastern Front. The chaos which followed the March
Revolution appalled millions of Russians as well, particularly those who
came from the wealthier classes. Lockhart predicted in the days immediately following the Tsar's abdication that there would take place in
the coming months 'a great struggle between the bourgeoisie and the
proletariat'.[95] Although some of the most active opposition to the Tsarist
regime had come from middle-class liberals who had no intention of
bringing about a social as well as a political revolution, the collapse of

the old structures of authority –particularly when combined with the growing strength of radical revolutionary parties like the Bolsheviks – meant that a stable 'bourgeois' political settlement was never likely to emerge from the anarchy of 1917. By the middle of the year many Russian officers and financiers were beginning to discuss the possibility of restoring order in their country via some form of military coup designed to crush the various revolutionary parties and, if necessary, the Provisional Government itself.[96]

Buchanan had already told the Foreign Office at the end of May that 'Talk begins to be heard about desirability of appearance of a Dictator to consolidate power and bring order, and Admiral Kolchak [in charge of the Black Sea fleet] has been mentioned as the man whose resolute character, energy and undoubted patriotism fit him for the part'. The Naval Attaché at the Embassy had been approached by Kolchak's flag officer a few days earlier, who asked if the British would provide transport to bring a Russian division to Petrograd from France, apparently in order to help stage a coup d'état designed to instal a new government capable of prosecuting the war with greater vigour.[97] The approach was rebuffed by the Embassy, where diplomatic staff were reluctant to become so directly involved in the internal affairs of Russia, and unwilling to be put in a situation where they could be accused of plotting against the government to which they were accredited. Nevertheless, it seems that Kolchak's representatives had already discussed the whole question at some length with the British liaison officer assigned to the Black Sea fleet, suggesting that at least some of Britain's military representatives had fewer scruples about such matters.

Although nothing came of the discussions that took place in May, during the weeks following the suppression of the July Rising there was a renewed debate among British representatives and Russian officers alike about the best means of restoring order in Russia. Two weeks after the collapse of the uprising, General L. G. Kornilov was appointed by Kerensky as Commander-in-Chief of the Russian army. Kornilov had for some months been identified as a vigorous opponent of the various revolutionary groups that sought to undermine military discipline, and his appointment was welcomed by British officials as evidence that the Provisional Government at last intended to take a tougher line with its opponents. The General made his acceptance of the post conditional on the introduction of a series of measures designed to rebuild military discipline, including the restoration of the death penalty and complete independence for the army command when making appointments and promotions. These proposals were leaked to the press and immediately created a storm of protest, both among the extreme revolutionary organisations and among less radical groups whose members still believed that the army should be organised on consensual lines, in which officers led their men by the power of persuasion rather than through the imposition of iron discipline. Yet while Kornilov's proposals appalled many on the left in Russia, they were predictably endorsed by the British. Buchanan urged Ministers in the Provisional Government to implement the General's proposals, telling them that further military aid from London would be conditional on their introduction.[98] During an interview with Kerensky at the end of August, he indignantly told the Prime Minister how distressing it was

> to see what was going on it Petrograd. Our soldiers were shedding their blood for Russia and in [the] United Kingdom every man, woman and child were working for the war. Here on the contrary there was no drill. Soldiers were loafing in the street, fishing in the river and riding in the trams while owing to the absence of police robberies were on the increase and German agents were everywhere.[99]

Some British military representatives still did not think that the Ambassador was being forceful enough in his representations to the Prime Minister, and wanted London to authorise even greater pressure to make Kerensky and his colleagues accept Kornilov's demands. This perception was almost certainly unfair: Buchanan was in fact something of a 'hawk' when compared with some other senior diplomats at the Embassy. Frank Lindley, in particular, did not believe there was any point in trying to keep Russia in the war against the will of its people, and advised a change of policy before popular resentment exploded into even worse civil disorder that would be certain to propel the Bolsheviks to power.[100] Throughout August and early September, however, that is during the period leading up to Kornilov's ill-fated attempt to seize power and restore order in Russia, the differences between Buchanan and Lindley were as nothing when compared with the growing breach between Britain's civilian and military representatives about the extent to which they should intervene in the country's internal affairs.

The historian Michael Kettle has presented compelling evidence to suggest that Kornilov was from early August trying to persuade Commander Oliver Locker-Lampson to use his Armoured Car Squadron in support of any moves which the General might make to take over the reins of power. The Englishman responded with alacrity to these overtures and decided to relocate his base to the town of Brovari, on the eastern side of the River Dneiper, from where it would be comparatively easy for him to join up with Kornilov's forces further north.[101] Locker-Lampson had always been something of a 'loose cannon' while on service in Russia. His friendship with members of the Royal Family gave him considerable prestige and allowed him to operate with a good deal of independence, while the Admiralty (to which he was nominally accountable) was in practice unable to exercise much effective control over his actions. Perhaps for this reason, Buchanan had always opposed the presence of the Armoured Car Squadron in Russia and constantly agitated for its withdrawal.[102] The suspicion was mutual. While Locker-Lampson knew from early August that Kornilov was considering some form of military action against the Provisional Government, he failed to pass the information on to British diplomats in Petrogad. It is not clear to what extent other British military officials knew that Kornilov was considering the use of force to influence the political situation – and harder still to know whether they gave him their tacit approval and support. General Sir Charles Barter, who replaced Hanbury-Williams as British representative at the *Stavka* in the spring of 1917, certainly had an idea that some kind of plot was afoot. On 20 August he informed the Chief of the Imperial General Staff in London that Kornilov had just told him that he was:

> out of patriotism considering expediency of adopting, if necessary, a vigorous political initiative which, should foreign diplomatic action fail, is, in his opinion, the only way to save the army and the country.[103]

It was presumably on the basis of this information that the Foreign Office wired Buchanan a few days telling him that 'British Military authorities believe that General Korniloff may be contemplating a *coup d'état*',[104] though Barter himself apparently neglected to inform the Ambassador direct. Two weeks later, on 6 September, Barter once again wired London, noting that Kornilov had now told him that he definitely intended to 'declare a state of siege in Petrograd in four days' time'. The General, however, begged the War Office that 'this information be kept entirely secret, especially from our Ambassador in Petrograd',[105] presumably since he feared that Buchanan would inform Kerensky who might then take steps to forestall Kornilov.

The Ambassador had in fact been told on the previous day that a coup was imminent, when a Russian visitor to the Embassy, the industrialist A. I. Putilov, asked him to place Locker-Lampson's Armoured Car Squadron at the disposal of the General. (This was of course something of a 'courtesy' request, since Locker-Lampson had apparently already made preparations to join with Kornilov.) Buchanan indignantly refused to have anything to do with the whole escapade, condemning it as a certain prelude to civil war. The Ambassador was shrewd enough to understand that the conspirators were flying in the face of the popular mood and had little prospect of success in their attempt to restore order. He did, however, agree not to inform the Provisonal Government about the existence of the plot, in spite of the fact that such silence could be construed as a breach of diplomatic protocol. Perhaps surprisingly, the Ambassador's strong opposition to military action was not entirely shared at the Foreign Office in London, where at least one official noted that he did not 'quite understand why Sir George Buchanan is so strongly opposed to a coup d'état. There will certainly be bloodshed before discipline in the army is restored and it seems that it is only through the Army that the Soviet can be abolished and discipline restored'.[106]

While it seems certain that some British military officials in Russia supported military measures to restore order in Russia, the position of Alfred Knox at the Embassy is harder to discern. He was certainly a great admirer of Kornilov and strongly supported the Commander-in-Chief's call for the restoration of greater discipline in the army.[107] A few days before the General's abortive march on Petrograd, Knox returned to England where he was asked to brief the War Cabinet about Russian affairs and comment on the possibility of a military putsch in the coming weeks. He told Ministers that he did not know what preparations were being made for a coup, but commented in his usual forthright fashion that 'A force of 10,000 loyalists would be enough to subdue Petrograd – the main source of the disorder – for the Russians are cowards'. The Attaché may of course have been lying when he said that he did not know what preparations were underway. Certainly, like every other foreign representative in the capital, he had heard many rumours about an impending coup. He also 'strongly urged' that the allied governments should impress on the Russian government that 'General Korniloff should be fully supported in the measures which he wished to take to restore discipline'.[108] Knox was, however, intensely loyal to Buchanan, and deeply imbued with the traditional ethos that the first loyalty of a British Military Attaché while on posting abroad was to the Head of the Mission rather than his military colleagues. It therefore seems doubtful whether Knox, like Barter, deliberately kept information about Kornilov's activities from the Ambassador. It seems even less likely that he was actively involved in the preparations for the coup itself.

It is still not entirely clear whether the Kornilov putsch which took place in the second week of September was directed against the Provisional Government itself, or whether the General's attempted march on Petrograd was at least initially supported by Kerensky who hoped to use it as a means of crushing the more extreme revolutionary groups in the capital.[109] A great deal of confusion was caused by the activities of a certain V. N. Lvov who, in acting as a 'go-between' between Kerensky and Kornilov during these fateful days, simply succeeded in sowing enormous doubt and mistrust between the two men. It is possible that Kornilov genuinely believed that he was acting with Kerensky's support when ordering his troops to move on the Russian capital, being taken by surprise when the population rallied to mount a successful defence of the city. Yet given his behaviour over the previous few weeks, there is little doubt that the General was prepared to go ahead with his plans even without the approval of the Prime Minister. Following the inconclusive outcome of the Moscow Conference, which was summoned by Kerensky at the start of September in a vain attempt to unite the Russian population behind the policies of the Provisional Government, Kornilov can hardly have believed that the political situation was going to become any more stable in the weeks ahead. Certainly, in the immediate aftermath of the Conference he told General Barter that 'a crisis was inevitable unless [the] government took [the] immediate steps demanded by moderates'.[110] Staff at the British Embassy were not of course in a position to unravel a series of events which still remains obscure to historians eighty years later. Colonel James Blair, an assistant Military Attaché at the Embassy, rightly noted a few days after the failure of the putsch that 'prodigious lying has been going on', which made it almost impossible to unravel the truth behind the whole bizarre affair.[111] Buchanan, as was seen earlier, opposed Kornilov's actions from the beginning and had little doubt that the coup was directed against the Provisional Government as well as revolutionary groups in the capital. Lindley similarly believed that the General had intended 'to declare himself dictator' should he have been successful in seizing the capital, though he was certain that the whole escapade had been 'doomed to failure' given the logistical problems involved in moving troops to Petrograd from their base ninety miles outside the capital.[112] Colonel Blair agreed, noting in his report that the coup could never have been successful as long as it did not command the general support of the army.

Whatever their individual views about the Kornilov affair, almost all British officials in Russia, whether military or civilian, recognised that its ignominious failure in the face of massive popular resistance from the populace of Petrograd virtually destroyed any real prospect for restoring order across the country. Lindley wrote in his account of the ill-fated putsch that although it had in the past been possible to 'regard a Bolshevik rising with a certain confidence in its failure ... now that the gathering forces of order have been split from top to bottom it would be a bold man who would predict the result of such a rising which has become more probable than ever before'.[113] Blair agreed, suggesting that a Bolshevik coup 'at no very distant date is almost a certainty'.[114] Like most British observers, the Colonel did not believe that any of the moderate political parties would be able to 'extricate the country from the chaotic state into which it has drifted'. Diplomats at the Embassy were shrewd enough to realise that the Kornilov rebellion had failed in large part because a majority of workers and soldiers in the city were opposed to it, even though the middle and upper classes fervently hoped that the General would be successful. This division, argued Lindley, had 'aggravated the situation and made the position of the officers in the army and that of the Bourgeoisie in the towns extremely critical'.[115] It had also made the position of British officials in the Russian capital more difficult. Diplomatic staff began to put in place detailed plans to defend the Embassy. They even considered asking the Admiralty in London to send two submarines to moor in the river opposite the building to act as a deterrent against attack.[116] Although British officials continued to walk the streets unmolested, they were increasingly fearful of the dangers they faced in a city where a large section of the population blamed Russia's allies for keeping the country in the war against the will of its people.

The Bolsheviks benefited enormously from the failure of Kornilov's attempted coup. The Party's members played a leading role in organising the successful defence of Petrograd against attack by the General's troops, and the prestige which it brought them helped to restore their fortunes following the calamity they suffered after the ill-fated uprising in July. The Ambassador and his colleagues were well aware that the revival in the Bolsheviks' fortunes had deep roots and was not simply a consequence of the organisational genius and charisma of Lenin and the other leaders. Lindley noted in early October that the Bolsheviks had succeeded in gaining a majority in the Petrograd Soviet for the first time since it had been established six months earlier, which destroyed any lingering prospects for effective cooperation between the Soviet and the Provisional Government. The same pattern was observable in other major cities across Russia, where the Bolsheviks' success led to 'a growth of class hatred and impatience of all restraint' which appalled staff at the Embassy.[117] During the final weeks before the Bolshevik coup, reports flooded into the Embassy from around the country detailing the breakdown of authority throughout the provinces. Lockhart told Buchanan in the final week of September that although 'perfect order' still prevailed in Moscow, 'the wildest rumours circulate and there is very great uneasiness among the better classes'.[118] He went on to suggest that 'Moscow will almost certainly fall into line with any action taken by ... the Bolsheviks'. Picton Bagge in Odessa, who had reported at length during July and August on the failure of the Russian army's ill-fated offensive against the Austrians in the west of his district, wrote to Buchanan on 19 September that military discipline had now collapsed entirely. As a result, he saw 'no hope of Russia being able to prolong the war ... [the Russian] has no backbone, is easily swayed along the line of least resistance, and is practically devoid of patriotism'.[119] A few weeks later, Bagge also reported on the breakdown of law and order among the civilian population in his district, telling the Ambassador that 'The local press is daily filled with reports of disorders of every kind'.[120] Patrick Stevens wrote in a similar vein from Batum, noting that 'the state of the Caucasus has gone from bad to worse, and the actual situation is anything but reassuring ... Murders, robberies, burglaries are being constantly reported from many localities'.[121] These reports reinforced the bleak mood of staff at the Embassy, helping to cement their belief that some dramatic dénouement to the crisis facing Russia would take place before the autumn was over. On the last day of September, Buchanan told the Foreign Office that the Bolsheviks 'are in a decided minority', but such optimistic reports were the exception among the constant flow of pessimistic telegrams and dispatches sent to London from the Russian capital. A month later, Lindley recorded in the final 'Summary of Events' to be written before the Bolshevik coup that:

> From all parts of Russia pillaging by peasants and soldiers behind the lines is reported, and burglaries become daily more common in the towns. In Petrograd itself the Bolsheviks are officially reported to be planning a coup d'état, and in the factories agitators are busy preaching to the men the doctrine of class hatred.[122]

British officials realised that they were powerless in such circumstances, although some British soldiers still chafed against their impotence. While Buchanan continued to ask the Provisional Government to introduce energetic measures to restore order, his demands became increasingly ritualistic and empty. A few weeks after the failure of Kornilov's coup, the representatives of several major allied powers met members of the government, including Kerensky, in order to express formally their hope that in future all Russia's energies would be concentrated on fighting the war. The Prime Minister met the delegation coldly, blaming the allies for failing to provide enough supplies to allow the Russian army to perform effectively in the field.[123] In the weeks that followed, relations between Buchanan and Kerensky broke down still further, the Ambassador complaining on a number of occasions that he was treated with a high-handedness that was inappropriate for the representative of a major power. Kerensky for his part believed that the British government was plotting with leading military figures to overthrow him, and threatened to retaliate by providing support to Sinn Fein activists in Ireland. Just before the Bolshevik coup took place at the end of the first week in November, personal relations had become so bad that the Prime Minister even demanded that Buchanan should be replaced as British Ambassador to Russia since he was too 'identified with the old regime'.[124] Such squabbles had in reality become immaterial and were evidence of little more than the psychological frustration and fatigue of all those who were caught up in the momentous events of 1917. It was clear by the beginning of November that the Provisional Government had failed to establish its authority in Russia. The only question that remained concerned the precise way in which its forlorn existence would finally be brought to a close.

5

Robbery and Murder

George Buchanan and his staff were largely resigned to the Bolshevik seizure of power which eventually took place on the night of 6–7 November, when a small number of Red Guards, under the direction of Leon Trotsky, occupied strategic points across the Russian capital. The Ambassador had long since given up hoping that the Kerensky government would take effective action to crush the Bolsheviks, but his concern about the political situation was ameliorated by his belief that the insurgents would not be able to hold on to power for any significant length of time. On the day of the coup itself, Buchanan told the Foreign Office that Petrograd displayed 'an almost normal aspect' in spite of the drama unfolding across the city. The atmosphere was calm enough to allow him to walk unhindered through the streets of the capital and watch the preparations that were underway to storm the Winter Palace, where Ministers of the Provisional Government were surrounded by troops loyal to the Bolsheviks. On the following day, the Ambassador was even able to enter the palace itself, which had finally been taken in the early hours of the morning, where he saw at first hand the damage done overnight by 'the soldiers and workmen, who looted or smashed whatever they could lay their hands on'.[1]

A few hours before the Bolshevik seizure of power began, Buchanan had told the Foreign Office that even if it were successful the new government could 'not be of long duration and would before long provoke counter-revolution', a view that was shared by most foreign diplomats in Russia.[2] The events of the next few days appeared to confirm his prediction. Although most Ministers were captured when the Winter Palace was taken, Kerensky remained at liberty and left Petrograd in order to rally forces loyal to the Provisional Government.[3] Two days later, the former chairman of the Duma, M. V. Rodzyanko, sent a message to the Embassy telling the Ambassador that there was already forming in the south of Russia a 'considerable organisation all ready to strike' against the Bolsheviks.[4] The belief that the Bolshevik coup was simply a passing phase in the turbulent world of Russian politics encouraged British representatives in the capital to respond with surprising calm to developments. There was of course a degree of nervous tension at the Embassy, as well as some apprehension about the fate of those Russians who had actively opposed the Bolsheviks. On the day following the uprising, General Knox had to intervene with the new authorities in order to save both the honour and the lives of more than a hundred young female soldiers enrolled in the so-called Women's Batallion, who had been taken prisoner while defending the Winter Palace. For the most part, however, the Ambassador and his staff were confident that the situation would soon return to the comparative 'normality' which had existed before 7 November. Only Frank Lindley really believed that the Bolsheviks might have the determination and popular support to establish themselves in power and survive the attempts that would inevitably be made to oust them.

Within a few days of the Bolshevik coup, the tone of Buchanan's reports began to change as his early optimism dissipated, particularly once it became clear that the Bolsheviks had no intention of cooperating with more moderate socialist parties whose leaders were anxious to continue the war against Germany. On 16 November he told London that he was still confident that the members of Lenin's new government would 'discredit themselves before many weeks are over', but also ruefully admitted that the 'Situation is becoming more and more hopeless. Bolshevists are masters in the North and according to latest reports are regaining the upper hand at Moscow' (where fierce street fighting had been taking place for a number of days). As a result, he suggested that the British would soon 'have to enter into unofficial relations with it as the only de facto authority'.[5] The prospect of the Bolsheviks surviving for any significant length of time transformed the diplomatic situation across Europe, particularly since one of the new government's first acts was to issue a decree demanding that all the belligerent nations begin talks to discuss peace terms.[6] The whole question of Britain's relationship with the Bolshevik regime, which was to become such a central issue in British foreign policy over the next few years, was placed firmly on the political agenda once it became apparent that Lenin and his followers had no intention of surrendering their precarious hold on power without a struggle.

Buchanan's attitude towards the Bolsheviks during the final weeks of 1917 was not entirely consistent, but his dispatches to London were informed by a number of well-defined assumptions and insights. In early December he told the Foreign Office that he had recently received a message from a prominent Octobrist member of the fourth Duma, warning against the 'fatuous optimism' of those who believed that the Bolshevik government was about to collapse. The erstwhile deputy noted that the 'upper and middle classes' were only concerned with 'their personal interests' and could not be relied upon to take effective action to destabilise the new government; he also pointed out that the Bolsheviks had shown themselves to be remarkably successful at establishing their position in other major cities across Russia.[7] Buchanan endorsed these views, adding that the army was solidly in favour of the new administration since it promised to create the peace that was so desperately wanted by the vast majority of soldiers. He therefore reiterated his support for an immediate de facto recognition of the new government, even though he despised the principles espoused by its members, since it would help to ensure 'the safety of our subjects' and allow their orderly evacuation from Russia.

The Ambassador's suggestion was a logical corollary to an argument he had put forward to London a few days earlier, when he proposed that Russia should be released from its treaty obligations to continue the war against Germany. Since Buchanan thought it was impossible to 'force an exhausted nation to fight against its will',[8] he hoped that the removal of allied pressure might make the Russian people recognise more clearly that the war against Germany was in their own interests, which would in turn actually encourage them to continue the struggle. At the very worst, the Ambassador believed, his proposal might lead to Russia becoming a benign neutral whose government would at least not actively support the Germans in their struggle against Britain and its allies. This attitude was predictably treated with contempt by most senior British military representatives in Russia, though Knox as usual supported Buchanan loyally. General Barter at the *Stavka* was convinced, like most other British military officers in Russia, that the Bolsheviks were in German pay and that it would be an act of folly to release them from their treaty obligations. General Poole, who was responsible for supervising the transfer of British military supplies to the Russians, angrily denounced the Ambassador as 'a not very strong but charming gentleman' who was failing to provide the 'strong and resolute handling' demanded by the situation.[9] More junior officers, who, like their superiors, were convinced that Petrograd would soon be occupied by the Bolsheviks' German patrons, simply confined themselves to irreverent visions of 'General von Sauerkraut in his carriage being dragged down the Nevski by Sir George and Knox while Lady G. and Meriel wave palm branches over his head'.[10] Buchanan's advice in fact showed once again that he had a better insight into the realities of Russian political life than Britain's military representatives in Petrograd, recognising as he did that it was quite impossible to keep Russia in the war against the wishes of its people. By the end of 1917, however, the British government's policy towards Russia was being made with little reference to the opinions of its Ambassador in Petrograd.

In the days immediately following the Bolshevik seizure of power the British War Cabinet did not discuss the Russian crisis in any detail, perhaps because the breakdown in telegraphic communications with Petrograd meant that little detailed information actually reached London. Once it became clear that the new government was not about to collapse, leading politicians and their advisers began to give great attention to the whole question of Britain's relations with Russia. The Bolsheviks' demand for a general European peace posed an immediate and serious problem for the British government, since any refusal by the Russians to continue fighting would allow the Germans to divert men and material from the Eastern Front to France. It was also widely feared in London that the Germans might come to some agreement with the Bolsheviks, allowing them to exploit Russia's natural resources in its struggle against the allies; there was particular alarm at the prospect of the Germans gaining control of millions of tons of war material that had been sent to Russia during the previous three years, most of which was stored at the ports of Archangel and Vladivostok. Opinion was divided among leading politicians as to whether the Bolsheviks really were German agents. Nevertheless, even those who did not believe this was the case still feared that the new Russian government, by failing to offer effective opposition, would allow German forces to move eastwards and to extend their country's power and influence across vast tracts of Europe.

Although it has often been suggested that British policy towards Soviet Russia was from the beginning driven by ideological hostility to the Communist principles espoused by its government, the truth was in fact a good deal more complex. During the final weeks of 1917 members of the War Cabinet were concerned above all else with the impact which the Bolshevik Revolution might have on the progress of the war. At the same time, certain Ministers, such as the Parliamentary Under Secretary of State at the Foreign Office, Robert Cecil, made little secret of their desire to support any 'responsible body in Russia that would actively oppose the Maximalist movement' (the name by which the Bolsheviks were habitually referred to at this time in official circles in London).[11] As a result, the British War Cabinet drifted inexorably towards a policy of intervention in domestic Russian affairs, agreeing at the end of November to provide millions of pounds of support for the Cossack leader General A. M. Kaledin, who was reported (on no very good authority) to be organising a large force to attack the Bolsheviks in the south west of the country.[12] In the first week of December, the Chief of the Imperial General Staff also asked the War Cabinet for permission to sound out the Japanese and Americans about the possibility of sending troops to Vladivostok 'for police purposes'.[13] It is in reality very difficult to disentangle anti-German and anti-Bolshevik sentiment inside British foreign policy-making circles during this period, since so many politicians and officials were convinced that the success of Lenin and his followers necessarily strengthened the German position. The War Cabinet that met on 7 December noted that Britain had two options when deciding on its policy towards the Bolsheviks: it could either 'make the best possible arrangements with them', along the lines previously suggested by Buchanan; or it could 'refuse to recognise them, and take open and energetic steps against them'.[14] By offering financial support to Kaledin, while sim-ul-taneously declining to withdraw all its representatives from Petrograd, the British government was following two directly contradictory policies.

This policy of ambivalence was elevated to a statement of principle in a celebrated memorandum prepared by the Foreign Secretary, Arthur Balfour, discussed at the War Cabinet which met on 10 December.[15] Balfour noted his strong dissent from the view that 'the Bolsheviks could only be regarded as our avowed enemies'. Unlike Robert Cecil, he believed that Britain should 'avoid, as long as possible, an open break with this crazy system', and went on to observe that 'If this be drifting then I am a drifter by deliberate policy'. The Foreign Secretary was anxious to avoid an open breach with the Bolsheviks for two main reasons. He was concerned about the fate of British officials and citizens in Russia, whom he feared would be placed in jeopardy from mob violence if relations between Petrograd and London declined further. The Foreign Secretary was also afraid that if Britain was too open in its support for the enemies of Bolshevism it would simply force Lenin and Trotsky to turn to the Germans for support, allowing Berlin to establish its influence over the new government in Petrograd. Although Balfour was as appalled as the rest of the Cabinet by the Bolshevik government's blithe refusal to observe conventional diplomatic proto-cols and procedures, he was certain that a policy of open hostility towards Lenin and his colleagues would be counter-productive.

The Balfour memorandum, with its overt support for the principle of deliberate 'drift', laid the foundations for Britain's whole policy towards Russia through until the Armistice of November 1918. It was also, in a sense, the harbinger of British policy towards the Bolsheviks in the period after the end of the war, though by 1919 the drift and indecision lacked the elegant rationale which Balfour articulated in 1917, simply reflecting disagreements between politicians in London and among representatives of the victorious powers meeting in Paris. Britain's policy towards Soviet Russia during the years between 1917 and 1921 was one of indecisive enmity. The Bolshevik regime was viewed as a threat both to Britain's national interests *and* to the values of civilised society, encouraging the government in London to offer material and moral support to its opponents. At the same time, British politicians were reluctant to take the decisive steps required to overthrow the Bolsheviks once and for all, although Winston Churchill tried hard to promote more active measures once he became Minister of War early in 1919. This half-hearted and contradictory policy inevitably made life very difficult for Britain's civilian and military representatives and soldiers in Russia. In the first part of 1918 they were expected to maintain relations with the Bolshevik government while simultaneously preparing the ground for its downfall. From the middle of 1918 onwards they were asked to implement policies designed to undermine the Bolshevik regime, while never being given either the material or political support required to bring about its final collapse. As a result, they found themselves sucked into the vortex of a bitter civil war in which their role was ill-defined, but in which all sides looked to the British to play a decisive role.

The Bolshevik leadership was still a surprisingly unknown quantity to British officials at the time of the November Revolution. Staff at the Embassy followed domestic political developments with great attention following the coup, reporting in detail to London on Lenin's attempts to broaden the base of his government by securing an alliance with the left Socialist Revolutionaries. They remained convinced that Russia would eventually 'pass into a phase of violent anarchy' whatever the political strategy adopted by the Bolsheviks.[16] During the final weeks of 1917, all British officials in Petrograd went through a 'very anxious time' as the new government began to mount violent attacks on Britain in the press, at the same time refusing to give permission to British nationals to leave the country. A military guard was on duty in the Embassy at all times, though the handful of soldiers could not in practice have done much to prevent a determined effort to storm the building.

Buchanan himself was a favourite target for the vitriolic attacks which appeared in the newspapers. It was known at the Embassy by early December that Trotsky, who had been appointed Commissar for Foreign Affairs, was planning to arrest both the Ambassador and the Military Attaché in reprisal for the British government's refusal to release two leading Bolsheviks held in prison in London. Buchanan bravely refused to consider leaving the Russian capital, even though he had been given permission to do so by the Foreign Secretary, arguing that his presence was necessary to reassure members of the British colony. Although warned by his own staff not to risk taking his usual daily walk through the streets of Petrograd, since it would make him vulnerable to arrest, he declined to listen to such advice on the grounds that it 'bored him to be told constantly that his throat was going to be cut: if it was it was, and that was an end to it'.[17]

The position of staff at the Embassy was made more vulnerable by the ambiguous policy which the British government pursued towards Russia following the November Revolution. Buchanan and his colleagues were undoubtedly responsible for channelling money to the nascent anti-Bolshevik forces in the south of the country, even though the Ambassador had specifically advised London that his staff should not be asked to carry out such work for fear that it might compromise their safety.[18] Colonel Terence Keyes, who was employed by Buchanan to collect 'political intelligence' in Russia, played a central role in promoting these financial dealings despite the fact that he and his colleagues 'would certainly have [been] shot' if the Bolsheviks had obtained definite proof of their activities.[19] In spite of the threatening atmosphere, British officials managed to escape falling foul of the authorities during the months immediately following the Bolshevik seizure of power, though they were often forced to witness scenes of considerable violence, including the brutal killing of a Russian army officer right in front of the Embassy building. The anti-British rhetoric of Trotsky and other members of the new government was in large part designed for Russian domestic consumption, intended to bolster domestic support by portraying the Bolsheviks as the advocates of peace in the face of determined opposition by the 'imperialistic nations'. A more potent threat to the safety of British officials in Petrograd came from the general break-down in law and order, which led to a huge rise in street crime and theft. Meriel Buchanan recalled many years later how:

Nobody troubled to clear away the snow in the streets. Little boys used the slopes of the bridges over the canals as toboggan slides, cannoning carelessly against people, utterly unheedful whether they knocked them down or not. Others again would use the pavements as skating rinks, and walking in the streets became a thing fraught with many dangers, ridiculous and otherwise.[20]

The antics of the young Petrograd ragamuffins were, however, far less sinister than those of their elders in the Red Guards who:

> [stood] round huge, blazing fires, stopping every motor that passed to ask questions, and sometimes turning the occupants out if the answers did not satisfy them; ready at any moment on the slightest excuse to fire off the rifles that were tied round them with a piece of string or a dirty piece of red ribbon.[21]

The chaos which had so appalled British officials and their families during the days of the Provisional Government became worse than ever, as the new regime failed to restore any semblance of public order. A few weeks after the November Revolution, the wine cellars of the Winter Palace were ransacked. Several of the looters were drowned after firemen flooded the building in an attempt to disperse the mob. On the streets of the capital, 'robbery and murder' became 'daily and nightly occurences'.[22] Colonel Keyes recalled many years later that a simple stroll could be dangerous since 'one never knew ... when the street in which one happened to be walking might be splayed by machine-guns from an armoured car'.[23] The Colonel was himself threatened on one occasion by a crowd of hostile sailors armed with bayonets, while other Embassy staff faced the ordeal of having the car in which they were travelling commandeered at gunpoint.[24] The wife of the acting Naval Attaché expressed the fear felt by all those associated with the Embassy when she wrote to her sister that she and her husband 'await being clapped into the Fortress of Peter and Paul, or else having our throats cut'.[25] Nor were British officials immune from the material deprivations that afflicted the whole population, which naturally increased the misery of their situation. In the immediate aftermath of the Bolshevik takeover, the electric supply in Petrograd was constantly interrupted, with the result that Embassy staff had to 'wander about with candles which are almost unprocurable'.[26] Communications were also difficult since the telephones often failed to work, while newspapers that criticised the new government were quickly suppressed, making it impossible for officials to obtain much accurate information about affairs either in Russia or abroad. The British Embassy did at least have a bigger stockpile of food than most of its counterparts, but there was still a good deal of concern about what would happen when it ran out

since there were so few supplies in the shops. By the beginning of
December it had become clear that there was little point in maintaining
a full-scale British diplomatic presence in Russia. Foreign representatives who remained in the country faced considerable personal
danger while having little real opportunity to influence the developments taking place around them.

George Buchanan's health was already fragile before the Bolshevik
coup, having been undermined by years of worry and stress. The events
which followed the Bolsheviks' seizure of power finally took their toll,
as the Ambassador laboured to protect his staff and fellow nationals
while simultaneously trying to manage the burgeoning crisis in Anglo-
Russian relations. In the middle of December he had a serious attack
of vertigo and was told by his doctor that he was 'at the end of my
tether'.[27] His wife put a somewhat different interpretation on her husband's illness, writing in a private letter that 'George has had rather a
nervous breakdown',[28] which forced him to remain in bed for several
days. Even though he was reluctant to abandon his post, Buchanan
decided to seek permission to return to London on leave (which was
quickly granted by the Foreign Office). On Christmas Day 1917 the
Ambassador doggedly held the traditional party for staff from the
various British missions in the Russian capital, complete with a concert
and 'sit-down supper'. In spite of the air of apparent normality, the
festivities were in reality something of a masquerade that could not
conceal the radically changed position of British officials in a country
where the social rituals of the Old Diplomacy seemed increasingly
arcane and out of place. Just a few days after the Christmas celebrations,
Buchanan and a number of his colleagues, including General Knox,
made the difficult car journey through the January snows to the Finland
Station, where Lenin had arrived just nine months earlier following his
triumphant return from Switzerland. Here the party boarded a train
bound for Scandinavia, ignoring the objections of the Bolshevik government which was still trying to prevent any British citizens from
leaving Russia. There was in truth something slightly pathetic about
this final journey. Buchanan had arrived in Petersburg in 1910 amid
the pomp and ceremony befitting the representative of one of the
world's great powers. He left the city like a fugitive from justice,
scurrying to escape from Russia while there was still time for foreign
citizens to avoid being caught up in the maelstrom of revolution. His
departure marked a symbolic recognition by the British government
that the institutions of conventional diplomacy were no longer capable
of managing relations with a regime whose leaders were committed to

the social and political transformation both of their own country and the countries that surrounded them.

George Buchanan was in many ways a surprisingly successful Ambassador to Russia, particularly since nothing in his background and early career had prepared him for the turbulent years he was to spend in the country. The man he left behind in charge of the Embassy, the Counsellor Frank Lindley, also showed himself to be an adaptable and competent official who carried out his duties with a considerable degree of skill and dedication. During the eighteen months that followed Buchanan's departure from Petrograd, Lindley played an important role in Russia, first as Chargé d'Affaires at the Embassy and later as British Commissioner in north Russia, the territory around Archangel and Murmansk occupied by British troops in the second half of 1918. Lindley's views about the whole Russian situation were not very different from those of his former chief. Within a few days of Buchanan's departure from Petrograd, his successor wired the Foreign Office suggesting that 'we enter into relations with all the de facto regional authorities in the country',[29] including the Bolsheviks, whom he argued should be treated as the effective government in the northern part of Russia. A number of his colleagues at the Embassy disagreed with this proposal and continued to oppose any form of recognition. In spite of this opposition, Lindley held firm to his position over the following weeks, maintaining that whatever the distaste felt by British officials for the Bolshevik leaders and their ideas, it was necessary to have 'a frank exchange of views with Trotsky in an attempt to come to a modus vivendi with him on the basis of assisting him against the Germans'. However, Lindley himself seems in practice to have pursued contradictory strategies during the three months he was in charge at the Embassy, though like other British representatives in Russia he was placed in an impossible position by the ambiguous policy adopted by his own government. He was on the one hand opposed to the principle of supporting the anti-Bolshevik forces of Kaledin in south Russia, at least via the Embassy, on the grounds that it would make the position of the staff there 'most precarious'.[30] At the same time, he was closely involved in an extraordinary scheme, organised by Colonel Keyes and General Poole, to take control of a number of Russian banks in order to use them to channel funds to the counter-revolutionary movement in south Russia.[31] Quite how Lindley was able to reconcile these two contradictory courses of action in his own mind remains unclear.

The British officials who remained in Russia after Buchanan's departure at the beginning of 1918 were something of a motley crew from an organisational and administrative point of view. In addition to Lindley and his small staff at the Embassy, most consular officials remained at their post, since it had been agreed in London that they should become the principal means of maintaining informal contacts with the Bolsheviks.[32] The staff of General Poole's Supply Mission also stayed, although their position was increasingly anomolous once the British War Cabinet had decided to send no further military supplies to Russia. Poole himself decided that his Mission's new role should be to prevent the stocks of war material already in the country from falling into German hands.[33] Indeed, during the first few weeks of 1918, as the Cabinet in London slowly adopted a more conciliatory policy towards Lenin and his colleagues, a number of British and other allied military officers based in Russia actively cooperated with the Bolsheviks in helping to move stocks of war material away from locations that might be occupied by the Germans.[34] Peace negotiations had started between the Russians and the Germans at the town of Brest-Litovsk in early January, but they dragged on for many weeks as Trotsky and his delegation refused to accept the punitive terms demanded by the representatives from Berlin, threatening instead to pursue a policy of 'neither peace nor war' designed to avoid the restoration of hostilities while avoiding as far as possible the surrender of territory.[35] In this diplomatic No Man's Land, Britain's civilian and military representatives struggled desperately, like their political masters in London, to devise and implement policies that would secure Russian opposition to German demands while at the same time avoiding any action that could be interpreted as a firm offer of recognition or moral support to the Bolshevik government.

The British government's response to its diplomatic dilemma was to send Lockhart back to Russia to establish 'unofficial relations' with the Bolshevik government, a decision taken by Lloyd George and Lord Milner at the end of 1917. Lockhart had returned to London on Buchanan's advice shortly before the Bolshevik Revolution, in order to put an end to a liaison with a Russian woman that was threatening a scandal serious enough to affect his career and damage the reputation of other British officials in the country.[36] Yet while the affair caused something of a stir in the close-knit foreign community in Petrograd, it did not create any lasting impression in London. In any case, the Prime Minister and Secretary of State for War, who had both been greatly impressed by Lockhart's consular dispatches from Moscow over the previous few years, believed that he was the ideal man to be given the job of establishing informal contacts with the Bolsheviks. Lloyd

George was by instinct distrustful of professional diplomats, while Lord Milner considered even the Foreign Secretary to be a 'harmless old gentleman' who lacked the insight and skills required to deal effectively with the situation in Russia.[37] As a result, both men were happy to choose a representative from outside the upper reaches of the Diplomatic Service. Even so, Lockhart was still an astonishing choice to carry out such an important mission. His appointment caused considerable irritation at the Foreign Office. Not only was he very young – he was only thirty at the time he returned to Moscow early in 1918 – but he was not even a member of the regular Diplomatic Service. The resentment at the Foreign Office which followed the announcement of an outsider's appointment to such an important job had considerable ramifications in the months that followed.

Lockhart certainly possessed many of the talents required for developing 'unofficial relations' with the Bolsheviks, not least of which was a boundless self-confidence that on occasions proved rather tiresome to senior officials in London. He spoke excellent Russian, while his entire career in Moscow between 1912 and 1917 had been a testimony to his aptitude for developing contacts with individuals in positions of power and influence. The memorandum setting out the role of his Mission, which was given the entirely misleading title of the British Commercial Mission to Russia, was surprisingly vague, noting simply that its 'main object is to form an unofficial connecting link between His Majesty's Government and the existing Bolshevik Government in Petrograd'.[38] Lockhart was instructed to work 'through the Embassy and be subordinate to the head of the Mission', but was also told to house his small staff in a separate building in order to emphasise their unofficial status. The precise nature of Lockhart's role was never entirely clear to British officials already in Petrograd, who reacted with resignation when they first heard about its members' impending arrival. Frank Lindley, who had no particular animus against Lockhart, but no great liking for him either, wearily told the Foreign Office that he would cooperate with the scheme 'however unworkable it may seem to be'.[39] The staff at General Poole's Supply Mission reacted with a predictable mixture of stony indifference and sullen hostility to the news that yet another of the despised civilians was about to try his hand at grappling with the endless complexities of Britain's relationship with Bolshevik Russia.

Although it is not clear exactly what role Lloyd George and Lord Milner envisaged for Lockhart, the Head of the British Commercial Mission had no doubts about his task. From the day of his arrival, he devoted his time and energy to persuading the Bolshevik government that they should refuse to come to terms with Berlin and instead accept allied assistance to carry on the struggle against Germany.[40] Given the scale of the demands made by German negotiators at Brest-Litovsk, which involved the surrender of vast areas of territory in the south west of the country, such a policy appeared to make considerable sense. Lockhart knew perfectly well that the Bolshevik government was deeply divided about whether to accept the terms offered by Berlin, and was therefore eager to support Trotsky in his determined refusal to cave in to German demands. During February and March Lockhart sent a long stream of telegrams to London arguing that as long as the Bolshevik leaders were treated 'tactfully' by the British, they would prove to be a 'very valuable asset against Germany'. He criticised the 'dual' policy which the British government was pursuing towards Russia, and suggested that it should end 'support of counter-revolutionary movements' and concentrate on winning the trust of the Bolsheviks in order to encourage them to continue the struggle against Germany.[41] He also attacked the widespread notion that the Bolshevik leaders were German agents, bitterly criticising British Secret Service agents in Russia who devoted much of their time and energy to a futile search for documents proving that Berlin was the paymaster of Lenin and Trotsky.[42]

Lockhart's belief that he could persuade the Bolshevik leaders to renew hostilities against Germany was at least in part based on his naive conviction that he was developing a genuine rapport with Trotsky, who had made a favourable impression on him from the time of their first meeting.[43] The Commissar shamelessly encouraged the young British official in this belief, recognising that the fragile position of the Bolshevik government meant that there was no point in making foreign enemies needlessly. When the Commissariat of Foreign Affairs was moved to Moscow in March, following a decision to transfer the seat of the new government away from Petrograd, Lockhart and his party were invited to travel on the same train as the Commissar himself, where they were treated with a 'politeness and courtesy which would not have been exceeded under the old regime'.[44] Not surprisingly, Lockhart was at this time a shrill critic of any move by the allied powers to begin direct military intervention on Russian soil, particularly by the Japanese in the Far East,[45] a policy that was being discussed urgently in London and other allied capitals as a way of guaranteeing allied control over the stockpiles of military goods held at Vladivostok. He believed instead that it was still possible for the British government to establish a *modus vivendi* with the Bolshevik government, based on their shared interest in preventing the expansion of German power and influence eastwards towards the heart of Russia.

Lockhart's attitude towards the Bolsheviks was reviled by many officials in London, particularly military men like General Knox, who was by this time exercising a significant influence on the government's deliberations over its policy towards Russia. The General attacked Lockhart for failing to deal forcefully enough with the Bolsheviks, stridently declaring in a paper prepared for the War Cabinet that 'The policy of flirtation with the Bolsheviks is both wrong and immoral'.[46] He went on to demand the recall of the Commercial Mission, suggesting that the energy of the British government should be devoted to bringing about Japanese intervention in the Far East rather than establishing some kind of unofficial understanding with the government in Moscow. Such attitudes were echoed by other senior army officers, both in London and Russia, though General Poole in Petrograd surprisingly remained in favour of recognising the Bolsheviks throughout the months before he left for London in the spring of 1918. One notoriously anti-Bolshevik officer in the British army, who had great experience of Russia, spoke for many of his colleagues when he tersely observed that Lockhart was 'either a fool or a traitor' who should be hanged. Opinion at the Foreign Office was more restrained, but here too senior officials expressed concern that Lockhart was far too sanguine in believing that it might be possible to establish any real understanding with the Bolshevik government.

Although Lockhart was certainly a particularly strong advocate of collaboration with the Bolsheviks during the early months of 1918, many other civilian officials in Russia expressed similar ideas at the time. The views of Frank Lindley prior to his departure from the Embassy in early spring, in a dramatic dash across the Finnish frontier,[47] have already been discussed. Oliver Wardrop, the new Consul-General in Moscow, was a strident critic of 'the least interference in [the] purely internal affairs of Russia',[48] a position that was echoed by Woodhouse in Petrograd. During the first few weeks of 1918, when the Bolsheviks had still not finally come to terms with the Germans, it made diplomatic sense to pursue a policy based on the search for cooperation and accommodation in the hope that an alliance of convenience could be forged between the erstwhile allies, based on their common hostility to the Central Powers. The vicious criticism which Knox and other senior military men made of Lockhart was therefore not entirely justified, and the 'unofficial representative' was of course being entirely truthful when he declared that he had absolutely no sympathy with Bolshevik ideals.[49]

The same was not true of the official used by the French in a similar capacity to Lockhart, Captain Jacques Sadoul, who eventually declared himself to be a Communist and a sympathiser with the Bolshevik regime.[50]

While Lockhart was undoubtedly gullible in failing to realise that Trotsky's friendliness was motivated by a calculated desire to enhance his government's diplomatic freedom of manoeuvre, the Head of the Commercial Mission was driven above all by a strong sense of realpolitik when recommending to London that Britain should avoid pursuing an overtly anti-Bolshevik foreign policy. He believed that the country's overriding goal should be to secure the rapid defeat of Germany, and argued that any ideological scruples about cooperating with the Moscow government should under the circumstances be put aside. Lockhart was often his own worst enemy when seeking to influence the formulation of British policy, sending imperious telegrams to London demanding that his Mission be accorded more status and that all British officials in Russia be told to 'work in conjunction with it'.[51] A number of civilian and military officials based in the country, as well as many of those who dealt with Russian policy at the War Office and Foreign Office in London, remembered Lockhart from his days as a junior consular official in Moscow. They did not take kindly to the high-handed attitude displayed towards them by their former colleague.

When the Bolsheviks finally acceded in March 1918 to the draconian German terms demanded at Brest-Litovsk, the situation of allied representatives in Russia was transformed. Since the Bolshevik leadership was at first bitterly divided over whether to accept the German demands, Lockhart and a number of other British officials continued to hope for a few weeks that the new agreement between Moscow and Berlin would quickly fall apart. By the middle of May, however, it was clear that Lenin's readiness to make huge concessions in order to win peace had triumphed over the doubts of his colleagues, with the result that there was little point in trying to encourage the Russians to reopen the Eastern Front. Lockhart's view of the Bolshevik government continued to be determined by the whole question of the war. While he had initially believed that it was possible to come to terms with the Bolshevik leadership, and warned against any form of allied intervention or support for counter-revolutionary forces, he quickly reversed his position once the signing of the Brest-Litovsk treaty made it clear that other ways would have to be found to contain the eastward expansion of German power and influence. By the end of April he had begun to call for British military intervention in the north of Russia to safeguard the stores at Archangel and prevent any possible German advance in the area, intervention which he suggested to London should take place with the support of the Bolsheviks if possible but 'if not the allies must impose it'.[52] Lockhart worked hard to secure such an invitation from the government in Moscow throughout April and May, but by the end of that time he had no doubt that it should take place whatever the views of the Bolshevik leaders. By early June he was even threatening to resign if British intervention did not occur in the immediate future.[53] This rapid volte-face caused a good deal of confusion at the Foreign Office. In March officials had been used to receiving telegrams from Britain's unofficial representative warning against any action that might offend the Bolsheviks; just two months later, Lockhart had become more hawkish than many of the military men who had once criticised him for his supposed pro-Bolshevik sentiments. Arthur Balfour could scarcely conceal his bewilderment, chiding Lockhart for his failure to understand the political complexities and tensions surrounding the whole question of allied military intervention in Russia.[54] These critic-isms were understandable, though Lockhart could hardly be blamed for his ignorance of the diplomatic machinations that took place across the globe, as the major powers desperately tried to agree on a common response to the upheavals that had taken place in Moscow over the previous year. All the allied representatives in Russia – whether British, French or American – became absorbed during 1918 in the day to day intricacies of their work, and were inclined to forget that their political masters often viewed the Russian situation through a very different prism from themselves.

Lockhart's support for British intervention in Russia was not only driven by his frantic desire to create opposition to the Germans on the former Eastern Front. He also believed that the arrival of British troops on Russian soil would have a big impact on Russia's *domestic* politics, suggesting to London in May that it could 'produce a counter-revolution which may easily be successful', a perception that was shared by a number of other British officials in Russia, including Woodhouse in Petrograd.[55] In February and March Lockhart's reports on Russia's domestic politics had emphasised the solidity of the Bolsheviks' hold on power.[56] Within a few weeks, he was arguing that they lacked 'any wide-spread popularity'. By the end of May, he was convinced that 'during the past few weeks the power of the Bolsheviks has been slowly diminishing',[57] and in early June told London that even the leaders themselves now believed that 'their reign is coming to an end'.[58] There was of course a large element of wishful thinking in this analysis, although the summer of 1918 was certainly a critical time for the Moscow government as opposition continued to grow in outlying parts of the country, while the economic situation in both the towns and the countryside deteriorated rapidly. Having seen his early attempts to encourage the Bolsheviks to oppose the German advance come to nothing, Lockhart was now apparently determined to bring down the Moscow government by any means possible – a hugely ambitious project for a young official representing a government that could not itself develop a coherent policy towards Russia.

The exact scope of Lockhart's activities in Moscow during the early summer of 1918 is still not entirely clear. He had started to develop contacts with various opposition groups as early as late April, but at this stage his main aim was apparently to encourage them to support the Bolshevik government in any new outbreak of hostilities between Russia and Germany.[59] By June his principal objective had changed, and he began to devote his energy to supporting the kaleidoscope of organisations that sought to overthrow the Bolshevik government in Moscow. Like most other British civilian representatives based in Russia during 1918, Lockhart was inclined to believe that the groups best placed to destabilise the Bolsheviks were comprised of left-leaning liberals and socialists of various kinds, rather than the 'White' reactionary officers of the old Tsarist army who were beginning to cluster together in various towns and cities on the periphery of Russia. Although he developed close links with White organisations active in the Russian capital, including the elusive 'National Centre', he also devoted a good deal of time and energy to cultivating contacts with groups like the Union for the Regeneration of Russia (URR), whose members were mainly drawn from the ranks of former Cadets and Socialist Revolutionaries. By July Lockhart was channelling considerable funds to individuals active in these organisations, though French officials based in Russia provided even greater amounts of money, particularly to the former Minister of War in the Provisional Government, B. V. Savinkov, who was identified by a number of allied representatives as the most significant opponent of the Bolshevik government.[60] Nor was Lockhart alone among British officials in carrying out such clandestine actions. Captain George Hill, who had worked closely with the Bolsheviks in the weeks following the November Revolution, in order to help them move war material away from areas where it might be captured in a German advance, went 'underground' in Moscow during the late spring of 1918. Over the next few months, he helped to establish an elaborate clandestine organisation designed to promote anti-Bolshevik propaganda and provide the British with information about developments in Moscow and Petrograd.[61]

The Naval Attaché at the Embassy, Captain Francis Cromie, also played an important role in offering support to the Bolsheviks' opponents. Cromie was a bitter critic of Britain's wavering policy towards Russia in the months following the Bolshevik Revolution, writing angrily to the head of Naval Intelligence in London to denounce the chaos and conflict that existed between the various British Missions in the country. The departure of Lindley and the remaining Embassy staff in March 1918 made the problem worse, and the Naval Attaché repeatedly called for the 'home authorities to consider sending a *responsible* man with a *definite* policy to direct our straggling efforts'.[62] Cromie himself played an important role in providing funds and advice to members of the URR during the summer of 1918, in order to help them to carry out a successful uprising at the northern port of Archangel, which was in turn designed to provide the allies with a bridgehead from where their troops could intervene in support of various anti-Bolshevik forces across Russia. He also helped to disseminate propaganda designed to foster 'the growing discontent of the Esthonian and Lettish elements at Kronstadt', and sent agents to the Black Sea fleet to carry out similar work there. Cromie's work was clearly quite incompatible with his quasi-diplomatic position, but the Naval Attaché was still reasonably confident in July 1918 that 'I have enough friends to get me out even if it comes to flying'.[63] He was quite wrong. Cromie was killed just a few weeks later when the Bolsheviks launched a dramatic raid on the British Embassy building in Petrograd.

The infamous British 'master-spy' Sidney Reilly was also active in Russia during the summer of 1918, though his movements are even harder to follow than those of Hill and Lockhart.[64] Reilly was instructed by the Secret Intelligence Service in London to concentrate on propaganda activities. He quickly established a number of projects, including one designed to use the Orthodox Church as a means of mobilising opinion against the Bolsheviks.[65] However, Reilly also pursued his own private war against the Bolshevik government, promoting an elaborate scheme designed to bring down the government by inciting key regiments to mutiny. Although many of his operations remain mysterious to this day, there is little doubt that they eventually helped to compromise Lockhart in the eyes of the Bolshevik authorities. Lockhart was doubtless unwise to establish close relations with the various anti-Bolshevik groups active in the Russian capital, since he was abusing the de facto diplomatic immunity which had been granted to him after his arrival in Russia; nor is it clear to what extent his actions were sanctioned by London, though there is a good deal of evidence to suggest that the Head of the Commercial Mission was often acting on his own initiative in building contacts with opposition groups. However, the ambiguous nature of Britain's entire policy towards the Bolsheviks created a climate in which such activities could flourish. In the early summer of 1918 it was not clear whether Britain and Russia were enemies or not. The British officials who remained in Moscow and Petrograd were expected to conduct some kind of dialogue with the Bolshevik authorities, while being under little illusion that policy-makers in London were drifting towards decisions that would make a final breach between the two countries irreversible. A normal existence was hardly possible in this twilight world, though staff at the various Missions continued to do their best to maintain the fabric of their former lives, attending the opera, playing poker and challenging the members of other allied Missions to games of football.[66] Since communications with London were poor, and the instructions sent to officials stationed in Russia ambiguous, individuals like Lockhart had to form their own judgement of the most appropriate course of action to follow. It was not surprising that the distinction between legitimate diplomatic activities and clandestine operations became less clear than ever under such circumstances.

Although Lockhart was an acute and intelligent observer of the changing political scene in Russia, he sometimes lacked the reflective capacity and breadth of historical knowledge required to put the tumultuous changes taking place around him in their proper context. These qualities were, by contrast, exactly the ones which Oliver Wardrop, the Consul-General in Moscow, brought to his work during the first part of 1918, before ill-health and strain took a toll on his judgement. Wardrop was a highly intelligent man, an expert on Georgian history and culture, who provided London with a perceptive if idiosyncratic series of dispatches reflecting on the historical significance of the Russian Revolution and its aftermath. His views on British policy towards Russia were in many respects similar to those of Lockhart, veering from opposition to any form of allied intervention in the early spring of 1918 to strong support for it a few months later. While Lockhart's opposition to intervention in the first few weeks of 1918 had been based on a pragmatic desire to avoid driving the Bolsheviks into the arms of the Germans, Wardrop opposed it because he believed that the Bolshevik Revolution was a natural outcome of Russia's historical evolution that could not be reversed by outsiders.[67] Unlike most British officials, the

Moscow Consul-General did not believe that the November Revolution was simply the work of a few men of 'iron will', but argued that it was a product of deep-seated tensions in Russian society.

Since Wardrop was sure that the November Revolution had deep roots, he was certain that the Bolsheviks were far more firmly established than either their domestic opponents or foreign critics wished to ac-knowledge. He also suggested that there was considerable popular support for the new government, and argued that 'any armed inter-vention' against the wishes of the population would be 'a fatal mistake'. This acknowledgement of the complex origins of the revolution was a perceptive one, which was not sufficiently understood by most British officials in Russia or London, who were too ready to cite the demonic energy and determination of Lenin and his colleagues as the main well-spring of the Bolsheviks' success. The Consul-General's shift on the question of intervention only came about in the late spring, once he began to recognise the full extent of the 'class war' preached by Lenin, which he feared would 'reduce Russia to mere barbarism'.[68] By August the stress of life in revolutionary Russia was starting to tell on Wardrop, particularly after the Bolshevik authorities in Moscow launched a raid on his Consulate and temporarily imprisoned several of its staff. The tone of his dispatches became far more hysterical, and he began to condemn the Bolshevik Revolution as 'an international Jewish coup' which was above all the work of 'unscrupulous Jews like Trotzky'.[69] He told London of his continuing faith in Russia's 'great future',[70] writing that the country would before long 'find herself again, purified, chastened, reverent, repentant', just as soon as the cancer of Bolshevism had been removed from the body politic.[71] It is not clear what officials at the Foreign Office in London made of these later dispatches. Their hysterical tone was presumably charitably ascribed to the stress under which their author was working, since Wardrop was given further important overseas postings once he finally left Russia in the autumn of 1918.

It was inevitable that British representatives in Russia would sooner or later fall foul of the Bolshevik authorities, given both the downward spiral of relations between London and Moscow and the questionable activities in which a number of them were engaged. The crisis finally broke in the middle of 1918. In early August the British landed a small detachment of troops at Archangel, having previously been instrumental in instigating a coup there designed to overthrow the local Bolshevik administration. The atmosphere across Russia had been very tense for a number of weeks, since it was widely known that some form of military intervention was pending. Within a few hours of the news arriving from Archangel the Consulate-General in Moscow was invaded by armed guards. The staff in the building rushed to destroy all incriminating documents and cyphers, though it is not clear whether they managed to complete their task before being arrested and taken off to a local prision.[72] Although they were all released within a few days, by now the Bolshevik government considered British officials in Petrograd and Moscow to be representatives of a country that was virtually at war with Russia. The local press furiously denounced the intervention at Archangel, and published sensationalist accounts of imaginary pitched battles between British and Bolshevik forces in the area. The papers poured scorn on the idea that intervention was was being 'undertaken not against the Russian revolution, but against German imperialism', and raged against the attempt by the forces of international capital to crush the 'workers' revolution'. The tone of the articles was distinctly threatening for all allied officials who remained in territories controlled by the Bolsheviks. One address to the 'toiling masses of England, America, France, Italy and Japan', published in *Izvestiya*, proclaimed that:

> Too long have we calmly endured the mockery of the representatives of Allied imperialism; we allow people who once licked the boots of Tsarism to remain in Russia although they do not recognise the workers' Government. We took no reprisals against them, although the hand of their military missions was visible in every counter-revolutionary plot ... We are certain that every measure taken against those who on Russian territory hatch plots against the Russian revolution will meet with your sincere sympathy, for these plots are directed against you as well as against us.[73]

Lockhart and the other remaining British officials began to plan their departure from Russia, since it had become clear that they could no longer serve any useful purpose and were simply putting their lives in danger by remaining. Before they could complete their arrangements to leave, however, news came through on the last day of August that an attempt had been made on the life of Lenin by a young woman belonging to the Socialist Revolutionary Party, Fanny Kaplan, which had left the Bolshevik leader with serious chest wounds. Although there is no evidence whatsoever to suggest that any British official was involved in the incident, Lockhart and his staff quickly realised that the assassination attempt was likely to have severe consequences both for themselves and their fellow countrymen who remained in Bolshevik Russia.

The reprisals by the Bolshevik government against allied representatives began almost at once. Following Kaplan's attempt on Lenin's life, Bolshevik troops stormed the British Embassy in Petrograd, which was crowded with staff from the various Missions who were due to collect their pay. The exact course of events in the next few minutes remains confused, but within a short time Captain Cromie, who had tried to resist the invaders, lay dead at the bottom of the main staircase. The Bolshevik Secret Police were well aware of the Naval Attaché's various activities during the previous few months, though it is not certain whether he was deliberately singled out for assassination. Cromie was undoubtedly expecting some kind of crisis and had previously destroyed the more incriminating papers in his possession, 'since the Embassy is no longer safe'.[74] British nationals in the Embassy building were prevented from offering help to the dying Captain, and were instead quickly rounded up by the troops who fanned through the building, though a few officials remained at liberty long enough to destroy at least some of the Embassy cyphers and other sensitive documents.[75] Two British consular officials who had been driving to the Embassy at the time of the attack tried to escape, but their car was intercepted at a nearby road-block; they were, surprisingly, eventually allowed to go on their way. In the hours that followed the raid, many other British subjects in Petrograd were arrested and, along with the male staff at the Embassy, hauled off to prison.[76] The tensions between Britain and Bolshevik Russia, which had constantly threatened to explode over the previous nine months, had finally claimed their first victim.

The position of Lockhart and his small staff in Moscow was even more precarious. The Head of the British Commercial Mission was arrested at gunpoint in the early morning of 1 September and taken to the Lubyanka, the headquarters of the notorious Cheka (Secret Police), which had been established a few months earlier under the leadership of the Pole Felix Dzerzhinsky. While he was in captivity, Lockhart managed to destroy some of the material which implicated him in the provision of funds to various anti-Bolshevik groups. He was released a few hours later without any formal charge being made against him. In the next few days, the papers were full of details of the so-called 'Lockhart Plot', which had supposedly involved bribing a number of officers in various Lettish regiments so as to encourage them to stage a mutiny and overthrow the Bolshevik government. The press had no doubts that Lockhart was the main instigator of the whole affair, accusing him of acting 'under the cover of diplomatic immunity' in order to bring about the 'capture of the Council of People's Commissars and the proclamation of a military dictatorship in Moscow'.[77] The Bolshevik authorities were aware that Sidney Reilly had played an important role in the plan to encourage a revolt by the Lettish regiments but, at least publicly, maintained that he was simply working on Lockhart's orders.

The realities behind the 'Lockhart Plot' are still obscure, though Lockhart himself was undoubtedly less than honest in the published account which he wrote many years later.[78] Although he claimed that he was not fully aware of Reilly's attempts to foster a mutiny against the Bolshevik government, the evidence strongly suggests that Lockhart was deeply involved in the plan. Reilly certainly played the most important role in supervising the detailed organisation of the uprising, but Lockhart had meetings with at least some of those concerned – though it seems unlikely that he was actively involved in any attempt to assassinate Lenin and the other Bolshevik leaders. Captain Cromie in Petrograd was also implicated in the affair and provided the funds that were needed to finance the 'heavy' expenses of the whole scheme.[79] Unfortunately for Lockhart and his colleagues, the Cheka was from the beginning able to use its undercover agents and agents provocateurs to follow the development of the plot. The attempt on Lenin's life, along with the successful assassination of a leading Bolshevik official in Moscow around the same time, forced the Bolshevik government to move against British representatives in Moscow and Petrograd sooner than it had intended. The note of hysteria in the press over the next few days, in which numerous articles appeared calling for vengeance against Lockhart and others, was not simply an attempt to justify an unprovoked attack on the representatives of the 'capitalist powers'. The Moscow government's decision to arrest British (and French) officials at the beginning of September was an outcome of the previous months of uncertainty and confusion. Lockhart's involvement in the plot was doubtless a reflection of his desire to salvage something from the wreckage of his mission, so that it would not be seen as an unmitigated disaster. Officials at the Foreign Office in London knew that he was providing help and support to opponents of the Bolsheviks, but it seems unlikely that they had much detailed knowledge of his activities, not least because of the constant interruptions to the telegraphic traffic between Moscow and London which became increasingly severe as the summer of 1918 progressed. Reilly had for years been treated with suspicion by officials in London and there was even a fear in some quarters that he was a double agent, though there is no evidence that he was ever guilty of anything more than extreme recklessness.[80] While the behaviour of both men was very naive, resting as it did on an exaggerated view of the weakness of the Bolshevik regime, their actions were understandable given the difficult circumstances under which they operated. Since politicians and officials in London were by the summer of 1918 effectively treating the Bolsheviks as a hostile government, their representatives in Russia naturally felt justified in using any and every opportunity to bring about the downfall of the regime.

The conditions endured by British prisoners in Petrograd following the raid on the Embassy building were grim, though less so than for the thousands of ordinary Russians swept up in the first wave of the Red Terror unleashed by the Bolshevik government in the summer of 1918. The Dutch Minister at Petrograd, William Oudenyk, who had nominally been responsible for the British Embassy since Frank Lindley's departure a few months earlier, worked hard to secure the release of the prisoners.[81] The storming of the Embassy caused outrage among western diplomats in the Russian capital; even the German diplomatic representative attended Cromie's funeral in an ostentatious display of contempt for a regime which threatened the 'civilization of the whole world'.[82] Most of the British prisoners in Petrograd, along with a number of French diplomats and army officers arrested around the same time, were transferred to the infamous Peter and Paul fortress, which had been used in Tsarist times to house the most dangerous members of the revolutionary movement. Conditions in the prison were poor. In a letter smuggled out to the Dutch Minister, the prisoners complained of the absence of food, clothing and medicine. They feared that they would 'sooner or later starve to death' – if they did not first fall victim to disease caused by insanitary conditions where 'The w. c. periodically refuses to work and the atmosphere is appalling'.[83] The Dutch Minister and his English-born wife worked tirelessly, however, to provide the prisoners with enough food to keep them alive, interceding constantly with the Soviet authorities to bring about their release.

Oudenyk also travelled to Moscow to demand the release of Lockhart, who was arrested for a second time by the Cheka in early September. Although subjected to endless questioning about his role in the 'Lockhart Plot', the conditions in which he and other officials in Moscow were held were good when compared with the ones endured by the prisoners in Petrograd. The interrogation sessions mostly took the form of a 'bantering cross-examination' conducted by the deputy head of the Cheka, Jacob Peters, while the guards were at worst 'surly and hostile' rather than brutal in their treatment of the prisoner. After several days confinement in the Lubyanka, Lockhart was removed to the Kremlin where he was provided with an apartment, complete with 'a sitting room [and] and diminutive bedroom'. He was allowed to read, and voraciously devoured books ranging from H. G. Wells's *The Island of Doctor Moreau* to Thomas Carlyle's *The French Revolution*. The food was poor, but no worse than the meals provided for members of the Cheka themselves. Yet while Lockhart's condition was in reality quite comfortable, there was great concern about his situation among western diplomats in Russia and British officials in London, since rumours kept circulating that he was about to be shot. There was also fear in some quarters that he would 'disclose something damaging to England' – presumably details of his links with anti-Bolshevik forces or information about British intelligence networks in Russia.[84] In the third week of September the British Minister in Norway told London that refugees entering the country assured him that Lockhart was compromised and 'had little chance of escaping alive',[85] though he was more hopeful about the fate of other British officials held by the Bolsheviks. Other reports that reached Stockholm about the same time were more optimistic.[86]

Throughout September, complex negotiations took place across Europe to secure the freedom of allied prisoners held in Russia, in exchange for the release of a small number of Bolsheviks and Communist sympathisers imprisoned in Britain (including the future Commissar of Foreign Affairs Maxim Litvinov).[87] Swedish, Danish and Dutch diplomats acted as 'honest brokers', desperately trying to reach an agreement that would be observed both by the Bolshevik government and by the governments of the two allied powers. The negotiations proved to be extremely difficult and tortuous, since each side feared that the other would fail to keep its side of any agreement. The reluctance of one of the detainees held in Britain to return to Russia also caused endless problems. Even so, the British government eventually agreed to release Litvinov and his fellow prisoners, who were taken by sea to Norway in preparation for the exchange. Because a good deal of confusion remained in both Paris and London over the exact number of British and French nationals held by the Bolsheviks, considerable delays resulted as efforts were made to check whether the Moscow government was intending to release all the prisoners arrested during August and September. The French were anxious that a number of their army officers were not on the list of those scheduled for release, while the British heard rumours that at least two of their military representatives might still face the death penalty. On 7 October, however, news reached the Foreign Office that Lockhart and Wardorp had been allowed to travel to Stockholm with all the members of their respective Missions. Three days later, the British representative in the Swedish capital telegraphed to say that the prisoners seized in the Embassy raid had also been released. It is still not entirely clear whether the Bolsheviks ever intended to do real harm to their prisoners. They certainly had detailed knowledge of Lockhart's underground activities during the summer, while the attacks on the Embassy and Moscow Consulate probably yielded evidence indicting other British officials of pursuing activities incompatible with their quasi-official status. The Bolsheviks' restraint still seems curious, given the brutal treatment that was being inflicted on members of counter-revolutionary organisations in Russia at this time. Lenin and the other leaders appeared reluctant to incur the wrath of the 'civilised world', even though allied troops in north Russia were already engaged in skirmishes with troops loyal to Moscow.

The death of Cromie and the imprisonment of other official representatives appalled public opinion in Britain, helping to establish more firmly than ever in the mind of the country's political class that the Bolsheviks were 'a menace to the whole civilised world' who refused to be bound by the rules of normal diplomatic intercourse and behaviour.[88] One British consular official who returned home in the autumn of 1918 spoke for most of his erstwhile colleagues, both civilian and military, when he wrote that:

> The most disquieting feature of all is the infectious nature of the Bol-
> shevist disease. All weak minds which come into contact with Bolshevism
> are liable to catch the infection, and it is alarming to observe the spread
> of Bolshevism at this time ... In my view, international intervention is
> the only satisfactory way of dealing with the crisis ... Russia must be in-
> ternationally policed if the civilization of Europe is to be protected'[89]

These views were echoed by a number of politicians in London. Winston Churchill, in particular, used the murder of Cromie to justify his demand for a more vigorous anti-Bolshevik policy after becoming Minister of War at the beginning of 1919.[90] There was something ironic about the enormous attention that was paid to the murder of one British official, and the imprisonment of a few dozen others, at a time when the Russian government was launching a brutal assault on its own population that was not to be exceeded in scale until the height of the Stalinist excesses in the 1930s. A number of British officials in Russia, including Lockhart and Cromie, were directly involved in a whole series of activities that directly threatened both the interests and the survival of the Bolshevik government.[91] Few governments would have been willing to tolerate such activities on their territory by representatives of foreign powers. It would, in retrospect, have made greater sense if the British government had withdrawn all its officials from Russia in March 1918, at the time when Frank Lindley and most other diplomats at the Petrograd Embassy returned to London. Yet the desire to revive some kind of Eastern Front, combined with the mistaken belief that the Bolsheviks' hold on power was so fragile that it would soon disintegrate, meant that British officials were kept in Russia for many months after they had ceased to perform a clear role. While Cromie was certainly a victim of the ruthless disregard for human life that was increasingly a hallmark of Bolshevik rule, he and his colleagues were also victims of their own government's ambiguous policy towards Russia, which placed all the country's representatives there in an impossible position during the turbulent summer of 1918.

6

The Worst Horrors in History

British troops had started to appear on Russian territory several months before the arrest of Lockhart and the other officials in Petrograd and Moscow during September 1918. A small detachment of marines had gone ashore from HMS *Suffolk* at Vladivostok in April, alongside a larger number of Japanese troops, in order to defend the military stores and protect British citizens in the town against violence. A few weeks before this, British naval forces at the northern port of Murmansk had begun to cooperate with the local Bolshevik authorities in order to repel an expected attack by the Germans. These moves took place with the support, or at least the grudging acquiescence, of the government in Moscow. British intervention in Russia was, as has already been seen, an incremental process that lacked a single rationale. In the first months of 1918, it was still primarily viewed in London as a means of increasing opposition to the Germans along the former Eastern Front. Yet given the open distaste of the British government for the Bolsheviks, the presence of its forces on Russian soil was always likely to slide imperceptibly into an anti-Bolshevik crusade. As Russia descended into the barbarism of the so-called Civil War – which was in reality a series of intermittent battles and skirmishes between forces loyal to the Bolsheviks and a disparate group of opponents – it was inevitable that British forces would be sucked into the vortex.

The problems faced by the British government when putting in place a coherent policy towards Bolshevik Russia were made more difficult by the complexities of the international political situation. As the French and Americans were also concerned about the long-term fate of Russia, the whole question became one of the most vexed issues between the representatives of the victorious powers who met at Versailles following the signing of the Armistice in November 1918. Although the allied governments committed themselves rhetorically to the Russian people's right to self-determination, they were in practice intensely concerned about the potential challenge posed by the government in Moscow to the peace and stability of the European continent. The disintegration of the old Tsarist Empire also seemed to provide opportunities as well as threats for the outside world, which ironically had the effect of creating further disagreements among the allies. Even when hostilities against Germany were still in full swing, a good deal of tension developed between London and Paris over policy towards Russia, since both governments were anxious to promote their power and influence on Russian territory in the hope that it would yield economic and political benefits once peace was declared. This tension continued to fester during the period of allied intervention. While British and French army officers cooperated moderately well for most of the time, the uncertainties and divisions between their political masters back home undoubtedly hampered operations. The arrival of American troops in north Russia and Siberia in the second half of 1918 made the problems still worse, since President Wilson was by instinct suspicious of the intentions of the old 'imperialist' powers and their local representatives.[1] The diplomatic uncertainties surrounding Britain's military intervention in Russia, when combined with the lack of a clear consensus in London about the proper role of the country's forces there, created a climate of confusion which even the most energetic commander or civilian official on the ground could not overcome.

Britain's civilian officials and soldiers who served in Russia during the period of allied intervention were drawn from a wide range of backgrounds, marking a further fragmentation of the British presence there. Senior army officers posted to the country had mostly been in active service on the Western Front, but lacked the knowledge required to understand the complex political circumstances that governed the deployment of British forces sent to Russia. Although there had been endless debates in London during the 1914–18 war about the best means of defeating the Central Powers, there was at least a clear enemy against whom campaigns could be directed by army and naval commanders on the ground. By contrast, military commanders in Russia faced the problem of planning and conducting operations without knowing the exact goals they were expected to achieve. Since the Lloyd George government in London was reluctant to acknowledge publicly its desire to see the collapse of the Bolshevik regime, and was in any case quite unwilling to make available the resources required to bring it about, the strategy of Britain's forces in Russia was for the most part limited to providing material help and training to the various anti-Bolshevik forces that clustered around the periphery of the old Tsarist Empire. As the Bolsheviks' opponents were bitterly divided, however, they proved to be quite unable to establish either viable forms of civilian administration or effective military organisations capable of conducting sustained operations against troops loyal to the government in Moscow. British commanders were therefore forced to deal with politicians and *ersatz* governments who could not even agree among themselves about their objectives and policies. Partly as a result, many senior British army officers fell into the trap of putting too much faith in 'White' Generals, mostly drawn from the old Tsarist army, who shared the characteristic military conviction that complex social and political problems could be resolved by the simple expedient of marginalising civilian politicians and concentrating instead on technical operational matters.[2] This proved to be a fatal error, since the White Generals failed throughout the Civil War to win widespread support among the Russian population, which in turn meant that British forces were left trying to prop up armies whose claim to represent the interests of ordinary Russians rang increasingly hollow.

The handful of British civilian officials who served in areas where intervention took place were more sensitive to these problems than their military counterparts. They were not, though, in a position to exercise much real influence over the reactionary White Generals and their political advisers, who became increasingly dominant in the anti-Bolshevik movement from the autumn of 1918 onwards. Nor were they able to exercise any effective control over the activities of British army officers, who steadfastly insisted that they were responsible directly to the War Office rather than to civilian representatives from the Foreign Office, most of whom were in any case rather junior and drawn from the ranks of the Consular Service. Although a series of ad hoc measures were put in place to resolve many of these conflicts and divisions, they could not overcome deep-seated problems that were rooted in the ambiguities and uncertainties surrounding Britain's whole ill-fated attempt at intervention in Russian affairs.

Any account of British involvement in Russian affairs in the years immediately after 1917 faces the risk of becoming submerged in what one historian of the period has rightly called 'the bog of history'.[3] George Kennan observed wryly in his own magisterial work on the subject that 'Anyone who sets out to give in brief compass an adequate picture' of the subject 'imposes on himself an almost impossible task'. Since the former Tsarist Empire went through a period of complete political and social disintegration in the years between 1918 and 1920, it is even difficult to talk with any confidence of 'Russia' itself as a cohesive entity. The pages that follow make no pretence at providing a comprehensive discussion of the views of British civilians and military men unfortunate enough to be charged with the job of executing an ill-considered policy devised by a government whose members had no real understanding of the vast changes sweeping across Russia. There is no room to discuss the role of the British army officers and civilian officials who played a crucial role in the political development of the ill-fated Transcaucasian states, which managed for a few brief years to establish their independence from Moscow. Nor is there any space to examine the way in which British naval personnel sought to influence the course of events in the Baltic region, where a number of new states emerged out of the chaos of 1917. It is not even possible to consider in depth the problems faced by the various British commanders who found themselves thrust into the alien world of the White Generals, a milieu dominated by petty rivalries and personal vanities that ultimately proved fatal to the cause of anti-Bolshevik resistance. The best that can be done is to provide an insight into the minds of a small group of men condemned to witness at first hand the chaos and brutality that accompanied the birth of the world's first socialist state.

In May 1918 General Frederick Poole was sent by London to Murmansk as 'British Military Representative in Russia', with instructions to pave the way for a possible influx of much larger forces, whose precise role was at this time still left undefined.[4] Over the next few months, Poole became a strong advocate of large-scale allied intervention in Russia, even though he had previously been sceptical about its likely outcome. The General's arrival in north Russia marked a clear stage in the deterioration of the relationship between Moscow and London, since Lenin and his colleagues feared that any allied troops sent to north Russia would be used to foment opposition to their rule rather than to spearhead resistance against a possible German advance. Around the same time that Poole arrived in Murmansk, Frank Lindley was once again posted to Russia, this time as Commissioner in north Russia, charged with taking 'general charge of British interests' in the region.[5] His appointment was furiously opposed by Lockhart,[6] who was of course at this stage still at liberty, even though the Foreign Office sought to reassure him that the move was not intended as an attack on the way he had performed his duties over the previous few months.[7] Ironically, Lindley himself was very doubtful about the wisdom of taking on the job. Since he had only been able to leave the country in March with the greatest difficulty, he made his acceptance of the post conditional on a guarantee that his wife and family would be provided with a pension in the event of his death. He also facetiously told Balfour that he was only willing to accept the 'uninviting job' on condition that it was understood he could 'do no good when I got to Russia'.[8] In the event, Lindley never arrived in Moscow as had originally been planned. He instead joined other senior allied diplomatic representatives who had previously retreated to the town of Vologda, 200 miles north east of Petrograd, where they believed themselves to be safe both against German attack and any possible threat from the Bolshevik government in Moscow.[9] Here the foreign diplomatic corps lived for some time in a diplomatic *demi-monde*, unwilling to move to Moscow but unable to return home, spending its time in desultory discussion with representatives of anti-Bolshevik forces about possible ways of destroying Lenin's government. In the weeks following Lindley's arrival, Britain's diplomatic and military representatives inside Russia were therefore effectively divided into three main groups. The first group consisted of the officials in Petrograd and Moscow who were eventually rounded up and imprisoned at the beginning of September 1918, while the second comprised General Poole and his military aides in north Russia. The third set of officials was made up of Lindley and his staff at Vologda.[10] Shortly before British troops occupied the port of Archangel at the beginning of August, Lindley and his party began to make their way to north Russia where, in the following months, they played a crucial role in organising the British presence in the region.

There is no doubt that the British were responsible for engineering the coup that took place in Archangel in early August, when the town's Bolshevik authorities were overthrown in a well-planned operation led by a Russian officer, Captain G. E. Chaplin, who had previously been provided with funds and a false passport by the British Embassy in Petrograd.[11] During July a number of British and Russian officers travelled between Archangel and Petrograd in order to liaise with Captain Cromie, who played an important role in preparing the groundwork for Chaplin and his colleagues to seize power. The coup took place in the face of vehement opposition from the radically-minded British Consul in the town, Douglas Young, who bitterly condemned the 'put-up job between the Moscow White Guard and the Allied Missions'.[12] Young's dispatches were ignored in London, however, since his advice was at odds with the prevailing political mood there, which now firmly favoured intervention in north Russia in order to safeguard the region against a possible German advance from the Baltic Republics or Finland. General Poole's forces, which arrived in Archangel shortly after Chaplin's coup, were comparatively small in number – far smaller than desired by advocates of large-scale intervention like Lockhart – but they were still sufficient to deter any attempt to retake the town by local forces loyal to the Bolsheviks. Once it was confirmed that Archangel had been secured, Lindley and his staff entered the town. There they quickly discovered that Poole's high-handed manner and arbitrary administrative methods had already infuriated the new government, which was largely made up of veteran non-Bolshevik socialists who had been in close touch with allied representatives since the middle of 1918.[13] The General had also managed to stir up a good deal of local resentment by requisitioning some of the best houses as accommodation for his senior officers.

Over the next few weeks, the relationship between Lindley and Poole went from bad to worse. The tension did not reflect any difference about the *principle* of intervention, which both men had supported for some time. It was instead the product of a profound disagreement about the correct role of British forces in north Russia and their relationship to the local population. Poole was frankly contemptuous of the local administration, regarding its socialist leaders as a nuisance who posed a potential challenge to his own authority and the smooth running of the town; he was also contemptuous of British civilian officials, even though his instructions expressly required him to report to the senior British diplomatic representative as well as the War Office.[14] His behaviour was in Lindley's view more suited to the commander of a military force in an occupied country rather than a leader of an army that claimed to be the liberator and protector of the local population.[15] Lindley himself, by contrast, believed that Britain's intervention in north Russia could only be successful if it commanded widespread popular support in the area. He admired the President of the new Archangel government, N. V. Chaikovsky, whom he described to London as a man whose character was 'beyond reproach' and whose programme 'suited my ideas perfectly'.[16] Throughout August Lindley used all his considerable talent in an attempt to improve the relationship between the local government and allied diplomats and officers, hoping to repair some of the damage done by Poole. He also sent numerous telegrams to the Foreign Office bitterly complaining that the General was refusing to follow any advice or instructions with which he disagreed.

In early September an attempted coup took place against Chaikovsky's government, led once again by Captain Chaplin and other former Tsarist officers who despised the radical political values and administrative ineptitude displayed by Ministers over the previous few weeks.[17] Lindley was appalled by this turn of events, fearing that political instability would spread across the region if a government that commanded widespread popular support was replaced by a more reactionary administration. The representatives of the other allied powers were equally dismayed since, with the partial exception of the French Ambassador Joseph Noulens, they generally endorsed Lindley's views on political and administrative questions. It was only with great difficulty that allied diplomats eventually asserted their authority and successfully demanded that the rebels release the Ministers and allow them to return to their posts. Lindley was immediately suspicious that General Poole and his officers had played a part in this clumsy attempt to destroy the Chaikovsky government. He told the Foreign Office that, while he accepted the General was not directly implicated in the conspiracy, he believed that more could have been done to prevent it from taking place.[18] He also threatened to resign unless something was done to improve his position vis à vis the whole British military establishment in Archangel. Lindley was even less restrained in his memoirs, in which he made no secret of his belief that Poole's staff 'were in' on the plot to overthrow Chaikovsky. The government in London eventually sided with Lindley in the dispute and Poole was recalled to Britain for indefinite 'consultations',[19] though his standing remained intact at the War Office. His replacement was General Edward Ironside, a young career soldier who proved to be a shrewder and less abrasive figure than his predecessor. As a result, the tension between British civilian and military officials in Archangel subsided after the failure of the attempted coup, although the relationship between the allied powers and the local Russian government continued to be a difficult one.

British forces stayed in Archangel for more than a year, though the government in London first decided on their withdrawal as early as the spring of 1919, following prolonged and bitter discussion in the War Cabinet, where Winston Churchill argued in support of a more active policy of intervention designed to destabilise Bolshevik rule.[20] These splits and divisions were echoed at the Peace Conference in Paris, where the victorious powers proved quite unable to formulate a consistent and united policy towards Russia, proposing mediation between the warring factions while at the same time offering moral and material support to one side.[21] During this period, British army officers and civilian officials alike were initiated into the arcane world of post-revolutionary Russian politics. In Archangel, as in most other major cities where the Bolsheviks lost control, there emerged complex constellations of different groups and organisations whose members were united only by their shared hostility to the government in Moscow. The local Russian government itself underwent many changes in composition and nomenclature during the year of allied 'occupation', which did little to make it an effective administrative and political force. After Chaikovsky left to attend the Paris Peace Conference, early in 1919, even Lindley acknowledged that few of the Ministers who subsequently held office were men 'to inspire enthusiasm, or go outside the customary bounds of bureaucratic procedure'.[22] General Ironside was still more scathing in his criticism, noting in a report written in the second half of 1919 that the government 'originally presided over by Chaikovsky deteriorated rapidly after his departure'.[23] The General was incensed by the failure of Ministers to counter the propaganda war launched by the Bolsheviks, which was designed to encourage the local population to rebel against the intervention forces. The Archangel government was also quite ineffective at setting up a viable system of local administration, a source of enormous frustration to all allied military and civilian representatives in the region. Many of the comments made by British officials and soldiers about its incompetence during 1918–19 bore an uncanny resemblance to the ones their predecessors had made about the Provisional Government in Petrograd during 1917. This failure to establish effective patterns of local administration was in part due to the difficulties faced by any government on taking power, a problem that was exacerbated by the new Ministers' almost complete lack of administrative experience. However, the squabbling which characterised the Russian political process in Archangel also damaged the cause of good administration, since it diverted Ministers' attention away from the mundane problems of restoring the fabric of normal life in the region and focused it instead on petty personal rivalries and jealousies. The tension between socialist members of the civilian government and reactionary officers from the former Tsarist army, who flocked to Archangel in their thousands, also created an endless source of instability. As a result of all these problems, British military and civilian representatives in north Russia soon found themselves sucked into organising much of the basic framework of civilian life in the region. It was not a task for which they had either the resources or the expertise.

By the spring of 1919 Lindley had virtually given up hoping that the local Russian population would ever manage to establish a government whose members were not 'very ill-provided with financial knowledge and administrative capacity', though he continued to oppose attempts to establish a new and more conservative administration for fear that it would forfeit any prospect of commanding popular support.[24] Long before this date, various departments in London had

seconded civilian officials to north Russia in the hope that their expertise could be used to reestablish the framework of normal life in
the region. Lindley had also been able to hand-pick the officials who
accompanied him back to Russia in the early summer of 1918. The
members of this talented young team worked eighteen-hour days in
Archangel in a desperate attempt to help the local authorities cope
with the problems facing the region. Particular attention was given to
the dreadful state of the economy, which had been devastated by the
dislocation and chaos that resulted from years of war and revolution.
Elaborate plans were made to launch a new currency in the region,
after the paper roubles issued by the Tsarist and Bolshevik governments
lost all their value, but the scheme proved unsuccessful since the
shortage of goods meant that few Russians were prepared to accept
paper money in exchange for products that could be bartered more
profitably. These attempts by the British to help rebuild the economy
were in any case often looked at with deep suspicion by sections of
the local population, as well as by representatives from other allied
powers, who feared that they were designed to turn the region into a
colony providing cheap supplies of timber and other local products
for export to Britain. In reality, while British officers and civilian
representatives in north Russia were certainly well aware of the economic potential of the area, they were hardly in a position to implement
the kind of policies needed to turn it into an economic fiefdom. During
the months and years that followed the Bolshevik seizure of power in
Petrograd, officials in both Archangel and London often discussed the
economic opportunities which the break-up of the old Tsarist Empire
might provide for Britain. In practice, it was quite impossible for any
country to extract real economic benefits from the confusion and
anarchy of the Civil War. The British, like the other allied powers who
intervened in Russia in 1918–19, simply lacked the manpower and
resources to turn any significant part of Russian territory into a well-
defined sphere of influence.

During the period of intervention in north Russia British army
officers, like their civilian counterparts, became closely involved in the
day to day problems of civil administration, as well as conducting
military operations against forces loyal to Moscow. The shortage of
military manpower across the region meant that they had to employ
thousands of Russian civilians on projects such as the construction of
barracks and the repair of rail communications. This was a particularly
fraught issue since the Treasury's determination to keep the cost of
intervention to a minimum meant that British commanders were seldom

given the resources to pay their workers regularly. One local commander was even advised by Treasury staff to use a stock of pickled herrings to pay for the labour he required, a suggestion which graphically illustrated how little officials in London understood about the situation on the ground in north Russia.[25] Under these conditions, the local work-force quickly became easy prey for the propaganda distributed by underground Bolshevik agents, who argued that Russian workers were being exploited by the British for their own imperialist ends. The problems were particularly acute in Murmansk, where 'strike followed strike in heartrending succession',[26] souring relations between the British intervention forces and the local population. The commander in the town, General Charles Maynard, valiantly tried to overcome the problem by borrowing funds from other allied officials in order to pay his workers. Even so, the financial problems greatly damaged the prestige of the British and made it difficult for the General to perform his duties effectively. Ironically, British military and civilian officials were in practice no more successful than the Russians at setting up viable administrative structures in north Russia.

Most senior British military officers posted to north Russia viewed the local political scene through a prism that was more akin to that of General Poole than that of Frank Lindley. Indeed, the attitude of the British officers on the ground, who exercised a predominant influence on the day to day course of allied intervention, was on occasions a matter of concern to other governments who had troops in the area under British command. The American government was particularly unhappy with the behaviour of Poole during his time in Archangel, a sentiment which played a part in bringing about his recall to London.[27] General Maynard in Murmansk acknowledged that the original role of his forces was to secure the town against German attack, but made little effort to conceal his hostile attitude to the Bolsheviks either at the time or when writing his memoirs several years later. In March 1919 he wrote to the War Office in London about the need to 'smash the Bolshevik power at Petrograd', though he reluctantly recognised that political divisions in London meant that the necessary resources were unlikely to be made available to achieve such a goal. In a talk given to his senior officers a few days later, in which he ordered them to take care that their men were not influenced by Bolshevik propaganda, he bitterly attacked 'the most autocratic form of so-called government the world has ever seen', and went on to argue that it only remained in power since those who lived under it were constantly in 'fear of death'.[28] He was preaching to the converted. Maynard's immediate subordinates shared their senior officer's bitter hatred of Lenin's government, as well as his frustration over the hesitant policy towards Russia adopted by the Cabinet back in Britain, which failed to set down clear objectives for the intervention forces. The same was not true of ordinary British soldiers and sailors in north Russia, many of whom bitterly resented being kept in uniform long after the hostilities in western Europe had come to an end.

Although the fighting between British forces and Bolshevik troops in north Russia was quite limited, there were a number of brutal skirmishes in which almost 200 British troops lost their lives. British diaries and letters reflect deep frustration and bitterness at the poor conditions in which they were forced to live. One wireless operator based in Archangel itself complained bitterly about the shortage of fresh vegetables and milk, though he was at least able to comfort himself with the thought that he was in a better situation than men posted up the line who had no bread to eat and had 'to munch biscuits as hard as any brick'.[29] The hideous cold of the northern winter, in which temperatures plummeted to forty degrees below zero, also sapped the morale of troops forced to live in inadequate temporary accommodation that did not provide proper shelter against the elements. Even the end of the harsh winter did not bring much relief, since the hot weather that followed led to plagues of mosquitoes that 'torture us to death'. Things became worse than ever once the British and other allied troops began their preparations to leave north Russia in the middle of 1919, since their impending departure encouraged serious outbreaks of disorder among the local population. Few British soldiers were particularly sympathetic to the Bolsheviks, and there were no mutinies on the scale of the ones which affected French forces in the region. Nevertheless, the state of morale was a source of endless concern for the British officer corps, who feared that discontent in the ranks might make their men susceptible to the barrage of propaganda distributed by Bolshevik agents. Considerable efforts were made to bolster the troops' spirits, but by the early months of 1919 a corrosive cynicism had set in that could not easily be countered even by the most enthusiastic and energetic commanding officer.

While certain groups in north Russia did support the allied presence, most of the population was indifferent or actively hostile to the intervention forces.[30] Few local men joined the regiments set up to fight the Bolsheviks, while any concerted attempt to introduce conscription was bitterly opposed. The British military authorities devoted huge resources to a propaganda campaign designed to win the support and trust of the local population,[31] warning them against the horrors of Bolshevism, but its impact on popular sentiment was very limited. There was in reality a considerable degree of support among the working class in Archangel and Murmansk for the Bolshevik government in Moscow, while the peasants in the countryside simply wanted to be left alone by all outside forces. Although the occasional outbursts of civilian unrest were sometimes instigated by Bolshevik agitators, they more often reflected a real tension between the local population and the thousands of foreigners who had appeared in their midst. Senior British army officers did not increase their popularity by the harsh way in which they often responded to these problems – a reflection, perhaps, of their own sense of frustration at the impossible role which they were expected to perform by their civilian masters back in London. On one occasion, when Russian troops nominally loyal to the allies mutinied at a barracks in Archangel, British soldiers were instructed to turn machine guns on them.[32]

The only really consistent support for the allied presence in north Russia came from former Tsarist army officers and the handful of wealthy Russian civilians who made their way to the region seeking a safe refuge from the Bolsheviks. Since these groups represented no more than a small section of the population, British soldiers and civilian officials alike were in time forced to accept that they were not seen as liberators or heroes by most local people, but rather just a part of the shifting human kaleidoscope that was such a hallmark of Russian society in the years after 1917. When the allied presence began to be run down in the summer of 1919, the resentment of the local population against their 'protectors' became transparent: officers and NCOs had to plan the deployment of their men so as to defend them against attack by the people they were meant to be protecting. Although Frank Lindley, along with most other British representatives in north Russia, opposed the War Cabinet's decision to withdraw its forces from the region, his views were motivated above all by concern over the fate of Russian nationals who had helped the allies during their sojourn in Archangel and Murmansk. By the summer of 1919, not even the most gung-ho British army officer in the region could believe that his presence was helping to protect either the Russians or the rest of the world against the menace of Bolshevism.

British military intervention in Siberia and the Urals took a different form from the intervention in north Russia, even though the rationale behind each was originally the same: to increase opposition to Germany along the Eastern Front, while at the same time preventing the Kaiser's armies from gaining access to the stocks of military materials sent to the country by Russia's allies. In reality, fears about the danger of a large-scale German advance eastwards were exaggerated, while the hope expressed by certain Ministers in London that Japan could be induced to send troops several thousand miles along the Trans-Siberian railway to do battle with the German armies in Europe was never more than a pathetic illusion which ignored clear diplomatic signals to the contrary sent by Tokyo.[33] Yet since the government in London was also concerned about the need to protect British economic interests in Siberia,[34] by the middle of 1918 the case for some form of military intervention in the region seemed a plausible one to most members of the War Cabinet. In the event, British intervention in Siberia and the Urals between 1918 and 1920 proved to be modest both in scale and consequence. In north Russia, the British were the dominant outside force in the area throughout the period of military intervention. By contrast, only a small number of British troops were sent to Siberia, where they were easily outnumbered by other allied forces.

At the time of the November Revolution, the War Cabinet and Foreign Office in London were not in a position to gauge the likely impact of the Bolshevik seizure of power on the vast territories east of the Ural mountains. Although consular officials in the region had filed regular reports throughout the war, they concentrated for the most part on economic rather than political questions. It was largely for this reason that a decision was taken early in 1918 to send the radical Member of Parliament, Colonel Josiah Wedgwood, on a secret visit to Siberia to produce a report about conditions there. The instructions given to Wedgwood were very vague,[35] but the primary role of his mission was to persuade 'the inhabitants of Siberia' about 'the worthlessness of German promises and the results which must ensue from the economic domination of Russia by Germany'. The Colonel was also told to emphasise 'the sympathy which exists between England and Russia and the efforts which we have already made on her behalf'. Given the chaotic state of Siberian society following the Bolshevik seizure of power in Petersburg and Moscow, it is not clear how Wedgwood was expected to carry out his instructions, particularly since he was also told to 'avoid publicity as far as possible'. In the event, the presence of his small mission made virtually no impact on the political situation in Siberia, but the report he submitted on return to London did provide a good deal of useful information about the state of popular feeling in the region.[36] He confirmed that 'German influences are at work in Siberia', which he believed were 'in some cases supported by Bolshevik elements, in others opposed ... many Bolsheviks are German agents, but many others are honest and sincerely hate Germans'. Wedgwood was optimistic that, in cases where local Bolsheviks had taken power, their 'misrule' was increasingly 'recognised as intolerable' by the population. The Colonel therefore strongly opposed any form of direct intervention, suggesting that outside forces were unlikely to have much impact on the political sentiments of the Siberian population. He concluded that the only hope of preventing the Bolsheviks from establishing deep roots in Siberia, with a possible subsequent increase in German influence across the region, lay in the 'recognition by the Russian people themselves of the distinction between liberty and licence, and in their support of the forces standing for the establishment of order and the protection of life and property'.

Wedgwood's observation that outsiders could not exercise significant influence on the chaos unfolding across Siberia failed to have much impact on the making of British policy towards Russia during 1918, as the War Cabinet drifted towards its policy of half-hearted and ill-considered intervention. In the summer of 1918 a British Military Mission under General Knox was dispatched to Vladivostok, with instructions to liaise with other allied military forces in the area.[37] Other British forces soon followed. Although the role of British military personnel in Siberia was never properly defined, most of their time and energy was spent helping to train the anti-Bolshevik forces that began to take shape in the second half of 1918. Unlike their counterparts in north Russia, they were involved in few direct engagements with troops loyal to the Bolshevik government in Moscow. A short time after Knox's arrival, Sir Charles Eliot, the former Principal of Hong Kong University, was appointed High Commissioner to Siberia, charged with the thankless task of coordinating the British presence there. British consular officials also continued to serve in a number of the most important towns in the region, ranging from Vladivostok on the Pacific coast to Ekaterinburg in the Urals, where they played an important role in keeping London informed about local political developments.

The task of all these officials, both civilian and military, was made extremely difficult by the complexity of the political situation that developed in Siberia and the Urals following the collapse of Bolshevik rule there in the middle of 1918.[38] In the immediate aftermath of the November Revolution, the Socialist Revolutionaries emerged as the most powerful political force across much of the region, but they quickly lost ground to the Bolsheviks in the first half of 1918. The political map was transformed in May, however, when several thousand Czecho-slovak soldiers, in transit homewards from prisoner of war camps, rioted following a clash with Hungarian prisoners of war who were being transported in the opposite direction along the Trans-Siberian railway.[39] Tension between the Czechoslovak Legion and the Bolshevik govern-ment had been growing for some weeks, since it was widely known that the allies were planning to use the Legion as an important element in their intervention strategy in north Russia. Although the riot itself was comparatively trivial, it signalled the final break between the two. Over the next few months, the Czechoslovak Legion's presence in Siberia had a great impact on the region's political life, since it began to form a nucleus of opposition to the Bolsheviks across large swathes of Russia. In the confusion that followed, several new regional governments emerged in Siberia and the Urals, all pledged to resist any attempt by the Bolshevik government to assert its authority in the area. Chaos reigned in the second half of 1918 as each of these anti-Bolshevik governments, which varied considerably from one another in political complexion, tried to organise military opposition to forces loyal to Moscow. In large parts of the region there was no effective authority for long periods of time, but rather just a prolonged descent into complete lawlessness and anarchy. Throughout the latter half of 1918 and the first half of 1919 Siberia became the setting for some of the bloodiest fighting of the whole Russian Civil War, as Red and White armies and partisans battled to establish control over the eastern ter-ritories of the former Tsarist Empire. Britain's civilian officials and soldiers serving in the region were forced to witness acts of brutality and carnage that rivalled anything seen on the battlefields of Europe during 1914–18.

The political views of British army officers who served in Siberia between 1918 and 1920 were generally similar to the ones held by their counterparts in north Russia. They were horrified by the chaos that spread across the region during the summer of 1918, following the revolt of the Czechoslovak Legion and the disintegration of Bolshevik rule in cities such as Ufa and Ekaterinburg. At the same time, they welcomed the collapse of Bolshevik power in the region. The Labour Member of Parliament, John Ward, who served as a Colonel in the Middlesex Regiment which arrived in Eastern Siberia in July 1918, was typical in regarding the Bolsheviks as a 'disgusting gang of cut-throats, whose sole business in life appears to be to terrorise ... the peasant and worker and make orderly government impossible'. Like other British army officers, he was appalled by 'the broken structure of human society' in Siberia, recalling in his memoirs that 'Russian society had been ripped up by the roots, and the whole country reduced to a huge human jungle. Human life was at a discount, in fact was the cheapest thing in the country'.[40] General Knox shared these views. He treated the various governments that sprang to life in Siberia in the second half of 1918, many of which were headed by socialists of various kinds, with the same kind of brusque impatience that he had treated the Provisional Government in Petrograd during the previous year. He did not believe that their civilian members were determined enough to restore social and political order in the areas under their control, and feared that they lacked both the inclination and will to implement the measures required to resist a Bolshevik advance. Like British army officers in north Russia, both Ward and Knox instinctively believed that some form of dictatorship was needed to establish order across Russia and to prevent any further descent into anarchy. However, with so few British forces in the region, they hardly seemed to be in a strong position to influence the course of Siberian politics, particularly since the diplomatic complexities of foreign intervention meant that they had to be cautious before taking any action which might cause offence to their allies.

Providence appeared to answer the concerns of senior British military officers in the autumn of 1918, though it is still not altogether clear whether they provided it with a helping hand. In the third week of November, a coup took place in the Siberian city of Omsk, directed against the so-called All Russian Provisional Government that had been formed a short while before out of an uneasy combination of liberals and erstwhile members of the Socialist Revolutionary Party. Following the coup, which was carried out by army officers hostile even to the moderate socialist coalition that controlled the All Russian Government, Admiral Alexander Kolchak was appointed 'Supreme Ruler of Russia' (though the title was in truth rather more grandiloquent than the reality, since Kolchak never succeeded in establishing his authority over all the various anti-Bolshevik forces across Siberia let alone the rest of the country). The Foreign Office in London was appalled by the events in Omsk, since the British government had been on the point of recognising the Directory – the name by which the All Russian Government was more commonly known – believing that it commanded wide support among the local population. Britain's civilian officials in the area, including Sir Charles Eliot, also reacted with concern when they first heard about the coup.[41] The sentiments of British army officers closer to the scene were more ambivalent, particularly since the

Admiral's commitment to the restoration of order and the defeat of Bolshevism so closely reflected the views repeatedly expressed by many of them. The senior French commander in the area, General Maurice Janin, had no doubt that British military personnel were actively involved in preparing the coup,[42] as had been the case in Archangel a few weeks earlier. The evidence for his claim is not entirely conclusive, though rumours certainly reached the Foreign Office in London that two officers from the Military Mission were playing an over zealous part in Siberian politics. Both Colonel L. Steveni and Captain J. F. Nielson had close personal ties with some of the plotters who overthrew the Directory, and may have given them the mistaken impression that the British government would welcome the destruction of the All Russian Government.[43] Nor should it be forgotten that Kolchak had since the middle of 1917 been engaged in discussions with various British military representatives about ways of establishing greater social and political order in Russia. Whatever the exact circumstances surrounding Kolchak's coup, many British officers certainly rejoiced at the demise of the ill-fated Directory, whose members were condemned by Ward as 'the most unmitigated failures that even poor distracted Russia had so far produced'.[44] General Knox was more concerned about the possible consequences of Kolchak's rise to power, since he knew that the new government was unlikely to attract much popular support. Nevertheless, he remained an unashamed admirer of the Admiral, praising him for the possession of 'two characteristics uncommon in a Russian – a quick temper which inspires a useful awe among his subordinates, and a disinclination to talk merely for talking's sake'.[45] On another occasion, he bluntly told the War Office that 'I confess that all my sympathy is with Kolchak … You have to take what you can get in Russia, and if you find an honest man with the courage of a lion he should be supported although he may not appear to have the wisdom of a serpent'.[46]

Many British army officers in Siberia believed, or at least made themselves believe, that Admiral Kolchak was by instinct a constitutionalist who did not share the rabidly reactionary views expressed by so many of the former Tsarist officers who flocked to his headquarters. Their conviction was not always shared in London, particularly at the Foreign Office, where there was a good deal of concern about the Admiral's political views,[47] a concern which was not assuaged by his repeated protestations of support for a liberal political order based on the equality of all Russians before the law. Nevertheless, from a purely strategic point of view, Kolchak's seizure of power appeared to be vindicated during the first half of 1919, as his forces staged a series of impressive advances westwards helped by a generous supply of weapons and other material from abroad. By late spring, it even seemed possible that troops loyal to Moscow would before long be driven from Siberia altogether. The attack petered out in the middle of the year, however, as the Red Army, which was becoming an increasingly professional and effective force under the direction of Leon Trotsky, regrouped and counter-attacked, eventually driving its opponents back into the eastern-most provinces of Siberia. A long and agonised debate took place in London throughout these months about the wisdom of formally recognising the Kolchak government as the government of the whole of Russia (an issue that also greatly exercised the leaders of the various anti-Bolshevik movements scattered across the country). Opinion was divided among politicians and officials at the Foreign Office and War Office, but the reversals which took place on the battlefield in the second half of 1919 made the whole question somewhat academic. It was decided in August to suspend the delivery of supplies to Kolchak's retreating armies so as to concentrate help on the forces of General Denikin, which were fighting the Bolsheviks with rather better results in south Russia. Although British civilian officials and soliders remained in Siberia, symbolically reflecting the Foreign Office's assertion that the decision to end supplies did not mean that Britain was 'disinteresting itself in the Siberian situation', the refusal of the allies to provide Kolchak with large-scale material assistance and military aid meant that his armies could not resist the Bolshevik advance for long. A few months later, the Admiral fell into the hands of the Bolsheviks when their forces captured the town of Irkutsk, where Kolchak had established his headquarters following a long retreat by his armies from central Siberia. He was executed by his captors in February 1920, his body being thrown unceremoniously under the ice of the river which flowed beneath the site where he was shot.

Kolchak's failure to establish either an effective government or an army capable of defeating the Bolsheviks showed how wrong British army officers were to put their faith in the benefits of 'dictatorship'. Although it is easy to understand why they believed that a 'strong man' was required to impose order on the chaos of Siberia, their political views were in reality extremely naive and failed to take into account the complexities of post-revolutionary Russia. While large sections of the Siberian population intensely disliked the Bolsheviks, they were equally suspicious of those who sought to turn the clock back to the days of the Tsarist *ancien régime*. The reactionary army officers who

flocked to Omsk in the first half of 1919 had no desire to respond to
the clamour for land-reform which was the main concern of the local
peasantry; nor were they temperamentally inclined to work with officers
belonging to the Czechoslovak Legion, who were often comparatively
radical in their politics. Although Kolchak's own political ideas were in
reality quite moderate, at least in the sense that he accepted the
impossibility of a 'return to the regime which existed in Russia before
1917', Colonel Ward was right in observing that the officers in his army
were monarchists 'almost to a man'.[48] Ward was also correct in noting
that many of the officials appointed to Kolchak's government held
reactionary political views, while at the same time lacking all the basic
administrative talents that were so desperately needed to restore effective government across the region. By the middle of 1919, British army
officers knew that the Kolchak government was hugely unpopular with
large sections of the Siberian population, and recognised that allied
forces were frequently viewed 'with hostility' as a result of their association with it. They also knew that Kolchak's troops 'had undoubtedly
been guilty of atrocities' against the civilian population.[49] At least some
British officers posted to Siberia were shrewd enough to understand
that the economic collapse in the region, and the poor living standards
that resulted from it, provided fertile ground for Bolshevik agitators.
As a result, while members of the British Military Mission in Siberia
worked hard to equip and train White forces in Siberia throughout
1918 and the first part of 1919, many of its members knew in their
hearts that they were fighting a losing battle. Even the boundless energy
and optimism of General Knox could not instil in his staff a real belief
that their efforts would have a lasting impact on Russia's future.

British civilian officials who served in Siberia during the Civil War
were never so hopeful as their military counterparts that Kolchak's
armies could offer effective resistance to armies loyal to the Bolsheviks,
in large part because they were more sensitive to the depth of the
tensions that had undermined the traditional social and political fabric
over the previous few years. But while Frank Lindley had been at least
partly successful in establishing his authority over the British presence
in north Russia, Sir Charles Eliot never managed to exercise so great
an influence from his base in Omsk. British intervention in Siberia was
more purely military in form and ethos than was the case in Archangel
and Murmansk. There were fewer civilian officials in Siberia than in
north Russia and they were far less involved in providing their Russian
'hosts' with help and advice about administrative questions. Eliot himself
had a certain amount of respect for Kolchak, whom he acknowledged

as 'an honest and brave man', but he was appalled by the Admiral's administrative ineptitude and failure to appoint competent officials. He told Lord Curzon, who replaced Balfour as Foreign Secretary in 1919, that the high level of corruption in Kolchak's armies played a crucial role in undermining morale, since the ordinary troops refused to obey officers 'who desert their regiments and make money out of the men's food'.[50]

Eliot was also fearful that the reactionary views of Kolchak's advisers would alienate large sections of the population and make them look more favourably on the Bolsheviks. His deputy in Vladivostok, William O'Reilly, was even more appalled by the behaviour and policies adopted by Kolchak's government as it tried to establish and maintain its authority across Siberia during 1919, bitterly criticising the Admiral for appointing as Provincial Governors 'brigands' who behaved in an arbitrary and despotic manner which destroyed popular support.[51] Both men were shrewd enough to recognise that there was a good deal of support for radical socialists among the Siberian population. O'Reilly himself noted in the summer of 1919 that a genuinely free election in the region would probably result in the establishment of a left-wing government composed of Socialist Revolutionaries.[52] The only way he could see to change the situation was for Britain and other allied countries to supply large quantities of economic aid, in order to persuade the population that their material interests would best be served by continuing to oppose the Bolsheviks. Such a policy was of course unlikely to be forthcoming at a time when the economic strains of the First World War were still making themselves felt throughout Europe. As a result, by the final months of 1919, following the collapse of Kolchak's forces, British officials could only watch in horror as refugees fleeing the fighting flooded into the major cities where they were forced to live 'in appalling conditions'.[53]

While British army officers and civilian representatives in Siberia were certainly not blind to the cruelty of Kolchak's armies or of the other White troops in the region, they were even more appalled at the barbarism displayed by the various Bolshevik forces. The reports sent to London from Siberia during 1918–19 played an important role in cementing in the mind of official Britain a conviction that the Bolsheviks were a menace to the entire civilised world. Some of the most graphic accounts of their brutality were collected by Thomas Preston, who served as British Consul in the city of Ekaterinburg, which was liberated by troops from the Czechoslovak Legion in July 1918 a few days after the Tsarist Royal Family had been put to death there. Dozens of eyewitnesses told Preston of the ghastly events that had taken place during the months when the Bolsheviks had been in control of the town and the surrounding area, including numerous cases of murder and rape.[54] They had taken hundreds of hostages as security against attacks by the local population, many of whom were tortured horribly before being trampled and bayonetted to death. In one village, the retreating Bolsheviks 'pricked the local miller with needles to get money from him and violated his wife before his eyes. They cut off the fingers, nose and lips of the station-master and killed him'. The worst treatment was reserved for those who either fought against the Bolshevik troops or refused to join them in their battle against their opponents. One peasant was torn in half between two horses for refusing to fight, while a captured officer in the Czechoslovak Legion was nailed to a tree, blinded and sprinkled with benzine, before being burnt alive. The systematic disfiguration of corpses was a frequent occurrence. The government in London published some of the accounts sent from Siberia to Britain, so as to help mobilise domestic opinion against the Bolsheviks and reduce the appeal of their ideas to workers in the major industrial cities.[55] While many of these published reports were disturbing enough in their own right, the most grizzly were kept in Foreign Office archives, judged to be too grotesque for distribution to a wider audience.

The execution of the Russian Royal Family in the town of Ekaterinburg in July 1918 inevitably commanded the attention of British officials throughout Siberia and the Urals for many months after the event, though the whole affair was even at the time surrounded by enormous controversy and confusion. For the outside world, the murder of Nicholas and his family quickly came to symbolise the cruelty of the Bolshevik leadership and its rejection of the values of civilised society. Inside Russia itself, by contrast, the fate of the Royal Family aroused surprisingly little reaction. Thomas Preston in Ekaterinburg made numerous representations demanding guarantees about the welfare of the Tsar and his family once they had been brought to the town from Tobolsk in the late spring of 1918. This interference was naturally unwelcome to the local authorities: on one occasion the Ekaterinburg Town Soviet even passed a resolution condemning the Consul to death for his attempts to intercede on behalf of the doomed Emperor. (Nothing in fact happened, except on one occasion when the Consulate was invaded by a dozen drunken Hungarian prisoners-of-war, armed with knives and hand-grenades, who told Preston they were looking for anyone guilty of holding 'anti-Bolshevik sympathies'.)[56] On the night of 16 July, as forces from the Czechoslovak Legion approached the town, Red troops placed machine-guns at strategic points across the centre of Ekaterinburg, as well as around the Ipatiev house itself where the Royal Family was being held captive. Although the account Preston gave in his memoirs of the events which followed was very detailed, at the time he knew virtually nothing about the tragedy that was taking place a short distance from his home. On the morning of 17 July, the Ural Soviet publicly declared that the Emperor had been killed – though no mention was made of the rest of his family – and various meetings were held across Ekaterinburg to announce the fact to the local population.

Preston himself attended some of these assemblies, where he was predictably treated with a good deal of hostility as an 'English spy'. He was unable to send news of the murder to the outside world, since his telegram to the Foreign Secretary in London was intercepted by the Bolsheviks and never transmitted. It was only when troops from the Czechoslovak Legion liberated the town a few days later that the Consul was able to transmit his report to Sir Charles Eliot, who had recently arrived in Siberia to take up his duties as High Commissioner. By this time, the town was already buzzing with rumours, many of which were relayed in Preston's telegrams, including one which noted that although the Tsar himself had been shot on 17 July, the members of his family had been burnt alive. A number of senior British officials and soldiers, among them General Knox, arrived in Ekaterinburg over the next few weeks to judge for themselves what had happened. Eliot visited the town in September and was shown the cellar in the house where the murders had supposedly taken place, complete with bullet holes in the walls and blood-stains on the floor. The Russian soldier who showed the High Commissioner around the building dismissed the shootings as 'fabrications', a belief that was already taking hold among a large part of the town's population.[57] Eliot did not share this optimism and discounted rumours that certain members of the Royal Family had been taken alive from the town by train. Like other British representatives in Russia, he had no doubt that the Bolsheviks were quite capable of adding regicide to their long list of crimes against the values of civilised society.

Thomas Preston recalled in his memoirs that the murder of the Royal Family did not cause 'a great sensation ... amongst the inhabitants' of Ekaterinburg.[58] He believed that this apathy was testimony to the success of the anti-monarchist propaganda that the Bolsheviks had churned out relentlessly over the previous few months. But he was also realistic enough to acknowledge that the first concern of the population in

Ekaterinburg and the surrounding area was to 'save themselves from a violent death at the hands of the Bolsheviks', with the result that they had little energy left over to worry about the fate of others. Reports from other British Consuls across Siberia during the middle of 1918 certainly suggested that the end of Bolshevik rule was almost invariably met with 'great approval'.[59] Some consular officials were too inclined to fall into the trap of believing that popular hatred of the Bolsheviks would automatically translate into support for their opponents. In reality, the majority of the population of central and eastern Russia were 'Whites' only in the sense that they sought liberation from the oppression and brutality of the 'Red' government in Moscow. The Czechoslovak Legion was welcomed by the population of towns like Ekaterinburg during 1918 precisely because its leaders were believed to possess radical political instincts, unlike the more conservative politicians and officers who followed in their wake. British officials like Clement Nash, a Vice-Consul based in the city of Irkutsk, were guilty of poor judgement when suggesting that the Russian people 'have become accustomed to the whip and it is a big mistake to think they can do without it'.[60] The dramatic events of 1917 had changed Russian society for ever. The population was no longer willing to be ruled by 'the whip'. The muted reaction to the Tsar's murder illustrated starkly the changes in popular attitudes that had taken place over the previous few years, and helps to explain why the Bolsheviks' opponents found it so difficult to mobilise public support behind their crusade to overthrow Lenin's government in Moscow.

William Gerhardie, who served under General Knox in the Military Mission to Siberia, gave the title *Futility* to his autobigraphical novel about life in Vladivostok after the Russian Revolution – a suitable word to describe the British government's half-hearted attempt to influence the outcome of the Civil War in the region. Gerhardie seldom went far from the Pacific coast and was spared some of of the more grizzly experiences of his colleagues who ventured into the Siberian hinterland. Life at the headquarters of the British Military Mission was comparatively comfortable, at least for the officers, though the work was endless and General Knox drove his small staff extremely hard.[61] It was, however, quite impossible for any foreigner on Russia soil entirely to escape the horrors taking place across the country. When the Czechoslovak General Rudolf Gaida staged an ill-fated coup in Vladivostok against the rule of Kolchak's government of 'butchers and political assassins', in the autumn of 1919, Gerhardie saw at first hand hundreds of men 'lying in horrid postures, dead or dying. Those who were not dead, when discovered were finished with the bayonet by the "loyal" troops, amid unspeakable yells'.[62] The sight challenged even Gerhardie's habitual sense of irony and detachment, making him question whether the White forces supported by his government were in any way more civilised than the Bolsheviks against whom they were fighting. During more peaceful times, though, staff at the Mission headquarters were at least able to enjoy a social life of sorts, mixing with the faintly raffish mélange of foreign troops and Russian noble refugees that provided Gerhardie with the inspiration for his best-known novel.

The author of *Futility* was of course hardly a typical figure among the British army officers who served in Siberia. Even so, his sense of the absurdity of Britain's efforts to support 'a band of disgruntled adventurers', fighting to restore a mythical national Russia, was shared by a number of his colleagues in the Military Mission, at least in the final months of 1919, when it had become clear that all their efforts over the previous year were in vain. The allied forces which clustered on the Pacific shore around Siberia were never able to influence developments taking place thousands of miles away in the heart of the country in Omsk or Ekaterinburg. The handful of British troops and civilian representatives in both eastern and western Siberia were simply powerless observers of an elemental process of social and political change that was taking place across Russia. Gerhardie's sense of the essential pathos of the allies' hope that they could control events was for a long time resisted by his superiors. In the end, even the indefatigable Knox had to admit defeat, wearily telegraphing to London in the early spring of 1920 that 'General Knox presumes that his further stay here can serve no useful purpose and recommends recall to England'. London agreed.[63] The return wire simply noted that 'General Knox's presumption is correct'. British intervention ended in Siberia as it ended in north Russia: with a whimper rather than a bang. The Military Mission was gradually run down as its members were recalled to other duties in Britain. The other allied powers also scaled down their presence as it became clear that they could serve no useful purpose. The determination of the Bolsheviks to gain control of Siberia eventually won out against the opposition of a myriad of divided and squabbling forces. Neither the British nor anyone else could do anything to prevent it.

The fate of south Russia had been of concern to the British government from the moment the Bolsheviks seized power, in November 1917, and was of far more immediate interest to London than events in distant

Siberia.[64] The 'Great Game' between Britain and Tsarist Russia during
the nineteenth century had in large part been a battle for power and
influence over the countries lying between Turkey and India, the defence of British interests throughout the region being one of the
traditional leitmotifs of the country's foreign policy. Yet the early support given by the British War Cabinet to Ataman Kaledin at the end
of 1917 failed to have any lasting impact on the local political and
military situation. The Cossack leader himself committed suicide in
February 1918 when it became clear that his forces were not strong
enough to resist the Bolshevik advance. During the year that followed
the Bolshevik Revolution in Petrograd, the political situation across the
southern and south-eastern territories of the former Tsarist Empire was
so complicated that it taxed the understanding of even the most diligent
British representative or Foreign Office official. The Ukraine oscillated
between Bolshevik control and the control of a nominally independent
national government which was in practice dependent on the German
army for its survival, while the Transcaucasian provinces took advantage
of the confusion created by war and revolution to declare their independence (though the new governments which emerged were never in
practice capable of establishing effective control over their respective
territories). Throughout 1918 there were two distinct centres of anti-
Bolshevik opposition in south Russia. As well as the army of the Don
Cossacks, there also emerged the so-called Volunteer Army, established
at the end of 1917 by former Tsarist army officers and politicians who
had fled south after the Bolsheviks succeeded in establishing their power
in Moscow and Petrograd. Relations between the Don Cossacks and the
Volunteer Army were at first very strained, in large part because some
Cossack leaders were willing to seek German support in pursuit of their
goal of independent statehood, while the military and political leadership of the Volunteer Army was solidly committed to maintaining the
territorial integrity of the old Russian Empire. Nevertheless, the existence of a common opponent in the Bolsheviks forced the two armies
to come to a grudging agreement with one another and, during the
second half of 1918, their leaders began to cooperate on a range of
military and administrative questions. By the time the Armistice was
signed in November, it was clear that south Russia might once again
become one of the most important centres of anti-Bolshevik resistance.

There had been a considerable British military presence in the Transcaucasus and Persia during the First World War, sent there to prevent
the Germans and their allies from establishing control over the Near
East. The confusion which followed the signing of the Armistice meant

that a good deal of uncertainty remained about the fate of German troops who had advanced south eastwards in the wake of the Treaty of Brest-Litovsk of March 1918. Supporters of British military intervention in south Russia were therefore still able to point to a potential German challenge in the area, though even the most zealous among them usually acknowledged after the beginning of 1919 that this was now more likely to take the form of a struggle for economic power and political influence rather than a battle for territory. In reality, British involvement in south Russia was always more straightforwardly directed against the Bolsheviks than in Siberia or north Russia, since operations there only really began once the Armistice with Germany was already signed. In November 1918 the British government dispatched a Military Mission to the Volunteer Army, which was by this time headed by a former Tsarist officer, General A. I. Denikin. Although Denikin was a competent soldier, he shared Admiral Kolchak's disastrous ignorance of the basic principles of both civil and military administration.[65] To make matters worse, many of the politicians and officers associated with the Volunteer Army shared its commander's impatience with mundane administrative questions. As a result, while the anti-Bolshevik forces in south Russia seemed on paper to be formidable at the end of 1918, the political and administrative realities of the local situation meant that their position was a good deal more fragile than it appeared.

The Military Mission sent to south Russia at the end of 1918 recommended that Britain should offer supplies and other assistance to Denikin's army rather than offer direct military support, a proposal that was quickly endorsed in London.[66] General C. J. Briggs, appointed as Head of a new Mission to be attached to Denikin's headquarters, was instructed to identify the material requirements of the Volunteer Army and report accordingly.[67] Over the next twelve months or so, Britain's civilian and military representatives in south Russia showed themselves to be far stauncher advocates of intervention in the region than the vast majority of politicians in London, where members of the Lloyd George government oscillated as ever between their desire to see the defeat of Bolshevism and a reluctance to put in place the policies designed to bring about such a goal. Although they were well aware of the shortcomings and downright brutality which often characterised the activities of White forces in south Russia, they were convinced that support for Denikin was vital both to defeat Bolshevism and to secure British interests in south-east Europe against the other major powers. In carrying out their work, however, they faced the same problems as Britain's representatives elsewhere in Russia. The British government's reluctance to make clear decisions about its policy towards Russia meant that soldiers and civilian officials 'on the ground' were confused about their exact role. While they could occasionally use London's ambivalence as a means of increasing their own independence and influence, more often than not it simply meant that they lacked the resources to exercise any sustained impact on the local military and political situation. Although British intervention in south Russia was marginally less catastrophic than intervention by French forces in the region, which culminated in an ignominious withdrawal from Odessa in the spring of 1919, it proved in the end to be no more long-lasting in its effects.

The Great Russian nationalism of General Denikin and the White leadership associated with the Volunteer Army was a cause of particular concern in London. Britain's foreign policy had, since the end of 1917, been based on a tacit willingness to accept and even welcome the process of political fragmentation in the borderlands of the old Russian Empire, providing that the successor states could be prevented from falling into the German sphere of influence. To this end, the de facto independence of Finland and the Baltic states was accepted without undue concern during 1918, in part because it was feared that a rise of nationalist sentiment in the region might otherwise encourage their leaders to seek German help to secure independence. It was, however, in the south of the country that the whole question of the territorial integrity of Russia became a particularly vexed issue for British foreign policy. General Denikin and his advisers instinctively opposed the declarations of independence made by the new governments in the Transcaucasus, insisting that the whole region should continue to form an integral part of Russia. When Lord Curzon became British Foreign Secretary, in October 1919, he was inclined to champion the claims of these small states to obtain independence from Russia;[68] the same was even more true of Oliver Wardrop, appointed as High Commissioner to Transcaucasia following his traumatic return from Moscow in the autumn of 1918. Winston Churchill at the War Office was, by contrast, indifferent about the fate of the Transcaucasian states and quite unwilling to allow the issue to complicate Britain's relations with Denikin.

During 1919 Britain's military *and* civilian representatives throughout south Russia enthusiastically endorsed the Minister of War's position. Picton Bagge, who had by now become the British Commercial Representative in Odessa, forcefully told the Foreign Office in March that 'Economically these small States will never be able to exist as independent States'.[69] He also warned London against any policy that might facilitate the break up of Russia, since it would enable the Bolsheviks to present themselves as champions of the country's territorial integrity. General H. C. Holman, who headed the British Military Mission to Denikin's headquarters in the second half of 1919, similarly made little secret of his mistrust of 'the shifty politicians' of the Transcaucasus, and urged the government in London not to allow disagreement over the region's future to colour its policy towards the Volunteer Army. Holman was even inclined to play down the notorious antisemitism of the White forces in south Russia. While he could hardly avoid acknowledging the existence of anti-Jewish atrocities in many areas where Denikin's forces were in control, he told London that 'nearly all the Bolshevik leaders are Jews' and suggested that the Jewish population was exaggerating the extent of the pogroms directed against them.[70] The omnipresent General Poole, who went to south Russia early in 1919 on a mission to examine the material requirements of White forces in the area, also dismissed the significance of the reactionary views held by the senior commanders in the Volunteer Army.[71] In fairness to Holman and Poole, neither man had any real sympathy with the political instincts characteristic of the White leadership in south Russia. Their willingness to disregard some of the more distasteful pronouncements of Denikin's aides was animated above all by a belief that the struggle with Bolshevism justified offering support even to those whose conduct would in more normal times have made such a policy seem quite unacceptable. Like many senior British army officers in north Russia and Siberia, they were certain that strong government was required to establish order and lay the foundations for successful resistance against forces loyal to the Bolshevik government in Moscow.

Even though Britain's civilian and military representatives in south Russia were willing to view the activities of the White leaders in the best possible light, they could not ignore the massive weaknesses of the administrative structures established by Denikin, which undermined the strength of the Volunteer Army and hampered its ability to benefit from the material help given by London. Poole noted during his visit that, although the calibre of Denikin's General Staff was quite high, 'the Administrative services do not strike me as efficient and, in some cases, notably the medical services, are deplorably bad'. He condemned the lack of 'grip' and 'method', and suggested that one of the most important tasks of British army officers should be to provide the Volunteer Army with advice about administrative questions.[72] Even the best efforts of the British Military Mission did little to improve matters, in spite of Poole's early optimism that the application of a little Anglo-Saxon 'method' would soon overcome the Russian genius for disorganisation. In September 1919, a Major attached to the Mission sadly noted that material supplied by the British 'never reaches the fighting troops and is either left lying at the base, given to troops doing garrison duty, or is fraudulently disposed of'.[73] Another officer bitterly complained about the level of 'thieving and peculation' carried out by staff officers.[74] Despite these problems, Britain's civilian representatives and soldiers in south Russia worked hard to encourage their government to provide still more support for Denikin, though their efforts were largely in vain. More or less from the moment the Military Mission arrived at Denikin's headquarters in the city of Ekaterinodar, the decision had effectively been taken to keep the scale of direct British involvement in the area to a minimum, notwithstanding a decision in the summer of 1919 to divert to south Russia material that had originally been destined for Kolchak's forces in Siberia.[75]

Although Winston Churchill railed against this policy of gradual disengagement, he could do little more than reduce the speed of British withdrawal from Russia. Perhaps encouraged by the Minister of War's stance, officials like Bagge continued to argue throughout 1919 that 'the only rational policy in south Russia consists in utmost military and economic support of volunteer army'.[76] In September 1919, at a time when Denikin's forces were rapidly advancing northwards towards Moscow, Bagge was confident that the Bolshevik armies would 'suddenly melt away like a heap of snow under a hot sun' when confronted by determined opponents. He also believed that the Russian population was willing to 'accept Denikin's dictatorship and cooperate in the establishment of law and order' – a claim for which he did not in fact have a shred of evidence.[77] This optimistic perspective was echoed by army officers like Holman, who repeatedly assured London that Denikin would be able to 'make good the promises' which its leaders had given to the British about the Volunteer Army's ability to contain and confront Bolshevism.[78] It was only with the final collapse of the White position in south Russia, at the end of 1919, that British army officers and civilian representatives in the region began to recognise that no outside force could hope to control the forces of chaos and disintegration that had been unleashed in Russia over the previous two years.

The character of the British military presence in south Russia was rather different from its counterparts in Siberia and north Russia. The Mission to Denikin's headquarters was composed entirely of volunteers, many of whom were eager to remain in uniform following the end of hostilities in Europe. One young Captain who served in south Russia recalled many years later that he had volunteered in order 'to escape the boredom of the demobilisation period', and observed ironically that most of his colleagues were similarly 'in no hurry to return home to the bosom of their families'.[79] Many were 'pure adventurers' who chafed against the passive role assigned by London to members of the Military Mission, preferring to grab any opportunity to engage in direct hostilities with the Bolshevik forces.[80] Not surprisingly, the whole Mission was treated with a good deal of suspicion by other British army units. Friction was particularly great with military headquarters at Constantinople, which 'did not see eye to eye with the British Military Mission in south Russia'.[81] Officers in Constantinople openly expressed a view that their counterparts attached to Denikin's staff were 'quite potty', and obsessed with countering the threat posed by the Bolsheviks, while members of the Mission in turn bitterly complained at the control that Constantinople attempted to exercise over their activities. In spite of these problems, cooperation between the various forces in the region was still good enough to allow the establishment of a formidable intelligence gathering network.[82] British intelligence officers in south Russia acquired a great deal of information about the activities of Bolshevik agitators and sympathisers in territories nominally controlled by Denikin, even though they could not normally do very much to counter their activities. As was the case in Siberia and north Russia, much of the population in south Russia looked with a good deal of suspicion at the activities of White army officers and politicians, and were seldom willing to help them in their struggle against forces loyal to the government in Moscow.

The irritation felt by Britain's representatives in south Russia over the half-hearted policy adopted by the Lloyd George government found echoes in certain quarters back home in Britain. Winston Churchill's anger at the passive policy adopted by his Cabinet colleagues towards Russia was shared, in private at least, by a number of officials and politicians in London. During the course of 1919 several 'semi-official' initiatives were therefore put forward from various sources to promote a more assertive British policy in south Russia. The most important of these was an extraordinary plan designed to establish British control over the major banks in south Russia, in the hope that it would enhance Britain's economic interests *and* stabilise the economic position in territories controlled by White forces. The proposal was enthusiastically promoted by some of those with personal experience of the region, including Picton Bagge, though it was treated with considerable scepticism by his colleagues at the Foreign Office.[83] The plan was extremely ambitious, involving the establishment of a 'Central Trust' designed to serve not only as a financial holding organisation but also as a medium for gathering intelligence and disseminating propaganda. The trust was to be staffed by young Englishmen from a public school background, trained to form a nucleus of quasi-colonial administrators possessing expert knowledge about Russian economic and political conditions.[84] The proposal was at least in part the brainchild of Sidney Reilly, who, after escaping from Bolshevik Russia at the end of 1918, had been sent by British Intelligence to work in the area controlled by Denikin's forces. The Polish finacier Karol Jaroszynski, who had participated in the earlier attempt by British officials to wrest control of the Russian banking system at the end of 1917, was also involved in the new scheme. There was in truth something altogether fantastic about the whole plan, which reflected Reilly's penchant for the dramatic and theatrical, and it was on the face of it surprising that a sober-minded official like Bagge should have become so involved in the whole affair. In the event, the British government's policy towards Russia was far too indecisive to allow a grandiose scheme of the kind put forward by Bagge and Reilly to get off the ground. While the political drift in London created a climate in which officials were able to pursue their own idiosyncratic plans, the financial resources and political determination needed to make them work was never likely to be forthcoming.

Bagge's involvement with Reilly in the first half of 1919 illustrates once again the lack of a clear boundary between consular and diplomatic work on the one hand and intelligence work on the other, a distinction that became even more confused in the chaos of post-revolutionary Russia. Both Reilly and George Hill were sent to south Russia at the end of 1918, where they joined members of the British Military Mission attached to Denikin's headquarters. Reilly spent most of the next three months promoting trade and economic reconstruction in the region, as well as sending confidential reports back to London about the state of the Volunteer Army. The two men were also involved in monitoring the activities of Bolshevik agents in south Russia and – a much harder task – compiling reports about the areas of Russia under Bolshevik control. Following the withdrawal of British officials from Moscow and Petrograd in the final months of 1918, it became much harder to get news about 'what is going on in Great Russia'.[85] Although George Hill dispatched numerous couriers to different parts of the country, some of them were captured while others came back with little concrete information. The paucity of material meant that great attention was given to such scanty reports as did get through about the 'hardship, privation and repression' that was becoming the stuff of everyday life in Bolshevik Russia. The British did have a few successes in placing intelligence officers of various kinds in Moscow and Petrograd. Colonel Terence Keyes went behind 'enemy lines' on one occasion, when trying to further plans for securing British control over the Russian economy and financial system, and had to bluff his way out of trouble when arrested by a Cheka officer curious to know why a foreigner was walking the streets of Moscow with £25,000 in notes. The quick-witted Keyes pretended to be an Irish revolutionary committed to the overthrow of the imperialist British government, an unlikely cover story that for some reason seemed to satisfy the authorities.[86]

The most notable achievement in gathering clandestine information came when the redoubtable Paul Dukes was successfully placed inside Bolshevik Russia, where he led an extraordinary life under a variety of assumed names after being sent to the country at the end of 1918 to pick up the pieces of the organisation established by Captain Cromie in 1917–18.[87] Dukes had spent many years in Russia, first as a student and then as a Red Cross volunteer, with the result that he spoke the language fluently and possessed a wide range of contacts that he was able to exploit during his time in the country under the codename 'ST 25'. He established an elaborate system of couriers who smuggled his dispatches across the Finnish border, making use of a special British naval unit established for the purpose.[88] The content of Dukes' reports to London is still unclear, though it seems they contained both specific information about military and industrial affairs and more general reflections on the political situation. One report smuggled out in April 1919 painted the familiar portrait of hunger and poverty, particularly among the educated classes for whom life under Bolshevism had become in Dukes' opinion 'literally intolerable'. Although Dukes did not believe that Lenin and his colleagues could remain in power for very long, he was pessimistic as to whether their disappearance from the political scene would bring much real relief to a country that had for decades been riven by social division, cynicism and passivity. He believed instead that the chaos and anarchy that had overtaken the country had far deeper roots which would take generations to expunge:

> With an intelligentsia devoid of will, character, love of industry or political understanding, often vain and capricious; with a 'semi–intelligentsia' devoid to boot of an elementary sense of patriotism, a 'herd of sheep' driven by a handful of upstarts; with a rural population of millions of illiterates, impelled by instincts of revenge and avarice, the prospect of the coming inevitable change brings little hope of any lasting settlement, or comfort other than that any system of administration will be less intolerable than the present.[89]

The British also received intelligence reports from the periphery of the territories controlled by the Bolsheviks, particularly in Central Asia, where it proved comparatively easy to reestablish the era of the 'Great Game' by dispatching agents to cities such as Tashkent and Bokhara. Colonel F. M. Bailey of the Indian army spent more than a year underground in the territory around Tashkent, where he was involved in a series of elaborate plots to destabilise Bolshevik rule in the area.[90] He also established a series of 'runners' who carried vital information about the activities of the Bolsheviks in Central Asia to British officials based at the Consulates in Kashgar and Meshed, which had both been important intelligence gathering centres during the late nineteenth century. British officials in Finland and the Baltic states similarly received a good deal of information on developments in Russia from individuals fleeing Bolshevik rule. British Missions in these countries became important centres for collecting secret intelligence about Bolshevik Russia after 1918, although their activities had to be conducted with considerable discretion for fear of offending the sensitivities of host governments. British Missions in Warsaw and Prague also became important centres for gathering political information about developments in Moscow and its environs. Yet while the flux of the Civil War meant that there was considerable movement of people both in and out of Bolshevik controlled territory, in marked distinction to the situation which existed in later years, it was still difficult for British officials based in the periphery of the old Tsarist Empire to obtain much detailed knowledge of developments in the Bolshevik heartland. All they could do was to report to London the scraps of information that were passed to them by emigrés fleeing from Bolshevik rule.

The year 1920 was a particularly difficult one for British civilian representatives and soliders who remained on Russian territory, including south Russia, since they were forced to witness at first hand the panic that accompanied the final collapse of the White forces across the country. Several thousand Russians who had played a prominent role in assisting the British were evacuated by warship from south and north Russia amid scenes of desperation and chaos, but little could be done for the large number of refugees who sought to escape the advancing Bolsheviks. The wealthy were best placed to flee, since they could afford to pay huge sums for places on trains and boats, while the less fortunate were forced to travel more slowly by cart or on foot.[91] Colonel Keyes, who had by now become the Senior Political Officer attached to Denikin's headquarters, told London in early April that the 'Remnants of [the] Russian army and civilian refugees can no longer be considered as normal. Horror of last two years has so demoralized them that they should be treated as suffering from complete nervous breakdown'.[92] Keyes was undoubtedly right. Although the morale of the White forces rose slightly following the replacement of Denikin by General Wrangel in April 1920, it was far too late to save the situation. In February the British Consul in Odessa, when describing the fall of the town to the Bolsheviks, noted scathingly that the men of the Volunteer Army had 'degenerated into a rabble' who were incapable of defending the town even though they were numerically superior.[93] Once the White forces in south Russia had lost confidence in their ability to secure any kind of victory on the battlefield, they simply fell apart and abandoned any pretence at resistance. It was not only the local population that fell victim to the stress of the situation. A number of senior British army officers in south Russia, including Keyes himself, were ordered home in the first few months of 1920, since they were believed by the War Office to be in need of 'a change' after the strain of the previous months.[94]

The sense of futility and despair felt by British soldiers and civilian representatives in Russia during the final months of the Civil War was quite understandable. They had been placed in an impossible position by their government which, even after the reversals faced by Denikin's forces in the final months of 1919, still failed to grasp the real complexity of the situation on the ground. At the end of 1919 the government had finally agreed to appoint a High Commissioner for south Russia, a move which members of the Military Mission had called for many months earlier. The instructions given to the new Commissioner, the distinguished London University geographer and Liberal MP Sir Halford MacKinder, revealed starkly the contradictions of Britain's policy towards Russia throughout the whole Civil War. While Lord Curzon confirmed Britain's desire to see the 'establishment of constitutional government in Russia', he frankly acknowledged that it was impossible to provide the resources needed to promote such a goal.[95] Even so, the Foreign Secretary still blithely instructed the High Commissioner to encourage Denikin and his aides to come to terms with the governments of the Transcaucasian republics, to secure the end of anti-Jewish pogroms, and to establish better relations with the Poles and Ukrainians. It was of course quite impossible for any foreign representative to exert much real influence in such a chaotic situation – particularly if they were not in a position to offer substantial material incentives. MacKinder bravely went to south Russia as instructed, though only after a frustrating delay caused by bureaucratic sloth at the Foreign Office,[96] but realised on arrival that he could not hope to achieve anything. He therefore quickly tendered his resignation.

In a report prepared for the Cabinet early in 1920, the High Commissioner listed the familiar litany of reasons for the Volunteer Army's failure: bad administration; the lack of widespread popular support; and the absence of sufficient funds to buy equipment.[97] MacKinder was not able, however, to put forward any effective suggestions for salvaging the situation, though he was tartly critical of staff at the British Military Mission attached to Denikin's headquarters whom he believed were not among 'the very best'.[98] He proposed that Britain should continue to reject any agreement with the Bolshevik government for fear that if it were allowed to 'enjoy its present triumph' it might grow stronger and destroy the chance of any 'peace for the world'. MacKinder also suggested that Britain should encourage some form of anti-Bolshevik alliance between the countries of eastern and central Europe, in the hope that it would encourage the spirit of resistance to Bolshevism in Russia itself. He feared that if the Bolshevik government were simply left to 'decay of itself', Russia would become:

> an immense monotonous plain, inhabited comparatively thickly by an illiterate peasantry, a few decayed towns, speculators, mostly hated Jews, supplying such manufactured articles as could be absorbed at extortionate prices; no educated class, or none capable of diffusing more than a glimmer of light; an impoverished and superstitious Church, and bands of marauders flowing the country. Out of such a welter history might produce again, as so often before from these very plains, some great leader of nomads who would gather the bands together and fall now on this border region and now on that. Asia and Europe alike would have to maintain military borders.[99]

In the event, MacKinder's proposals had no influence on British policy towards Russia, particularly since Lloyd George was already in the process of deciding that the collapse of the White forces across the country meant that the western powers should acknowledge the reality of Bolshevik power and seek a partial normalisation of relations. The High Commissioner's views were in fact fairly typical of the attitudes displayed by many of the British army officers and civilians who had served in Russia over the previous eighteen months or so. Although Colonel Keyes may have been a particularly outspoken and zealous critic of Lenin and his government, few of his colleagues seriously dissented from the view that:

As the destructiveness of the Bolshevik creed exceeded that of any former movement, so have their hostilities far surpassed the worst horrors of any revolution in history ... The evidence of wholesale executions, without enquiry, carried out by brutal and clumsy ways, of the cold-blooded and refined tortures carried out by Chinese experts and the revolting Sadism of young Jewesses is irrefutable ... the aim of Bolshevism [is] to induce revolution in all countries in order to destroy the very roots of Christian civilization.[100]

By 1920 the Bolsheviks had become for many Britons in Russia – and in London as well – the latest incarnation of the age-old tradition of Russian savagery and barbarism.

While many British civilian officials and military men posted to Russia after 1917 believed that Bolshevism was a natural expression of Russian culture, most of them were also paradoxically inclined to dismiss the idea that the November Revolution had deep historical roots. As a result, many of the reports sent to London between 1918 and 1920 were filled with predictions of the Bolshevik government's impending demise – predictions which time and again were proved to be wrong. Too many British representatives in Russia were ready to account for the Bolsheviks' survival in the Civil War simply by reference to the 'iron will' displayed by their leaders. The ruthless reorganisation of the economy to serve military needs, when combined with Trotsky's transformation of the Red Army into an effective and disciplined fighting force, certainly played an important role in allowing Lenin and his colleagues to hold on to power.[101] There was a greater measure of popular support for the Bolshevik government than most British soldiers and many civilian officials were prepared to acknowledge. More importantly, there was a real distaste among the population for the reactionary policies adopted by the White Generals who dominated the anti-Bolshevik resistance, particularly after the Omsk coup in November 1918 signalled the virtual defeat of the moderate socialist and liberal opponents of the Moscow government as an effective political force. A handful of individuals, such as Frank Lindley, were intelligent enough to understand that the events of 1917 had transformed Russia for ever, making it difficult to impose order by force on a population that relished its new economic and political freedoms. However, the withdrawal of virtually all members of Britain's diplomatic corps in the first half of 1918 removed the most skilful political observers from Russia. Many of the civilian officials who remained behind, like Lockhart and Bagge, lacked the judgement and experience characteristic of more senior professional diplomats. Army officers posted to Russia were even less adept at understanding the changes taking place around them; they were conditioned by their training to trust in the virtues of order and hierarchy, and were too inclined to believe that a strong leader provided with adequate resources could impose order on a turbulent country. In reality, the various White Generals and politicians did not lose the Civil War simply because of political divisions and poor administration. They lost it because no individual or group among them managed to attract any genuine measure of popular support.

Even though the Bolsheviks had all but won the Civil War by the early summer of 1920, at least in the sense that they had defeated the main White armies, many British officials responsible for monitoring Russian affairs still doubted whether Lenin and the other Bolshevik leaders would be able to retain power in the years ahead. Lockhart, who was appointed to the Consulate in Prague following his return from Moscow at the end of 1918, held numerous meetings with Russian emigrés who had fled to the city in an attempt to escape the turmoil in their own country. Their reports led him to believe that the 'appalling' economic conditions in Russia would in time provoke a revolution against the Bolshevik government, even though the population currently showed 'complete apathy' about all political questions.[102] Similar dispatches were sent by British diplomats and consular officials in the Baltic, emphasising the fragility of Bolshevik rule despite the success of the Red Army in the Civil War. Information obtained by agents of the Special Intelligence Service (SIS) inside Russia also suggested that the position of Lenin and his colleagues was increasingly insecure. One SIS report even suggested that the Moscow government might provoke a war with its neighbours in order to divert the population's attention away from their atrocious living conditions.[103] British officials watching the country from abroad were therefore not particularly surprised at the eruption of widespread social disorder in the first few months of 1921. The SIS compiled numerous reports about the crisis, detailing the outbreak of peasant riots and a sharp rise in the number of urban strikes which followed the government's decision to reduce food rations. The author of one these reports spoke for many of his colleagues in both the Intelligence and Diplomatic Services when he observed that the problems facing Lenin and his colleagues were 'almost impossible' to resolve.[104] The eruption of a serious rebellion in March 1921 among sailors at the Kronstadt naval base, which had provided one of the bedrocks of support for the Bolsheviks since the heady days of 1917, appeared to confirm the depth of the crisis. The SIS even managed to place one of their agents inside the base, who reported in detail on the strength of the men's discontent and their determination to bring about changes in the policies and composition of the Moscow government.[105]

Although the situation of the Bolshevik government's was without doubt extremely parlous in the first months of 1921, the reports sent to London still often fell into the trap of underestimating the resilience of Lenin and his colleagues. The revolt at Kronstadt, along with the strikes and riots in Petrograd, were certainly an ominous sign that the Bolshevik leadership could no longer rely on the support of the class in whose name it had seized power in 1917. The disorders that swept the country early in 1921 were, however, for the most part uncoordinated and unplanned. The British representative in Helsingfors (Helsinki), George Kidston, rightly noted that the information which percolated through to the outside world about events in Russa was not very reliable, since most of the informants were White emigrés desperate to convince themselves and others that the Bolshevik government was on the point of collapse.[106] In the event, the Moscow government was eventually able to use loyal troops to put down the Kronstadt rebellion, brutally killing 'hundreds, if not thousands' of sailors in the process. The strikes in the major cities also gradually subsided, while a certain degree of order was restored to the Russian countryside. Once again, the Bolsheviks had confounded their critics by surviving against apparently insurmountable odds. Nevertheless, although the regime survived the immediate crisis, Lenin and at least some of the other Party leaders had become aware that they needed to act decisively to defend their position. The early spring of 1921 marked a watershed in the history of Bolshevik Russia, as the Soviet leadership began to adopt new policies and tactics designed to secure its position while at the same time laying the foundation for the development of a socialist society in Russia. British officials who returned to the country in the summer of 1921, charged with establishing a new de facto relationship with the Bolshevik government, were witnesses to one of the most important stages in the development of Soviet society.

7

A Very Ordinary Bureaucracy

It was clear by 1921 to even the most virulent anti-Communist observer that the Soviet regime was not in danger of imminent collapse, even if hopes continued to run high in some circles that Lenin and his colleagues could not maintain themselves in power indefinitely. The White armies had been smashed by troops loyal to Moscow, while British and other allied forces had retreated ignominiously in the wake of their failure to exercise any lasting impact on Russia's political development. The survival of Lenin's government therefore elevated to the forefront of international attention the vexed question of its relationship with the other governments of Europe. It was not a situation that either side had expected to confront. The Bolsheviks had been confident that the seizure of power in Petrograd in 1917 was the first act in a worldwide revolution that would quickly lead to the establishment of friendly socialist governments across the globe. On being appointed Commissar of Foreign Affairs, Leon Trotsky had even felt sanguine enough to suggest that his only role in his new job would be to issue a number of decrees setting out the Bolsheviks' aims and objectives, after which he could 'shut up shop' and wait for world revolution to destroy the forces hostile to the new regime in Moscow.[1] The governments of western Europe and America, by contrast, could never quite bring themselves to believe that the Bolshevik seizure of power was anything more than an unpleasant episode that would soon come to an end once sanity and common sense prevailed again among the Russian people. By the end of 1920, however, both sides were increasingly having to face the reality of the situation and rethink their attitude towards one another.

British policy towards Russia during the 1920s was confused and contradictory, in large part because it was vulnerable to the influence of domestic political passions that hindered the pursuit of consistent foreign policy objectives. In 1921 the Lloyd George government extended de facto recognition to the Bolshevik government when it negotiated a Trade Agreement with Moscow. Yet far from ensuring the development of harmonious relations between the two countries, the next three years were marked by ill-tempered disputes and quarrels. The appointment of a minority Labour government in 1924 led to the rapid de jure recognition of the Moscow government by Britain, but the publication of the infamous Zinoviev Letter at the end of the year helped bring about the return of a Conservative administration whose members looked with grave suspicion at the Soviet leadership. Formal diplomatic relations continued for the next two and a half years, despite the challenge posed by events such as the 1926 General Strike, which was widely believed in London to be funded and organised from Moscow. In time, however, the influence of the diehard anti-Communists in Cabinet began to exert a decisive influence. Diplomatic relations between Britain and Soviet Russia were broken off in May 1927, following a dramatic raid by the Metropolitan Police on the headquarters of the Soviet trade organisation Arcos, in search of evidence that officials working there were engaged in espionage activities.

The formulation of British policy towards Russia during the 1920s reflected wider changes in the way that foreign policy was made in London in the years after 1918.[2] The outbreak of the First World War had discredited the claims of professional diplomats that they alone knew how to manage international crises effectively. Lloyd George's dislike of professional diplomats, whom he believed were invented 'simply to waste time',[3] also meant that the Foreign Office and Diplomatic Service, which were merged into a single organisation in 1919,[4] found it increasingly difficult to retain their power and authority in the aftermath of the Great War. Although the extent of diplomats' loss of influence vis à vis politicians has sometimes been overstated, the reality of the change cannot be doubted. This was particularly true when foreign policy issues were politically sensitive, as was the case with almost all questions involving Russia during the 1920s. The position of the Foreign Office was especially difficult in 1924, when a minority Labour government came to power, since many of the new Ministers were instinctively suspicious of the privileged world of the professional diplomat.[5] Even so assertive a figure as Lord Curzon, who served as Foreign Secretary from 1919 to 1924, found the diminution of power and influence associated with his post to be frustrating.[6] The situation was a little easier for Austen Chamberlain, when he went to the Foreign Office at the end of 1924, since the Prime Minister, Stanley Baldwin, took far less interest in foreign affairs than had Lloyd George.[7] Nevertheless, as Chamberlain quickly found out when he tried to pursue a policy towards Russia that came into conflict with the 'russophobic' instincts of his Cabinet colleagues, no Foreign Secretary who held office after 1918 could hope to enjoy the independence and influence of his nineteenth-century predecessors. The same was even more true for his officials.

The origins of the Trade Agreement that was signed in March 1921 between Soviet Russia and Britain went back more than a year, to the first weeks of 1920, when a considerable number of British troops were still stationed in the south of the country. Lloyd George recognised that the Bolsheviks' impending victory in the Civil War meant that Lenin and his colleagues would soon be firmly established in power. He therefore proposed to the Allied Council in Paris that the economic blockade of Russia should be suspended in order to rebuild trade across Europe.[8] Although the Prime Minister's proposal was inspired by a sense of realpolitik rather than any sympathy for the Moscow government, it met with little support from the other countries represented at Paris, where the majority still favoured maintaining an economic and diplomatic *cordon sanitaire* around Russia. Even so, Lloyd George persisted in his efforts, with the result that a Soviet delegation arrived in London in the middle of 1920 to discuss possible terms for a bilateral Trade Agreement. The negotiations proved difficult, not least so because they were interrupted by the crisis which developed when Britain offered material support to the Polish government following its unexpected decision to launch an invasion of Russia in an ill-fated attempt to take advantage of the confusion there. Nevertheless, an agreement was eventually reached, though only in the face of strong opposition from Lord Curzon, who was reluctant to come to terms with a regime that was actively disseminating revolutionary propaganda in many parts of the British Empire.[9] From the perspective of the Soviet government, the attractions of the Trade Agreement were obvious, since it provided them with a form of de facto recognition by the most important power in Europe, as well as holding out the possibility of obtaining foreign loans to rebuild an economy shattered by years of war and revolution. For the British government, by contrast, the rationale was more complex, though the prospect of increased trade was certainly appealing at a time of rising unemployment, an argument that was put by activists in the 'Hands-Off Russia' movement who sought to promote a more positive policy towards Moscow.[10]

Lloyd George and his colleagues also hoped that a Trade Agreement would help to limit Soviet propaganda and reduce Moscow's support for revolutionary groups operating in areas of particular sensitivity to the British. Reports from the Special Intelligence Service based on material obtained in Reval indicated that the Soviet government was funding Sinn Fein 'germ cells' in Dublin,[11] while it was also known in London that the Bolsheviks were providing active support for revolutionary groups in India via the provision of special training facilities at the town of Tashkent in Central Asia.[12] However, Lloyd George's most important motive for promoting the Trade Agreement was his hope that closer international economic integration could tame the excesses of the Soviet regime both domestically and abroad, since the Moscow government would be fearful of the costs of antagonising its trading partners. In a speech to the House of Commons, the Prime Minister expressed his conviction that 'Commerce has a sobering influ- ence ... The simple sums in addition and subtraction which it inculcates soon disposes of wild theories'.[13] He rejected the idea that Russia should be excluded from the international economy, arguing that a continuation of the blockade would simply play into the hands of the extremists in Moscow. Although the Prime Minister was not well liked in the Foreign Office, his support for developing and maintaining some kind of relationship with the Bolshevik government was widely endorsed by senior officials there in the years that followed. The belief that sustained contact with the Soviet government, however distasteful, was more likely to serve British interests than a complete rupture in relations informed countless memoranda by Foreign Secretaries and officials alike throughout the 1920s. The principle was supported even more enthusiastically by British representatives serving in Soviet Russia itself.

The fiction that the Trade Agreement established purely commercial relations was sustained by the title chosen for the small group of individuals selected to go to Moscow in 1921 to develop a new relationship with the government there: 'The British Commercial Mission to Russia'. The man chosen to head the new Mission was Robert Hodgson, who had been Acting High Commissioner in the Siberian city of Omsk for a short time following the departure of Sir Charles Eliot in 1919. The instructions issued to Hodgson noted that, while economic questions would form the major part of its work, his Mission was expected to perform other quasi-diplomatic tasks as well. The new 'Commercial Agent', as Hodgson was styled, was given considerable latitude to define his role, so that he could respond as necessary to 'the peculiar conditions prevailing in Russia'. He was reminded to 'bear in mind the necessity of His Majesty's Government being kept fully informed on questions of political, social and industrial importance'.[14] The task assigned to the

Mission was a difficult one, and Hodgson was in some ways a surprising choice to serve as its Head. In spite of the importance of his new post, he was not a professional diplomat by background, having spent most of his working life in the much derided Consular Service – something which could not of course be avoided by the British government given its determination to avoid establishing formal diplomatic relations. Nevertheless, Hodgson undoubtedly possessed a number of skills and attributes that were to prove of value in his new role. He had served in Russia continually since 1906, working mostly at the British Consulate in Vladivostok, where he developed a first-class command of the Russian language and a good knowledge of the social and political tensions besetting the Tsarist Empire. He had also acquired a reputation for being a diligent and helpful official,[15] though it was only with the onset of the Civil War that he was given an opportunity to carry out any significant political and diplomatic functions. The enthusiasm and skill with which he performed his work during this crucial period made a considerable impression at the Foreign Office and presumably accounted for the decision to send him back to Russia in 1921.

Hodgson worked hard to carry out his duties throughout his six years in Moscow, driven at times by an almost missionary zeal to protect the relationship between Britain and Russia from the political storms that constantly threatened to pull it apart. Nevertheless, his task turned out to be almost impossible – given the level of suspicion and hostility between the two governments. Hodgson's lack of experience did show itself on more than one occasion, and he sometimes incurred the wrath of senior Foreign Office officials frustrated by his failure to understand the subtleties of diplomatic protocol.[16] His determined efforts to defend the Anglo-Soviet relationship against attack by the anti-Communist zealots in the Cabinet occasionally caused him to overstep the boundaries of normal diplomatic practice. When formal diplomatic relations between Britain and Russia were established in 1924, and the status of the Commercial Mission was upgraded, Hodgson was trusted enough in London to be kept on in Moscow as Chargé d'Affaires. The feeling nevertheless remained in some quarters that he was something of a 'plodder' who lacked the talents and skills required to make a really successful diplomat. It was doubtless for this reason that, when he finally left Russia in 1927, Hodgson was 'rewarded' with the distinctly unrewarding post of British Minister in Albania.

The other British officials posted to Russia during 1921–27 shared many of Hodgson's characteristic virtues and vices. They were all drawn from the ranks of consular and commercial officials, rather than the

regular diplomatic corps, and most of them displayed the same combination of diligence and occasional naivety as the Head of the
Commercial Mission himself. As a result, while Hodgson's colleagues
were for the most part reasonably well-equipped to report on the
economic and political changes that took place in Soviet Russia during
the 1920s, they sometimes struggled when drawn into the complex
world of diplomacy and international relations.[17] Thomas Preston, who
served as the British Official Agent in Petrograd, already had considerable experience of Russia when he arrived in the city in 1922. Like
Hodgson, he had worked as a consular official in Russia for a number
of years prior to the outbreak of war in 1914, before moving to Siberia
during the traumatic period of allied intervention. While at Ekaterinburg and Omsk, he was required to write numerous reports about the
local situation, a skill which proved useful after his return to Russia
when he was expected to keep both Hodgson and the Foreign Office
informed about political developments in the country's second biggest
city. William Peters, who served as deputy to Hodgson at the Moscow
Mission, did not by contrast have very much personal experience of
Russia when he first arrived in the country in 1921 (though he had
been a member of the ill-fated Commercial Mission sent to the country
in 1918 to explore the possibility of establishing trading links with the
Bolsheviks). He was a formidably intelligent and hard-working official,
who quickly adjusted to the demands of his new surroundings. Over
the next six years, Peters produced a large number of detailed memoranda about the state of the Soviet economy – an astonishing feat given
the paucity of reliable statistics made available by the government in
Moscow. He also served as an effective stand-in whenever Hodgson
returned to Britain on leave. Peters was in fact the only senior official
posted to Russia in 1921–27 who had not previously worked in Russia
in some capacity. The former Consul in Moscow, Montgomery Grove,
spent two years at the Mission between 1921 and 1923, before being
replaced by John Waite, another old 'Russia hand', who had worked at
various Consulates in the south of the country since the early 1890s.
George Paton, who took charge in Vladivostok, also knew Russia well.
This wealth of experience undoubtedly helped officials to settle down
in their new posts. At the same time, the society that Hodgson and his
staff once knew so well had largely disintegrated by the 1920s, blown
apart by the trauma of war and revolution. As a result, they were seldom
able to rely on old contacts when seeking information about the new
world growing up around them, being instead forced to develop new
methods of working in order to carry out their duties effectively.

Although one of the most important functions of the Moscow Mission was to supply the Foreign Office with information about economic and political affairs in Soviet Russia, the job turned out to be a complex one that made the difficulties faced by British diplomats in Russia before 1917 seem almost straightforward by comparison. The Mission's members at first found it difficult to come to grips with the nuances of Bolshevik psychology. It took time for them to grasp the delicate interplay of ideological commitment and pragmatic action that was the hallmark of the Moscow government during its first decade. Yet the greatest obstacle they faced when trying to make sense of events was simply the lack of hard information on which to base their reports. Although the culture of official secrecy only reached its heights in the 1930s, after Stalin had assumed absolute power over the country, it was already well-established by the time Hodgson and his staff arrived in Moscow.

The most important figures in the Soviet leadership seldom deigned to have any dealings with the British Mission. Lenin and the other Bolshevik leaders looked askance at the institutions and conventions of regular diplomacy, preferring to rely on organisations such as the infamous Comintern to further the interests of Soviet Russia and promote global revolution.[18] They did not even ascribe much importance to their own Commissariat of Foreign Affairs, which was charged with conducting 'formal' diplomatic relations with other countries.[19] Hodgson and his staff understood the dual nature of Soviet foreign policy perfectly well, and spent a good deal of time reporting to London on the activities of the Comintern and other revolutionary instruments of Soviet foreign policy. Nevertheless, most of their routine dealings were in practice with the Commissariat of Foreign Affairs, particularly its two leading figures, Georgy Chicherin and Maxim Litvinov.[20] Although neither man occupied a particularly influential position in the Soviet hierarchy, they were the most senior officials that staff at the British Mission met on a regular basis. Chicherin was the scion of a wealthy Russian family who had, like many of his peers, rebelled at an early age against the privileged world into which he was born. As a young man he had worked for a time in the Tsarist Foreign Ministry, but left it when he became an activist in the Menshevik Party. During the First World War he attracted the attention of Lenin, who was sufficiently impressed by his abilities to appoint him as Commissar for Foreign Affairs in March 1918, after Trotsky vacated the post to take charge of the Red Army. Chicherin was a decidedly eccentric individual, whose irregular working habits and penchant for night-time meetings frequently drove his subordinates to fury. In a private letter to London, the Head of the British Mission described him as:

> a strange individual ... extraordinarily shy and nervous. He is to be met at odd times in the disgusting staircases of the Commissariat for Foreign Affairs, wandering about with a telegram or looking for a bit of blotting paper – too shy to send for the office boy or the Soviet substitute for one. He has no idea of time or space – is quite likely to promise to come and dine and change his mind on your doorstep and go home again.[21]

Hodgson was, by contrast, reasonably at home with Litvinov, a more outgoing and ebullient character than his master. One Soviet diplomat who defected a few years later recalled that 'it would be difficult to find two men so different in character' as Chicherin and his deputy,[22] and it seems certain that there was a good deal of tension between them. These problems were not, however, evident to officials at the British Mission, who managed to maintain a reasonable working relationship with both men throughout the six years that Hodgson was in charge.

Like other foreign representatives, the Mission's staff were banned from having direct dealings with Soviet officials outside the Commissariat of Foreign Affairs, which made it hard for them to obtain information about economic and political questions. The closed nature of Soviet officialdom would have mattered less to British representatives if they had been able to rely on alternative sources of information, but this proved in practice to be very difficult. The press had been heavily censored from the time the Bolsheviks seized power in 1917. By 1921 no publications were permitted that directly criticised the government and its policies. Censorship was more relaxed when technical economic issues were under review, and William Peters made extensive and intelligent use of specialised Soviet publications when preparing reports for dispatch to London. A close reading of the press also provided Hodgson and his colleagues with insights into other areas of Soviet political life, especially since the speeches of prominent leaders were often reproduced verbatim in the newspapers. Staff at the Mission quickly learned to cultivate the 'Kremlinological' skills that became so important for later generations of western diplomats and academics, learning how to identify the significance of apparently trivial pronouncements by individuals in the Soviet leadership. It was never an exact science. The Soviet government's control of the media allowed it to downplay the importance of such domestic catastrophes as the famine which broke out in the early 1920s. Censorship also made it possible to minimise the significance of the outbreaks of popular disorder which broke out from time to time.

A number of the Mission's members had personal contacts dating from their years of service in the old Tsarist Empire, which they used to acquire information that could not be obtained elsewhere. The reports sent to London were quite often based on 'private sources' that could not be named for fear that a copy might fall into the hands of the Secret Police.[23] Most of the people they knew before 1917 had long since fled the country, however, while those who remained were almost invariably excluded from positions of power and influence. It was in any case difficult for British officials to persuade nervous Soviet citizens to have any dealings with them. When Preston arranged to visit an old acquaintance in Petersburg soon after his arrival in the city towards the end of 1922, he was forced to don the clothes of a workman and make his way secretly to his friend's apartment so as to avoid compromising the family.[24]

The difficulty of developing personal links with Soviet citizens was exacerbated by the close scrutiny which the Secret Police maintained on all foreign Missions. The British Mission's staff usually felt themselves to be quite safe throughout the 1920s, despite the 'spontaneous' street demonstrations that took place at times of particular tension in Anglo-Soviet relations. Hodgson himself believed that the Soviet government was fearful of the consequences that might follow if any harm should come to the representatives of a major foreign power.[25] The representatives of smaller powers could, by contrast, find themselves in a rather more perilous situation, as one unfortunate Estonian official discovered in 1923 following the death of a Communist activist in the custody of his government. A hostile crowd formed outside the Estonian Consulate demanding that the Consul be handed over for the imposition of summary justice by drowning in the nearby River Neva. Since the Soviet authorities made little serious effort to intervene, the unfortunate representative was fortunate to escape with his life by fleeing through a back entrance.[26] The demonstrations that took place outside British official premises were usually far more ordered and ritualistic affairs, carefully orchestrated by the authorities to bring pressure on the British government at times of tension between London and Moscow. In any case, members of the Secret Police were usually on hand to make sure that the protesters did not get out of hand.

Given all of these problems, the day to day organisation of the British Mission was an important question from the moment Hodgson first arrived in Moscow. Although Peters had been sent ahead to sort out the housing of the Mission, when Hodgson and the remaining officials reached the Soviet capital in June 1921 they found that the building allocated to the Mission was far too small to provide sufficient accommodation.[27] To make matters worse, the authorities had already put in place their own domestic staff, who had clearly been instructed to report on the activities of the new occupants. A permanent guard of eight soldiers was posted just outside the building in order to deter any visitors from entering it.[28] After a few weeks, Hodgson succeeded 'in chasing out' the servants so thoughtfully provided by his Soviet hosts,[29] but there was little he could do to get rid of the soldiers at the gate, even though the close watch that was kept on the Mission proved to be a source of enormous frustration to all its occupants.

Harassment by the authorities did not correspond in any obvious way with the peaks and troughs in the Anglo-Soviet relationship, and some of the worst problems occurred in 1924, shortly after the MacDonald government had extended de jure recognition to the Moscow government. In May of that year, Hodgson wrote privately to Litvinov complaining about the treatment endured by his staff over the previous three years. He described how Soviet citizens working at the Mission had been blackmailed and threatened by the Secret Police, in order to make them spy on the activities of the British officials based there. Those who refused were told that they 'would disappear into jail and never get out' – a threat which usually had the desired effect.[30] The rationale behind many of these attempts to penetrate the Mission was not always obvious. The elderly woman who supplied Hodgson with second-hand furniture was asked to submit a report on her client, even though she had no access to information of any possible value. Rather more sinisterly, the Soviet government also used *agents provocateurs* in an attempt to implicate British officials in activities that were incompatible with their official status. On one occasion, a man turned up at the Leningrad Consulate falsely claiming to be a representative of a certain Colonel Boyce, who was at this stage a senior official in British Intelligence operating out of the Baltic states. The staff in the building fortunately refused to have anything to do with their unexpected visitor, which was not surprising since they almost certainly had no knowledge of Boyce's activities.[31] As far as can be ascertained, considerable care was taken by the British government throughout the 1920s to avoid contacts between their regular representatives in Russia and individuals working in the country on behalf of the Special Intelligence Service.

It was not only the Moscow Mission and Preston's Petrograd office that attracted the attention of the Secret Police. The Soviet authorities also sought to infiltrate the Consulate in Vladivostok, on one occasion trying to force a young female typist who worked there to report on the activities of George Paton. She bravely refused to cooperate and told her employer about the incident, who promptly relayed details to Hodgson in Moscow. Amazingly, Hodgson brought the incident to the attention of Litvinov, who sportingly promised to hold a full inquiry into the affair. Not surprisingly, the luckless typist fled across the border to the Chinese city of Harbin rather than waiting for Soviet justice to take its magisterial course, presumably cursing her erstwhile employers as she went.[32] In this nervous atmosphere, in which foreigners were treated as virtual enemies, Soviet citizens quickly recognised the risks involved in having any dealings with British officials; indeed, even officials at the Commissariat of Foreign Affairs tried to keep their contacts with foreign representatives to a minimum, for fear that they might be accused of betraying their country. Hodgson worked hard to encourage visitors to his Mission, and a few brave souls did arrive to play tennis or attend one of the occasional musical evenings that were held there, but attendance at these functions could prove costly. One young woman was imprisoned after visiting the Mission to enquire about the possibility of emigrating to Canada, while others were arrested for attending parties there.[33] Preston was even convinced that some of his visitors in Petrograd paid with their lives for their audacity, though Hodgson was inclined to doubt this claim – at least before the final break between London and Moscow in 1927, when the Soviet authorities brought capital charges of espionage against a large number of individuals who had made some form of contact with British officials over the previous six years.

One of the biggest obstacles faced by Hodgson and his colleagues when reporting on domestic affairs in Soviet Russia was the same one that dogged their predecessors before 1917: the sheer size and diversity of the country. The difficulties were compounded by the Soviet government's reluctance to allow the establishment of posts outside Moscow. Hodgson found these constraints almost insuperable during his first year in Moscow and furiously lobbied the Foreign Office to find some way of establishing an official presence in other major cities.[34] Even when Thomas Preston obtained permission to take up residence in Petrograd at the end of 1922, he immediately encountered the same difficulties faced by staff at the Moscow Mission when seeking access to reliable information. Nor was it possible to overcome these problems by sending British officials on 'fact-finding' tours around the country. The workload at the Moscow Mission was so great that no individual could be spared for any significant amount of time. In any case, the Soviet authorities were reluctant to authorise trips that might give foreign representatives an opportunity to obtain information that the government wanted to keep secret. One of the few exceptions came in 1925, several years after the Mission was first established, when Hodgson and a senior official from the Foreign Office's Northern Department, Owen O'Malley, obtained permission to travel through southern Russia in order to see conditions there at first hand. The idea for the trip was originally Hodgson's, who wrote to London at the end of 1924 noting that the Mission needed access to a wider range of information if it was to provide the kind of detailed reports demanded by the Foreign Office.[35] He had already spoken unofficially to Chicherin, who had given permission to make the journey. O'Malley was a logical choice to accompany Hodgson, since he had dealt with Russian affairs for some years at the Foreign Office and possessed the kind of knowledge and experience required to make him an ideal observer. In any case, senior officials at the Foreign Office were increasingly keen in the 1920s that staff based in London should have more opportunity to acquire more direct experience of the countries with which they dealt. The Assistant Under Secretary there, J. D. Gregory, noted that 'Many of our mistakes arise from our being unable to visualise the countries and peoples with which we deal'. He also observed that the arrival of a fresh pair of eyes at an overseas post could help to overcome the parochialism of 'the diplomat permanently established in foreign parts', who often lacked the broader perspective and knowledge possessed by those based in London.[36] O'Malley therefore set off for Moscow in April 1925 to 'observe and remember the sights and words which governments cannot conceal or silence'.

O'Malley's official account of the journey provided a vivid panorama of a country racked by poverty and a permanent sense of psychological siege.[37] Like so many British visitors to Russia, he found that 'the romantic view of the Russian character and nation' could not survive 'close contact with the country and its people'. The filth of public buildings, including the hotels and railway stations, appalled him; so too did the dreariness of the propaganda posters which covered every inch of spare wall-space in the major cities. Although O'Malley's official report on his trip did not yield any new statistics or startling information about Soviet policy, it provided his colleagues at the Foreign Office with a lively summary of the kind of material that the Mission had been sending to London over the previous few years. Despite this success, Hodgson and his staff were still not able to find the time and energy to make further trips of a similar kind. Their experience of Russia during the 1920s was always limited to a small number of major cities and a tiny handful of unrepresentative contacts, which did not provide them with much real opportunity to sense the mood of the country or the state of popular morale.

Given the conditions in which they lived and worked, daily life at the British Mission in Moscow and the Consulates in Petrograd and Vladivostok was far from easy. The atmosphere of restrained hostility surrounding them was inevitably debilitating and depressing, and could only be partly relieved by trips back to Britain on leave. Thomas Preston recalled in his memoirs how on arrival in Petrograd he was 'rudely told that no bourgeois were allowed to enter' the hotel in which he was due to stay, since it was filled by hundreds of delegates attending a Comintern Conference, who jeered him as he retreated out into the night.[38] The unfriendliness of Soviet officials, and the terror of ordinary citizens at the prospect of any dealings with foreign representatives, meant that British officials had to rely on each other for company. Although they met regularly with representatives from the few countries that had diplomatic relations with Moscow, there were none of the grand receptions or informal *soireés* that had made life bearable in pre-revolutionary Russia. Most officials left their families back in England, since they were reluctant to expose them to the rigours of life in Soviet Russia, but this just served to enhance the sense of loneliness and isolation. The few officials who brought their wives to Moscow could not find decent accommodation in the city and were forced to live 'in relative discomfort' in the cramped Mission building itself, while unmarried men were 'obliged to sleep two to a bedroom'. The poor living conditions inevitably took a toll on the nerves of the staff, even though Hodgson worked hard to make things as easy as possible for his colleagues. Life at the Mission was far less hierarchical than was normal at British posts abroad. O'Malley wrote after his 1925 visit that 'Mr Hodgson has organised the life of his establishment without regard to the official and social distinctions observable at other diplomatic posts. The Head of the Mission, his diplomatic and consular officers, archivists, clerk and steward sit down to every meal at a common mess with a disregard of convention which naturally renders the Moscow Mission quite unlike any other Embassy or Legation'. The visitor was inclined to ascribe this informality to the peculiar circumstances in which the Mission staff found themselves.[39] In fact, the egalitarian tone came far more easily to Hodgson than it would have to an official who had spent his life in the Diplomatic Service. Everyday life at British Consulates in Russia during the pre-war years had always been a far more relaxed affair than at the Petersburg Embassy.

Conditions were if anything worse for the handful of staff in Petrograd and Vladivostok than they were for their colleagues in the capital. Because their numbers were so limited, they could not create a private life built around professional relationships, as happened at the Moscow Mission. Thomas Preston knew that he was immensely privileged when compared with the Soviet population, but still could not help feeling that the building in which he worked was a 'luxurious prison'. Even in Moscow, where he spent several months before moving to Petrograd in 1922, he was assailed by a feeling of 'extraordinary loneliness', despite the fact that the Mission there was 'like an oasis in the desert'.[40] The situation was still bleaker in Vladivostok on the Pacific coast, where the sense of isolation was more stark and corrosive than ever. Like their colleagues in Moscow, British officials in Petrograd and Vladivostok could not by the very nature of their work separate their private and professional lives. Although they struggled to make their reports as objective and dispassionate as possible, the daily concerns and worries under which they laboured inevitably influenced the way they viewed the dramatic changes which took place in Soviet Russia during the 1920s.

The British government did of course have access to sources of information about Soviet political life other than reports compiled by Foreign Office staff posted to the country. A number of journalists representing major western newspapers were based in Russia, and their reports were carefully studied in London before being filed for future reference. The Foreign Office also acquired copies of the numerous books written in the 1920s by visitors to the Soviet Union, in the hope that they might provide useful information about daily life in the country. In general, Foreign Office staff preferred not to rely too much on accounts by casual visitors, particularly since many of them were avowed supporters of the Soviet regime. Diplomatic posts in countries bordering the Soviet Union continued to serve as a vital source of information. The reports of travellers and emigrés collected there were transmitted regularly to London. British Missions in the Baltic states were particularly important as listening posts,[41] along with Consulates in central Asia such as the one at Kashgar, which provided London with detailed reports about disorders and rebellions against Soviet rule in the region.[42] A number of these posts, including the ones at Reval and Kashgar, were also involved in work carried out by the Special Intelligence Service, which was surprisingly successful at acquiring sensitive material about Russia during the early 1920s.[43] Documents were obtained showing the extent of the Soviet government's ongoing concern about the level of domestic opposition, particularly in areas such as the Ukraine, where the imposition of Communist rule from Moscow challenged the nationalist sentiments of large sections of the population.[44] Other material obtained by the Special Intelligence Service showed the Soviet government's anxiety over possible unrest among the working-class population of the major cities,[45] as well as its fears about the ease with which anti-Communist activists were able to enter and leave the country via the Baltic states.[46] The SIS also predictably gave a good deal of attention to monitoring the composition and activities of the Secret Police.[47] None of this material emanated from the highest reaches of the government in Moscow. It did, nevertheless, provide the Foreign Office in London with a useful insight into the insecurities and doubts of Lenin and his colleagues at a critical time in the development of the Soviet state.

During the years between 1921 and 1927, British officials in Russia reported on a massive array of topics ranging from the success of the so-called New Economic Policy through to the officially sponsored attack on religious belief. Although Bolshevik rule still seemed comparatively fragile when Hodgson and his staff arrived in Moscow in the summer of 1921, they never shared the view, common in some quarters in London, that the Bolshevik government was on the point of collapse. Just a few months after his arrival, during one of the periodic crises in Anglo-Soviet relations, Hodgson emphasised his belief in the solidity of the regime in a dispatch to London. He told Lord Curzon that there was no chance of 'an internal movement [causing] the downfall of the present regime', since 'The country is too depressed, too apathetic and too miserable to allow of anything more than sporadic outbursts of discontent to take place. The organisation of counter-revolution on a scale which could seriously menace the Soviet government is hardly conceivable'.[48] Although Hodgson reported in detail over the next few years on the huge economic and political problems confronting Soviet Russia, and provided details of military rebellions and public protests against the government in Moscow, he never wavered in his conviction that the regime could crush any serious threat to its survival, a fact which he considered made it more important than ever to retain some form of official Anglo-Soviet relationship. In putting forward this view, the Head of the Commercial Mission showed himself to be shrewder than many officials and politicians in London. He was further from the mark when he insisted in the autumn of 1921 that 'the [Soviet]

Government is becoming communist in little but name', a theme that similarly ran through many of his dispatches during the following years. Hodgson's certainty that the ideological zeal displayed by Lenin and his colleagues would fade away as they confronted the practical problems of government proved to be his greatest error of judgement during his years in Moscow.

While the Mission's staff never believed that the Soviet regime could be dislodged by force or direct challenge, they were under no illusions about the desperate condition of the country at the time of their arrival in the summer of 1921. Soviet Russia seldom made a good first impression on British officials. Hodgson and his colleagues were struck from the time of their arrival in Moscow by the decay which afflicted all the major cities:

> The general aspect of the town of Moscow is deplorable. There are a few small provision shops open, a café here and there, some ladies' hat shops and a florist or two. There are also a fair number of little shops where repairs of almost every conceivable article are carried on ... The appearance of such as are open is pitiable in view of the almost complete absence of goods for sale. Whole streets of offices and shops show nothing but windows broken and boarded up, with chaos and rubbish inside. Many houses have been destroyed as the result of civil war and no effort has been made to rebuild them or to repair the buildings which have suffered.[49]

The news which filtered through to the Mission about life in the countryside during the middle of 1921 was even bleaker, since famine was killing huge numbers of people in rural areas. Hodgson told the Foreign Office in August that in the Volga region children were being abandoned without food or clothes, while the adults were eating 'grass, bread made of roots, horses and other rubbish'.[50]

Preston's impressions of Soviet Russia at the time of his arrival a year later were little better, even though by this time the state of the countryside was improving and the level of economic activity was higher than a year earlier. A 'feeling of depression' came over him when he looked at passers-by in the streets of Moscow who all 'appeared to be in rags'.[51] Many members of formerly well-to-do noble families were desperately trying to hawk the remnants of their possessions on the streets in order to buy food, since they were barred from any form of employment by the Soviet government. The material conditions of the population were quite dreadful, since they lived in 'extremely bad and dirty flats and, in winter, owing to the high cost of fuel, frequently in temperatures bordering on zero'. Within a few weeks of his arrival in Moscow, Preston found that 'The novelty of Soviet Russia is beginning to wear off, and I am fast reaching that stage of "depression" that pervades the air'.[52] Things were even worse in Petrograd, where he took up his new post in November 1922. The city was 'shabby and dead', disfigured both by the street fighting that had taken place during the revolution and the failure of the local authorities to carry out any repairs to public buildings. The grand houses which lined the English Embankment along the Neva River were dilapidated and occupied by squatters, who had destroyed their contents in a desperate search for firewood or *objets d'art* that could be exchanged for food.[53] While prolonged exposure to the dreary conditions of Soviet Russia meant that Hodgson and his colleagues became at least partly inured to their surroundings, they could never entirely ignore the depressing environment in which they had to live and work.

The Mission's staff arrived in Moscow just a few months after the Tenth Party Congress, where Lenin had announced the launch of the New Economic Policy (NEP), a desperate attempt to kick-start the economy and build political bridges to the peasantry by restoring a measure of private ownership and trade. The policy was a controversial one for the Soviet government. It ran counter both to its ideological commitment to establishing state control of the means of production, as well as to its deep-seated conviction that the peasantry was irredeemably petty bourgeois and hostile to the principles of socialism and communism. The Mission's staff recognised the ambiguous nature of the NEP,[54] but were convinced that its adoption proved that the Communist Party leadership was abandoning its traditional principles in the face of economic and political reality. Hodgson rejected Lenin's own assertion that the policy was simply a tactical retreat, a view that was endorsed by his colleagues. Peters prepared a long report on the NEP even before the majority of the Mission's staff first arrived in Moscow, arguing that it represented a 'complete change' in the policy of the Soviet government that would soon lead to closer economic relations between Russia and the major western countries.[55] His chief was certain that there was no alternative to the NEP, writing in one of his dispatches that the state of economic collapse was so severe that at some stage 'the Soviet Government will come back to the old system of private ownership' as the only means of overcoming the crisis.[56] The Mission's staff were reasonably sanguine about the results of the modest measures introduced in the first half of 1921: the Situation Report for the first two weeks in August noted that there was 'appreciable change ... from week to week in the streets of Moscow. Where there was one shop a fortnight ago, there are now half-a-dozen; daily each shop that is open increases its window front'.[57] Hodgson and his colleagues recognised that an influx of western capital and technology would be required to increase the momentum of economic development, being optimistic that the Soviet government was itself trying hard to encourage foreign investment in the country. They were well aware that justifying NEP posed formidable ideological and practical problems for the leadership, but had little doubt that Lenin and the other Soviet leaders were 'prepared to accept any compromise' to stay in power,[58] even if it meant adopting policies that were at odds with the principles they had es-poused for decades.

Hodgson was too ready to be impressed by evidence of the early economic changes wrought by the NEP, failing to understand that a small-scale revival of urban trade did not necessarily signify either a rapid restoration of the economy or the Soviet government's abandon-ment of its commitment to the eventual elimination of private ownership. The Head of the Commercial Mission and his colleagues were struck even more powerfully by the cultural and social conse-quences of the NEP. The revival of private trade allowed a few individuals to accumulate a considerable degree of private wealth, which they then used to purchase luxury goods and entertainment. Early in 1922 the Mission's fortnightly report noted that there had appeared in Moscow during the previous few months a new bourgeoisie that,

> can now spend their evenings in cabarets and cafés where they can mix with tchekists and their women friends. High prices are paid for wines, but this does not deter 'Limon Milliardovitch' from his evening's enjoy-ment. As his name implies, he now thinks in milliards. He usually gains them, as of old, by knowing the right people, and sailing as close as possible to the wind. One of these establishments has an almost European appearance. It is known as the Empire Café, and it even boasts waiters in evening dress, an astonishing anachronism in the present regime, when prominent members of the Government, like M. Trotsky, dine at various diplomatic missions in top boots and short tunics.[59]

Preston was struck by the same phenomenon in Petrograd. Diners at the Europe Hotel, which had been one of the most elegant in the city in pre-revolutionary times, were served in 1922 'by the same Tatar waiters in their white suits as we had been accustomed to see them in the old days'. A string orchestra played excellent music, listened to by guests who paid a pound for a bottle of German wine and almost three times as much for a bottle of French champagne – vast sums at the time. There were even a number of licensed casinos in Petrograd, controlled and operated by the state which took a percentage of the turnover.[60] Both Hodgson and Preston noted the curious social composition of the patrons found at such establishments. Senior officials in the bureaucracy rubbed shoulders with members of the old nobility and so-called *nepmen,* who made their money from shrewd trading and bartering of commodities in short supply. The spectacle of such people enjoying themselves contrasted sharply with the poverty and deprivation of the general population, many of whom had to struggle desperately just to find enough food and fuel to keep alive. Even Hodgson, who believed that the NEP represented a partial return to sanity on the part of the Soviet government, could not conceal his distaste at the coarse taste displayed by many of the individuals who proved to be its greatest beneficiaries.

While British officials welcomed the NEP they were under no illusions that its adoption signalled the Soviet government's complete reversion to 'normal' standards of behaviour. Hodgson and his colleagues were convinced that the Soviet leaders had privately acknowledged 'the failure of Communism in Russia', but feared that their background and mentality would mark their future careers for ever:

> They are, to a man, conspirators, ex-convicts or fugitives from justice, who have spent their lives as outcasts. They have the tortuous brain of the conspirator, his suspiciousness and the inability to be straightforward themselves or to understand the straightforwardness of others.[61]

Hodgson argued that this distinctive mentality helped to explain the Soviet government's appalling brutality towards many of its own citizens, particularly its use of the dreaded Cheka to prevent any conspiracy against its rule.[62] Throughout the early 1920s, the reports of British officials in Russia were filled with accounts of savage executions, such as the killing of an entire family that took place at Smolensk after one of its members made a disparaging remark about the Secret Police.[63] Just a few weeks after he first arrived in Moscow, Hodgson was already sending details to London of the fear which the Cheka evoked among the population by its use of 'arrests and summary executions'. He had few doubts that the Soviet leadership's readiness to use terror against the population would become even more pronounced in the future, as its members struggled to maintain themselves in power while simultaneously abandoning the principles they had espoused four years earlier at the time of the Bolshevik coup.

The Soviet government's vicious treatment of the Russian Orthodox Church during the early 1920s was a matter of particular concern for British representatives, not least because it attracted considerable attention and public disquiet back in London. Hodgson reported at length on the expropriation of church property, as well as the trial and execution of members of the clergy who tried to prevent it from taking place.[64] Preston wrote in detail about the anti-religious demonstrations that took place from time to time in Petrograd, at which 'effigies of the gods of various religions were beheaded and burnt' before a jeering crowd.[65] British officials were in private rather dismissive of the Orthodox Church, condemning its 'ignorant' priesthood for inculcating in their congregations a religious world view founded 'upon superstition [rather] than upon a reasoning belief'.[66] Nevertheless, they were appalled by the savagery of the government's assault on the church, which they believed symbolised both the brutality of the Soviet leadership and its willingness to flout the norms of civilised behaviour. By 1923, after he had been in the country for almost two years, even the optimistic Hodgson was beginning to acknowledge that he had been too hopeful in believing that the Soviet government would rapidly adopt more pragmatic foreign and domestic policies. Yet when a major crisis developed in Anglo-Soviet relations in the spring of that year, he doggedly continued to insist that Britain should maintain some form of official relationship with Moscow.

The 1923 crisis developed over the old and vexed question of Soviet propaganda. Lord Curzon had always been dubious about the wisdom of maintaining relations with Moscow. Once it became apparent that the clause in the Trade Agreement banning the dissemination of propaganda was not being observed, he saw little point in keeping official representatives in Russia. Needless to say, his feelings were shared by a large number of Conservative MPs, who throughout the 1920s kept up constant pressure on the government to review its policy towards the Soviet Union. In April Curzon wrote to Hodgson that the 'barbarities committed by the Soviet Government', along with its refusal to desist from spreading propaganda, 'have led me to doubt whether the mission which we maintain at heavy expense in Moscow has any real justification'.[67] He went on to ask for Hodgson's views about the whole question of Anglo-Soviet relations. The reply was predictable. While Hodgson acknowledged that the Trade Agreement had not yielded the commercial results which had been anticipated two years earlier, he argued that 'a rupture would tend for a time to throw power more completely into extremist hands'. He was convinced that 'The mission has a strong moderating influence and good standing; it has, moreover, accumulated knowledge and [experience] which it would be a misfortune to lose'.[68] He concluded by warning Curzon against instituting a break in relations.

It seemed at first that such counsels of moderation were unlikely to prevail, given the political climate in London, and detailed preparations were put in motion for the withdrawal of the Mission. In the event, a breach was avoided, though this owed little to Hodgson's advice and far more to the Soviet government's surprisingly conciliatory response to an Official Note from Curzon complaining about repeated violations of the Trade Agreement.[69] While the immediate crisis passed, and Hodgson and his staff remained in Russia, the Anglo-Soviet relationship remained tense. The year following the 1923 Curzon Note was a critical time for relations between Britain and Russia. In January 1924 Lenin died after long bouts of ill-health. In the same month, Ramsay Mac-Donald's minority Labour government came to office in London and promptly extended de jure recognition to the Soviet government. British representatives in Russia were kept busier than ever in the years that followed, managing the intricacies of the Anglo-Soviet relationship and keeping London informed about the political battles that took place in Moscow following the death of Lenin.

Hodgson and his staff found it difficult to follow the titanic struggle for power that began after Lenin had his first stroke in 1922, and that led after seven or eight years of bitter in-fighting to the triumph of Joseph Stalin over his rivals in the Soviet leadership. The Mission consistently underestimated the General Secretary's political skills and his ability to exploit his position in the Party bureaucracy to build up enormous powers of patronage. When Lenin was still alive, Hodgson was certain that the Soviet leader was a force for moderation within the government, believing that his pragmatic desire to hold on to power would lead him to ignore the ideologues and extremists within the Communist Party. In the spring of 1922, the Head of the Commercial Mission sent to London a document obtained from a 'confidential source', which argued that Lenin's personality and authority were alone preventing the fragmentation of the Party and the triumph of a radical faction willing to launch a revolutionary war against the major powers of Western Europe.[70] The Soviet leader's illness in the summer of that year was therefore a matter of considerable concern to officials at the British Mission. Hodgson had no doubt that Lenin's removal from day to day politics strengthened the position of the extreme wing of the

Party, telling Curzon in July 1922 that 'the irresponsible Communists, who form the left wing of the party, have been given a freedom which they would hardly have enjoyed had Lenin's cynical genius been able to exercise a wise restraint'.[71] By the beginning of 1923 he was certain that the extremists were in complete control of the Party. However, Hodgson's views were not entirely shared by his deputy, who continued to insist that 'the Soviet Government is guided entirely by Real Politik'.[72] Peters' analysis certainly appears to be the more accurate of the two, for there is little evidence that Lenin's frequent illnesses and withdrawal from politics during the final years of his life led to the adoption of more radical foreign and domestic policies. Hodgson was in part confused by his ignorance of the ideological outlook of the other major Soviet leaders. He remained convinced throughout 1923 that Nikolai Bukharin was a standard-bearer of the extreme left and that Trotsky was something of a moderate who, like Lenin, was willing to set aside Communist principles when they threatened the Communist Party's hold on power.[73] In reality, Bukharin had some years earlier begun to move towards the right wing of the Party, while Trotsky was by 1923 firmly attempting to present himself as a revolutionary hero committed to defending the spirit of the revolution against the forces of bureaucratisation and ideological compromise. Hodgson's confusion was understandable, given the complexities of Soviet politics during these years, but it made it harder for him to follow the intricacies of the power struggle that unfolded in the years after 1924.

By the end of 1923, a few weeks before Lenin's death, British officials in Moscow and Petrograd had come to realise just how deep were the divisions within the leadership, even if they still did not entirely understand the significance of them. Thomas Preston recognised that the 'indefatigable and enthusiastic' Zinoviev had emerged, along with Stalin and Kamenev, as a key figure who was likely to exercise considerable power in the future.[74] In November Hodgson wrote incredulously that 'the loyalty of even Trotski himself was no longer proof against attack', describing a Central Committee meeting in which Bukharin and Zinoviev had launched a bitter attack on the architect of the Red Army's triumph in the Civil War.[75] The Mission had apparently acquired a reliable and accurate source who provided information about the battles within the leadership, which Hodgson saw as evidence of a growing 'slackness' that indicated the Party was losing its 'most precious possession ... the rigid discipline which has brought it through the hours of stress and set it where it is now'.[76] He remained convinced, nevertheless, that the divisions within the Party were not a harbinger of its imminent demise; he instead saw them as evidence of a division between an 'Old Guard', who were trying to ensure that they could maintain their power and influence once Lenin died, and a 'New Guard' that was seeking to establish its own claims to power and influence. By siding with the New Guard, suggested Hodgson, Trotsky was distancing himself from the old leadership and launching a concerted attack on their authority and status.

Lenin's death in January 1924 had little real impact on the struggle for power, since the battle between Trotsky and his rivals had been raging for at least a year. Hodgson was frankly contemptuous of the abilities of almost all the surviving Soviet leaders. Although he had no knowledge of Lenin's celebrated 'Testament', written the previous year, in which the Bolshevik leader savagely criticised all his colleagues, the language used by the Head of the Commercial Mission was remarkably similar:

> Shorn of its two leaders [Lenin and Trotsky] the party cuts a sorry figure. Zinoviev, a poor creature at best, finds his influence rapidly waning ... Kamenev is a depressing personality incapable of giving inspiration to the mass; Stalin, 'the man of steel', a narrow-minded, obstinate Georgian, entangled in the intricacies of party doctrine; Bukharin, a fanatic, popular with the working man, but without the makings of a leader. Of the others among the old Communists none is of eminence, while the 'Young Guard' of Communism is barren.[77]

Nevertheless, in spite of his low opinion of Lenin's heirs, Hodgson went on to recommend formal diplomatic recognition of the Soviet government, citing the familiar argument that its 'revolutionary mentality' would be diminished by 'closer relations with the outside world'. Lord Curzon was not disposed to listen to such a plea, but by the time this particular report reached London the new Labour government was already in office. The MacDonald government's extension of de jure recognition to the Soviet government was not of course prompted by Hodgson's dispatch. Although Ramsay MacDonald, who served as both Foreign Secretary and Prime Minister in the new government, was no admirer of Soviet Communism, there was still enough residual leftist sentiment among his colleagues to make recognition of the government in Moscow seem a natural policy. In any case, attitudes had been changing for some time even within business circles in Great Britain, as many firms looked hopefully at the potential market that could be opened up by establishing closer relations with Soviet Russia.[78]

In the event, formal recognition had a smaller impact on Anglo-Soviet relations than might have been expected. It was quickly decided not to send an Ambassador to Moscow, in part because George V objected to the idea that such an honour should be accorded to a government that had murdered his cousin. Hodgson instead was appointed Chargé d'Affaires in Moscow and the status of the Commercial Mission upgraded. Attempts to negotiate a formal treaty to resolve the outstanding differences between the two countries were more problematic. Although an agreement was eventually reached in August, after long and complicated negotiations, the fall of the Labour government in November 1924 meant that it was never ratified.[79] The Mission's staff therefore found that the advent of formal diplomatic relations between the Soviet Union and Britain had little effect on their daily work. Nor did the Chargé d'Affaires believe that the extension of de jure recognition would have much impact on the course of Soviet domestic politics, even though it was a prize that had long been sought by the Moscow government. In one of his first dispatches to MacDonald, Hodgson told the new Prime Minister that it was certain that power would in the future remain firmly in the hands of the triumvirate of Stalin, Zinoviev and Kamenev.[80]

Hodgson and his colleagues feared that the death of Lenin would mark the beginning of a harsher domestic policy in which the Secret Police became more active and powerful than ever. Their reports were increasingly filled with accounts of imprisonments and executions, as well as the more petty persecutions that made life so difficult for large sections of the population. Hodgson observed in one of his dispatches that Lenin's death caused the Soviet government to fall into a 'nervous and excitable state in which any untoward circumstance is magnified into a peril threatening the very existence of the Peasants' and Workers Republic'. In April 1924 he described how:

> Women and girls are being dragged from their homes at night and conveyed to the headquarters of the secret police in batches, for no apparent reason and with no apparent qualification, except that they belong to the old aristocratic families; arrests are being carried out seemingly without rhyme and reason, and a state of complete panic prevails among all classes.[81]

The Chargé d'Affaires and his staff were particularly struck by the assault on the educated classes, who faced the twin challenges of economic privation and social marginalisation. In universities and schools, non-Party members were often thrown out of their jobs to be replaced by loyal Communists, a fate that was frequently shared by bourgeois specialists in industry, whose skill and knowledge was no longer deemed to be essential for the development of the Soviet economy. Such people also found it increasingly difficult to find accommodation in Moscow, since the loss of their jobs prevented them from participating in the house committees that allocated living space in the city. Members of the British Mission in Moscow were naturally appalled by these developments, though they continued to hope that Lenin's heirs would before long realise the absurdity of their behaviour and have recourse 'to saner measures'.

Thomas Preston in Petrograd was also struck by what he perceived as a shift towards a more repressive domestic policy during 1924. He was convinced that the new 'extreme left wing' leadership was determined to destroy the NEP and begin mass arrests of all those who were suspected of any possible opposition to their rule. As a result of the new hard line, 'As many as 1000 persons have been arrested in one night. The prisons are full and it has even become necessary to turn a sugar factory into a temporary gaol in order to accommodate the overflowing stream of prisoners'.[82] Preston also described how the decision to exclude students of bourgeois origins from the universities had led to many suicides, a phenomenon that was equally visible among faculty members who were unable to cope with the discrimination and persecution they faced at the hands of the authorities.[83] Preston and Hodgson both commented at length on the increasingly proletarian character of the Soviet regime, which they believed was the consequence of a recruitment policy deliberately designed by the leadership to promote 'an ignorant herd which can be driven in whatever direction the interests of the dominant oligarchy may desire'. Hodgson was particularly struck by the changing nature of the Communist Party itself:

> The last few years ... have brought into existence a new generation of worker, immature youths who have been brought up on ill-digested theories of Marxism, class animosity and the negation of the humanities. They form a rancorous, truculent and intolerant mass which cries out for the textual execution of the theories in which it has been educated.[84]

This analysis was a shrewd one. It recognised the significance of Stalin's attempt to broaden the base of the Communist Party in order to dilute the influence of older members who were less willing than new recruits to accept uncritically the growing power of the General Secretary.

The idea that the Soviet government was moving rapidly to the left in 1924 seems on the face of it to be rather curious. Following the virtual eclipse of Trotsky by the end of 1923, Stalin began to turn his attention to defeating Zinoviev and Kamenev, who had become his most formidable remaining rivals. In doing so, he successfully championed the cause of a moderate domestic and foreign policy based on the retention of the NEP and the avoidance of unecessary conflicts abroad; 1924 therefore represented, at least in one sense, the nadir of radicalism in the USSR. Officials at the British Mission were, however, in many ways less concerned with questions of policy than with the changes taking place in the culture and tone of Soviet public life. They were appalled by the growing emphasis on 'class hatred' in the speeches and articles of leading officials. Hodgson and his colleagues were fearful that the government's 'war against the intelligentsia' would soon 'threaten all that is left of culture in Russia' and lead to untold horrors for the educated bourgeoisie.[85]

The return of a Conservative government at the end of 1924 meant that the conciliatory views of Hodgson and his staff on Britain's relations with Soviet Russia were less likely than ever to be taken into account in London. The election campaign that led to the Conservative victory was dominated by the publication of the 'Zinoviev Letter', a document purporting to contain detailed instructions from the Head of the Comintern to the British Communist Party demanding the establishment of revolutionary cells in the British army. The truth behind the whole affair remains deeply mysterious. The document itself was almost certainly a forgery, possibly produced in Poland by anti-Soviet activists who wanted to make the British government adopt a harder line towards Moscow. It also seems certain that members of the British Special Intelligence Service played a role in ensuring that the letter was passed to the government (and perhaps in leaking a copy to the press).[86] Whatever the exact status of the document, there is no doubt that similar material had already been intercepted on a number of previous occasions by the intelligence services. It was well known in the Foreign Office and Home Office that members of the Comintern maintained contacts with left-wing organisations in Britain. Even so, the sensational publication of the Zinoviev Letter helped to change the climate of opinion among at least a section of the British public, since it appeared to confirm the claims made by Conservative anti-Communist diehards that the Soviet government could never be trusted. Anglo-Soviet relations plunged into a state of crisis which lasted for the next five years. The 1925 Locarno Treaty, in which Britain offered a guarantee to France against German attempts to expand the country's borders westwards, but not eastwards, was inevitably viewed in Moscow as evidence of the formation of an anti-Soviet bloc in the west of the continent. By contrast, Soviet involvement in the 1926 General Strike was seen by Ministers in London as proof that the Soviet government was seeking to destabilise the social and political fabric of British society. Against such a background, the role of British officials in Russia became more difficult than ever, since they were dealing with a regime that was viewed by many members of the government they represented as a pariah in the international community.

During his final two years in Russia, Hodgson continued to defend the views that he had expressed since 1921, arguing that the Soviet government would in time abandon the ideological principles which it publicly promulgated. He also remained a staunch advocate of the need to maintain formal diplomatic relations between London and Moscow. In putting forward these views, Hodgson was taking a position that commanded a good deal of support back at the Foreign Office, most notably among officials in the Northern Department, who were throughout the 1920s strongly opposed to any policy that might lead to a breach between Britain and Russia. The new Foreign Secretary, Austen Chamberlain, was also firmly in favour of maintaining formal relations between London and Moscow, even though on taking office he came under a great deal of pressure from some of his Cabinet colleagues to revoke the recognition of the Soviet government made by the MacDonald government a few months previously.[87] Like his officials, the Foreign Secretary instinctively endorsed the notion that British foreign policy towards Russia should be based on a pragmatic realpolitik, which accepted the existence of the Soviet regime as an unavoidable if unpleasant fact of international life. Such a principle was, however, entirely rejected by many leading Conservative politicians in London, who were convinced that the ideological challenge posed by Soviet Communism was so great that no meaningful form of diplomatic dialogue could take place between Britain and Russia. British policy towards Russia during the mid 1920s therefore became the subject of a complex political and bureaucratic battle, in which the Foreign Office sought to defend its primacy in determining foreign policy against the pressure of both public and political opinion.

The events that took place in Russia during 1925 represented a critical stage in the power struggle inside the Soviet leadership, since it was during this year that Stalin managed to outmanoeuvre both Zinoviev and Kamenev, who had been his allies in the earlier battle with Trotsky. Yet the General Secretary remained an enigmatic figure to British officials in Moscow, who found it impossible to gauge the true extent of his power and influence. The Mission was initially inclined to treat the eclipse of Zinoviev as a victory for the cause of moderation. In March 1925 Hodgson wrote to Chamberlain suggesting that a recent decision to reduce the staff of the Comintern was evidence of a growing realism on the part of the Soviet leadership, since it indicated that they were unwilling to come into conflict with foreign governments whose 'benevolence is essential to them if they are to extract Russia from her [economic] difficulties'. He went on to note optimistically that by the time the economy was restored it was 'fairly certain that the light of battle will have gone from them, and the process of metamorphosis which is now going on will have transferred them into innocuous bourgeois like you and I'.[88] Hodgson was at least consistent in taking this view, though the evidence to support it was no stronger in 1925 than it had been four years earlier. The reduction in the size of the Comintern staff was in reality largely driven by Stalin's desire to reduce the power and prestige of an organisation with which Zinoviev was so closely associated. Nor was Hodgson alone in believing that the General Secretary was a force for moderation. One official at the Foreign Office, who had considerable experience of Soviet affairs, observed in a departmental minute that Stalin was 'not beloved of the left Comintern extremists nor of the Cheka whose excessive brutality he has on occasion denounced'.[89] Although the idea of Stalin as a moderate and a critic of excessive brutality sounds ridiculous to later generations, in the mid 1920s the General Secretary was still portraying himself as a stern critic of Trotskyism and other forms of 'left deviationism'. In the final stages of his battle with Zinoviev and Kamenev, which were followed carefully by British officials in Russia, the General Secretary took care to defend the moderate New Economic Policy and attack those who called for an 'adventurist' foreign policy. It was therefore not surprising that staff at the Mission managed to convince themselves that he was a cautious pragamatist opposed to the adoption of extreme left-wing policies.

Since Hodgson and his colleagues believed that Stalin's growing power was evidence of the triumph of moderation over radicalism, they were frustrated by the antics adopted by 'diehard' critics of the Soviet government in London, which they feared would destroy the fragile diplomatic relationship between the two countries. So committed indeed was Hodgson to improving Anglo-Soviet relations that he occasionally engaged in activities that overstepped the boundaries of diplomatic protocol. It was of course entirely permissible for the Head of a British Mission abroad to put forward his views on policy to the Foreign

Secretary, and Hodgson did so tirelessly during his final two years in Russia. Yet while a senior British representative was entitled to a degree of independence when dealing with the government to which he was accredited, there were strict limits to the level of autonomy that was permissible. In the autumn of 1925, Hodgson engaged in an extraordinary bout of 'private diplomacy' when home on leave in London, apparently coming close to deceiving his colleagues at the Foreign Office in the process. With the Foreign Secretary abroad in Italy at the time, Hodgson took advantage of his absence to visit the Soviet Mission in London. After the visit, he told senior officials at the Foreign Office that the Chargé d'Affaires at the Mission, Arkady Rosengoltz, had proposed informal talks to resolve some of the outstanding differences between the two countries. Although Hodgson urged his colleagues at the Foreign Office to respond positively to this gesture, they proved reluctant to do so without the express permission of Chamberlain. A few days later, a senior official therefore visited the Soviet Mission in order to explain to Rosengoltz that it would not be possible to respond formally to his offer of talks until the Foreign Secretary returned from Italy. Much to the official's surprise, Rosengoltz replied that the proposal for talks had come from Hodgson himself.[90] The whole incident was soon forgotten, at least officially, though it caused considerable irritation to senior staff at the Foreign Office, who felt that they had been misled by one of their own colleagues. It was not the only occasion when Hodgson faced criticism for taking personal initiatives without first obtaining the permission of his superiors. By the end of 1925 he was gaining a reputation in some quarters for being far too eager to seek accommodation with the Soviet government. The British Ambassador to Germany, Lord d'Abernon, noted acidly in his diary following one meeting with Hodgson in Berlin that his visitor was 'more disposed to make concessions in order to get on better terms with the Soviets than I had expected'.[91]

The General Strike in May 1926 inevitably gave an enormous impetus to critics of the Soviet Union who wanted to bring about an end to diplomatic relations between London and Moscow, since they were able to play on the widespread popular fear of the 'Red Menace' to mobilise support for their cause. Money from the USSR was undoubtedly channelled to the British labour movement during this period, though the Soviet government insisted unconvincingly that the funds were sent by private citizens rather than official sources. While there is little serious evidence to suggest that the labour movement was in any sense directed from Moscow – if anything the General Strike took the Soviet government by surprise – it was easy for the Cabinet diehards and their supporters to make propaganda out of supposed Soviet involvement in internal British affairs. Shortly before the strike began, Hodgson sent a long memorandum to Chamberlain setting out yet again his views on the whole question of Anglo-Soviet relations. Although he said nothing substantially new, the language he employed was unusually forthright. The memorandum sharply criticised the British government for pursuing a 'purely negative policy' towards Russia and took issue with those who believed that the Soviet regime was about to collapse, claiming instead that it was 'in spite of many troubles, gaining ground, and winning through to solidity'. However, argued Hodgson, this stability did not signify a triumph for radical socialist principles. He instead suggested that:

> The Soviet Government has been continually in conflict with the conceptions to which it owes its being – to cope with practical exigencies it has had to recede little by little from the ideas which inspired the revolution, and one of the difficulties which confronts it to-day is so to camouflage its continual retreat so as to allow a trusting proletariat to cherish the illusion that it, and not a very ordinary bureaucracy, governs Russia.[92]

Hodgson went on to argue that, as the Soviet government started to adopt a more pragmatic foreign policy, it would increasingly behave like its Tsarist predecessor, with the result that British policy should be guided by traditional diplomatic principles rather than ideological passion. He also argued that any attempt to isolate and exclude the Soviet Union within Europe, which was essentially the policy favoured by Chamberlain, would simply heighten the siege mentality of the Soviet government and make it a more dangerous foe. The memorandum concluded with a call for closer economic and diplomatic ties between London and Moscow, in the hope that such a policy of constructive engagement would weaken the revolutionary principles of the Soviet leadership.

These ideas were close to ones expressed by officials in the Northern Department of the Foreign Office. A few months before Hodgson wrote his May memorandum, a First Secretary in the Northern Department, Charles Orde, had written a memorandum for the Cabinet warning against the dangers of pursuing a harsh anti-Soviet policy. Like Hodgson, he believed that the Soviet government's 'revolutionary ardour' would fade over time as it continued to grapple with mundane economic and administrative problems. Such views did not count for much, however, during the political drama of the General Strike. At a Cabinet meeting held on 11 June, shortly after the collapse of the Strike, the Home Secretary, William Joynson-Hicks ('Jix'), argued fervently that the British government should end diplomatic relations with Moscow in protest against the Soviet government's attempt to fund the miners and other sections of the British labour movement. His proposal was supported by several of his Cabinet colleagues, including Churchill and Birkenhead, as well as by many Conservative MPs who took advantage of a debate in the House of Commons during the last week of June to call for a tougher policy towards Russia. Members of the Foreign Office had to work hard to counter this pressure. Chamberlain himself insisted in Cabinet during the middle of June that 'the moment was not opportune for the rupture of diplomatic relations',[93] a position he defended in the House a few days later by referring to the need for a careful and understated policy towards Russia that was not driven by fleeting passions and passing emotions:

> I conceive that it is better that a Foreign Secretary should study rather to understate the case that can fairly be made than to press it to its full extent, and I have deliberately adopted language always courteous, though it has never been cordial, and I have never gone in any official utterance beyond that of which I was certain by information which I had in my hand.[94]

The Foreign Secretary went on to warn that a break with the Soviet Union would challenge the stability created at Locarno, and give free rein to the 'political uncertainties and sense of political insecurity' by which 'All Europe is harassed and perplexed'. This position was supported by his officials, including Charles Orde, who in June wrote a second memorandum for the Cabinet, warning that a break with Moscow would make it harder than ever to exercise any effective leverage over the Soviet government.[95] The contrast between the position of the Foreign Office and the position of the Cabinet diehards and their parliamentary supporters could hardly have been more stark. The one side believed that the challenge posed to Britain by the Soviet Union was exaggerated and could in any case be countered within the framework of traditional diplomacy. The other side was convinced that the Russian Revolution had given birth to a new phase in international relations, in which 'diplomacy as usual' was no longer able to guarantee British interests and security.

The voice of Hodgson and his staff was increasingly drowned amidst the clamour in London, although the Chargé d'Affaires still reported diligently on Soviet domestic affairs while doing all he could to encourage the cause of moderation in London.[96] Staff at the British Mission and Consulates continued to be appalled by the economic and human misery facing the country, which they believed was absorbing most of the Soviet government's time and energy. In a dispatch sent to London at the end of May 1926, Hodgson told Chamberlain about the terrible social problems 'that would be considered a disgrace in a more civilised community':

> The hordes of homeless children, originally the product of the war, the famine and concomitant ills, that roam the big towns show no signs of decreasing. Every now and then thousands are rounded up and cleared from the streets, but thousands still remain, and but a small proportion are willing to remain in the 'homes' in which they are placed. Most are bodily and mentally defective, and are suitable only for concentration in special psychopathic institutions, which do not exist. Drug taking, prostitution, thieving are but a few of the vices to which they are addicted: the murder by them of their companions or of peaceful citizens is common.[97]

The situation was little better in the countryside, where epidemics of syphilis and rabies were ravaging the population.

The impressions of Thomas Preston in Petrograd (now renamed Leningrad) were equally bleak. He reported in April 1926 that the situation 'cannot be regarded otherwise than as catastrophic'.[98] There was a critical shortage of food and fuel across the city, with the result that popular discontent was on the rise, even taking the form of occasional bombings and attacks on Party officials. The ritual assertions of Soviet power continued unabated, although British representatives were struck by the increasing hollowness and formality of the marches and demonstrations that took place in support of the government. The only public officials who performed their duties with any real zeal belonged to the Secret Police, whose brutal activities continued unabated.[99] Hodgson and Preston reported in detail on the final stages of the power struggle between Stalin and the so-called 'Left Opposition' grouped around Zinoviev and Kamenev, a battle which they continued to believe was as much about personalities as principles. The Chargé d'Affaires noted that Stalin's victory left him as 'the dominant figure' in Soviet political life, but was still convinced that the bitter conflict within the Communist Party was of little relevance, since whichever faction won it would have no choice but to adopt more pragmatic policies in order to avert economic catastrophe.[100] He also believed that the gradual disintegration of the Party 'monolith' made it less of a threat to the outside world than ever before, since its members were concerned above all with the struggle for power and had little energy to spare for the cause of promoting world revolution. At a time when the diehards in London were arguing that the Soviet government posed a direct challenge to its neighbours, Hodgson suggested that it was becoming more inward-looking than at any previous point in its stormy existence.

There was in fact something contradictory about the picture of the Soviet Union which Hodgson portrayed in his dispatches during the final months before the break in diplomatic relations that eventually took place in the spring of 1927. He repeatedly argued both that the Soviet regime was becoming more firmly established *and* that it faced a social and economic crisis of enormous proportions. Since Hodgson's views commanded little attention in London, the potential ambiguity of his position mattered little. He wrote periodically to the Foreign Office during the second half of 1926, complaining about the anti-Soviet tone of speeches made by prominent Conservative MPs and Ministers,[101] but his protests had no impact. Although the Cabinet diehards had not been able to bring about a break with Moscow at the time of the General Strike, their failure simply encouraged them to redouble their efforts. Their incessant pressure eventually paid off. During the second half of 1926, a number of senior officials *within* the Foreign Office itself were themselves beginning to reconsider their earlier moderate position. In July, the new Permanent Secretary, Sir William Tyrrell, had already argued in a paper circulated to the Cabinet that the Soviet government posed a substantial threat to Britain, since the overthrow of the Empire was 'the chief aim and object of Moscow'.[102] At this point, Tyrrell still defended the traditional Foreign Office position that the best protection against the Soviet challenge was to be found in patient diplomacy rather than dramatic gestures. By the end of the year, however, the Permanent Secretary was becoming increasingly anti-Soviet in his outlook, noting in December that he would like nothing better than a chance 'to catch the Soviets in a case of *flagrante delicto* which will enable us to clear them out of this country with almost universal content'.[103] Although these views were not shared by many junior officials in the Foreign Office, some of Tyrrell's senior colleagues were coming round to a similar position.

In December 1926 Gregory drew up a detailed memorandum setting down the pros and cons of a break with Russia, concluding that they 'are to some extent evenly balanced'.[104] While the overwhelming majority of British Ambassadors *en poste* abroad urged the need for continued restraint, it was clear that there were fissures even within the diplomatic establishment. In the first weeks of 1927 concern over the Soviet government's behaviour grew still further at the Foreign Office, since it was believed there that Moscow was directly responsible for a sharp rise in the level of anti-British sentiment among a significant section of the Chinese population.[105] Although largely untrue, the issue increased tension between London and Moscow and dominated Cabinet discussions for a considerable period of time.[106] Chamberlain himself began to support a more confrontational policy, dispatching a Note of Protest in February following the discovery that the Soviet government had been tampering with the diplomatic bags of foreign powers.[107] Although the Foreign Secretary and his senior officials still hoped it would be possible to avoid a final break in diplomatic relations, the Foreign Office's shift to a tougher stance made it harder for them to resist the pressure of those who wanted to bring about a rupture. Once he had taken the decision to send a Note of Protest, Chamberlain's whole position had become extremely ambivalent: he was openly acknowledging that the behaviour of the Soviet government abroad was unacceptable, while at the same time insisting that formal relations should remain intact. The Foreign Secretary worked hard to defend his position in Cabinet, claiming that although Britain had *grounds* for recalling its representatives from Russia, it was not in British *interests* to do so. Not surprisingly, such arguments failed to convince the diehards. Robert Hodgson, who was at this time back in Britain on leave, desperately tried to prevent the dispatch of the February Note of Protest, recognising that once it was sent Anglo-Soviet relations would enter a downward spiral that would be hard to escape from. His efforts met with little success, as even the good-natured Chamberlain noted with some irritation that Hodgson was saying nothing new, but simply repeating arguments he had made many times before over the previous few years.

Once the Note of Protest was sent, the Cabinet had effectively acknowledged that a breach of relations was almost inevitable unless the Soviet government rapidly changed its behaviour.[108] Although Chamberlain continued to call for caution, the political battle was now effectively over, and it was clear that even the most minor incident would be seized on by likes of 'Jix' and Birkenhead as an excuse to end diplomatic relations with Moscow – whatever the views of the Foreign Office. In the event, the incidents which finally sparked the break are still shrouded in mystery. At the end of March MI5 received detailed information about Soviet espionage activities in Britain, a revelation that came on top of an announcement by Chamberlain a few weeks earlier that the Special Intelligence Service had obtained details concerning Soviet interference in British domestic affairs.[109] While there was no doubt that all this information was genuine, Joynson-Hicks, the Home Secretary, was reluctantly forced to acknowledge that it would be difficult to use it in open court due to the sensitive nature of the material. A few weeks later the Home Secretary was informed by the War Office that it had received information indicating that a member of the Soviet trade organisation (Arcos) in London had obtained a copy of a secret army signals training manual. 'Jix' was in no doubt that the information was serious enough to justify the issue of a warrant to search the premises of Arcos, even though the quasi-diplomatic status of the organisation meant that the legal foundations for such a decision were questionable. He quickly notified the Prime Minister and the Foreign Secretary about the impending raid and, on 12 May, a large number of officers from the Metropolitan Police and Special Branch descended on Arcos headquarters in Central London to conduct a search for the missing training manual. They never found it.

Although the missing manual was not recovered, the Special Branch report indicated that material had been recovered showing that employees of Arcos were involved both in espionage activities and the spread of propaganda in Britain and abroad.[110] The report's claim that the evidence proved the complicity of the Soviet Mission in espionage was more controversial. This naturally posed a problem for Ministers who wanted to use the documents recovered in the Arcos raid as an excuse for ending diplomatic relations with Russia. Perhaps significantly, the draft of the Special Branch report was amended to read, unlike the original version, that the chief of the Soviet trade delegation, who was formally accredited to the Soviet Mission, had been personally aware of the illegal activities taking place at Arcos. Even so, some junior Foreign Office officials in the Northern Department remained sceptical about the link, insisting that 'unless further proof of the complicity of Rosengoltz and the Soviet government is forthcoming, it seems ... that we have very flimsy reasons for breaking off diplomatic relations'.[111] This was to miss the point. Since a majority in the Cabinet had already decided to end relations with Moscow, they could always find some kind of evidence to justify the move if they were sufficiently determined to do so. Given that the Arcos raid had yielded little material of interest, it was decided to authorise the publication of secret documents about

Soviet activities in Britain that had been obtained previously from intelligence sources. On 23 May the Cabinet took the formal decision to expel Soviet diplomats from London, a decision that Chamberlain defended manfully three days later in the House of Commons, in spite of his lingering doubts about the wisdom of such a move.

Since Hodgson was still in Britain, it was left to William Peters to organise the withdrawal of British officials from Russia. Although the Soviet government naturally denied the charges made by London, it made little effort to interfere with the process,[112] though a number of demonstrations did take place outside the Leningrad Consulate. Peters was warned in advance that a break in diplomatic relations was about to be announced, so his colleagues were able to destroy the Mission's cyphers and a large number of documents in readiness. He also told consular staff to take the same precautions, an instruction that was quickly carried out by Preston in Leningrad, who had in his files numerous letters 'which might be compromising vis à vis our Russian acquaintances'.[113] The actual withdrawal took place largely without incident, but in the weeks following the Mission's departure the Soviet government moved quickly to round up and execute a large number of individuals accused of being British spies. The issue caused considerable controversy in Britain during the months that followed, with Hodgson and his staff all going to great lengths when back home to deny the allegations.[114] Most of the evidence produced by the Soviet authorities was certainly of a very circumstantial character, based on selective and misleading quotations from letters intercepted by the Secret Police. Yet while Hodgson and Preston were doubtless being entirely honest when they denied the spying charges made against them by their erstwhile hosts, they had over the years built up a number of contacts and acquaintances which could all too easily be cited as proof that they were engaging in activities incompatible with their diplomatic status. In a letter to the Norwegian Minister in Moscow, the former Chargé d'Affaires admitted his relief that the authorities had only been able to produce evidence of a very tendentious nature that effectively amounted to giving the Mission 'a flatteringly clean bill of health'. Since British representatives had been required by the Foreign Office to report on a closed society in which the authorities were unwilling to make any information freely available, Hodgson and his colleagues were forced over the years to develop strategies to circumvent these constraints. In doing so, they had undoubtedly shown a degree of curiosity and persistence that was not congenial to the Soviet authorities.

The absence of British officials in Russia during 1927–29 at first threatened to make it much harder for the Foreign Office to interpret the economic and political developments taking place in the Soviet Union. This was potentially a serious problem, since it was during these years that Stalin finally established his supremacy within the leadership – defeating the so-called 'Right Opposition' associated with Nikolai Bukharin – and used his power to set in motion fundamental changes destined to transform Russia. The Foreign Office quickly learnt to exploit new sources of information and expertise, however, drawing more heavily than ever on reports originating at Embassies and Consulates in countries bordering the Soviet Union. The erudite and intelligent Norwegian Minister in Moscow, Dr Jan Urbye, also provided London with detailed dispatches on a whole range of economic and political questions. The articles written by foreign correspondents in Moscow, particularly those of Paul Scheffer in the *Berliner Tageblatt*, were similarly read with great attention. As a result, the absence of a British Mission during 1927–29 was not necessarily as great a handicap as might be imagined. The American government, which had invested heavily in establishing a 'listening post' in the Baltic city of Riga, believed indeed that it was easier for its officials to collect accurate information about the Soviet Union when they were not subject to the day to day constraints faced by foreign representatives actually resident in Moscow.

During his six years in Moscow, Robert Hodgson was committed to the view that the ideological zeal of the Soviet government was something of an illusion, consistently arguing in his reports that a retreat to more orthodox economic and foreign policies was inevitable once the leadership recognised that its revolutionary dogmas could never be instituted in real life. In reality, the final triumph of Stalin over his rivals signalled the beginning of the 'Third Revolution', the launch of a programme of massive economic transformation and, in its wake, the beginning of the infamous Great Terror which destroyed the lives of millions of Soviet citizens. Hodgson was a diligent official, who worked hard to keep London informed about the changes taking place in Russia during the 1920s. He richly deserved Chamberlain's praise for his resilience in the face of six years spent in 'trying conditions, physical and moral'.[115] The Foreign Secretary was also right to compliment the former Chargé d'Affaires for the 'tact with which you carried out your instructions'. Yet while Hodgson was correct to emphasise throughout his time in Moscow that the Soviet regime was reasonably secure against the threat of any violent internal challenge, both he and his colleagues ultimately failed fully to understand the extent and significance of the changes that had taken place in Russia during the previous decade. British officials in Russia, and at the Foreign Office in London, were too inclined to believe that the force of circumstances would inculcate a pragmatic instinct in a leadership that had come to power committed to the promotion of dramatic social and political revolution. It was largely for this reason that they failed to understand the full significance of the power struggle that took place among Soviet leaders following the death of Lenin, wrongly believing that the outcome would have few consequences for foreign and domestic policy. By the time British representatives returned to the Soviet Union in 1929, the country was on the threshold of dramatic social and political changes that were far greater than anything that had taken place since the Bolshevik seizure of power twelve years earlier.

8

A Grotesque Vision of Life

The election of a second Labour government under Ramsay MacDonald in the summer of 1929 paved the way for a restoration of diplomatic relations between London and Moscow.[1] Although the new Foreign Secretary, Arthur Henderson, was anxious to assert that the new government would pursue a different foreign policy from its predecessor, the disagreement between the two main political parties over Russia was less stark than at first appeared to be the case. The Baldwin government had itself put out a number of tentative feelers to Moscow following the break in diplomatic relations over the Arcos affair, confident that it had proved once and for all its determination to oppose the expansion of Soviet influence both in Britain and overseas. Conservative Ministers therefore hoped that the Moscow government would be willing to participate in the construction of a new economic and political relationship, while refraining from the kind of activities that had caused so much anger in Britain during previous years. Similarly, although the new Labour government placed considerable importance on establishing a *modus vivendi* with Soviet Russia, the principal concern of its more senior members was with mundane questions of trade and security. Despite the fact that some radicals in the Labour Party continued to look favourably on the 'great experiment in socialism' taking place in the Soviet Union, they seldom had much impact on the making of foreign policy.[2] The mechanical aspects of re-establishing diplomatic relations did create a certain degree of tension between Ministers in the new government, largely reflecting disagreement over whether a formal exchange of Ambassadors should precede or follow the resolution of outstanding problems between the two countries. In the event, it took less than six months between the election of the second MacDonald government and the arrival in Soviet Russia of a fully-fledged British Ambassador, the first since Sir George Buchanan had left Petrograd twelve years previously.

Even though the 1930s were a turbulent time in both Britain and

Soviet Russia, the diplomatic relationship between the two countries proved to be rather less troubled than in the previous decade, at least before the dramatic announcement of the Nazi-Soviet Pact in August 1939 turned the world of European politics upside down. This was in part due to Hitler's rise to power, since the threat posed to the security of Europe by Nazi Germany quickly came to dominate the attention of both London and Moscow. In addition, the mere fact that the Soviet government had managed to survive the numerous challenges it faced during the first decade of its life meant that it was by the early 1930s an increasingly accepted, if resented, part of the international scene.[3] While there were still numerous bad-tempered disagreements between London and Moscow, on topics ranging from trade to propaganda, the *principle* of maintaining diplomatic representation in the Soviet capital was only really seriously challenged on one occasion, when the arrest in 1933 of a small number of British engineers working in Russia threatened to bring about a rupture. The USSR's entry into the League of Nations in 1934, a policy closely associated with Maxim Litvinov at the Commissariat of Foreign Affairs, symbolised a growing recognition both in Moscow and abroad that the country needed to be integrated more effectively into the global order.[4] Although the Soviet government never abandoned the revolutionary rhetoric of its early years, it was increasingly willing to participate in an international system whose elaborate procedures and rules had once been dismissed caustically by its spokesmen as the hallmark of a bourgeois order doomed to imminent collapse.

While the diplomatic relationship between Britain and Russia may have been more harmonious during the 1930s than in the previous decade, the period was without doubt one of the most dramatic and painful in the entire domestic history of the Soviet Union. The collectivisation of agriculture that took place in the first few years of the decade turned out to be one of the bloodiest episodes of the twentieth century. Tens of thousands of peasants died at the hands of troops and shock brigades sent into the countryside to enforce the new policy, which was designed to drive the peasantry into massive state-run collective farms where their labour could be exploited by the state. Millions more died in the famine caused by the massive social and economic upheavals that subsequently took place across rural Russia. At the same time, the changes in the countryside helped to make possible the dramatic industrial expansion of the 1930s, which followed the introduction of the celebrated Five Year Plans designed to alter the economic face of the country in the space of a single decade. Even though the results never lived up to the dreams of the planners, the construction of vast new industries transformed the Soviet Union into an urban and industrial society quite unlike the peasant land of 1917.

The brutality of this massive process of economic and social dislocation was exacerbated by the development of the whole ghastly apparatus of political terror, directed with increasing vigour by Stalin against both his erstwhile colleagues and the general population as a whole. The show trials of leading Party figures, such as Nikolai Bukharin and Grigory Zinoviev, represented only the tip of an iceberg. For every leading politician condemned to the macabre process of a public 'trial', that consisted in practice of nothing more than a set-piece theatrical performance in which the accused were forced to confess their complicity in the most absurd crimes, dozens of less prominent bureaucrats were condemned to death in secret by administrative order. For every minor functionary who was executed, dozens of ordinary citizens were swept up in the cycle of arrest and punishment. Although it is dangerous to focus too much attention on the pathological nature of Soviet society in the 1930s, ignoring the extent to which everyday life continued in some ways much as before, it was without doubt a period of quite extraordinary brutality and upheaval. British diplomats who served in the country were witnesses to some of the most dreadful events of the century. Although they were themselves largely isolated in a privileged diplomatic cocoon that protected them from the worst horrors taking place around them, even the most detached could not help but be appalled by the experience.

While the Foreign Office worked hard to keep abreast of the changes that took place in Russia after the Hodgson Mission left the country in 1927, the break in diplomatic relations inevitably made it difficult for the officials who returned to the country at the end of 1929 to make sense of the important changes which had taken place over the previous two and a half years. The Soviet government's tacit decision to abandon the NEP in favour of one designed to facilitate more rapid economic development came while there was no official British representation in Moscow. In addition, the contacts which Hodgson and his staff had made with Soviet citizens and officials during the 1920s were of little value to their successors, since many of these people had either been rounded up in the spy scandal of 1927 or were so intimidated by the whole affair that they refused to renew their links with the Embassy. Most important of all, the diplomatic and consular staff who travelled to Moscow at the end of 1929 were for the most part new to Russia and Russian affairs, with the result that it took them time to adjust to their new environment. George Paton, who returned to the country to take over as Commercial Secretary, was the only senior official with extensive experience of service in Soviet Russia.

The new Ambassador, the suave and debonair Sir Esmond Ovey, had dealt with Soviet affairs during his time at the Northern Department of the Foreign Office in the early 1920s, but he lacked any first-hand knowledge of the country, having served in Mexico and Argentina prior to taking up his duties in Moscow. Ovey was a typical product of the British diplomatic establishment, combining professional reticence with an ability to charm all those who came into contact with him.[5] Although dogged by ill-health during his three years in Moscow, he was a single-minded individual who came to the country committed to improving commercial relations between Britain and Russia – a subject that filled dozens of his dispatches.[6] The new Ambassador was initially disoriented on first arriving in Russia, since he had to come to terms not only with the political rituals of Soviet society but also with the alien quality of Russian life. His first impressions as he arrived by train from Poland were comparatively favourable: he believed that the dilapidated state of the towns and villages was no worse 'than that which distinguishes many of the smaller towns and the outskirts of the larger towns in North America'.[7] A few days of closer acquaintance with the realities of Soviet life soon changed his mind. The Ambassador quickly came to realise that 'one is undoubtedly living in a city and country which either are or imagine themselves to be in a state of siege', ruled over by a government committed to a 'quasi-religious war' against large sections of its own people.[8] Ovey's confusion in the face of such an alien political and ideological landscape was shared by his staff. Senior staff at the Embassy, such as the acting Counsellor Frank Ashton-Gwatkin and the First Secretary Colin Patrick, had gained most of their previous diplomatic experience in countries like Japan and Switzerland and were ill-equipped to understand the nuances of social and political life in a post like Moscow. Edward Walker, who took over as First Secretary in the summer of 1930, had previously served at Riga and at least had the advantage of knowing Russian when he arrived in the country, but only a few of his colleagues shared this advantage.[9] The Foreign Office's long-standing reluctance to allow senior diplomatic staff to remain in a particular country for any great length of time made it difficult for individual officials to develop their expertise, though it did help them to retain a broad perspective and flexibility that was of value in their peripatetic lifestyle. Nor did things become any easier for British diplomats and consular officials posted to Russia in the later 1930s, since few of them served there for more than three or four years at a time, which meant that they were often transferred at precisely the moment when they had started to develop a knowledge of the country and its people. When the 'steady and sound' Lord Chilston replaced Ovey as Ambassador at the end of 1933, he too faced all the problems encountered by his predecessor in adjusting to a complex new environment, since his previous postings had been in the very different settings of Vienna and Budapest.[10] In fairness to the Foreign Office, Moscow was a desperately unpopular post throughout the 1930s. Only one individual volunteered for service there during the whole of the 1930s,[11] while many others made little secret of their distaste for the country. Most of those sent to the Moscow Embassy or one of the Consulates were therefore only too keen to be relieved of their duties at the earliest possible moment.

The situation of British officials was particularly difficult during the first half of the decade, before the diplomatic community in Moscow had a chance to develop the collective experience needed to cope with the problems faced by its members. The British government had continued to lease the building used by the Hodgson Mission, in the years following the break in diplomatic relations, and it was quickly reoccupied by Ovey and his staff after their arrival in Moscow at the end of 1929. As the house was not large enough to provide suitable accommodation for a full-scale diplomatic residence, negotiations were started with the Soviet government to obtain a new building capable of meeting the needs of the Embassy. This proved to be a matter of considerable difficulty, since there was a shortage of all kinds of accommodation in Moscow. The Soviet authorities invariably demanded very high rents from foreigners (which naturally caused grave concern at the Treasury in London). It was eventually agreed that the Embassy should move to new premises in 'the ugly grandeur of a former sugar merchant's house', located on the banks of the Moscow River directly opposite the Kremlin.[12] The ornate building was finally occupied by the British Embassy at the beginning of 1931, following extensive repairs and improvements costing more than £18,000.[13] The old Hodgson house was kept on to provide accommodation for the Moscow Consulate and the Commercial Secretariat. A fourteen-room house in Leningrad was rented from the Finnish government to provide accommodation for the new Consulate there.[14]

Before the new Embassy building in Moscow was ready, life for British officials in the Soviet capital was extremely uncomfortable. Since there was little spare accommodation for them in the Hodgson house, the majority were forced to live at the Savoy Hotel which, in spite of its grand name, offered its patrons poor accommodation and 'meals so revolting ... that we preferred to live on tinned food in our rooms'.[15] The establishment did not, however, shrink from charging a small fortune for its services. One young consular official, Leslie Pott, was appalled by the expense of his accommodation, and repeatedly wrote to London to 'wail about the cost of living' and request an increase in his allowances – a demand that was echoed by many of his colleagues.[16] The financial situation of British officials during the early 1930s was made worse by the fact that, unlike representatives from every other country, they were instructed by the Foreign Office not to buy any of the black-market roubles which could be obtained from unofficial sources at a rate far more favourable than the one offered by the state bank. As this inevitably made it difficult for them to afford many of the basic necessities of life, a few officials even felt they had no choice but to ignore the instructions. The experienced and dignified Consul-General in Leningrad, Reader Bullard, wrote somewhat shamefacedly to the Foreign Office in London that if he had not bought black-market roubles his family would have faced the indignity of 'living on our relations', since his salary was quite insufficient to pay for his own expenses and those of his wife and children back home in England.[17]

The financial crisis which forced the British government to make savage public expenditure cuts in 1931 brought the whole question of expenses to a head, particularly given the high cost of maintaining a diplomatic establishment in Moscow. Ovey himself was bitterly opposed to any suggestion that diplomatic staff should be expected to make use of black-market roubles to keep down expenditure, even though his Counsellor, William Strang, was certain that the Soviet authorities would turn a blind eye to such transactions.[18] As usually happened when caught between a conflict of principle and parsimony, the Foreign Office was eventually swayed by considerations of cost. The Embassy was therefore authorised to acquire black-market roubles, though care was taken to ensure that the Soviet government should not obtain any definite evidence of such transactions. Ovey was also forced to consider some other rather undignified schemes for saving money, including renting out spare garage space at the new Embassy in order to raise cash. The whole question of diplomatic expenses continued to rumble on, leading to something of a crisis in 1932 when the Soviet authorities arbitrarily decided to stop allowing diplomats access to special shops where they could obtain scarce goods priced in roubles.[19] They insisted instead that foreign representatives should use hard currency for such transactions, which of course largely undermined the rationale for obtaining black-market roubles. Many of these practical problems became easier as the decade wore on, but even in the late 1930s it was still hard for newly-arrived officials to find decent accommodation at a price they could afford. One British Military Attaché found that his plight was only resolved when the Soviet Ministry of Defence took pity on him and helped to find a suitable flat, while as late as 1935 the Embassy was still desperately looking for extra accommodation to house its married staff.[20]

In spite of the money spent on converting the ornate new Embassy building, it was still not well suited to its role.[21] The Embassy was situated near a large vegetable market, 'with the result that in the summer, with the wind in certain quarters, there is an almost unbearable stench'. The rising waters of the Moscow River also threatened to flood the downstairs rooms each spring, following the annual thaw of snow. The building itself was large and rambling. The attics and cellars were so big that officials were quite unable to keep track of the large numbers of Tatar *dvorniky* (caretakers) and their families who lived there, many without the residence permit that was a legal requirement for all inhabitants of Moscow. The heating system constantly broke down, forcing Chancery staff to wear their overcoats throughout the winter, though the situation improved when a new oil-fired system was installed in 1932. The stoves in the two wings of the house, where a number of diplomatic and clerical staff had private apartments, were not ventilated properly and on occasions leaked dangerous fumes, much to the concern of the occupants. Many of the doors and windows fitted very badly, which made the building extremely drafty and uncomfortable in autumn and winter. The quality of fittings was also poor, even in rooms used to accommodate important guests – a matter of particular concern and embarrassment to the aesthetically-minded Lady Chilston when she arrived with her husband at the end of 1933. As a result, while officials posted to Moscow in the early 1930s generally preferred to stay either in the Embassy or at the Hodgson house, rather than face the rigours of one of the city's luxury hotels, their living conditions were for the most part still spartan and uncomfortable. Although a steady supply of domestic servants helped them to cope with the trials of everyday life, their lifestyle was far less luxurious and ceremonial than the one enjoyed by their colleagues at other British Embassies in Europe.

The supply of food for employees at the Moscow Embassy and Consulate was a source of concern in the early 1930s, particularly as there was considerable uncertainty about the terms on which the Soviet government would allow diplomats to have access to scarce goods. There

were few provisions available in the shops and the ration card to which
each foreign representative was entitled only allowed for the daily
purchase of a few hundred grammes of black bread. Stores were normally purchased centrally by the Embassy, the Chancery car being
dispatched several times a week to collect supplies from the special
shops reserved for diplomats and privileged employees of the Soviet
government. Large quantities of tinned food were also shipped in from
Britain, while the weekly messenger brought more perishable items
such as meat and vegetables. Despite these efforts, the absence of
refrigerators and ice meant that the diet of officials in Moscow was very
monotonous, which in turn led to 'the digestive troubles from which
most of the staff have suffered'. The arrival of a consignment of English
sausages was enough to send William Strang into raptures of delight
in 1930, leading to an impromptu dinner party with a Russian friend
to celebrate the arrival of such scarce delicacies. The shortage of decent
food also occasionally led to petty and bad-tempered squabbles, particularly among diplomatic spouses, who on occasion 'used to measure
the beetroot tails with a tape-measure' in order to make sure that they
received their fair share.

A poor diet was not the only trial faced by Ovey and his staff during
the early 1930s. They also lacked opportunities to enjoy the 'ordinary
human distractions' which William Strang believed were vital for the
'mental well-being' and morale of all foreign representatives forced to
confront the grim reality of Soviet Russia at first hand. The Embassy
had its own tennis court that was used for tennis parties in summer,
before being frozen over during the winter months to make a skating-
rink. A number of officials also went skiing, though the absence of hills
around Moscow meant that this was usually of the nordic rather than
alpine variety. In summer Embassy staff were able to bathe in the river
using the facilities of the Dynamo Club (which was also the sporting
club of the Secret Police). Officials who had access to a car could also
drive out of the city to enjoy the peace of the countryside although, as
Strang mournfully noted, the landscape was flat and not very pictur-
esque. The favourite form of entertainment for the foreign diplomatic
corps was, without doubt, the theatre.[22] The quality of Soviet produc-
tions remained fairly high throughout the 1930s, although an
unhealthily large proportion of new plays staged in the capital were
either 'propagandistic' dramas of uncertain quality or performances of
older works staged in a way designed to promote the policies of the
Soviet government. When Sir Esmond Ovey attended a performance
of *Carmen* soon after his arrival in Russia, he was dismayed to see that

the back of the stage was covered with a vast red banner calling on the audience to volunteer for extra work shifts during their holidays.[23] Visits to the opera and ballet were also popular with foreign representatives, particularly since they could obtain with ease the scarce tickets that were so eagerly sought by the general public. A few of the younger members of staff at the British Embassy even attended parties put on by members of the city's cultural elite, providing them with a rare chance to meet Soviet citizens in person. Nevertheless, these diversions could not outweigh the general hardship of diplomatic life, particularly in the first half of the 1930s, when the number of foreign diplomats and journalists in the capital was still too limited to provide much of a social milieu. While more staff brought their wives to Russia than in the 1920s, many of these diplomatic spouses so disliked the country that their presence often just had the effect of creating even greater stress for their husbands. While a strong esprit de corps did develop, which helped to protect officials against the pressures of daily life, living and working so closely together also created its own tensions – tensions that could on occasion even erupt in physical violence.[24] Strang wrote in 1931 that no British representative should be posted to Soviet Russia for more than six months without a break. He suggested that any tour of duty there should be strictly limited, since a lengthy posting might create a level of stress that would damage the physical and psychological health of the individual official.

The material conditions faced by British officials in Moscow during the 1930s improved considerably as the decade progressed, though the situation always remained rather grim in Leningrad. The accommodation in the Embassy and Hodgson house was gradually improved. The import of food supplies from abroad became better organised and officials were able to buy luxury goods for their own consumption. By the late 1930s, the diet of British officials in Moscow was not very different from the one enjoyed by their counterparts in Paris or Berlin; indeed, it was the only foreign Mission in Moscow, other than their own, where the fastidious staff of the American Embassy felt able to eat with a fair degree of confidence that they would not fall victim to food poisoning.[25] The most difficult feature of life in Moscow for the whole diplomatic corps continued to be the lack of the kind of social amenities that existed in other major European cities. The number of restaurants and nightclubs in Moscow was very small, and the quality of the food and entertainment provided in such establishments was usually dismal. For this reason, the foreign community had to rely heavily on one another for company and amusement. In some respects, diplomatic life in the capital was more normal in the 1930s than the 1920s, since a larger number of countries now had representatives in Moscow.[26] Each of these Ambassadors and Ministers brought their own coterie of officials with them, creating the basis for a diplomatic milieu that was at least at first glance not utterly unlike the ones which existed in other major capitals. One British diplomat posted to Moscow in the late 1930s recalled how 'Night after night we would put on our white ties and go and dine at one or another Embassy or Legation, sitting next to the same people, discussing the same topics'.[27] Relations were particularly close between staff at the British Embassy and their American counterparts, among whom were such talented young officials as George Kennan and Charles Bohlen, who both later played important roles in determining US policy towards the Soviet Union after the end of the Second World War.[28] British officials also frequently met with staff from the German Embassy, despite the political tension that existed in the second half of the 1930s between London and Berlin.[29] A few foreign representatives, including several at the British Embassy, rented country cottages or *dachas* outside the city where they could retreat at slack times. In this more relaxed atmosphere, the formal world of white tie receptions was left behind and it was possible for foreign diplomats and journalists to build friendships that helped to keep at bay the grim realities of Soviet life. Even so, the development of a private network of friends could not prevent a sense of *ennui* descending from time to time over the entire foreign diplomatic corps in Moscow. The daily life led by most foreigners in Russia, cut off as they were from any meaningful communication with the people around them, could at times become horribly tedious and and insular.

Although this closed world of diplomats and journalists was in most respects highly artificial, it did provide an important network for obtaining information. Several foreign Missions in Moscow proved to be more adept than the British at gleaning insights into the changes taking place in the USSR. Many Polish diplomats were able to pass themselves off as Russians, which gave them an opportunity to engage in the kind of informal conversations with Soviet citizens that were seldom possible for the tongue-tied British. Staff at the American Embassy were also better trained and prepared than their British counterparts for work in Moscow, since the US State Department placed far greater emphasis than its counterpart in London on encouraging staff to develop expert knowledge of a particular country or region. Once selected for service in Russia, they were sent to universities in Europe to undergo intensive postgraduate language training, before being posted to Baltic cities like

Riga where they had an opportunity to improve their linguistic skills and develop greater knowledge of Russian culture and history.[30] The American Embassy in Moscow was also more generously funded than the British Embassy, allowing its staff to travel frequently around the country in order to obtain information about the changes taking place there. However, since the various Embassies were on the whole ready to pool their information on an informal basis, the British were fortunate enough to benefit from the expertise and professionalism of other members of the diplomatic corps.

Staff posted to the British Embassy and Consulates in Russia during the 1930s did not find it any easier than their predecessors to report on the changes taking place around them, even though they had a number of advantages over officials who had served in the country during the 1920s. There had always been something rather makeshift about the Hodgson Mission, reflected both in the lowly status of Hodgson himself, as well as the Foreign Office's reluctance to provide him with the resources needed to carry out his work effectively. The resources made available to Ovey and Chilston were by contrast considerably more generous, despite the constant threat of expenditure cuts throughout the early 1930s. The level of clerical support was greater than in the 1920s, since a number of typists and receptionists were recruited both locally and in Britain to carry out some of the more mundane administrative work. Several senior officials were also provided with cars to help them carry out their duties (a virtual necessity given the appalling state of public transport in Moscow). Following an agreement between the Soviet and British governments in 1934, Military, Air and Naval Attachés were posted to the Moscow Embassy for the first time since the Bolshevik Revolution of 1917, providing London with a valuable new source of information. Nevertheless, an increase in staff could not alone overcome the problems involved in following economic and political developments in a country where the government was determined to prevent foreign officials from finding out the truth. Throughout the 1930s, British diplomats and consular officials had to spend an enormous amount of time and energy trying to penetrate the layer of secrecy with which Stalin and his minions attempted to shroud the whole of Soviet Russia.

Embassy and consular staff continued to rely heavily on personal observation and a detailed reading of the Soviet press when searching for information, since their contacts with senior Soviet officials were still for the most part fleeting. The most important members of the

Politburo remained 'in almost monk-like seclusion',[31] avoiding direct contact with the staff of foreign Missions. Ovey found Maxim Litvinov, who finally took over as Commissar for Foreign Affairs in 1930, difficult to deal with, writing in an early dispatch to London that he was 'more innately fanatical than I had expected', though 'not without a sense of humour' that made him quite congenial company in face to face meetings.[32] British officials were treated with courtesy whenever they visited the Commissariat but found that the promises made to them by officials there were often broken, without explanation or apology, while much of the information they were given about Soviet domestic affairs proved to be quite unreliable. The Embassy had almost no regular dealings with Soviet officials working outside the Commissariat or Burobin, the bureau responsible for maintaining its buildings. When the Commissar of Defence, Marshal Voroshilov, attended the British Embassy for dinner with the Ambassador in 1932, the visit was almost without precedent.[33] The occasion passed off extremely well, but was not followed by many other informal meetings of a similar kind. Perhaps surprisingly, the various Military Attachés who served in Moscow from the mid 1930s onwards were often more successful than their civilian counterparts at developing a working relationship with their Soviet hosts. Although sometimes treated with suspicion when visiting training establishments or watching military manoeuvres, they found that Red Army officers could on occasion be quite open about their activities. A certain military camaraderie seems to have prevailed despite the ideological hostility and tension between their political masters.

Embassy and consular staff found it even harder to develop contacts with ordinary Soviet citizens in the 1930s than had been the case during the previous decade. Consular staff in Leningrad were almost entirely isolated from the people living around them. Their reports often referred to the impossibility of having even the briefest conversation with any of the city's residents (though one official did, quite astonishingly, form a liaison with a local woman that lasted for a considerable period of time). By the early 1930s Leningrad had become one of the most dismal and fear-ridden cities in the Soviet Union. William Strang observed with amazement that foreign travellers arriving in Moscow 'usually remark upon the air of vitality, activity and relative cheefulness of the capital as contrasted with the bleakness and sordidness of Leningrad'.[34] The air of greater relaxation in Moscow was in truth rather bogus but, during the early 1930s in particular, Embassy officials did have more opportunities than consular staff in Leningrad to develop contacts with ordinary Soviet citizens. These meetings often came about by chance. In the summer of 1932, for example, the Archivist at the Embassy, George Vincent, made the acquaintance of three Soviet mechanics who came to his assistance when his car broke down on the outskirts of Moscow. He invited the men to his apartment for a meal, at which they engaged in a bitter diatribe against the failings of the Soviet government and the brutality of the Secret Police, sentiments which Vincent believed were 'typical ... of the contempt and bitterness of the general workers for the present situation'.[35] Vincent's guests were exceptional in their frankness, however, and it was only on rare occasions that British officials were able to have such open discussions with Soviet citizens. It was generally believed at the Embassy that individuals who willingly had dealings with foreign diplomats were 'probably *agents provocateurs*'.[36] Every British official therefore took care to avoid any friendships or associations that might be construed as suspicious by the Soviet authorities.

During the first half of the 1930s the Secret Police's monitoring of the activities of British officials in Russia was, if anything, rather less overt than had been the case when Hodgson and his staff worked in the city.[37] Even so, senior staff at the Embassy recognised that 'there is no reason to doubt that the GPU have copious information as to our private lives and characters as a result of their interrogation of official and domestic servants'.[38] The Soviet authorities missed few opportunities to put pressure on individuals whom they believed could be of value to them – though the quality of information they received was on some occasions very questionable. One young woman from an Anglo-Russian family who had extensive dealings with the Embassy was recruited as an informant in the summer of 1931; however, her 'control' in the Secret Police apparently received few reports of interest from her, other than details of supper menus and reports about games of table-tennis.[39] Although Embassy staff eventually worked out that one of their guests was in effect spying on them, they reacted remarkably nonchalantly, accepting that such things were an occupational hazard that could not be avoided. British officials travelling outside the major cities were particularly conscious of the ubiquitous security men who followed in their wake, since the countryside and small provincial towns did not provide their shadows with much opportunity to conceal their presence. For some of the more junior British officials, dodging these tails became something of a game. When Fitzroy Maclean served as a young Second Secretary at the Embassy in the late 1930s, he made a number of lengthy trips through the provinces, during which he found himself followed by the inevitable 'minders' from the Secret Police. On one occasion he tried to elude his escort by jumping onto a passing lorry carrying bails of cotton. Unfortunately, this particular ruse failed since the vehicle stopped abruptly, allowing one of the security men tailing him to catch up again. Nevertheless, the athletic Maclean took a mischievous delight in continuing his efforts to shake off his pursuers, much to the dismay of the two security men who had to take 'a good deal more exercise than they liked'.[40] While more senior staff scorned such antics, they could not resist poking fun at the Soviet authorities for their attempts to monitor the activities of British officials. When Maclean was arrested later during his trip by an overly zealous border guard, a senior member of the Embassy wrote to Litvinov chiding the two representatives of the Secret Police for allowing their quarry to come to harm.[41]

The cat and mouse game also had its more serious side. A number of Russian staff who worked at the Embassy were arrested and, in spite of formal protests, their fate often remained unknown (a pattern that was repeated at the American Embassy following the brief 'honeymoon' in US-Soviet relations which took place after Franklin D. Roosevelt's decision to extend diplomatic recognition in 1933). One employee was detained for six months before being allowed to return to her old job at the British Embassy, where she told officials that her imprisonment had only come about because she had been mistaken for someone else. The situation was particularly bad in 1936 and 1937, when the Great Terror was at its height. In autumn 1937, for example, a young female clerk-translator named Nina Bengson failed to turn up for work as usual, prompting the Embassy to lodge a series of complaints with the Commissariat of Foreign Affairs demanding information about their erstwhile employee. A few weeks later, one of the hall porters who lived in at the Embassy also disappeared without warning. Such arrests were undoubtedly designed to make it difficult for the Embassy to carry out its work, by discouraging Soviet citizens from having any contact with foreigners.[42] Although agents of the Secret Police could not directly harm British citizens working at the Embassy,[43] who were for the most part protected by diplomatic immunity, they succeeded in spinning an invisible web of fear round the building which deterred most sensible Soviet citizens from having anything to do with its occupants.

Since the size of the British official presence in Russia was greater in the 1930s than the 1920s, staff at the Embassy did have rather more opportunity than their predecessors to travel in search of the kind of information that could not be obtained in Moscow. The Soviet government did not encourage such trips, though the poor state of the roads and the indifferent quality of the rail network also helped to deter many diplomats from travelling further than was absolutely necessary. Nor were the British as enthusiastic travellers as their counterparts at the American Embassy, where young officials and senior staff alike were positively encouraged to take every opportunity to visit the provinces. The most enthusiastic 'tourist' at the British Embassy was Fitzroy Maclean, who made a number of trips to Central Asia in the second half of the 1930s, attracted there by the romance of this fabled and exotic region lying on the border of Russia and China. Even though the majority of his journeys were made without obtaining permission from the Soviet government, the authorities usually became aware quite quickly that a foreign diplomat was roving unattended through the provinces, with the result that the familiar shadows from the Secret Police soon appeared. Maclean's reports about central Asia and Siberia provided the Embassy and the Foreign Office with genuine information about life in these little-known Soviet provinces,[44] and his vivid accounts quickly earned the young diplomat a reputation as a central Asian expert. Although the reports submitted by other British officials who travelled in the provinces were seldom as colourful as the ones submitted by Maclean, they too provided a host of valuable insights that could not be obtained by sitting at a desk in the Embassy. Soviet citizens living in the provinces were usually more forthright than the residents of Moscow and Leningrad. When John Vyvyan, a young Third Secretary at the Embassy, went on a week's visit to Crimea and the Ukraine in 1932, he was surprised by the 'apparent fearlessness, outspokenness and disregard for the authorities' displayed by many of those with whom he came into contact.[45] Two officials who toured in the Caucasus for three weeks in 1935 also found that 'the people in general are less afraid to talk to casual foreigners' than was the case in the more oppressive atmosphere of Moscow.[46] Maclean similarly reported that it was quite easy to strike up conversation with fellow passengers when travelling by rail in central Asia or Siberia in the late 1930s, even though his visits to these regions coincided with some of the worst moments of the Great Terror. While the evidence that could be culled from such casual conversations was of limited value, they did at least give the Embassy an insight into the views of the Soviet public at a time when the government systematically denied its citizens any opportunity to express their opinions openly.

Embassy staff also made regular visits to factories and collective farms, which gave them an opportunity to see at first hand the massive economic changes taking place across the country.[47] Since foreigners were carefully chaperoned on these trips, it was difficult for them to talk with anyone but hand-picked officials, who carefully refrained from expressing views other than those already laid down in *Pravda* or other organs of the Soviet press. All they could do was keep their eyes open and make a mental note of anything that could prove to be of importance. During his trip to the Ukraine in 1932, Vyvyan was initially surprised by the apparent health of the local population in an area supposedly ravaged by famine until, walking unchaperoned through the streets of Rostov, he saw 'two men lying on the streets – their faces covered with flies'. None of the passers-by took any notice of them, a tell-tale sign that death from malnutrition and disease had become so common in the region that it was no longer a cause for any comment or concern. In another town, Vyvyan watched as a passer-by eagerly scraped out the contents of an old sardine tin into which some used tea-leaves had been emptied. Almost every British official who travelled in the provinces during the 1930s returned with similar stories about the dreariness of daily life and the poor standard of living.[48] Perhaps surprisingly, they often found that the local authorities were chaotic in the way they conducted their business, reflecting the problems which the government in Moscow had throughout the 1930s in establishing an effective administrative system outside the major cities. Even the local GPU representatives sometimes appeared to be taken by surprise when foreign officials turned up on their doorstep asking for help in obtaining accommodation or travel documents, suggesting that the much-feared Secret Police was at least on occasions less efficient and omniscient than its reputation implied.

Although Embassy staff relied a good deal on personal observation when compiling their reports, they still had to depend on the Soviet press for much of their information. Lord Chilston pointed out in 1935 that, as foreign diplomats in Moscow could only have the most fleeting contacts with officials and ordinary Soviet citizens, 'the study of the Press has an importance which from the point of view of information – not only of what is happening but of what is the policy of the Government and its attitude in foreign and internal affairs – is perhaps greater than anywhere else'.[49] Since the state-controlled press was used to announce government policy, a careful study was potentially of far greater importance than in a country where newspapers were free from official control. As had been the case in the 1920s, a thorough reading of the more specialised publications often yielded information about the country's economic development. George Paton compiled many detailed reports based on material culled from technical economic journals and other similar publications. Embassy staff also painstakingly

followed the published proceedings of the various congresses and committees that took place from time to time, in the hope that they would
yield some political intelligence of value. Yet monitoring the press and
translating articles was a time-consuming affair, particularly since the
Embassy only had one official translator throughout most of the 1930s.
Lord Chilston therefore recommended that the Foreign Office should
establish a special training scheme under which members of the Consular Service would be seconded for a year to a university or college,
where they could learn Russian, before being sent to Moscow to help
Embassy officials in the mammoth task of reviewing the Soviet press.[50]
This apparently sensible scheme was scotched by the Foreign Office,
ostensibly on the grounds that it would be difficult to organise, though
in reality it seems certain that the expense was the real reason for
rejecting the proposal. Once again, the British Embassy in Moscow
found itself handicapped when compared with its more generously
funded American counterpart.

The Embassy naturally had dealings with the burgeoning Western
press corps in Moscow, since its members could on occasion provide
useful information of a kind that was not normally available to foreign
representatives in Soviet Russia. Malcolm Muggeridge, who represented
the *Guardian* in Russia during the early 1930s, recalled in his memoirs
that Ovey and his colleagues did not normally make much effort to
exploit the knowledge and expertise of foreign journalists.[51] This was
not altogether true. Muggeridge himself was asked for his opinion about
Soviet affairs on a number of occasions, even though he represented a
left-wing newspaper that was viewed with suspicion by most British
diplomats. The Embassy even canvassed the opinions of Walter Duranty,
the notoriously pro-Soviet correspondent who worked for the *New York
Times*.[52] The views of western academics and businessmen visiting Russia
were also assiduously sought, particularly during the second half of the
1930s, since staff there recognised the value of any scrap of information
in a country where so little was available. Nevertheless, British representatives were instinctively cautious about giving too much credence
to the reports of newspapermen and other foreigners visiting Russia.
They knew that the Soviet government had become extremely skilful
at managing foreign correspondents, with the result that even the most
diligent of journalists could occasionally be hoodwinked. In any case,
although the press corps in Russia during the 1930s was certainly
not made up of fellow-travellers, and some like the *Daily Telegraph*
correspondent A. T. Cholerton were extremely hostile to all things socialist, there was a fair sprinkling of individuals who were only too

willing to give the authorities the benefit of the doubt when reporting on the changes taking place in the country.

Most foreign diplomats posted to Russia in the 1930s were of course sheltered from the dreadful events on which they reported. Although staff at the British Embassy and Consulates were on occasion anxious about their own safety, the Foreign Office in London was confident that the Soviet government would not harm foreign diplomats even at times of international tension.[53] Nor did British officials have many close Soviet friends to worry about, though there was a good deal of concern about the fate of Russian staff at the Embassy who were unlucky enough to fall victim to the Secret Police. While British officials themselves faced little danger, the same was not always true of their fellow nationals living in Russia. The fate of the small British colony was a matter of constant concern at the Embassy and the Consulates. A number of British citizens were arrested during the 1930s. Dealing with their cases gave diplomatic and consular staff a vivid insight into the reality of Soviet power – and the powerlessness of those who were crushed by it. Members of the British colony in Russia fell into a number of categories. There was in the first place a small number of engineers and businessmen, employed by foreign firms who had won contracts from the Soviet government. A second group of British 'nationals' came from families that had been resident in Russia for many years. A large number of them spoke no English and did not even possess a British passport; indeed, consular staff in both Moscow and Leningrad had to spend a good deal of time trying to establish whether particular individuals were really entitled to help and assistance. Other British residents in Soviet Russia had been attracted to the country in the heady days after 1917, enthused by a desire to help build the world's first socialist state. Many became disillusioned by the events of the 1930s, however, and sought the help of the Embassy to return home – though some had been foolish enough to take up Soviet citizenship which meant that they could not be given much assistance or protection. The engineers and businessmen were by contrast usually safe, since they were carrying out work that was deemed by the Soviet government to make an important contribution to the country's economic development. Even so, they too could sometimes fall victim to the authorities, most notably in 1933 when a number of employees of the Vickers Company were arrested and put on trial accused of charges ranging from espionage to economic sabotage.[54] The Embassy was convinced of the men's innocence, but the case provided them with an insight into the workings of the Secret Police. Although the prisoners were treated quite well, the whole affair caused enormous tension between London and Moscow and threatened at one stage to lead to a complete break in diplomatic relations. It even played a role in bringing about the departure from Russia of Sir Esmond Ovey, who 'got himself recalled' towards the end of 1933 in large part because he did not believe that London was sufficiently resolute in protesting about the behaviour of the Soviet government.[55]

The fate of long-term British residents in the USSR was in many ways the most pathetic of all. The main threat to their welfare did not come from arrest and imprisonment, although a number did fall foul of the Secret Police, usually on the entirely bogus grounds that they had assisted officials at the Embassy to carry out espionage.[56] The real challenge came instead from poverty and deprivation, particularly since many members of the colony were old and frail. Unlike staff at the Embassy or employees of foreign companies, they did not have access to supplies of hard currency or special stores where scarce goods could be purchased. Many were looked after by the British Subjects in Russia Relief Association, a remarkable organisation set up by the indomitable Muriel Paget to provide money and assistance to those unfortunates who could not support themselves.[57] Lady Paget had long experience of Russia, dating back to pre-revolutionary days, when she had developed numerous close friendships among the upper reaches of the nobility as well as the foreign diplomatic corps. During the 1920s she had helped to establish a Relief Fund that was used by Hodgson and Preston to channel financial assistance to distressed British subjects. The Association itself was set up in 1930 and eventually developed quite an elaborate infrastructure, including a residential home in Leningrad and a small staff who organised the distribution of food and fuel to British residents in Russia who had no reliable source of income. Dozens of men and women, ranging from elderly governesses to retired footmen, relied on the organisation as their sole means of survival in an increasingly brutalised society, in which there was little sympathy for the plight of foreign nationals who had originally come to Russia to serve the privileged classes of the old Tsarist regime. The British government gave money to the Association via its officials in Leningrad, effectively delegating part of its consular functions to a private organisation.

Unfortunately, both Reader Bullard and his successor as Consul-General in Leningrad, Bernard Gilliat-Smith, loathed Lady Paget intensely, with the result that the relationship between the Relief Association and consular staff was always very tense. Bullard wrote bitterly to the Foreign Office, after one particularly stormy meeting, that Lady

Paget 'showed clearer signs of madness than ever, and a more determined lack of scruple'.[58] Other officials similarly blanched at the
prospect of any dealings with the Chairwoman of the Relief Association.
In the late 1930s, when it became clear that the organisation would
have to leave Russia after its members were accused of espionage by
the Soviet government, the British Consul in neighbouring Estonia
desperately tried to persuade the Foreign Office in London that the
country should not become the new base for Lady Paget's activities.[59]
The high-handed manner of the Chairwoman of the Association grated
on officials who resented the demands she placed on their scarce time
and resources. Nevertheless, while Lady Paget could undoubtedly be
imperious in manner, her organisation played a remarkable role in
providing assistance to members of the British colony in Russia at a
time when official representatives could do very little to help them.

In spite of the difficulties they faced when reporting on Stalin's Russia,
staff at the British Embassy and the two Consulates sent thousands of
reports to London during the 1930s, designed to keep the Foreign
Office informed about everything from high politics through to the
state of the Soviet construction industry. The picture they painted of a
country going through wrenching economic and social change remains
a compelling one, even if the restrained tone of their dispatches sometimes failed to capture the full drama of the events on which they
reported. In the second half of the decade, the horrors of the Great
Terror naturally dominated the dispatches sent by the Embassy to the
Foreign Office in London. During the first part of the 1930s, however,
the most common topic was without doubt the transformation of the
Soviet economy and the social changes associated with it. Stalin's attempt to rebuild the economy at breakneck speed, following his decision
to abandon the New Economic Policy, required the development of an
elaborate apparatus of central planning, the foundations of which were
laid down in the 1920s with the establishment of Gosplan (1921) and
the first Five Year Plan (1927).[60] It quickly became clear that the Soviet
leadership planned to use the government's enhanced control over the
economy to modernise and expand the country's farms and factories,
so as to overcome once and for all the legacy of Russia's economic
backwardness.

There were a number of motives behind the Soviet government's
decision to promote rapid economic development, though the most
important was undoubtedly the desire to build 'Socialism in One Country', while simultaneously developing the material wherewithal to

defendthe Soviet Union against possible invasion from abroad. William Strang suspected that the government's desire to adopt a rapid pace of industrial development was driven by its belief that 'there are limits to the period during which the population may be expected to endure the hardships inseparable from a policy of intensive and comprehensive reconstruction'.[61] During the early 1930s at least one official at the Embassy believed that the population was on the point of rebelling against the atrocious living conditions they suffered, the result of the collectivisation of agriculture and the diversion of resources to the construction of new factories,[62] though most of his colleagues were confident that the natural passivity of the Russian people in the face of their rulers would once again prevail.[63] Whatever the exact reasons for promoting a programme of crash modernisation, the audacious attempt to rebuild an an entire economy on new foundations attracted a great deal of attention beyond Russia's borders. The Great Depression of the 1930s, which highlighted the flaws in the free enterprise system, created an upsurge of interest in the possibility of planning economic activity so as to avoid the horrors of unemployment and mass poverty. A stream of foreign visitors arrived in the USSR throughout the decade, anxious to see for themselves how the government there was attempting to promote economic development. When British officials first returned to Russia at the end of 1929, they were immediately struck by the Soviet government's obssession with the state of the economy, which Ovey believed was 'the dominating political problem of the present moment'.[64] The Ambassador himself was agnostic as to whether the 'Great Experiment' set in motion by the Five Year Plans was likely to succeed or fail.[65] Like Stalin himself, he recognised that the economic and political survival of the Soviet government depended on its success in transforming the face of the Russian countryside.[66] Without dramatic changes in the agricultural sector, the whole elaborate programme of industrialisation was doomed to failure – and with it the edifice of Communist rule.

The collectivisation of agriculture which ripped apart the social and economic infrastructure of rural Russia in the early 1930s was always something of a second-hand experience for British officials. Since they were largely confined to two major cities, neither of which was situated in an important agricultural region, they rarely had the opportunity to see the process in action for themselves. This perhaps accounts for the curiously bloodless texture of the reports sent to London. The Embassy staff were initially inclined to treat collectivisation as an essentially economic affair: an attempt to increase agricultural productivity and output by creating large-scale farms in place of small and supposedly inefficient peasant holdings. Their early dispatches, in particular, were filled with dry reflections on such arcane technical problems as the supply of tractors and other agricultural machinery to the new farms. It took some time for them to realise that there was a vital political dimension to collectivisation, which was in large part a consequence of the Soviet government's desire to end once and for all the tension between town and countryside that had constantly threatened to undermine the regime in the 1920s. The destruction of the traditional institutions of rural society, and the creation of new large-scale *latifundia*, provided the government with an opportunity to extend Soviet power more effectively into rural areas. It also facilitated the grim business of dekulakisation, the deportation of the wealthier and more vocal strata among peasant society to the wastelands of central Asia and other similarly remote areas. Since the Embassy did not fully recognise the importance of these aspects of collectivisation, its members sometimes found it difficult to comprehend the sheer brutality and violence of the whole process.

A number of journalists and other foreign observers did provide the Embassy with descriptions of the collectivisation process,[67] but even these were of limited value since the authorities took care to ensure that few witnesses were present at the moment when whole villages were uprooted and 'urged' to move to one of the new collective farms. British officials in Moscow knew that special detachments of young workers were sent from the cities to help in the task, 'their departure being celebrated at the railway stations by speeches, bands, and bunting'.[68] They also heard rumours that some members of these 'shock-brigades' were apprehensive about their task, while others relished the prospect of helping to construct socialism in the Russian countryside. There was little love lost between many urban workers and their erstwhile cousins in the villages, particularly following the various food scares of the 1920s. The combination of ideological hatred and economic resentment allowed the Soviet government to mobilise a considerable degree of popular support for its collectivisation programme.[69] The Embassy was aware that troops often had to be called in to impose order in rural areas during the early 1930s,[70] though the staff there had little detailed information about the fate of millions of the deported kulaks, who were frequently left to die once they had been dumped unceremoniously thousands of miles from their homes. An assistant Archivist at the Embassy, C. H. Hardy, was by chance present at one railway station when a goods train pulled in crammed with kulaks bound for 'the great concentration camp at Vologda',[71] but it was rare for any member of the Embassy staff to be confronted in so immediate a fashion by the horrors taking place beyond Moscow. Although the Soviet government could not completely prevent foreigners from obtaining information about the agricultural revolution it had set in progress, it was for the most part able to keep the worst excesses secret from the representatives of foreign power.

If the process of collectivisation was brutal, the famine that followed was even more devastating, particularly in the Ukraine where millions died.[72] The social and economic disruption caused by the destruction of the traditional fabric of rural society led to a catastrophic fall in agricultural output, while the authorities seized a large proportion of the food that was actually produced in order to feed the burgeoning urban population. The Embassy was well aware that food production fell rapidly in the early 1930s, hearing rumours that many peasants destroyed their own animals rather than hand them over to the new collective farms.[73] Although a number of British officials, including George Paton and John Vyvyan, were able to tour a few of the farms, they were invariably taken to showcase establishments where the workers were well fed and food production was proceeding smoothly. Some of the best evidence of the famine's impact available to Embassy staff came from journalists like Malcolm Muggeridge, whose harrowing articles in the *Guardian* provided a graphic insight into the horrors taking place in the Russian countryside. A number of reports were also provided by Andrew Cairns, a Canadian working for the Empire Marketing Board, who wrote in painful detail of the suffering he witnessed during a trip through the Ukraine and South Russia in 1933. One unexpected source of information came from a mass of unsolicited and anonymous letters sent by Soviet citizens to the British Embassy and Consulates describing the horrors of their daily life. Some of these letters were heartbreaking. One anonymous author wrote in 1933 that in his region:

> The population would be glad to eat carrion but there is none to be found. They are digging up horses that have died from glanders, and people are also eating them and finally they have not only invented the method of killing and eating each other but also dig up dead bodies and eat them.[74]

Reports of cannibalism in the areas worst hit by famine were commonplace. Many correspondents spoke of the 'complete catastrophe' that had overtaken Russia, pitifully begging the Embassy and the British government to 'save us who are dying of hunger'.[75] A number of letters blamed the catastrophe on a Jewish conspiracy, accusing the 'Yids' of 'pumping out all the wealth of Russia, transferring it abroad'. Several correspondents were quite explicit in their views that there was only one way to destroy these 'Soviet-Jewish machinations', warning the Embassy that 'If you do not want the same thing to happen in England join the Hitler movement'.[76] The vast majority of letters were believed to be genuine by the Embassy, though it was recognised that some of them could be the work of *agents provocateurs*. Extracts from a few of the more literate letters were forwarded to the Foreign Office, to provide staff there with a graphic, first-hand insight into conditions in the provinces.

In spite of all this evidence, British diplomats based in the comparative comfort of the Moscow Embassy still found it difficult to comprehend the sheer scale of the tragedy taking place in the countryside; ironically, staff at the Foreign Office in London probably had a greater sense of the extent of the suffering, since they received reports about the famine from a large number of different sources. Even though William Strang heard rumours that up to ten million peasants had died during collectivisation and its aftermath, he seemed to find it hard to accept that this 'fantastic figure' was accurate.[77] A number of his colleagues also struggled to believe that such casualties could occur as a result of a deliberate policy adopted by a government indifferent to the suffering it created for millions of its own people, though Sir Esmond Ovey himself had few doubts that the Soviet government was determined to push through its rural revolution whatever the cost in human lives.[78] Malcolm Muggeridge later accused the British government of hushing up the scale of the famine during the 1930s. The charge has been echoed more recently by a number of historians, who have suggested that the Foreign Office wanted to improve the reputation of the Soviet government in Britain in order to focus public concern on the threat posed by the rising power of Nazi Germany.[79] It is difficult to substantiate these charges, not least because Foreign Office anxiety over Germany only really began to mount after the famine in the USSR was past its peak. If there was any such attempt to conceal the tragedy unfolding in Russia, it certainly took place in London rather than at the Moscow Embassy. While it is true that British diplomats based in the Soviet Union could sometimes appear curiously disengaged from the horrors on which they reported, they were members of an organisation whose professional culture emphasised the virtues of objectivity and detachment. In any case, although Embassy staff received hundreds of reports about the plight of rural Russia during collectivisation, they seldom witnessed the suffering with their own eyes, which perhaps tended to inculcate a degree of aloofness that could easily appear to outsiders as unfeeling indifference.

Embassy and consular staff generally found it easier to report on the country's industrial development than on changes taking place in rural areas. Moscow and Leningrad both expanded rapidly during the 1930s, as the number of factories in each city grew rapidly. While this gave British representatives an opportunity to witness some of the changes at first hand, the most dramatic growth took place elsewhere. Millions of Soviet citizens were mobilised to work on huge construction programmes across the country. New cities were built and old ones transformed beyond recognition, while power stations and hydro-electric dams mushroomed in regions that had once been virtually uninhabited. Many of the workers in these remote areas were young volunteers, attracted either by the prospect of high pay or fired with enthusiasm at the chance to participate directly in the construction of socialism. The British Consulate in Leningrad, however, also received numerous reports during the early 1930s indicating that forced labour was employed extensively in some of these projects, particularly by the massive timber industry that flourished in the isolated north west of the country.[80] Although it was impossible for consular officials to verify these claims in person, the reports were confirmed by the handful of western journalists who managed to get permission to travel in the region.[81] Embassy and consular staff were also occasionally given eye-witness accounts of the grim conditions in the labour camps by relatives of individuals unfortunate enough to be sent there.[82] Other accounts were provided by British nationals who had for one reason or another witnessed at first hand the plight of those who had fallen victim to arrest and deportation. One report handed to the Leningrad Consulate described in graphic detail the situation faced by those working on the White Sea Canal project, where the forced labour was comprised of a mixture of ordinary convicts and political prisoners. The barracks in which the workers lived were 'terribly overcrowded', while 'No proper sanitary or washing arrangements were installed' either in the mens' or womens' quarters. The flesh of the prisoners swelled dreadfully in the Arctic conditions. 'Men often returned from work so utterly exhausted that they sank down on the barrack-room floor and died.'[83] Although the *gulag* did not reach its full extent until the late 1930s, it was already well developed by the early years of the decade.

Officials from the Moscow Embassy sometimes travelled outside the city to see for themselves the vast new industrial projects that were springing up across the provinces. George Paton travelled with a party of

American economists through European Russia in 1930, visiting the huge new automobile factory at Nizhny Novgorod, four hundred miles east of the capital, where American engineers were helping to construct a new plant designed to produce 140,000 cars and trucks per annum.[84] Paton was struck, like the other visitors, by the gigantic size of the development. A new power station and training school for the workforce had been built alongside the factory, as well as a railway line to connect the plant with the rest of the rail network. It was also planned to build a 'Workers City' to house up to 50,000 workers and their families. After leaving Nizhny Novgorod, the party of western visitors went on to Stalingrad, where they visited an equally enormous tractor plant that was under construction in the city. While journeys like these did not provide foreign representatives with much detailed information about the development of the Soviet economy, they did impress on them the scale of the changes which were taking place. Following his 1930 trip, Paton was convinced that, despite the many economic difficulties facing the USSR, its government was utterly resolved to 'to carry out their plans for the industrial and agricultural development of the country'. His views were shared by most of his colleagues, who had no doubt that the Soviet leadership possessed both the ruthlessness and the determination required to ensure the realisation of its ambitious plans for the economy.

The enormous pace of industrialisation soon forced the Soviet government to introduce new measures to guarantee greater labour discipline and ensure that workers could be directed to the areas where they were most needed. The Embassy monitored the process in some detail, sending London detailed reports about the introduction of a new system of internal passports, which Ovey believed led to the 'virtual economic and political enslavement' of the population.[85] The Ambassador and his colleagues were also struck by the Soviet government's rejection of any semblance of wage egalitarianism, a policy that was of course designed to increase the material rewards for productive workers.[86] Most intriguing of all, however, was the rise of the Stakhanovite movement in the middle of the 1930s, a subject that filled many reports sent to London by the Embassy. The movement was named after a coal miner who, in the course of a single shift, overfulfilled his individual target by more than a 1000 per cent.[87] Soviet propaganda quickly seized on such feats of individual heroism, hoping that they could be used to inspire other workers to achieve similar results. Embassy staff were struck by the essential banality of Stakhanovism, with its quasi-military language and desperate attempt to construct a cult of proletarian heroism. Nevertheless, they recognised the potential social and political significance of a movement which, like so many initiatives of the Soviet government, was taken to an unreasoning extreme during the first flush of enthusiasm.[88] The principle was even extended at one stage to workers in scientific institutes, who were urged to imitate the example of industrial workers by extending their own intellectual creativity by a multiple of several times.[89] Lord Chilston pointed out in a dispatch sent to London in 1936 that the whole idea was absurd and could not 'be indefinitely continued without serious damage', since 'working at high tension' created 'overstrain and exhaustion' that in time became counter-productive.[90] The Ambassador was of course correct. Nevertheless, while such a phenomenon as Stakhanovism was in many ways little more than a creation of the Soviet propaganda machine, designed to create a culture of urgency and heroism capable of mobilising the population behind the industrialisation drive, it was also an integral part of the Stalinist system. Although the contribution of Stakhanovism to the massive rise in industrial output achieved in the 1930s was limited, the movement was an important symbol of the Soviet government's desire to portray the unity between its own goals and those of the population. In reality, industrialisation was achieved by adopting policies that required draconian labour legislation to ensure their implementation. In the fantasy world created by Soviet propaganda, though, the success of the industrialisation programme was due to the heroic efforts of the population inspired by the vision and leadership of Joseph Stalin.

It was hard for British representatives to make any detailed judgement about the success of the drive for industrial development, not least because failures were seldom reported in detail in the Soviet press, while the published figures were extremely suspect. George Paton shrewdly observed in 1932 that the biggest problem involved in assessing the Soviet economy concerned the yardstick to be used when measuring its performance. He poured scorn on the government's decision to seek to fulfil the Five Year Plan in just four years, pointing out that farms and factories were already finding it difficult to meet their existing targets. Even so, noted Paton, 'if even a matter of 50 or 60 per cent of the tasks laid down in the original plan are completed, the achievement is not one that can be scoffed at. A new Russia is being created'.[91] His view was endorsed by his colleagues at the Embassy. William Strang acknowledged as early as 1930 that, despite the many difficulties faced by the Soviet government, it still had 'a remarkable achievement to show' for its determined effort to establish the foundations of a modern industrial economy in the course of just a few years. By the second half of the 1930s the Embassy accepted as a *fait accompli* Russia's emergence as a major industrial power; indeed, Paton was increasingly concerned that it might prove to be an important commercial rival to Britain in many overseas markets. While the economic transformation of the 1930s was an extraordinarily brutal process that destroyed millions of lives, by the time the decade drew to a close the Soviet government had come closer to solving the age-old problem of Russian backwardness than any of its predecessors. Even though the population at large did not reap the benefits of the changes, they were living in a country that had become one of the world's major industrial powers.

Although officials like Paton found it difficult to produce reliable figures about the scale of industrialisation, they were in a much better position to assess its impact on at least one section of the Soviet population: the residents of Moscow and Leningrad. Although living standards in the major cities were higher than in the countryside, conditions remained grim throughout the 1930s. The rapid rate of urbanisation brought huge social problems in its wake, which the government tried to counter periodically by expelling groups of people in an attempt to alleviate some of the strain. Reader Bullard in Leningrad heard many reports of suicides among people told that they were about to be deported from the city. The same pattern was repeated in Moscow, where Ovey relied on his Soviet barber for information about the clampdown on illegal workers in the city. This desperation to remain in the two biggest Soviet cities seemed all the stranger to British officials given the poor conditions endured by most of the residents. From the moment Ovey and his staff travelled to Russia at the end of 1929, they were struck by the greyness of daily life in Moscow and Leningrad. After the Ambassador had been in post for a short time, he wrote to the Foreign Office that:

> One becomes used, after a few months, to the general aspect of dinginess which strikes one so strongly on arrival. The average appearance of the crowds becomes gradually less remarkable, and one begins to notice the outstanding figures – those who are, literally, in rags, and those whom, by a stretch of the imagination or forgetfulness, one can actually describe as well-dressed.[92]

He went on to describe the lack of food in the shops and the absence of almost any other goods available for purchase. The problems were particularly acute for 'the class of unfortunates ... priests, ex-business men, ex-employees of the police force and the secret police, former military and naval officers', who received no ration cards and could not afford the high prices of food sold on the open market. Although the

Ambassador occasionally intervened on behalf of such people with the Soviet authorities, he was abruptly told that their welfare was none of his business.

The situation was if anything worse in Leningrad, particularly during the early 1930s. Douglas Keane noted in the summer of 1930 that, while the city looked on the surface much as it had before the revolution, in reality the general conditions were desperate and 'All necessaries of life have become scarcer even during the short period I have been here ... Queues are now formed for almost every commodity, are of increasing length and begin to show less good temper than formerly'.[93] The shortages made the Consul's own life difficult, even though he was able to obtain food from the special stores reserved for foreigners. He had to spend two weeks scouring the city to find a broom-handle, let alone other more necessary supplies. By the beginning of the following year, disease was also becoming a big problem in the city, a consequence of bad food and poor housing that undermined the health of the population. Both Keane and his successors reported in detail on the frequent outbreaks of typhus and dysentery that took their toll on the population in Leningrad throughout the 1930s. The housing crisis was particularly acute, since the local authorities were quite unable to build enough new apartments to cope with the influx of people into the city. Reader Bullard described one case in which a single 'room contains five beds nearly touching, and each bed contains a family of two or more persons'.[94] William Strang in Moscow spoke for many of his colleagues in the summer of 1931 when he reviewed his impressions of Russia after one just year in the country:

> I must confess that after a year in the country I find more that makes for depression and less than makes for cheerfulness than I did a year ago. People seem less well-favoured (and many more positively ugly), less well-disposed, less buoyant.[95]

There was a remarkable consistency in the reports that emanated from the British Embassy and the Consulates over the years that followed, despite the considerable fluctuations in the country's economic fortunes. Although a massive programme of housing construction was in place throughout the 1930s, Lord Chilston noted in 1937 that living conditions in Moscow were still 'almost unbelievably bad', while the housing stock was shoddily constructed and quite unsuitable for 'the enormously increased number of families which now occupy them'.[96] Even though the food crisis in the cities eased as the decade progressed, officials continued to be overwhelmed by the shabbiness and dinginess of Soviet life. While

out-and-out starvation in the larger cities became much rarer, most of
the urban population appeared to be crushed and dispirited by the
cramped material conditions under which they lived. Officials who
travelled outside Moscow and Leningrad usually found that the situation
was even worse in provincial towns, where the rate of population growth
was higher and the absence of proper food and housing more noticeable
than ever. When Fitzroy Maclean visited the cities of Sverdlovsk and
Novosibirsk in 1937, he was struck by the 'uniformly depressed appearance' of the crowds and the 'shoddily constructed and very roughly
finished' new apartment blocks.[97] William Hayter and Noel Charles were
slightly more sanguine following a 1935 trip to the Transcaucasus, since
the Soviet regime there appeared to 'take a milder and more actively
benevolent form than elsewhere'. Even so, the material conditions faced
by the population were still dismal. Workers in Baku lived 'in the most
appalling plank hovels' while in Yerevan they had to make do with 'mud
huts'.[98] Since foreign representatives travelling in the provinces were
less protected from the rigours of everyday life than in Moscow, their
experience of the difficulties faced by the population was more immediate and personal than ever. A few days exposure to a diet of 'almost
inedible food' quickly served to depress the spirits of even the most
resilient official,[99] encouraging them to scamper back to the comparative
comfort of Moscow at the first opportunity.

There were a few exceptions to the seemingly universal pattern of
deprivation and poverty. After Stalin's strictures against the principle of
wage egalitarianism in the early 1930s, workers in certain key industries
were able to earn comparatively high wages that allowed them a much
higher standard of living than the rest of the population. Senior officials
in the state and party bureaucracies enjoyed an even more privileged
life-style. At the end of 1931, William Strang wrote to London that:

> one of the noteworthy developments in Moscow life during the past year
> or so is the emergence, perhaps temporarily, of a new urban *bourgeois*
> class. They are distinguishable from the mass of the population by being
> obviously better fed, and by being well and even, by local standards,
> smartly dressed ... They frequent the more expensive, if still modest,
> native restaurants, from which the poor and hungry are turned away.
> They live, by our standards, plainly, but in this country it is luxury to
> have enough.[100]

Reader Bullard noticed a similar phenomenon in Leningrad, where
Party officials and the labour aristocracy benefited from high wages
and shorter working hours, while luckless office workers 'often work

inhumanly long hours'. These reports about the emergence of a 'new bourgeoisie' were in many respects similar to the ones sent from Russia by Robert Hodgson and Thomas Preston during the early days of the NEP, though the social and economic composition of the privileged class of the 1930s was of course quite different from its predecessor. The striking differences in income and living standards became a source of repeated comment in reports sent to London from the Moscow Embassy throughout the 1930s. Strang observed in a 1932 dispatch that the privileges enjoyed by the small number of people able to patronise the new restaurants that had sprung up in Moscow were increasingly resented by the rest of the population, 'whose living conditions may vary from the passable to the almost intolerable'.[101] The Soviet government remained unconcerned about the whole issue and continued actively to promote wage differentials, particularly during the years when the Stakhanovite movement was in vogue. On the eve of the Great Terror, in 1936, Gilliat-Smith in Leningrad reported a sharp increase in the quantity of goods in the shops for the small number of buyers who had 'money to burn', and went on to note that cafés and restaurants were 'springing up all over the town' while:

> Other *bourgeois* tendencies, which two years ago would have been frowned on by the authorities, have now their benignant approval and support. Western dancing, predominantly jazz, is being actively fostered. Numerous schools of dancing have sprung up, and according to reports which have reached us are immensely popular and are frequented by young doctors, surgeons, clerks, engineers and technicians.[102]

Gilliat-Smith also approvingly observed that the authorities were trying to encourage the population to dress better, adding that the Soviet press was giving considerable prominence to descriptions of new fashions, a trend which would have been unthinkable a few years earlier. Lord Chilston in Moscow was so struck by the scale of the changes in the mid 1930s that he even felt compelled to send a lengthy dispatch to London early in 1936 rebutting the idea that they were the harbinger of an impending return to capitalism.[103] The Ambassador instead pointed out that, although the appearance of new privileged groups in the Soviet Union seemed at first glance to be somewhat ironic, given the Communist ideology espoused by its rulers, hierarchies of status and income were a natural feature of all societies; they did not signify that the Soviet government was abandoning its commitment to the construction of socialism. However, such messages did not always seem to be understood at the Foreign Office. One senior official, when reading Gilliat-Smith's report, scribbled on it that 'On the whole it [Russia] would appear to be moving slowly but surely towards a "Middle West" conception of life – a new aristocracy based on wealth, an inordinate enthusiasm for jazz music, disregard for the poor and unsucessful – all these are typically American characteristics'.[104] Staff at the Embassy and Consulates were fortunate enough not to see the minute, since their hearts would surely have sunk had they known how little real understanding of Russia their reports engendered among at least some Foreign Office officials.

The growth of inequality in Soviet society during the 1930s was not the only social change that took British representatives by surprise. They were also struck by the government's attempt to reverse many of the liberal social reforms that had been introduced in the 1920s – a development which one senior official suggested was as important a change in policy as the decision to abandon the NEP.[105] Following the 1917 revolution, at least some leaders of the new regime had vigorously attacked the traditional social structure based on the family as irredemiably bourgeois in character.[106] In the permissive climate of the 1920s, both the divorce rate and the abortion rate began to increase rapidly. By the mid 1930s, however, the Soviet government was increasingly concerned that these changes might undermine some of its most important policies, most notably the achievement of rapid economic growth. Lord Chilston reported on the issue at some length, noting the increased number of articles in the Soviet press denouncing the 'light-handed attitude to marriage' that was widespread in Soviet society.[107] The Embassy also provided London with copies of various decrees that were issued outlawing abortion and announcing financial rewards for mothers of large families. The Ambassador was uncertain about the real significance of the policy. Since the population was already growing at the rate of about three million a year, he could not understand why the Soviet government wished to increase it still further. He was sceptical about the argument that Stalin was 'taking a very long view', encouraging population growth in the hope that it would lead to an increase in Soviet economic and military power a generation down the line. The Ambassador was instead inclined to believe that the new socially conservative climate reflected the instincts of Stalin himself, as well as a shrewd calculation that 'married couples with large and young families are less likely than the old-fashioned Communist exponent of free love to wish for a violent overthrow of the existing Soviet order'.[108] As was usually the case in Stalinist Russia, concern about maintaining and extending the power of the leadership was the main leitmotiv of government policy.

If British diplomats in Russia found it hard to report on the country's economic and social transformation during the 1930s, the difficulties faded into insignificance when compared with the problem of monitoring the political changes that took place in the same decade. Joseph Stalin had by 1930 firmly established his position as the most powerful figure within the Soviet Communist Party, but there were still many individuals who could, and did, attempt to use Party committees and congresses to impose limits on his power.[109] Ten years later, virtually all possible rivals to Stalin were dead, while the Party organisation itself had been deprived of any real power and influence. Stalin instead exercised power through a complex ad hoc network of individuals and organisations that posed no corporate challenge to his position. The Soviet leadership had of course used force to destroy its opponents on many occasions before the infamous Great Terror of 1936–38, most notably in the years following the 1917 revolution and during the collectivisation process of the early 1930s. It was only as the decade wore on that terror began to be used systematically against leading figures in the Communist Party itself, however, as well as against those who occupied prominent positions in the economy, the military and the arts. Before the Great Terror, the Soviet political elite used violence primarily as a means of securing its position and advancing its chosen policies. Yet, at the very point when it had seemingly established its power absolutely, it began to destroy itself from within.

Hundreds of books and articles have been written trying to make sense of these events. For some historians, the key can only be found by focusing attention on Stalin's desire to establish a personal dictatorship over Soviet Russia.[110] Other writers have suggested that the process was more complex, reflecting above all the chaotic nature of the Soviet administrative system in which many different individuals and groups sought the opportunity to use force to destroy rivals or settle old grudges.[111] British representatives in Russia did not of course have the benefit of the two great advantages available to the historian: documentary evidence and hindsight. Even though their dispatches were filled with details of the trials and executions reported in the local press, they always struggled to understood the sheer scale of the destruction wrought by the Terror of 1936–38. The concentration camps of the Gulag Archipelago remained largely unknown to them, except through rumour and hearsay. So too did the vast number of executions of ordinary Soviet citizens, many of whom were indicted on no more solid a foundation than malicious denunciation by a jealous colleague or neighbour. Lord Chilston and his staff worked hard to understand the cataclysm that overtook Russia in the second half of the 1930s, but they were themselves often little more than bewildered observers of a process that seemed to defy rational explanation.

The Embassy reported in detail on the various trials and arrests which took place in the early 1930s, such as the Kondratiev trial of September 1930 and the arrest of three hundred GPU officers in June the following year.[112] Their reports also gave a good deal of space to the widespread accusations of sabotage that were made in the years that followed. Despite the social and economic upheavals of the early 1930s, the Embassy was for the most part convinced that the regime was well-established and secure against any internal threat to its existence. Strang wrote in the autumn of 1930 that although 'dissatisfaction is widely and openly expressed, it would not be wise to attach very great significance to this'. Even though plays were staged in the Moscow theatres satirising some of the 'personal and doctrinal absurdities, to which even good communists are prone', the willingness of the authorities to allow such ridicule suggested that 'they are in no great fear of a popular explosion'.[113] Both Strang and Ovey believed that at least some of the trials of 'wreckers and saboteurs' held in the early 1930s were intended to deflect popular criticism away from the government, by creating scapegoats who could be blamed for the the shortage of food and poor living standards.[114] This was a strategy which they suggested was on the whole quite successful, at least among urban workers hostile to the privileged cadres of engineers and officials who were the most frequent victims of the early show trials.

The Embassy was also certain that the position of Stalin was secure following the defeat of his 'Left' and 'Right' opponents during the long battles of the previous decade. Soon after his arrival in Moscow, Sir Esmond Ovey told the Foreign Office that although the Soviet leader was not 'regarded with affection by his followers, yet all the world knows and respects the terrific force of will which is his very being and which has raised him to the position of Dictator'.[115] During the 1920s Hodgson and his colleagues had sometimes failed to appreciate the extent of Stalin's energy and determination, but their successors never fell into the same trap. Indeed, they were if anything inclined to underestimate the extent of the opposition to Stalin that still existed in the early 1930s, though this was hardly surprising since few references appeared in print to indicate the existence of divisions within the Soviet government. Ovey rightly pointed out in 1932 that questions of personal character and strength were of great significance in an autocratic political system, and suggested that Stalin's position remained 'very strong' in spite of occasional rumours which circulated to the contrary.[116] The Ambassador suspected that the extent of the Soviet leader's power was becoming increasingly damaging for the country, however, since fewer and fewer people dared to 'tell the truth to Stalin' with the result that many serious problems were not properly addressed.[117] The General Secretary's character remained as elusive as ever to British officials throughout the 1930s. Since he lived in 'in complete seclusion somewhere behind the walls of the Kremlin',[118] and seldom made speeches or public appearances, it was impossible for them to obtain any insight into his motives. Ovey was convinced that the Soviet leader was driven by a 'single and fanatic purpose ... to perfect and fix for ever the principles of Marx',[119] though when Chilston served as Ambassador he was more inclined to believe that the search for absolute personal power was Stalin's main goal in life. Both men had a good deal of respect for the Soviet leader's ability, a view that was endorsed by the Foreign Office Minister Anthony Eden when he visited Moscow in 1935.[120] They also gave credence to the rumours that circulated about Stalin's brutality. When Reader Bullard in Leningrad was told by 'a fairly good source' that the suicide of Stalin's second wife in 1932 only took place after her husband had signed her arrest warrant,[121] it struck a chord with his colleagues who had no doubt that the Soviet leader was not a man to allow family sentiment to influence his behaviour.

The murder of the Leningrad Party leader Sergei Kirov, in December 1934, marked the beginning of a new phase in the use of terror in Stalin's Russia, coming as it did at a time when Soviet political life seemed to be more tranquil than for some years. Kirov was perhaps the most charismatic figure in a leadership that had become increasingly grey and colourless. His popularity among the Party rank and file during the early 1930s was considerable, whereas Stalin found that his own speeches at congresses and committees were, according to one dispatch, 'ill-received, evoking no spontaneous applause'.[122] It is still not clear whether Kirov was actively involved in any plot to get rid of Stalin, just as there are a few lingering doubts about whether the Soviet leader was directly responsible for his rival's death at the hands of a disgruntled young former Socialist Revolutionary.[123] Embassy staff knew that Kirov was very popular in the Communist Party, recognising that he might be a possible successor to Stalin.[124] They were, despite this, bemused by the brutal reaction that followed the murder, which Lord Chilston believed was a reflection of deep-seated 'panic amongst the Communist hierarchy'.[125]

The Ambassador regarded the arrest and immediate execution of

dozens of people for involvement in the plot to murder Kirov as a
puzzling over-reaction, since it undermined the government's desire to
promote the belief that 'the country was quiet, well-ordered and pros-
pering'. Stalin's decision to indict and imprison Zinoviev and other
former leading Communists for complicity in the Kirov assassination,
early in 1935, was at first assumed by Embassy staff to be an indication
that the political turmoil was likely to continue into the indefinite future.
In the event, the rest of 1935 turned out to be a year of comparative
tranquillity. The apparent lull fooled British officials, who were not of
course in a position to know that Stalin was putting in place across the
country a whole cohort of officials on whose political loyalty he could
rely in times of crisis and challenge. Lord Chilston did speculate in
one dispatch whether Stalin might be removed from power, but concluded that such an event was extremely unlikely. He pointed out that
an assassin would 'find his way beset by almost insuperable difficulties',
since the Soviet leader was well-guarded and seldom appeared in public.
He believed that a military coup d'état by Marshal Voroshilov or any
other senior army figure was also unlikely, since the GPU would hear
of it and, in any case, the senior officer corps would themselves be
divided over such a dramatic move.[126] The Ambassador similarly discounted the possibility of a 'palace coup', since the men who surrounded
Stalin were not 'of the calibre to carry through an intrigue of this kind'
and were in any case 'too jealous of one another'.[127] On the eve of the
Great Terror, Chilston and his colleagues were impressed both by the
solidity of the Soviet regime and Stalin's unrivalled place within it.
While they knew that the system of central and local administration
could be chaotic, the Embassy was convinced that the Soviet leader was
in a position to impose his will on the country.

The Embassy was in fact too impressed by the signs of 'normalisation'
that appeared in Soviet society throughout 1935 and early 1936, following the end of the brief orgy of arrests and executions which took
place in the wake of Kirov's assassination. The staff there recognised
that Stalin was still trying to eliminate any possible rival sources of
prestige and influence, which they believed accounted for his decision
to abolish the Society of Old Bolsheviks in the summer of 1935, since
its members had traditionally enjoyed 'a certain latitude in respect of
criticisms of the party line'.[128] In general, Chilston and his colleagues
were more struck by the rise of 'bourgeois tendencies' among the
population, along with the government's decreasing emphasis on ideological vigilance.[129] Far from sensing an impending crisis, they believed
that Soviet society was if anything more relaxed than it had been for

a decade. The Embassy's failure to predict the impending storm was not, however, evidence of any real negligence on the part of those who worked there. Stalin's preparations for the out-and-out assault on Soviet society, which began in the final months of 1936, were conducted in great secrecy, giving few clues to suggest the scale of the coming drama. Throughout that year, ordinary Soviet citizens also seem to have been oblivious to the cyclone that lay ahead, reflecting the care and caution with which the Soviet leader made his plans.[130] When the first show trial of leading Communist officials began, in the late summer of 1936, it took British diplomats largely by surprise. They were quickly forced to reassess their view that Stalin's Russia was evolving into an increasingly stable society.

Zinoviev, Kamenev and the other prominent political figures put on trial in August 1936 had of course long been under lock and key, and were therefore hardly in a position to threaten Stalin's position. The Embassy was uncertain about the significance of the indictment that was issued against them on capital charges, speculating that it might be designed to divert public attention away from the shortage of food in the shops or to justify increased repression by the Secret Police.[131] When the trial itself began, the Ambassador and his staff were immediately struck by the bizarre and ritualistic nature of the proceedings. The Soviet press as usual 'prejudged the issue by calling for the execution of the accused even before the trial opened'. The accused all declined legal representation and instead made full but wooden 'confessions' of numerous offences, including participation in a plot to kill Stalin as well as direct complicity in the murder of Kirov. The Public Prosecutor, Andrei Vyshinsky, a former Menshevik lawyer who had come to prominence during the trials of various wreckers and saboteurs early in the 1930s, conducted the prosecution with his usual ferocity, demanding the death penalty for the prisoners when they were found guilty.[132] Even when the drama of the trial was over, the Embassy still faced huge problems in trying to interpret the significance of the whole affair. Lord Chilston wryly observed in one dispatch that, 'The old description of revolution as a monster which devours its own children has seldom been so notably exemplified as in the witch-hunt now proceeding in the Soviet Union', and went on to note that 'I do not think that we shall ever know the real reasons for the holding of this trial; they can only be known to a few members of the inner circle who are unlikely to reveal them'. The Ambassador and his staff were convinced that the trial had strengthened Stalin's position, but only at the cost of making him more dependent than ever on the Secret Police.[133]

Embassy officials had still not at this stage fully grasped the scale of the violence that was about to begin, and were surprised by the extent of the purge that took place of the protegés of Zinoviev and his fellow-defendants in the weeks following the trial. The appointment of Nikolai Ezhov as head of the Commissariat of Internal Affairs at the beginning of October 1936 caused further confusion at the Embassy. It was at first believed that the change might signal a retreat from the hard-line policy of the previous weeks, but it soon became clear that the significance of the appointment was in reality quite different. Since Ezhov was 'one of M. Stalin's closest associates',[134] Embassy officials soon realised that his promotion was probably designed to limit the 'excessive independence' of the Secret Police and ensure that none of its members became too powerful. Far from signalling an end to the terror, the appointment simply represented an attempt by Stalin to assert his control over the whole process.

A few weeks after the victims of the first show trial were executed, a second trial of leading Soviet politicians began in Moscow. Among the victims on this occasion were individuals who had at one time been closely associated with Trotsky, including Karl Radek and Georgy Pyatakov. British officials were better prepared to follow the proceedings on this occasion, since they now understood that the court proceedings were simply 'the oral elaboration and formal concluding act of a process which had been going on for many months in the prisons of the GPU'.[135] The prisoners were again accused of a bizarre series of crimes, including cooperation with the Nazi regime in Germany and the 'Fascist' regime in Japan. The long harangue by Vyshinsky, which terminated the trial, was designed once more to heighten the sense of national paranoia and justify an even greater campaign of 'vigilance' against internal and external enemies. Lord Chilston and his staff still found it difficult to understand Stalin's real motives in holding such elaborate show trials, a sentiment shared by most of the diplomatic corps in Moscow. They were, however, more struck than ever by the vitriolic attacks on Trotsky, who had of course gone into exile many years earlier. Chilston speculated that these attacks were designed to reduce the influence of an individual who could easily become the rallying point of ideological purists opposed to Stalin, though he was not able to provide any concrete evidence to support this argument. The Ambassador gave little credence to the charges against the accused, writing to the Foreign Office that to 'take this case at anything approaching its face value involves an intolerable strain on the faculty of belief'. It was, he observed, inconceivable that men who had spent all their adult lives as revolutionaries would suddenly throw their lot in with reactionary powers like Germany and Japan.

All this raised the intriguing question of why the accused sat sheep-like in court, failing to seize the opportunity of proclaiming their innocence in front of an audience of foreign journalists and diplomats. Embassy staff who attended the trial were struck by the eerie and emotionless quality of the confessions, but found it impossible to account for the absence of any passion or fear on the faces of the prisoners. Although foreign observers naturally speculated as to whether torture had been used on the men, the Ambassador himself noted, perhaps somewhat surprisingly, that the Embassy had:

> no reason to believe that the present despot in the Kremlin has resorted to actual torture. The appearance of the prisoners did not suggest that they had been subjected to physical violence. On the other hand, their conduct in court was anything but natural. They confessed to the most heinous crimes without any hesitation or emotion, like a well-coached class being put through an oral examination on a familiar and not very interesting subject.[136]

Chilston also considered the possibility that the men had been drugged or hypnotised in order to extract confessions, or that they were cooperating with the authorities so as to protect members of their family against possible retribution. The Ambassador was not convinced by any of these explanations – but nor was he able to advance any others which were more plausible. His confusion was not surprising. The appeal of these staged confessions to the authorities was obvious, but to this day it is still not clear why condemned men with a proven record of courage and bravery should have cooperated so freely with those who sought to destroy them.

Since the attention of British officials was focused on the show trials in Moscow, their dispatches at first gave little attention to the growing number of arrests of ordinary people taking place across the country. This started to change in the spring of 1937, as the press began to be filled with details of a fantastic number of stories about plots and conspiracies to murder leading officials and create political turmoil. In February Gilliat-Smith wrote in his 'Report on Conditions in the Leningrad Consular District' that 'one is impelled to the conviction that organised terrorism is and will continue to be a chronic and endemic malady'.[137] The local authorities showed 'no signs ... of abandoning their Draconian methods of government', with the result that the public mood was becoming increasingly fearful. Lord Chilston and his colleagues in Moscow were also struck by the rising level of anxiety, in contrast to previous months when the population had seemed largely unmoved by the assault taking place on former members of the Soviet political elite. Embassy staff found it difficult to obtain details about the scale of the terror experienced by ordinary Soviet citizens, since only a fraction of the various indictments and arrests were reported in the newspapers. As virtually no Russians would have anything to do with foreign diplomats, they were not able to obtain much first hand information either. They knew that arrests were normally made in the middle of the night, and that the flat or house of the unfortunate victim was ransacked for 'evidence' before being sealed up to prevent any unauthorised entry. It was this mass dimension of the Great Terror which the Embassy found hardest to explain. While the destruction of Stalin's erstwhile political rivals and their supporters did at least have a grizzly political logic, the same could hardly be said of the imprisonment and execution of thousands of people who could by no stretch of the imagination have posed a challenge to the regime. One of the most thoughtful attempts to explain the whole phenomenon was made by the acting Counsellor, Douglas Mackillop, in a dispatch sent to the Foreign Office in April 1937 when he was temporarily in charge of the Embassy. Mackillop argued that there was in all advanced states a growing tension between the principles of individualism and community. While governments felt impelled to pay some form of lip-service to the notion of popular sovereignty and individual freedom, they also recognised that promoting economic welfare and national power usually required them to make 'the life of the common man ... much more planned, managed and regulated than it has been at any previous time'.[138] Although the Soviet regime took this process to an extreme, by using terror as an instrument for regulating the population's behaviour, Mackillop argued that the growth of state power to achieve economic goals was a phenomenon taking place across much of Europe. The move towards totalitarian government in the Soviet Union reflected deep social and economic tensions that were influencing political development across the globe.

In the second half of 1937 reports emanating from the British Embassy and Consulates were filled to a greater degree than ever before with accounts of arrests and executions. Staff reported at length on the persecution of 'bourgeois' nationalists in the various Soviet republics, who were accused of seeking to overthrow Communist rule and restore authoritarian regimes.[139] They also obtained details about the assault on Soviet cultural life that took place in this period,[140] though they apparently knew little of the imprisonment and death of leading writers such as Osip Mandelstam. The purge of the military was given particular attention. British officials had heard rumours early in 1937 that Mikhail Tukhachevsky, an extremely able and experienced officer appointed as a Marshal of the Soviet Union in 1935, was in 'serious trouble'.[141] A few months later, Tukhachevsky and a number of his colleagues were tried in camera and executed, a move that was quickly followed by a massive purge of the Soviet officer corps. Mackillop, who was still in charge of the Embassy at the time, had no doubts that 'these officers ventured to oppose the policy of the civilian leaders and ... have paid with their lives for their temerity'.[142]

The Embassy did not have any firm evidence about the extent of opposition to Stalin among the army leadership, since 'in this country the few who know how history is made do not whisper, and the many who whisper do not know'. The Military Attaché, Colonel Firebrace, noted that although it was impossible to know whether there had been 'any organised resistance to Stalin's policy ... Any deviation from the party line by senior officers of great influence in the army must appear to Stalin a great danger'. He also observed that the Soviet leader clearly placed the need for absolute political obedience above the requirement for military efficiency, and speculated that Tukhachevsky's real crime might have been his opposition to new measures designed to rein in the autonomy of army commanders by increasing the authority of the political commissars attached to every Red Army unit.[143] The loss of some of the Red Army's most talented officers undoubtedly helped to destroy the operational effectiveness of the Soviet military, reversing some of 'the great strides towards efficiency' that had been achieved over the previous few years. A subsequent assault on the Soviet navy had an equally pernicious effect. On the eve of the Second World War, British military experts at the Moscow Embassy were still convinced that the purges had undermined the ability of the USSR to defend itself effectively,[144] a view that appeared to be spectacularly vindicated in the summer of 1941 when German tanks moved swiftly eastwards following Hitler's decision to launch Operation Barbarossa.

Early in 1938, when the whole population had been traumatised by the wave of arrests and executions which had taken place over the previous year, the Soviet government began preparations for a third major show trial. An indictment was published against a number of individuals who had once been leading figures in the Communist Party, including Nikolai Bukharin and Aleksei Rykov, who had both been prominent supporters of the NEP in the 1920s. The indictment on this occasion was of particular interest to the British Embassy, since a number of the prisoners were accused of working for British Intelligence against the Soviet government. Before the trial began, Lord Chilston acknowledged that it would almost certainly take the usual course, in which ritualistic confessions of guilt by the accused were followed by a sentence of death. In the event, things did not work out as the authorities planned. The proceedings were followed with great care by British officials. Fitzroy Maclean was present during every day of the trial, along with representatives from other foreign missions in Moscow and members of the western press corps, and was joined on most occasions by Chilston himself. The trial began as normal when the twenty-one accused, 'paler and smaller, somehow, than normal human beings',[145] filed into court and listened as an official read out the charges against them. One by one they admitted their guilt, until it was the turn of Nikolai Krestinsky, a former senior official in the Commissariat of Foreign Affairs, who responded with spirit that he had 'never committed a single crime'.[146] The court was immediately adjourned in order to allow pressure to be brought to bear on the prisoner, but when it reconvened shortly afterwards the 'small, bedraggled' Krestinsky still refused to plead guilty to the charges against him. Once again the court was adjourned, and this time the authorities were more successful, apparently after threats were made against the accused's young daughter. On the following day, Krestinsky publicly admitted his guilt and accepted 'full responsibility for my criminal and treacherous behaviour'.[147]

The prosecutor may have won on this occasion, but the drama was not yet over. Later on in the trial, Bukharin also refused to play his assigned part in the performance, even though he had during the previous few weeks apparently begged Stalin to spare his life. When cross-examined by Vyshinsky, he began by admitting his full responsibility for all the supposed crimes of the 'Rightist-Trotskist bloc'. Yet, in spite of this admission, Bukharin persisted in talking in abstract terms and refused to admit any direct complicity in the specific crimes of which he was accused. He denied that he had ever sought to kill Lenin or been an agent for a foreign power. He also refused to incriminate his fellow-prisoners. This spirited refusal to play the game of elaborate recantation and confession destroyed the carefully planned psychological drama of the show trial. The reaction of defendants like Bukharin and Krestinsky undermined the authorities' attempts to represent its opponents as common criminals who took money from foreign powers in order to destroy the Soviet Union. The absurdities of the Soviet justice system were put on display in front of diplomats and journalists from around the world, all of whom, with the glaring exception of the American Ambassador,[148] had no doubt that the prisoners were innocent of the crimes with which they were charged. The outcome of the trial was of course predictable. The accused were duly condemned to death or long terms of imprisonment. The risks involved in pursuing such a strategy were recognised by the Soviet government, however, with the result that elaborate and high-profile show trials were abandoned in favour of the more reliable private world of administrative 'justice'. In any case, with the conclusion of the Bukharin trial, Stalin had eliminated almost all the leading old Bolsheviks who had been members of the Party since the time of the revolution.

Officials at the British Embassy were absorbed by the drama of the third show trial, though they found proceedings no easier to explain than before. Lord Chilston once again speculated that it was designed to provide the government with convenient scapegoats who could be blamed for any shortcomings in the economy.[149] Fitzroy Maclean, who drafted the Ambassador's reports on the subject, believed that the whole phenomenon of the show trials could only be explained by reference to the peculiar nature of the psychology of all those involved. For more than twenty years, everyone in the courtroom had been surrounded by 'the tense atmosphere of unreality, tension, oppression and suspicion' that was the hallmark of Soviet Russia. The accused had for months lived with the fear of execution and torture. The judgement of prosecution and defence alike had been warped by decades of propaganda. In this world of passionate commitment and passionate hatred, it became harder and harder to distinguish 'between the real and the unreal, the actual and the hypothetical'.[150] The actors began to believe that their parts were genuine, and even the defendants found it impossible to work out the extent of their 'guilt'. It was only when an individual like Bukharin departed from the prepared script that the absurd nature of the proceedings became obvious. By insisting on his innocence of particular crimes, and gently hinting at the idiocy of the idea he could ever have been responsible for them, he destroyed the illusory world so carefully constructed by the prosecution. Yet even Bukharin, whose intellect allowed him to run rings round the prosecution, remained a prisoner of his life-long commitment to Bolshevism. He could not find it in himself to renounce outright the system that he had helped to build, even at the moment it destroyed him. Like all the other victims of the show trials, Bukharin's ambivalence in the face of a frenzied assault helped Stalin in his quest to destroy all those who opposed him. The lingering myth of the Communist Party's infallibility provided its leader with a powerful tool to manipulate and crush anyone who had any shred of idealism or ideological belief left intact.

The end of the third show trial did not itself mark the end of the Great Terror, but within a few months of its conclusion the scale of the violence began to be scaled back. During the final period of the Terror, officials at the British Embassy continued their valiant efforts to understand the significance of the whole process, but without any greater success than before. If Maclean was accurate in suggesting that decades of propaganda had so distorted Soviet society that it was no longer possible for its members to understand their own motives, it was certainly quite impossible for any outsider to untangle the complex boundaries between truth and fiction. Chilston had no doubt, following the end of the trial, that 'those who hold supreme power in the Soviet Union no longer take into consideration the real interests of the country over which they are ruling, but subordinate the whole of their policy to their desire for unlimited personal power, however much national interests may thereby suffer'. While the Ambassador firmly discounted the idea that the purges were driven by ideological zeal, he remained uncertain about Stalin's true motives. Like later generations of historians, he could not decide whether 'the ruler of the Soviet Union is a cold and calculating tyrant ... or a homicidal maniac whose mania is exploited for their own ends by a band of bloodthirsty tyrants'.[151] Chilston was inclined to accept the former explanation, particularly after the scale of the terror began to wind down in the second half of 1938. The Embassy reported in detail on the growing number of attacks that appeared in the press on local officials who had exceeded their authority and become 'over zealous' in conducting arrests and executions of innocent people.[152] The Ambassador had already told the Foreign Office as early as February 1938 that Stalin and the Politburo were desperately trying 'to keep the machinery of terror from running away with its masters'.[153] Unlike many of those who watched events in the Soviet Union from abroad, British officials inside Russia were sensitive to the chaos and disorder of the Soviet administrative system, recognising that it was never as smoothly responsive to the injunctions of the leadership as was sometimes believed. Nevertheless, they acknowledged that the decision to reduce the role of terror in Soviet political life was itself evidence that Stalin remained in firm control of the country. The abrupt end of the Great Terror in the final months of 1938 was, in a curious way, itself testimony to the Soviet leader's dominance over his country.

Lord Chilston left Moscow with considerable relief at the beginning of 1939, confident that he had done his duty by representing Britain there during the last few turbulent years. The Ambassador's period of office had been a difficult one both for himself and his wife, who, like her husband, was never able to reconcile herself to the dinginess and cultural barrenness of Soviet society. Chilston was replaced at the Embassy by Sir William Seeds. Since the impending war was already casting its shadow across Europe, the new Ambassador was concerned above all with foreign affairs during his first few months in the country. He recognised that the foreign and military policy of the Soviet Union was intimately shaped by domestic circumstances, one of his first acts on arriving in Moscow being to ask his staff to produce a detailed series of reports about the state of the country. The reports they compiled painted a remarkably consistent picture of the Soviet Union on the eve of the Second World War. There was a general agreement among them that the regime was 'as firmly established as any regime can reasonably expect to be'.[154] Maclean told Seeds that:

> The point of view of this embassy has for some time past been that, except in the event of war or of a collapse of the economic system, there is no reason to anticipate anything in the nature of a political upheaval in the Soviet Union.[155]

This view was endorsed by the new Ambassador himself, who believed that the Soviet government even had a good chance of surviving a war intact, since compared with the 'Russia of the Tsars ... it possesses a stronger moral stamina to stand the strain arising from natural conditions and a certain inborn inefficiency'. Both men were certain that the government had nothing to fear from the Soviet population, despite the upheavals of the previous decade. Maclean was convinced that the long-standing passivity of the Russians in the face of their rulers meant that there was unlikely to be any spontaneous opposition or rebellion. He also pointed out that the Soviet people were now so cut off from the rest of the world that they had no standard by which to judge the extent of their privations: 'In short, twenty years of a totalitarian regime, coupled with hermetical isolation, have produced a nation which accepts blindly the existing system because it knows no other, and swallows the grotesque conception of life forced upon it because, unaided, it can conceive of no other'. The Military Attachés took a rather different view of the situation, since they recognised the damage done to the armed forces by the repeated purges of senior army officers over the previous two years. Even so, there was still general agreement among them that 'The Red army itself can be considered as loyal to the regime, and there is no question of its refusing to fight or of revolting in the early stages of the war'.[156]

The reports compiled by Seeds and his staff in the spring of 1939 were ironically a testimony to the success of Stalin. When Robert Hodgson arrived in Russia in 1921, it was generally assumed by the outside world that the Soviet regime was doomed to imminent collapse. At the time Sir Esmond Ovey was posted to Moscow at the end of 1929, the Soviet government appeared far more secure politically than eight years earlier, but the economic situation of the country was still extremely parlous. Just a decade later, the revival of Soviet power was such that the country was once again playing a pivotal role in determining the fate of Europe. The mobilisation of the country's vast human and material resources had made it one of the most formidable powers on the continent, desperately courted by the British and French as a possible ally in the coming war with Germany. As William Seeds noted in February 1939, 'the Soviet Government have achieved their main object of incorporating practically the whole population of this country in socialised activities and creating a framework for the large-scale operation of industry and agriculture'. Despite these successes, the Soviet Union that existed in 1939 bore little resemblance to the utopian society dreamt of by the revolutionaries who seized power in Petrograd in November 1917. Stalin's greatest achievement during the 1930s was to transform a backward economy at breakneck pace, while at the same time preventing the various social and political strains that accompanied the process from destroying the regime. The paradoxical nature of his triumph was captured by Seeds, when he wrote to London that although socialism had in once sense been achieved,

> it will be many a long day yet before communism as understood by Lenin is installed, or before the rulers of this country can claim with any show of truth that the great experiment has justified the appalling sacrifices which it has entailed, and before they can show to the world that the Soviet people as a whole enjoys a greater well-being than that enjoyed by the workman in capitalist states.[157]

Although the Communist regime survived in Russia for another fifty years, it never did succeed in producing the results needed to justify the 'appalling sacrifices' which it imposed on its own people during the 1930s.

9

Conclusion

The British Embassy's assessment of the internal condition of the Soviet Union described at the end of the last chapter took place at a most critical and sensitive moment in European history. Sir William Seeds' assertion that the Soviet government was secure against any internal challenge implied that the country could prove a useful ally in the approaching war with Nazi Germany, a war which became almost inevitable once the invasion of Czechoslovakia demonstrated so graphically the failure of the appeasement policy pursued by the British government over the previous few years. Although the doubts expressed by the Embassy's Military Attachés about the calibre of the Soviet armed forces suggested that the country might not be powerful enough to be a particularly important partner in the immediate future, it clearly still had an enormous potential that could in time allow it to play a central role in European politics. In the early summer of 1939 British and French representatives went to Moscow in a desperate attempt to persuade Stalin to throw his weight behind the struggle against Germany.[1] The spectacular failure of this policy in August 1939, following the signing of the Soviet-Nazi Pact, was not of course the responsibility of Seeds and his staff. The British Embassy in Moscow, along with its counterpart in Berlin, had reported throughout the 1930s on relations between German and Soviet officials, reflecting a widespread fear that the two great totalitarian powers of Europe might come to some kind of agreement despite their huge ideological differences. Even the most diligent and best-informed official could not hope to follow the secret negotiations that led to the Pact. The governments of both Soviet Russia and Nazi Germany were adept at keeping information secret, and the British Ambassador and his colleagues could not be blamed for failing to predict the actions of the Moscow government when they were hardly ever given the opportunity to meet its most important members.

The Nazi-Soviet Pact lasted, in practice, for less than two years. Germany's invasion of the Soviet Union in June 1941 destroyed instantly the fragile relationship between the two countries. Over the following few months, military necessity led to the establishment of the Grand Alliance between Britain, the United States and Soviet Russia – as curious a trio as has ever been assembled in the course of the twentieth century. However, this alliance also crumbled away in a few years, once its main adversary had been defeated on the battlefields of Europe. The Soviet Union emerged from the Second World War in 1945 as a far stronger power than ever before, despite the devastation suffered by its people in the struggle against Germany. The Red Army's advance westwards in the final months of the war helped to establish the country's power across half of Europe. The drawing of an Iron Curtain through the heart of the continent signified the start of the Cold War, and with it a fundamental transformation in the relationship between the Soviet Union and the major western powers. In the years after 1945 'Russia-watching' became a huge bureaucratic industry in both London and Washington. The British and American governments devoted vast re-sources to countering the threat posed by the Soviet Union, funding huge military establishments and elaborate intelligence agencies on a scale unimaginable in the interwar years. The institutions and processes of 'routine' diplomacy also benefited from an enormous increase in resources. In 1939 the British Embassy in Moscow was still a very modest organsation, employing a handful of accredited diplomats and a small number of support staff. Fifty years later it had become a large bureau-cratic institution employing officials concerned with everything from the promotion of trade to the organisation of educational exchanges.

The modesty of the resources available to the men responsible for keeping London informed about Russia's domestic affairs before 1939 has to be kept in mind when making a judgement about the success with which they carried out their reporting role. Officials had to rely a great deal on their native wit when collecting the kind of material required by the Foreign Office. They lacked access to the technology and manpower that was taken for granted by their successors who worked in the country at the height of the Cold War. During the years before 1914, the Petersburg Embassy served as the 'gatekeeper' of the authoritative information about Russia. Members of the Foreign Office and Diplomatic Service were united at this time in a belief that the foreign policy process should be confined to a small number of officials and politicians. Although Foreign Office staff did read the articles published by the handful of British journalists in Russia, most of their knowledge of the social and political crisis facing the country was derived from the reports sent back by the Embassy and the various

Consulates. The dispatches filed by British diplomats and consular officials during these years were on the whole acute in their analysis of the tensions which ripped the Tsarist Empire apart. Successive Ambassadors and their staff understood that the turmoil which faced the government of Nicholas II in years before 1914 was not simply created by a handful of revolutionary extremists from organisations like the Social Democrats and Socialist Revolutionaries. They recognised instead that deep-seated social and economic changes were undermining the traditional fabric of Russian society, as the growth of cities and the emergence of a new professional class chipped away at established patterns of authority. It was for this reason that Sir Charles Hardinge, Sir Arthur Nicolson and Sir George Buchanan all vehemently supported the cause of political reform during their time in Petersburg, since they hoped that the establishment of constitutional forms of government, when combined with firm measures to restore public order, would help to reduce the tension between state and society in Tsarist Russia. It is clear in retrospect that the Embassy did not fully understand that the cause of 'conservative reformism' was intimately bound up with the personality and career of Peter Stolypin. The assassination of the Prime Minister in the autumn of 1911 marked the effective close of attempts to promote the reestablishment of the government's authority via co-operation with the more liberal elements in Russian society. In any case, Stolypin's own drift towards a more authoritarian style of government during the years before his death reflected the virtual impossibility of bridging the gap between a Duma anxious to assert its powers and an Emperor who remained committed to the principle of autocratic rule. The Embassy's support for a 'constitutional solution' to Russia's domestic crisis in the years before 1914 may have been entirely logical, but the process was never likely to prove successful given the constellation of personalities and circumstances that existed during the vexed years of the Constitutional Experiment.

Following the outbreak of hostilities in August 1914, Sir George Buchanan and his staff struggled hard to maintain the Embassy as the principal source of information about Russia's internal affairs, but the task was a difficult one. The arrival of new civilian and military representatives in Russia, many of whom also reported home on political affairs, undermined the Embassy's 'gatekeeper' role. The decline of the Foreign Office's influence on policy-making eroded still further the significance of the reports emanating from its representatives in Russia. These changes were on balance damaging ones. During the years between 1914 and 1921, British diplomats and consular officials usually showed themselves to be shrewder judges of the Russian domestic situation than politicians in London and the assorted army officers who arrived in the country. Buchanan and his staff were well aware that the Tsarist regime did not simply collapse in March 1917 because of its chronic administrative inefficiency; it collapsed because the autocratic political system beloved of Nicholas II and his more conservative Ministers was unable to command the loyalties of an increasingly large section of the Russian population. The Ambassador and his staff were at first hopeful that the Provisional Government which emerged after the March Revolution might be more successful than its predecessor at attracting popular support, but they quickly became disillusioned by the failure of Ministers to establish a new political consensus based on liberal values and a commitment to vigorous prosecution of the war against the Central Powers. At the same time, civilian officials at the Embassy understood that the hesitations and vacillations displayed by the Provisional Government were not simply a consequence of its members' inexperience and lack of confidence: they also reflected the constraints placed on Ministers' freedom of action by the growing radicalism of the popular mood. By contrast, the British army officers at the *Stavka* who extolled the virtues of firm government in such a chaotic situation simply revealed their ignorance of the political realities confronting Russia's new rulers. The military mind seemed incapable of understanding that the Provisional Government was quite unable to restore order in the face of mounting popular unrest. The same pattern was repeated during the years of Civil War when most of Britain's senior civilian representatives in Russia, including Frank Lindley and Sir Charles Eliot, recognised that allied intervention was doomed so long as it was seen by the local population as little more than an attempt to support White leaders whose conservative political values commanded little popular support. The majority of senior British army officers, in contrast, could not grasp that operational questions were of secondary importance in a conflict that was in large part a battle for 'hearts and minds' of the population.

The men who reported on Russia between 1921 and 1939 also found it difficult to establish their status as the main source of information about the country's internal affairs, particularly since the Foreign Office and its staff never recovered the prestige and influence which they had enjoyed before 1914. The author of one Foreign Office memorandum written in the early 1930s observed sadly that because Britain's relationship with Russia was such a controversial political issue at home, it was virtually impossible to put in place a coherent and sustainable policy.[2] The problem was particularly acute during the 1920s, when Sir Robert Hodgson and his small staff struggled to make their voice heard above the uproar. The Hodgson Mission was in reality quite successful in following developments in Russia at a time when its members had few resources and little experience to fall back on. Its members' repeated assertion that the regime was secure against any internal challenge, although endorsed by the Foreign Office, struck little chord in conservative political circles, however, where hopes were strong that the Soviet government might be on the point of collapse. Nor was there a much warmer response in these circles for Hodgson's argument that a normal diplomatic dialogue should be maintained with Moscow – even though his position was once again strongly supported at the Foreign Office. By the early 1930s, Hodgson's views had more or less become the established political wisdom. Although Sir Esmond Ovey and Lord Chilston reported at length on the horrors that took place in the Soviet Union during these years, they never doubted that the regime was secure – an opinion that was almost universally accepted back in London, even among diehard conservatives fearful that Moscow was committed to seizing any opportunity to threaten Britain's security and, domestic tranquillity. The task facing the Embassy in keeping abreast of Soviet affairs during the 1930s was an enormous one. Since power was so heavily concentrated in the hands of Stalin and a handful of other leaders, British representatives could only speculate about the motives of the men who determined the country's fate. Even though officials posted to Russia between 1929 and 1939 reported as best they could on the economic and social changes sweeping the country, they were never able to provide London with much significant information about purely political matters. Before 1917 British representatives in Russia had at least been able to talk on occasion with the Emperor and his Ministers, which gave them some opportunity to judge the personalities and ambitions of the men responsible for guiding the destiny of the Tsarist Empire. The diplomats and consular officials who served in Soviet Russia after 1921, by contrast, viewed politics as complete outsiders; they were never able to rely on the kinds of contacts and inside knowledge which were the stuff of diplomatic life in most other posts.

There were of course many straightforward errors of fact and interpretation in the reports sent to London by representatives of the Foreign Office in the years between 1900 and 1939. As often as not, these proved to be of a comparatively trivial nature, concerned with events and personalities that were of little more than passing significance. In any case, most officials took a cautious line, warning against the problem of placing too much emphasis on a single report sent from a country where information was scarce and the pace of change rapid. Different individuals did of course express distinct views during their time *en poste*. There was both before and after the revolution a marked distinction between 'russophiles' and 'russophobes' among Foreign Office representatives in Russia. In the years before 1917, the 'russophiles' included individuals as disparate as Sir Arthur Nicolson, 'Benjy' Bruce and Robert Bruce Lockhart, while the most prominent russophobe was without doubt Cecil Spring Rice. Such labels are not, of course, exact ones. Some russophiles, like Arthur Nicolson, were concerned primarily with improving diplomatic relations between Britain and Russia; others, like 'Benjy' Bruce, qualify as russophiles on account of their love of Russian history and culture. In a similar way, Spring Rice's loathing of virtually every aspect of Russian society was complemented by his staunch opposition to the 1907 Anglo-Russian entente, while Viscount Cranley appeared to be perfectly happy at the prospect of an improvement in diplomatic relations between London and Petersburg even though he too seldom had a good word to say for the Russians.

The whole question was given a new twist by the events of 1917. Although few British diplomats had much respect for the old Tsarist regime, their dislike faded into insignificance when compared with the loathing they felt for the Bolshevik leaders who seized power just a few months after Nicholas's abdication. While it is true that almost every senior civilian official posted to Russia between 1921 and 1939 argued that Britain should maintain formal relations with Moscow, this simply reflected a general recognition that the Soviet Union was emerging as a significant power that could not be ignored indefinitely. The contrast between russophiles and russophobes continued to exist even in this new interwar world – though the contours were less sharp than before 1914. Robert Hodgson was a russophile in the sense both that he had a profound respect for Russian culture, or at least the culture that existed before the Bolshevik government began its determined assault on the intelligentsia, and that he displayed a zealous determination to promote the cause of Anglo-Russian relations. Fitzroy Maclean's fascination with Russia, which first drew him to the country in the 1930s, perhaps requires that he too should be treated as a russophile of sorts, even though his dislike of the Soviet regime meant that he had little interest in seeing the development of anything more than the most formal and correct diplomatic relations. Sir Esmond Ovey, by contrast, did not seem to have much interest at all in Russian history and culture;

he did, however, arrive in the country late in 1929 with a burning determination to improve political and commercial relations. The significance of this distinction between russophiles and russophobes during the first few decades of the twentieth century should certainly not be overestimated. The Foreign Office's emphasis on the virtues of balanced and cautious reporting meant that such 'prejudices' were seldom aired very openly. In any case, russophiles and russophobes were rarely at odds about the interpretation of developments inside Russia. When they did disagree with one another, it was usually about the significance of these developments for British foreign policy.

The reports about Russia's internal affairs compiled by British officials posted to the country were of course designed for a specific purpose: to provide policy-makers back home with the knowledge required to facilitate effective decision-making. It was recognised in London that the foreign policy of the Tsarist and Soviet governments, like that of all governments, was influenced both by the personalities of the leaders and the domestic constraints under which they operated. It was for this reason that British diplomats and consular officials posted to Russia after 1900 not only provided the Foreign Office with material relating directly to international questions, but also attempted to give a more rounded picture of the country's domestic life. As has been seen in previous chapters, Foreign Office representatives were generally successful at making some sense of the changes which swept across Russia in the first four decades of the century. It is less clear whether the knowledge and insights contained in their reports were always used effectively. During the years before 1914 – and particularly in the period between 1904 and 1910 – senior officials at the Petersburg Embassy exercised a significant influence on Britain's policy towards Russia. Charles Hardinge and Arthur Nicolson each played an important role in promoting the 1907 Anglo-Russian Convention in the face of considerable public opposition. For both men, like most of their colleagues in the Foreign Office and Diplomatic Service, an entente with Russia seemed a sensible policy, since it held out the prospect of reducing the threat to Britain's imperial possessions in Asia while simultaneously providing a bulwark against the continued growth of German power in Europe. This policy was, however, effectively predicated on the assumption that Tsarist Russia was a strong military power, capable of proving a formidable enemy and a valuable friend. Such an assumption was not unreasonable at the time when tentative negotiations for the Entente began in 1903, when Lord Lansdowne was still at the Foreign Office, but the Russian defeats in the war against Japan during 1904–5 showed that the Tsarist military machine was a good deal less formidable than it at first appeared. In addition, the upheavals of 1905 starkly demonstrated the fragility of the Russian government. Nevertheless, when Sir Edward Grey arrived at the Foreign Office at the end of 1905, neither he nor his senior advisers appeared concerned that Russia's frailty might reduce the value of an understanding with Petersburg. Sir Arthur Nicolson was instead dispatched to Russia with a mandate to pursue negotations as quickly as possible. Although there were occasions during 1906–7 when the Foreign Office was forced to recognise that political instability inside Russia might slow down the pace of negotiations, the potential benefit of an entente was never seriously questioned. The reasons for this curious failure to recognise the consequences of Russian weakness for British foreign policy are still not altogether clear. Anxiety about the growth of German power in Europe had emerged by 1906 as the dominant concern at the Foreign Office, with the result that a pursuit of better relations with another major European power, as well as France, seemed to make a good deal of sense to officials. In addition, the traditional reluctance of Foreign Office officials and members of the Diplomatic Service to interest themselves in the internal affairs of other major powers could on occasions drift perilously close to a belief that relations between the powers should somehow be insulated from the turmoil of domestic changes – a curious position in an age when the doctrine of the balance of power implicitly informed most thinking about international relations. The dispatches sent from the Petersburg Embassy to London before 1914 were full of information about the strength and weakness of the German faction at Court. There was much less discussion in these reports about whether it was sensible to make friendship with Russia a central plank of British policy at a time when the stability of the country's domestic institutions appeared to be in doubt.

The decline of professional diplomats' influence in the years after 1914 naturally affected the significance of the political reports filed by Foreign Office representatives in Russia. Since members of the Diplomatic Service and Foreign Office found it so much more difficult than before to influence the policy-making process, they were hardly in a position to make sure that their assessment of the Russian domestic situation was reflected in British policy towards the country. Sir George Buchanan found it difficult to convince politicians in London during 1914–17 that the Tsarist government was more vulnerable than commonly believed in London, while Robert Hodgson and the Foreign Office had an equally hard time in the 1920s persuading Ministers that its Soviet successor was in reality quite secure against the threat of internal upheaval. The same pattern continued in the 1930s, when the Embassy's reports detailing the growing economic and political strength of Stalin's Russia were once again not fully taken into account by those responsible for making British foreign policy. The position during the 1930s was indeed in some ways a mirror image of the one that existed in the years leading up to the First World War. Before 1914, Britain pursued a policy of friendship with Russia even though domestic unrest in the country was already threatening to undermine its value as an ally in the dangerous strategic environment created by the growing power of Germany. In the 1930s, by contrast, the British government proved stubbornly reluctant to seek closer relations with Moscow, even though a resurgent Germany was once again clearly a major threat to the international status quo.

Diplomacy has always been an essentially human affair, in which success cannot be reduced to simple formulas or guaranteed by elaborate training programmes. This is not of course to deny that the absence of professional training sometimes handicapped British representatives posted to Russia; it clearly did. Lack of appropriate linguistic skills and ignorance of local culture and traditions makes it harder for diplomats in any post to carry out their work. Effective political reporting is, however, an art rather than a science. It depends above all on the ability to distinguish important trends from the daily flux of economic and political life. The Foreign Office representatives posted to Russia in the first few decades of the century varied in their talents and aptitudes. Russia always remained something of a mystery for most of them – a violent and alien world quite unlike the countries of Western Europe to which they were accustomed. Nevertheless, while they never succeeded in solving the Russian riddle, they played a full part in helping their government to make sense of a country and a people that continues to this day to baffle the imagination.

Notes

Notes to Chapter 1: Diplomats and Russia

1. For a classic account of the evolution of diplomacy, see Harold Nicolson, *The Evolution of Diplomatic Method*. Nicolson was convinced that 'the principles of sound diplomacy' were 'immutable'.
2. Michael Hughes, 'In Praise of Folly? Traditional Diplomacy in a Modern World', *Paradigms*, 9 (1995), pp. 75–98.
3. It should perhaps be noted that such words were not typical of de Callières, who was by instinct wary of attempting to define ambassadorial virtues. For details of de Callières' ideas, see Keith Hamilton and Richard Langhorne, *The Practice of Diplomacy*, pp. 69–71.
4. Prince C. M. Lichnowsky, *Heading for the Abyss*, p. 87.
5. Quoted in John Dickie, *Inside the Foreign Office*, p. 13.
6. For useful comments on this theme, see Sir Geoffrey Jackson, *Concorde Diplomacy*, pp. 5–8.
7. Hamilton and Langhorne, *The Practice of Diplomacy*, pp. 32–33.
8. Quoted in M. S. Anderson, *Britain's Discovery of Russia, 1553–1815*, p. 41.
9. Anderson, *Britain's Discovery*, p. 14.
10. Guy de Miège, *A Relation of Three Embassies from the Sacred Majestie Charles II to the Great Duke of Muscovie, the King of Sweden and the King of Denmark in the Years 1663 and 1664*, p. 140.
11. Quoted in Francesca Wilson, *Muscovy: Russia Through Western Eyes*, p. 38.
12. Giles Fletcher, *Of the Russe Commonwealth*, pp. 26, 63.
13. A rather more positive view was expressed by Sir Thomas Smith, who went to Moscow as Ambassador in 1604; see Samuel Purchas, *Hakluytus Posthumous or Purchas his Pilgrimes*, vol. 14, pp. 132–51.
14. Charles, Lord Whitworth, *An Account of Russia as it was in the Year 1710*, p. 57.
15. *Imperatorskoe russkoe istoricheskoe obshchestvo sbornik*, vol. 91, Finch to Harrington, p. 107.
16. George Macartney, *An Account of Russia*, p. 40; Anthony Cross, *Russia under Western Eyes, 1517–1825*, p. 204.
17. *Diaries and Correspondence of James Harris, First Earl of Malmesbury*, vol. 1, p. 173.
18. *Diaries and Correspondence of James Harris*, vol. 1, p. 204.
19. For a useful discussion of the Anglo-Russian relationship in the eighteenth century, see chapter 8 of D. B. Horn, *Great Britain and Europe in the Eighteenth Century*.
20. For a lively description of this subject, see Peter Hopkirk, *The Great Game*.

21. The best discussion of this issue can be found in John Howes Gleason, *The Genesis of Russophobia in Great Britain*.

22. W. Jesse, *Notes of a Half-Pay in Search of Health: or Russia, Circassia and the Crimea in 1839–40*, p. v.

23. G. J. Hennington, *Revelations of Russia*, vol. 1, p. ix.

24. See, for example, Vigilans, *The Dualism of England and Russia in the Far East and its Consequences upon the General Political Situation in Europe*.

25. See, for example, W. Probyn-Nevins, *Apologia for Russia: Being an Answer to Popular Objections; An Examination of Her Naval and Military Position; and a Plea for a Permanent Anglo-Russian Alliance*; Philalethes, *A Dispassionate View of Anglo-Russian Dualism in the East* (response to Vigilans, *The Dualism of England and Russia in the Far East*).

26. C. A. A. Disbrowe, *Original Letters from Russia, 1825–1828*, p. 37.

27. *British Documents on Foreign Affairs*, part 1, series A, Russia 1859–1914 (henceforth *BDFA*, 1A), vol. 1, Napier to Russell, 17 February 1863.

28. Thomas Michell, 'Constitutional Government in Russia' (published anonymously), *Quarterly Review*, January 1863, pp. 60–95.

29. D. C. M. Platt, *The Cinderella Service: British Consuls since 1825*.

30. Lichnowsky, *Heading for the Abyss*, p. 84

Notes to Chapter 2: There Will be a Catastrophe

1. The description of the Embassy is based on documents located in the Public Record Office, WORK 10/25–1; see also FO 800/16 (various letters by Lascelles).

2. For three lively and competing interpretations of changes in British foreign policy during the early twentieth century see George Monger, *The End of Isolation: Britain's Foreign Policy, 1900–1907*; A. J. P. Taylor, *The Struggle for Mastery in Europe*, pp. 403–56; Paul Kennedy, *The Realities behind Diplomacy*, pp. 110–127.

3. For a valuable summary of the vexed debate about the 'myth' of splendid isolation, see Christopher Howard, *Spendid Isolation*, passim.

4. For details of the origins of the alliance, see Ian Nish, *The Anglo-Japanese Alliance: The Diplomacy of Two Island Empires, 1894–1907*; Monger, *End of Isolation*, pp. 46–66.

5. G. R. Searle, *The Quest for National Efficiency*, pp. 34–53.

6. See, for example, the views expressed in George N. Curzon, *Russia in Central Asia*, passim.

7. For radical views towards the 1907 Anglo-Russian Convention, see K. G. Robbins, 'Public Opinion, Press and Pressure Groups', in F. H. Hinsley (ed.), *British Foreign Policy under Sir Edward Grey*, p. 83; Max Beloff, *Lucien Wolf and the Anglo-Russian Entente, 1907–1914*; A. J. Anthony Morris, *Radicalism against the War, 1906–1914*, pp. 52–70.

8. The published documents relating to the incident and its aftermath are contained in G. P. Gooch and Harold Temperley (eds), *British Documents on the Origins of the World War, 1898–1914*, vol. 4, *The Anglo-Russian Rapprochement*, pp. 5–41.

9. FO 800/72, Grey to Spring Rice, 19 February 1906.

10. The best general discussion of the Diplomatic Service in this period can be found in the relevant chapters of Raymond A. Jones, *The British Diplomatic Service, 1815–1914*. On the Foreign Office (which was until 1919 a separate organisation), see Zara Steiner, *The Foreign Office and Foreign Policy, 1898–1914*.

11. *British Parliamentary Papers, 1914–16*, 11 (cd 7749), Royal Commission on the Civil Service. Appendix to the Fifth Report of the Commissioners (Evidence of Sir Arthur Nicolson), qu. 36,546.

12. *British Parliamentary Papers, 1914–1916*, 11 (cd 7748), Royal Commission on the Civil Service. Fifth Report, p. 15.

13. On Morel's views see Catherine Ann Cline, *E. D. Morel, 1873–1924*; on Angell's views see J. D. B. Miller, *Norman Angell and the Futility of War*.

14. For a comparative view of the changes in national diplomatic corps during this period, see Paul Gordon Lauren, *Diplomats and Bureaucrats*, pp. 34–78.

15. On the 1905 reforms in the Foreign Office see Ray Jones, *The Nineteenth-Century Foreign Office: An Administrative History*, pp. 111–35; Zara Steiner, 'The Last Years of the Old Foreign Office, 1898–1905', *Historical Journal*, 6 (1963), pp. 59–90; Sir John Tilley and Stephen Gaselee, *The Foreign Office*, pp. 152–71; Edward Corp, 'The Transformation of the Foreign Office, 1900–1907' (unpublished Ph.D thesis).

16. Useful accounts recalling the pressure of studying for the dreaded examinations can be found in Maurice Baring, *The Puppet Show of Memory*, p. 153; Sir

Geoffrey Thompson, *Front-Line Diplomat*, p. 43; The Earl of Onslow, *Sixty-Three Years*, p. 61.

17. Lord Hardinge of Penshurst, *Old Diplomacy*, p. 69.
18. Scott Papers, Add. Mss 52305, Note by Scott, June 1907.
19. Hardinge, *Old Diplomacy*, p. 69.
20. Onslow Family Papers, 173/1/1–9, 'History of the Onslow Family', p. 1997.
21. The Papers of Sir Henry Beaumont, P8/MCR/113, 'The Autobiography of Sir Henry Beaumont', p. 189.
22. Note Charles Hardinge's caustic comment that the Russians 'look upon him here as quite their own creature'; cited in E. T. Corp, 'The Transformation of the Foreign Office, 1900–1907', p. 71.
23. Beaumont Papers, 'Autobiography of Sir Henry Beaumont', p. 190.
24. Details of Hardinge's varied career are provided in the excellent biography by Briton Cooper Busch, *Hardinge of Penshurst: A Study in the Old Diplomacy*; for a more negative view of Hardinge, see Sibyl Crowe and Edward Corp, *Our Ablest Public Servant: Sir Eyre Crowe, 1864–1921*, passim.
25. See, for example, FO 65/1620, Memorandum by Hardinge enclosed with Scott to Lansdowne, 6 March 1901; FO 65/1640, Memorandum by Hardinge (on the 1902 budget) enclosed with Scott to Lansdowne, 6 March 1902.
26. Harold Nicolson, *Sir Arthur Nicolson, Bart, First Lord Carnock: A Study in the Old Diplomacy*, p. x.
27. Bernard Pares, *A Wandering Student*, p. 140.
28. W. Somerset Maugham, *Collected Short Stories*, vol. 3, p. 147.
29. R. H. Bruce Lockhart, *Memoirs of a British Agent*, p. 117.
30. H. J. Bruce, *Silken Dalliance*, p. 174.
31. Pares, *Wandering Student*, p. 238.
32. Beaumont Papers, 'Autobiography of Sir Henry Beaumont', p. 203.
33. Stephen Gwynn (ed.), *The Letters and Friendships of Sir Cecil Spring Rice*, vol. 1, p. 360.
34. Bruce, *Silken Dalliance*, p. 158.
35. Bernard Pares, *My Russian Memoirs*, p. 276.
36. Hardinge, *Old Diplomacy*, p. 69.
37. Both Montgomery Grove, the Consul in Moscow, and his deputy Robert Bruce Lockhart, turned to journalism and writing to raise money. See, for example, H. M. Grove, *Moscow* (a guidebook to the history and architecture of the city which in addition contained a number of observations about the contemporary political situation); R. H. Bruce Lockhart, *Memoirs of a British Agent*, p. 196.
38. Nevile Henderson, *Water under the Bridges*, pp. 37–38.
39. Nevile Henderson became British Ambassador in Berlin in the 1930s; Ronald Graham went on to serve as Ambassador in Rome; Lord Onslow, after serving with distinction during the First World War, served as Parliamentary Under Secretary in various Conservative Administrations during the 1920s.
40. Onslow Papers, 'History of the Onslow Family', pp. 1794–95.
41. FO 65/1678, Scott to Lansdowne, 7 January 1904.
42. Lockhart, *Memoirs of a British Agent*, p. 116.
43. Meriel Buchanan, *Ambassador's Daughter*, pp. 95–96.
44. Henderson, *Water under the Bridges*, p. 28.

45. Henderson, *Water under the Bridges*, p. 44.
46. FO 371/121, Hardinge to Grey, 12 January 1906.
47. See Hardinge's comments on Spring Rice in FO 371/121, Hardinge to Grey, 12 January 1906; Hardinge's comments on Parker in FO 65/1678, Hardinge to Lansdowne, 13 January 1904.
48. George Alexander Lensen (ed.), *Revelations of a Russian Diplomat: The Memoirs of Dmitri I. Abrikossow*, p. 111.
49. Agatha Ramm, *Sir Robert Morier, Envoy and Ambassador in an Age of Imperialism*, pp. 203–4.
50. Beaumont Papers, 'Autobiography of Sir Henry Beaumont', p. 190.
51. See, for example, RA W50/109, Wallace to Knollys, 9 December 1906; RA W51/59, Memorandum by Wallace on Audience with the Tsar. Such information was important, given that Nicolson found it particularly difficult to obtain audiences with the Tsar in the first year after his arrival in Russia.
52. Dominic Lieven, *Nicholas II: Emperor of All the Russias*, p. 54; for some further comments on this theme, see also the *Memoirs of Count Bernstorff*.
53. Sir George Buchanan, *My Mission to Russia and Other Diplomatic Memoirs*, vol. 1, p. 173; for a description of some of these royal festivities, see Bernstorff, *Memoirs*, pp. 32–34.
54. RA W47/204, Hardinge to Knollys, 12 September 1905.
55. See, for example, RA W42/16, Edward VII to Nicholas II (Edward R. to Nicky), 19 June 1901; RA W45/61, Nicholas II to Edward VII, 25 October 1904. Useful material about Edward VII's diplomatic interests and activities can be found in the first volume of Sir Sidney Lee, *King Edward VII: A Biography*; also see Gordon Brook-Shepherd, *Uncle of Europe: The Social and Diplomatic Life of Edward VII*.
56. The Embassy found it difficult to assess Nicholas's true character and political outlook from the moment he became Tsar. See, for example, FO 800/17, Lascelles to Chirol, 8 November 1894.
57. Onslow Papers, 'History of the Onslow Family', p. 1976.
58. Gwynn, *Cecil Spring Rice*, vol. 1, p. 458.
59. Onslow Papers, 'History of the Onslow Family', p. 1862.
60. *BDFA*, 1A, vol. 4, Annual Report for 1906.
61. For a valuable discussion of these changes in the context of foreign policy, see the unpublished dissertation by David Maclaren McDonald, 'Autocracy, Bureaucracy and Change in the Formulation of Russian Foreign Policy, 1895–1914', passim.
62. Lamsdorff was, though, generally perceived by the Embassy as being moderately anglophile in outlook, which naturally helped relations; see, for example, FO 800/141, Hardinge to Lansdowne, 15 September 1904; FO 800/72, Spring Rice to Grey, 16 February 1906.
63. RA X22/44, Memorandum by Hardinge on visit by Edward VII to Russia in 1908.
64. At the time of Izvolsky's appointment in the spring of 1906, there was a good deal of concern at the Embassy about his supposedly pro-German instincts; see, for example, FO 800/72, Spring Rice to Grey, 10 May 1906.
65. Izvolsky subsequently presented his own views about pre-war policy, including the Anglo-Russian relationship, in *The Memoirs of Alexander Iswolsky*.

66. Buchanan, *Mission*, vol. 1, p. 101.

67. On Stolypin, see M. S. Conroy, *Peter Arkadevich Stolpypin: Practical Politics in Late Tsarist Russia*; also see Alexander V. Zenkovsky, *Stolypin: Russia's Last Great Reformer*.

68. See the comments on Witte by Spring Rice in FO 800/72, Spring Rice to Grey, 1 March 1906.

69. Nicolson, *Lord Carnock*, p. 225.

70. RA X22/44, Memorandum by Hardinge on visit by Edward VII to Russia in 1908.

71. RA W51/59, Memorandum by Wallace on Audience with Nicholas II.

72. RA W51/110, Wallace to Knollys, 6 June 1907.

73. Beaumont Papers, 'Autobiography of Sir Henry Beaumont', p. 202.

74. Beaumont Papers, 'Autobiography of Sir Henry Beaumont', p. 237.

75. Beaumont Papers, 'Autobiography of Sir Henry Beaumont', p. 194.

76. Beaumont Papers, 'Autobiography of Sir Henry Beaumont', p. 231.

77. Henderson, *Water under the Bridges*, p. 44.

78. Beaumont Papers, 'Autobiography of Sir Henry Beaumont', p. 192.

79. See, for example, *BDFA*, 1A, vol. 4, Nicolson to Grey, 9 June 1906; *BDFA*, 1A, vol. 4, Nicolson to Grey, 16 June 1906.

80. The same was, for example, true of the German Embassy, particularly when Count Alvensleben and his glamorous wife were based in the Russian capital during 1901–1905. See Lamar Cecil, *The German Diplomatic Service, 1871–1914*, pp. 87–88.

81. *British Parliamentary Papers, 1914–1916*, 11 (cd 7749), qus 38,321–22 (evidence by Sir Arthur Hardinge).

82. Pares, *A Wandering Student*, p. 141.

83. Beaumont Papers, 'Autobiography of Sir Henry Beaumont', pp. 248ff.

84. *British Parliamentary Papers, 1914–1916*, 11 (cd 7749), qus 38482–85 (Evidence by Arthur Hardinge).

85. Nicolson, *Lord Carnock*, p. 212.

86. On the role of Consuls in Russia during these years, see Michael Hughes, 'Diplomacy or Drudgery: British Consuls in Russia in the Early Twentieth Century', *Diplomacy and Statecraft*, 6 (1995), pp. 176–95.

87. Lockhart, *Memoirs of a British Agent*, p. 64.

88. Lockhart, *Memoirs of a British Agent*, p. 78.

89. For a good discussion of the evolution of the Consular Service, see D. C. M. Platt, *The Cinderella Service: British Consuls since 1825*.

90. Colonel C. E. De La Poer Beresford, 'Kundschaftsdienste', *National Review*, February 1911, p. 954.

91. Aubrey Smith Papers (various letters).

92. Beresford, 'Kundschaftsdienste', p. 955.

93. The relevant papers are located in FO 371/1215.

94. Hardinge, *Old Diplomacy*, p. 108.

95. Full details about Stevens' activities are given in Hughes, 'Diplomacy or Drudgery?'. It seems probable that Aubrey Smith, who frequently visited relatives with property near Batum, was one of those who acted as a courier for the information Stevens sent back to London.

96. The information in this paragraph is derived from Henderson, *Water under*

the Bridges, pp. 29–33; Onslow Papers, *History of the Onslow Family*, pp. 1869ff; Hardinge, *Old Diplomacy*, pp. 107–8; HD 3/128, HD3/132, HD3/133.

97. Christopher Andrew and Keith Neilson, 'Tsarist Codebreakers and British Codes', *Intelligence and National Security*, 1 (1986), pp. 6–12.

98. For useful comments on this theme, see Reginald E. Zelnik, 'Russian Bebels: An Introduction to the Memoirs of the Russian Workers Semen Kanatchikov and Matvei Fisher', *Russian Review*, 35 (1976), pp. 249–89. The Embassy was also aware of the phenomenon; see FO 65/1659, Memorandum by Ronald Graham, dated 10 February 1903, on 'Condition of Russian Peasantry'.

99. On the agricultural crisis of the 1890s, see Lazar Volin, *A Century of Russian Agriculture: From Alexander II to Khrushchev*, pp. 57–76. For a critique of this interpretation, see James Y. Simms Jr, 'The Crisis in Russian Agriculture at the End of the Nineteenth Century: A Different View', *Slavic Review*, 36 (1977), pp. 377–98.

100. Among the vast literature on Russian liberalism during this time, the most useful accounts include Shmuel Galai, *The Liberation Movement in Russia, 1900–1905*; George Fischer, *Russian Liberalism*. For a rather different treatment of the subject, see Jacob Walkin, *The Rise of Democracy in Pre-Revolutionary Russia*.

101. On Nechaev, see Philip Pomper, *Sergei Nechaev*; Tibor Szamuely, *The Russian Tradition*, pp. 247–71.

102. FO 65/1620, Memorandum by Graham dated 20 March 1901. Over the next few years, Graham became the Embassy's resident expert on the rise of popular discontent. See, for example, his Memorandum, dated 10 February 1903, on the 'Condition of the Russian Peasantry' contained in FO 65/1659.

103. FO 65/1620, Scott to Lansdowne, 21 March 1901.

104. FO 65/1621, Memorandum by Michell on 'Labour Disturbances', enclosed with Scott to Lansdowne, 13 June 1901.

105. FO 65/1661, Scott to Lansdowne, 17 August 1903.

106. On Plehve's career at the Ministry of the Interior, see Edward H. Judge, *Plehve: Repression and Reform in Imperial Russia, 1902–1904*.

107. Spring Rice Papers, 1/20, Spring Rice to Chirol, 18 August 1904.

108. Gwynn, *Spring Rice*, vol. 1, p. 371.

109. Gwynn, *Spring Rice*, vol. 1, p. 447.

110. RA W44/103, Hardinge to Knollys, 25 May 1904.

111. RA W45/77, Hardinge to Knollys, 8 December 1904.

112. RA W45/77, Hardinge to Knollys, 8 December 1904.

113. RA W45/91, Hardinge to Knollys, 22 December 1904.

114. *BDFA*, 1A, vol. 3, Hardinge to Lansdowne, 23 January 1905.

115. Onslow, *Sixty-Three Years*, p. 114; Beaumont Papers, 'Autobiography of Sir Henry Beaumont', pp. 242ff.

116. *BDFA*, 1A, vol. 3, Hardinge to Lansdowne, 27 January 1905.

117. RA W45/105, Hardinge to Knollys, 1 February 1905.

118. Beaumont Papers, 'Autobiography of Sir Henry Beaumont', p. 244.

119. RA W45/105, Hardinge to Knollys, 1 February 1905.

120. Onslow Papers, 'History of the Onslow Family', p. 1986.

121. FO 800/141, Hardinge to Lansdowne, February 8 1905.

122. *BDFA*, 1A, vol. 3, Spring Rice to Lansdowne, 24 May 1905.

123. *BDFA*, 1A, vol. 3, Smith (Odessa) to Lansdowne, 8 July 1905.
124. *BDFA*, 1A, vol. 3, Report by Bosanquet (Nicolayev) to Smith, 26 September 1905.
125. FO 181/848, Murray to Hardinge, 26 August 1905.
126. FO 181/827, Grove to Spring Rice, 23 November 1905; FO 181/832, Stevens to Spring Rice 22 May 1905.
127. Hughes, 'Diplomacy or Drudgery?', pp. 183–84.
128. Henderson, *Water under the Bridges*, p. 39.
129. RA W45/105, Hardinge to Knollys, 1 February 1905.
130. RA W45/156, Hardinge to Knollys, 12 April 1905.
131. *BDFA*, 1A, vol. 3, Hardinge to Lansdowne, 4 July 1905.
132. RA W46/3, Spring Rice to Knollys, 2 May 1905.
133. Gwynn, *Spring Rice*, vol. 1, p. 456.
134. RA W46/3, Spring Rice to Knollys, 2 May 1905.
135. Spring Rice Papers, 1/20, Spring Rice to Chirol, 26 March 1905.
136. RA W45/120, Hardinge to Knollys, 1 March 1905.
137. Lieven, *Nicholas II*, p. 141.
138. Gwynn, *Spring Rice*, vol. 1, p. 456.
139. FO 800/141, Spring Rice to Lansdowne, 30 October 1905. The information was given to Spring Rice by the enigmatic *Daily Telegraph* correspondent E. J. Dillon, who was on very close terms with Witte throughout these critical months.
140. FO 181/827, Grove to Spring Rice, 23 November 1905.
141. FO 181/827, Grove to Hardinge, 25 December 1905.
142. The following paragraph is largely drawn from Eliyahu Feldman, 'British Diplomats and British Diplomacy and the 1905 Pogroms in Russia', *Slavonic and East European Review*, 65 (1987), pp. 579–608.
143. Onslow Papers, 'History of the Onslow Family', p. 1959.
144. See, for example, RA W46/36, Hardinge to Knollys, 6 June 1905, concerning rumours about mutiny among the Russian troops in Manchuria; RA W46/64, Hardinge to Knollys, 5 July 1905, concerning rumours about mutiny among the troops in Poland and south Russia.
145. RA W46/70, Hardinge to Knollys, 19 July 1905.
146. FO 800/72, Hardinge to Grey, 11 January 1906.
147. For a translation and analysis of the new constitution, see Marc Szeftel, *The Russian Constitution of April 23 1906*.
148. RA X21/17, Nicolson to Knollys, 3 July 1907.
149. Nicolson, *Lord Carnock*, pp. 224–25.
150. *BDFA*, 1A, vol. 6 (Editor's Introduction).
151. The most lucid discussion of Russia's flirtation with representative institutions during the years after 1905 is still to be found in Geoffrey Hosking, *The Russian Constitutional Experiment*.
152. RA W51/55, Wallace to Knollys, 28 March 1907.
153. *BDFA*, 1A, vol. 4, Nicolson to Grey, 3 September 1906.
154. *BDFA*, 1A, vol. 4, Nicolson to Grey, 14 October 1906.
155. RA W51/110, Wallace to Knollys, 6 June 1907.
156. RA W51/133, Wallace to Knollys, 20 June 1907.
157. *BDFA*, 1A, vol. 4 Nicolson to Grey, 17 June 1907.

158. RA W52/74, Wallace to Knollys, 5 December 1907.
159. A useful discussion of three particular areas of contention between the third Duma and the Tsarist government can be found in George Tokmakoff, *P.A. Stolypin and the Third Duma: An Appraisal of the Three Major Issues.*
160. *BDFA*, 1A, vol. 5, O'Beirne to Grey, 16 July 1908.
161. FO 800/177, O'Beirne to Bertie, 2 December 1906.
162. For details of Stolypin's agricultural reforms, see Volin, *A Century of Russian Agriculture*, pp. 94–116.
163. FO 800/73, Memorandum by O'Beirne, dated 14 August 1908.
164. *BDFA*, 1A, vol. 5, Annual Report for 1908.
165. *BDFA*, 1A, vol. 6, Buchanan to Grey, 28 March 1911.
166. *BDFA*, 1A, vol. 6, Buchanan to Grey, 6 March 1911.
167. *BDFA*, 1A, vol. 6, Buchanan to Grey, 20 September 1911.
168. RA GV P284a/4, Buchanan to George V, 22 September 1911.
169. The new Prime Minister recalled his experiences during these years in his memoirs, published in English under the title *Out of My Past.*
170. FO 371/1743, O'Beirne to Grey, 11 June 1913.
171. FO 371/1743, O'Beirne to Grey, 25 November 1913.
172. FO 371/2090, Woodhouse to Grey, 27 January 1914.
173. FO 371/2092, Buchanan to Grey, 29 March 1914.
174. FO 371/2091, Minute by Nicolson on Buchanan to Grey, 11 February 1914.

Notes to Chapter 3: Drawing Near the End

1. Keith Neilson, *Strategy and Supply*, p. 43.
2. For a rather different view see B. H. Liddell Hart, *History of the First World War*, pp. 72–73.
3. S. J. G. Hoare, *The Fourth Seal: End of the Russian Chapter*, p. 237.
4. Lindley Papers, MS 1372/2, p. 3.
5. Norman Stone, *The Eastern Front, 1914–1917*, p. 151.
6. FO 371/2444, Letter from War Office to Grey, 28 December 1915.
7. Useful insights into Hanbury-Williams' daily life at the *Stavka* can be found in his *The Emperor Nicholas II as I Knew Him*, passim.
8. The Papers of Sir Richard Phillimore, PP/MCR/C34, Letter by Phillimore to his wife dated 27 November 1915.
9. For details, see Keith Neilson, 'Joyrides? Intelligence and Propaganda in Russia, 1914–1917', *Historical Journal*, 24 (1981), pp. 885–906.
10. For details of these dispatches, see Hoare, *Fourth Seal*, passim.
11. FO 371/2749, Knox to Buchanan, 9 March 1916.
12. Ariadna Tyrkova-Williams, *Cheerful Giver: The Life of Harold Williams*, p. 164.
13. Hoare, *Fourth Seal*, pp. 241–42.
14. See the various minutes contained in FO 371/2447 on this subject.
15. For details see, Neilson, 'Joyrides', pp. 889–96; Rupert Hart-Davis, *Hugh Walpole: A Biography*, chapters 10–11.
16. Gerhardie's memories of his time in Russia during the period of the Revolution and Civil War can be found in William Gerhardi, *Memoirs of a Polyglot*, pp. 109–53; some further information is contained in Dido Davies, *William Gerhardie: A Biography*, pp. 53–90. It should, perhaps, be noted that neither Gerhardie himself, nor those who have written about him, have ever agreed on a definitive spelling of his name.
17. Lindley Papers, MS 1372/2, p. 3.
18. FO 371/2446, Buchanan to Grey, 20 December 1914.
19. FO 371/2747, French to Campbell, 18 February 1916.
20. FO 371/2746, Buchanan to Foreign Office, 20 January 1916. When making use of *unprinted* telegraphic communications in the Foreign Office archives, I have adopted the convention of describing them by the form of 'Sender to Foreign Office' or 'Foreign Office to Addressee'.
21. FO 371/2746, Admiralty to Philmore (*sic*), 15 February 1916.
22. FO 371/2455, Buchanan to Foreign Office, 30 October 1915.
23. For a useful discussion of the changing role of the Foreign Office, see Gordon A. Craig, 'The British Foreign Office from Grey to Austen Chamberlain', in Gordon A. Craig and Felix Gilbert (eds), The Diplomats, 1919–1939, vol. 1, pp. 15–48. See the comments made by Buchanan himself on this theme several years later contained in the Gosse Papers, Buchanan to Gosse, 20 February 1920.
24. For Lloyd George's view of Buchanan, see *The War Memoirs of David Lloyd George*, vol. 4, p. 1891.
25. Papers of Lieutenant J. R. Parsons, 73/123/1, Letter by Parsons to his wife dated 14 August 1916.
26. For a brief reference to the tensions which Grenfell's behaviour sometimes caused at the Embassy, see Lindley Papers, MS 1372/2, p. 3.

27. For useful comments on the Durnovo Memorandum, which reflected the anxieties of one senior official about the likely impact of war on Russia's social and political structures, see D. C. B. Lieven, *Russia and the Origins of the First World War*, pp. 78–82.

28. See, for example, FO 371/2096, Roberts (Odessa) to Grey, 23 October 1914; FO 371/2096, Bayley (Moscow) to Foreign Office, 23 October 1914.

29. FO 371/2095, Stevens to Grey, 31 August 1914.

30. FO 371/2448, Roberts to Grey, 6 February 1915.

31. FO 371/2448, Blakey (Kharkov) to Smith (Odessa), 21 March 1915.

32. FO 371/2095, Hanbury-Williams to Buchanan, 9 October 1914.

33. FO 371/2095, Hanbury-Williams to Buchanan, 6 December 1914 (referring to an earlier dispatch).

34. FO 371/2095, Hanbury-Williams to Buchanan, 15 December 1914.

35. Sir Alfred Knox, *With the Russian Army*, vol. 1, passim.

36. Neilson, *Strategy and Supply*, pp. 43–85.

37. FO 371/2446, Hanbury-Williams to Buchanan, 17 January 1915.

38. Bernard Pares, *My Russian Memoirs*, pp. 289–90.

39. Stone, *Eastern Front*, esp. pp. 144–164.

40. See, for example, Winston Churchill's 'A Further Note upon the Military Situation' which was prepared for the Cabinet in the summer of 1915, contained in CAB 37/130, 16.

41. FO 371/2447, Buchanan to Foreign Office, 24 February 1915.

42. FO 371/2452, Buchanan to Grey, 24 June 1915.

43. FO 371/2451, Roberts to Grey, 24 June 1915.

44. Maurice Paléologue, *An Ambassador's Memoirs*, vol. 2, p. 39. For Buchanan's views of Paléologue's somewhat histrionic character, see Gosse Papers, Buchanan to Gosse, 20 August 1920.

45. FO 371/2454, Buchanan to Grey, 6 August 1915.

46. On the Union of Towns, see W. E. Gleason, 'The All-Russian Union of Towns and the Politics of Urban Reform in Tsarist Russia', *Russian Review*, 35 (1976), pp. 290–302; on the Union of Zemstvos, see Thomas Fallows, 'Politics and the War Effort in Russia: the Union of Zemstvos and the Organization of Food Supplies', *Slavic Review*, 37 (1978), pp. 70–90.

47. Buchanan commented early in 1916 that the Zemgor alone had 'given proof of efficiency and capacity during the war'; see FO 800/75, Buchanan to Grey, 8 February 1916.

48. FO 371/2454, Lockhart Memorandum on 'Changes in Public Opinion in Moscow as Affected by the First Year of the War', enclosed with Buchanan to Grey, 12 August 1915.

49. FO 371/2454, Lockhart Memorandum on 'The Growth of the Industrial Movement in the Moscow Industrial District', enclosed with Buchanan to Grey, 12 August 1915.

50. FO 371/2450, Buchanan to Foreign Office, 8 September 1915.

51. Lindley Papers, MS 1372/2, p. 5.

52. The correspondence of the Tsar and Tsarina is contained in *Letters of the Tsar to the Tsaritsa, 1914–1917* and *Letters of the Tsaritsa to the Tsar, 1914–1916*.

53. FO 371/2454, Lockhart to Buchanan, 20 September 1915.

54. FO 371/2455, Lockhart to Buchanan, 27 September 1915.

55. FO 371/2454, Buchanan to Grey, 16 September 1916.
56. FO 371/2454, Buchanan to Grey, 22 August 1915.
57. FO 800/75, Buchanan to Foreign Office, 12 October 1915.
58. Lindley Papers, MS 1372/2, p. 25.
59. FO 371/2454, Buchanan to Foreign Office, 28 September 1915.
60. FO 371/2455, Buchanan to Grey, 16 October 1915.
61. FO 800/75, Buchanan to Foreign Office, 17 October 1915.
62. FO 800/75, Nicolson to Grey, 18 October 1915.
63. FO 800/75, Foreign Office to Buchanan, 18 October 1915.
64. Buchanan, *Mission*, vol. 2, p. 4.
65. FO 800/75, Buchanan to Foreign Office, 19 October 1915.
66. 'I am always careful to represent what I say as coming from myself personally'; FO 800/75, Buchanan to Drummond, 3 February 1916.
67. FO 800/75, Buchanan to Foreign Office, 20 October 1915.
68. FO 800/75, Buchanan to Foreign Office, 5 November 1915.
69. FO 371/2455, Lockhart to Buchanan, 10 November 1915.
70. FO 371/2455, Lindley, Summary of Events, enclosed with Buchanan to Grey, 11 December 1915. Lindley was more inclined to downplay the significance of the upheavals of 1915 in his memoirs, writing that 'There was no general feeling of coming catastrophe'.
71. FO 371/2745, Bagge to Buchanan, 9 December 1915.
72. Bosanquet Papers, various letters by Dorothy Bosanquet about her husband's working life.
73. Lindley Papers, MS 1372/2, p. 4.
74. Lockhart, *Memoirs of a British Agent*, p. 150.
75. Lockhart, *Memoirs of a British Agent*, p. 158.
76. Lindley Papers, MS 1372/2, pp. 6, 19.
77. Phillimore Papers, Letter from Phillimore to his wife, 27 November 1915.
78. Parsons Papers, various letters by Parsons to his wife.
79. Gerhardi, *Memoirs of a Polyglot*, p. 121.
80. Buchanan, *Mission*, vol. 2, p. 3.
81. Lloyd George Papers, E/3/23/4, Buchanan to Hardinge, 4 November 1916.
82. Buchanan, *Mission*, vol. 2, p. 3.
83. FO 371/2745, Lindley, Summary of Events, enclosed with Buchanan to Grey, 21 March 1916.
84. FO 371/2745, Buchanan to Grey, 28 January 1916.
85. FO 371/2743, Buchanan to Foreign Office, 4 February 1916.
86. Walters, *Secret and Confidential*, p. 360.
87. For a description of the situation in north Russia, see Young (Archangel) to Grey, 12 December 1916.
88. Parsons Papers, letter from Parsons to his wife, 14 August 1916.
89. Buchanan, *Mission*, vol. 2, pp. 16–17.
90. Walters, *Secret and Confidential*, p. 329.
91. Buchanan, *Mission*, vol. 2, p. 26; also see FO 371/2752, Buchanan to Foreign Office, 6 November 1916 for further details.
92. Lloyd George Papers, E/3/23/4, Buchanan to Hardinge, 4 November 1916.
93. Hoare, *Fourth Seal*, pp. 241–42.
94. FO 371/2748, Knox to Buchanan, 4 July 1916.

95. See, for example, FO 371/2745, Stevens to Buchanan, 20 July 1917.

96. FO 371/2995, Douglas (Kiev) to Bagge, 16 January 1917.

97. FO 371/2995, Walton (Mariupol) to Bagge, 22 November 1916.

98. FO 371/2745, Lindley, Summary of Events, enclosed with Buchanan to Grey, 28 October 1916.

99. FO 371/2745, Buchanan to Foreign Office, 2 November 1916.

100. Buchanan, *Mission*, vol. 2, p. 28.

101. Lloyd George Papers, E/3/23/4, Buchanan to Hardinge, 4 November 1916.

102. Buchanan, *Mission*, vol. 2, p. 41.

103. FO 371/2995, Lockhart to Buchanan, 21 December 1916.

104. FO 371/2995, Lockhart to Buchanan, 26 December 1916.

105. Neilson, *Strategy and Supply*, p. 231.

106. FO 371/2995, Lindley, Summary of Events, enclosed with Buchanan to Balfour, 18 January 1917.

107. A good description of the conference can be found in Neilson, *Strategy and Supply*, pp. 225–48. For Lindley's comments, see Lindley Papers, MS 1372/2, p. 28.

108. C. E. Callwell (ed.), *Field-Marshal Sir Henry Wilson: His Life and Diaries*, p. 315.

109. Hoare, *Fourth Seal*, p. 207.

110. *War Memoirs of David Lloyd George*, vol. 3, pp. 1587–89.

111. Buchanan had serious doubts about Protopopov's sanity, writing to Hardinge that he had once been treated 'for mental disturbance, and the story is that now he crawls about on all fours on the advice of Tibetan quack, who recommends a return to the natural life'. Lloyd George Papers, E/3/23/4, Lloyd George to Hardinge, 4 November 1916.

112. FO 800/205, Buchanan to Foreign Office, 4 January 1917.

113. FO 800/205, Foreign Office to Buchanan, 5 Janaury 1917.

114. Lindley Papers, MS 1372/2, p. 26.

115. FO 800/205, Buchanan to Foreign Office, 7 January 1917.

116. FO 800/205, Foreign Office to Buchanan, 8 January 1917.

117. Buchanan, *Mission*, vol. 2, p. 49.

118. Buchanan, *Mission*, vol. 2, p. 57.

Notes to Chapter 4: A Scene of Extraordinary Disorder

1. FO 371/2995, Buchanan to Foreign Office, 9 March 1917. The telegram was in fact sent before Buchanan's return to Petrograd, but was not recorded as such at the Foreign Office.
2. FO 371/2995, Buchanan to Foreign Office, 10 March 1917 (a telegram which was once again in fact sent before Buchanan's return to Petrograd).
3. FO 371/2995, Knox for DMI in Buchanan (*sic*) to Foreign Office, 10 March 1917.
4. Meriel Buchanan, *Petrograd: The City of Trouble, 1914–1918*, pp. 92–100.
5. FO 371/2752, Buchanan to Foreign Office, 14 December 1916.
6. FO 317/2995, Buchanan to Foreign Office, 12 March 1917.
7. FO 371/2995, Buchanan to Foreign Office, 13 March 1917.
8. FO 371/2995, Knox to DMI, in Buchanan to Foreign Office, 13 March 1917.
9. FO 371/2995, Buchanan to Foreign Office, 13 March 1917.
10. FO 371/2995, Buchanan to Foreign Office, 13 March 1917.
11. Lieven, *Nicholas II*, p. 232.
12. Both telegrams are in FO 371/2995, 14 March 1917.
13. CAB 24/7, GT 187, Hanbury-Williams to Robertson, 14 March 1917. In his memoirs, Hanbury-Williams said that he wrote the letter on the following day, but this seems to be an error.
14. FO 371/2995, Buchanan to Foreign Office, 15 March 1917.
15. FO 371/2995, Buchanan to Foreign Office, 15 March 1917.
16. FO 371/2995, Foreign Office to Buchanan, 17 March 1917.
17. CAB 23/2, War Cabinet 99, 19 March 1917.
18. An even more positive account was given by Hugh Walpole in his official report of the revolution, dated 20 March 1917. A copy is contained in Hart-Davis, *Hugh Walpole*, pp. 449–69. See also the comments of Lindley in FO 371/2996, Lindley to Clerk, 20 March 1917.
19. Glenesk-Bathurst Papers, 1990/1/2860, Letter by Lady Georgina Buchanan, 16 March 1917.
20. FO 371/2995, Buchanan to Foreign Office, 16 March 1917.
21. Lockhart, *Memoirs of a British Agent*, p. 173.
22. FO 371/2998, Buchanan to Foreign Office, 18 March 1917.
23. FO 371/2998, Buchanan to Foreign Office, 22 March 1917.
24. FO 371/2998, Foreign Office to Buchanan, 23 March 1917.
25. FO 800/205, Stamfordham to Balfour, 30 March 1917.
26. FO 800/205, Stamfordham to Balfour, 6 April 1917.
27. FO 800/205, Foreign Office to Buchanan, 13 April 1917. In his memoirs, Buchanan notes that the invitation to Nicholas was never formally withdrawn.
28. Hoare, *Fourth Seal*, p. 242.
29. On the whole question of Russian war aims during the first half of 1917, see Arno Mayer, *Political Origins of the New Diplomacy, 1917–1918*, pp. 61–97.
30. Knox, *With the Russian Army*, vol. 2, p. 564.
31. *FO 371/2995, Buchanan to Foreign Office, 15 March 1917.*
32. Hanbury-Williams, *The Emperor Nicholas II*, p.157.
33. FO 371/2995, Knox to DMI, in Buchanan to Foreign Office, 17 March 1917.
34. FO 371/2995, Buchanan to Foreign Office, 17 March 1917.

35. Hanbury-Williams, *The Emperor Nicholas II*, p. 172.
36. FO 371/2996, Lindley to Clerk, 20 March 1917.
37. FO 371/2995, Buchanan to Foreign Office, 26 March 1917.
38. Hanbury-Williams, *The Emperor Nicholas II*, pp. 211–12.
39. Knox, *With the Russian Army*, vol. 2, p. 569.
40. CAB 24/14, GT 890, Undated memorandum by Thornhill on 'Effects of the Russian Revolution'.
41. Knox, *With the Russian Army*, vol. 2, p. 599.
42. Knox, *With the Russian Army*, vol. 2, p. 582.
43. Buchanan, *Mission*, vol. 2, p. 108.
44. Buchanan, *Mission*, vol. 2, p. 114.
45. FO 371/2996, Knox to DMI, in Buchanan to Foreign Office, 9 April 1917.
46. The documents cited in this paragraph are printed in Robert Paul Browder and Alexander F. Kerensky, *The Russian Provisional Government*, vol. 2, passim.
47. FO 371/2998, Buchanan to Foreign Office, 14 May 1917.
48. See the message from senior figures in the Labour Party to the socialist members of the Provisional Government contained in FO 371/2995, 15 March 1917.
49. CAB 23/2, War Cabinet 144, 23 May 1917.
50. For a more positive account of Henderson's visit, see Mary Agnes Hamilton, *Arthur Henderson*, pp. 125–34; for a more general discussion of Henderson's views on wartime diplomacy towards Russia, including his subsequent resignation over the Stockholm Conference, see Arno Mayer, *New Diplomacy*, pp. 215–24.
51. FO 800/205, Bruce to Clerk, 26 May 1917.
52. FO 800/205, Knox to DMI, 26 May 1917.
53. CAB 23/3, War Cabinet 160, 11 June 1917.
54. Lockhart, *Memoirs of a British Agent*, p. 187.
55. Lindley Papers, MS 1372/2, p. 34.
56. Lockhart, *Memoirs of a British Agent*, pp. 187–88.
57. Parsons Papers, Letter by Mrs Parsons, 12 June 1917.
58. FO 800/205, Bruce to Russell, 15 June 1917.
59. Lindley Papers, 1372/2, p. 33.
60. FO 371/2996, Knox to DMI, in Buchanan to Foreign Office, 1 June 1917.
61. See, for example, FO 371/2996, Lockhart to Buchanan, 23 March 1917.
62. FO 371/2996, Buchanan to Foreign Office, 12 May 1917.
63. FO 371/2996, Report by Bagge to Buchanan, in Buchanan to Foreign Office, 10 May 1917.
64. FO 371/2996, Lockhart to Buchanan, 6 June 1917.
65. FO 371/2996, Brown to Bagge, 31 May 1917.
66. FO 371/2996, Brown to Bagge, 22 May 1917.
67. Buchanan, *Mission*, vol. 2, p. 110.
68. FO 371/2994, Woodhouse to Buchanan, 22 December 1916.
69. FO 371/2994, Buchanan to Foreign Office, 17 April 1917.
70. Lindley Papers, MS 1372/2, p. 9.
71. FO 371/2996, Woodhouse to Buchanan, 30 March 1917.
72. Knox, *With the Russian Army*, vol. 2, p. 575.
73. Lindley Papers, MS 1372/2, p. 29.

74. Meriel Buchanan, *Petrograd*, pp. 120–21.
75. For a more positive view of Lady Buchanan, see Parsons Papers, Letters by Mrs Parsons, 12 October 1917 and 7 November 1917.
76. FO 371/2997, Lindley, Summary of Events, enclosed with Buchanan to Balfour, 9 July 1917.
77. Lindley Papers, MS 1372/2, p. 31
78. For a useful discussion of Germany's attempt to intervene in Russia's domestic affairs during the war years, see Z. A. B. Zeman, *Germany and the Revolution in Russia, 1915–1918.*
79. FO 371/2996, Lindley, Summary of Events, enclosed with Buchanan to Cecil, 13 May 1917.
80. Gerhardi, *Memoirs of a Polyglot*, p. 130.
81. Glenesk-Bathurst Papers, 1990/1/2862, Letter by Lady Buchanan, 2 July 1917.
82. For a challenge to this view, see Richard Pipes, *The Russian Revolution, 1899–1919*, p. 426.
83. For two eyewitness accounts, see Buchanan, *Mission*, vol. 2, pp. 151–55; Meriel Buchanan, *Petrograd*, pp. 130–138.
84. Meriel Buchanan, *Petrograd*, p. 137.
85. FO 371/2997, Buchanan to Foreign Office, 17 July 1917.
86. Glenesk-Bathurst Papers, 1990/1/2863, Letter by Lady Buchanan, 22 July 1917.
87. FO 371/2997, Buchanan to Foreign Office, 18 July 1917.
88. FO 371/2997, Buchanan to Foreign Office, 17 July 1917.
89. CAB 24/22, GT 1619, Memorandum by Knox dated 22 July 1917 on 'Military Riots in Petrograd on 16th and 17th July 1917'.
90. FO 371/2997, Lindley, Summary of Events, enclosed with Buchanan to Balfour, 6 August 1917.
91. Knox, *With the Russian Army*, vol. 2, p. 671.
92. Knox, *With the Russian Army*, vol. 2, p. 618.
93. FO 371/12997, Buchanan to Foreign Office, 19 July 1917.
94. For details of Maugham's mission see Andrew, *Secret Service*, pp. 209–11; Geoffrey Swain, *Origins of the Russian Civil War*, pp. 102–10.
95. FO 371/2996, Lockhart to Buchanan, 23 March 1917.
96. Swain, *Origins of the Russian Civil War*, pp. 14–23.
97. FO 371/2996, Buchanan to Foreign Office, 30 May 1917.
98. Buchanan, *Mission*, vol. 2, p. 168.
99. FO 371/2998, Buchanan to Foreign Office, 31 August 1917.
100. Lindley Papers, MS 1372/2, p. 35.
101. Michael Kettle, *The Allies and the Russian Collapse: March 1917-March 1918*, pp. 36–105, esp. p. 56.
102. See, for example, FO 371/2746, Buchanan to Foreign Office, 20 January 1916.
103. CAB 24/24, GT 1828, Barter to Chief of Imperial General Staff, 20 August 1917.
104. FO 371/3015, Foreign Office to Buchanan, 24 August 1917.
105. Quoted in Kettle, *The Allies*, p. 80.
106. Buchanan's account of his meeting and the Foreign Office minute can be found in FO 371/3015, Buchanan to Foreign Office, 5 September 1917.

107. Knox, *With the Russian Army*, vol. 2, p. 680.

108. CAB 23/4, War Cabinet 229, 7 September 1917.

109. On this whole question see George Katkov, *The Kornilov Affair*; a number of relevant documents can be found in Browder and Kerensky, vol. 3, chapter 27. Kerensky's own recollections are printed in his *History and Russia's Turning Point*, pp. 341–99, in which he roundly condemns the allied representatives in Petrograd for encouraging Kornilov.

110. CAB 24/25, GT 1911, Barter to Chief of Imperial General Staff, 28 August 1917.

111. CAB 24/28, GT 2035, Memorandum by Blair on 'General Kornilov's Coup d'Etat', dated 15 September 1917.

112. FO 371/2997, Lindley, Summary of Events, enclosed with Buchanan to Balfour, 16 September 1917.

113. FO 371/2997, Lindley, Summary of Events, enclosed with Buchanan to Balfour, 16 September 1917.

114. CAB 24/28, GT 2035, Memorandum by Blair on 'General Kornilov's Coup d'Etat', dated 15 September 1917.

115. FO 371/2997, Lindley, Summary of Events, enclosed with Buchanan to Balfour, 16 September 1917.

116. Lindley Papers, MS 1372/2, p. 36.

117. FO 371/2997, Lindley, Summary of Events, enclosed with Buchanan to Balfour, 7 October 1917.

118. FO 371/2997, Lockhart to Buchanan, 26 September 1917.

119. FO 371/2997, Bagge to Buchanan, 10 September 1917.

120. FO 371/2997, Bagge to Buchanan, 17 October 1917.

121. FO 371/2997, Stevens to Balfour, 16 October 1917.

122. FO 371/2997, Lindley, Summary of Events, enclosed with Buchanan to Balfour, 1 November 1917.

123. Buchanan, *Memoirs*, vol. 2, pp. 191–94; Kerensky, *History and Russia's Turning Point*, pp. 387ff.

124. FO 800/205, Note by Sir W. Wisemann following a meeting with Kerensky. Kerensky was particularly critical of the 'environment' around the Ambassador, presumably the various military officers whom Kerensky believed were instrumental in supporting Kornilov's ill-fated putsch.

Notes to Chapter 5: Robbery and Murder

1. Buchanan, *Mission to Moscow*, vol. 2, p. 208.
2. FO 371/2999, Buchanan to Foreign Office, 6 November 1917.
3. Kerensky, *History and Russia's Turning Point*, pp. 438–44.
4. FO 371/2999, Buchanan to Foreign Office, 9 November 1917.
5. FO 371/2999, Buchanan to Foreign Office, 16 November 1917.
6. 'Decree on Peace, Passed by the Second All-Russian Congress of Soviets of Workers', Soldiers' and Peasants' Deputies', in Jane Degras (ed.), *Soviet Documents on Foreign Policy*, vol.1, pp.1–3.
7. FO 371/3000, Buchanan to Foreign Office, 2 December 1917.
8. Buchanan, *Mission to Russia*, vol. 2, p. 225.
9. Michael Kettle, *The Allies and the Russian Collapse*, p. 122.
10. Kettle, *The Allies and the Russian Collapse*, p. 109.
11. CAB 23/4, War Cabinet 289, 3 December 1917.
12. CAB 23/4, War Cabinet 286, 29 November 1917.
13. CAB 23/4, War Cabinet 294, 7 December 1917.
14. CAB 23/4, War Cabinet 294, 7 December 1917.
15. CAB 23/4, War Cabinet 295, 10 December 1917 (Paper GT 2932 attached as appendix).
16. FO 371/3000, Lindley Summary of Events, enclosed with Buchanan to Balfour, 27 November 1917.
17. Quoted in Knox, *With the Russian Army*, vol. 2, p. 728.
18. FO 371/3000, Buchanan to Foreign Office, 2 December 1917. For an interesting insight into Buchanan's views during these crucial weeks, see Swain, *Origins of the Russian Civil War*, pp. 119–21.
19. Keyes Papers, MSS Eur. F. 131/12a, Untitled and undated memorandum by Keyes reviewing his role in Russia during the revolution and its aftermath.
20. Meriel Buchanan, *Petrograd*, p. 224.
21. Meriel Buchanan, *Petrograd*, p. 228.
22. Meriel Buchanan, *Petrograd*, p. 235.
23. Keyes Papers, MSS Eur. F. 131/34, '"Rusty Bayonets": The Rise of the Bolsheviks. Russia 1917'.
24. Keyes Papers, MSS Eur. F. 131/12a. Untitled Memorandum by Keyes reviewing his role in Russia during the revolution and its aftermath.
25. Parsons Papers, Letter by Mrs Parsons, dated 17 November 1917.
26. Glenesk-Bathurst Papers, 1990/1/2865, Letter by Lady Buchanan, 13 November 1917.
27. Buchanan, *Mission*, vol. 2, p. 239.
28. Glenesk-Bathurst Papers, 1990/1/2866, Letter by Lady Buchanan, 16 December 1917.
29. FO 371/3298, Lindley to Foreign Office, 7 January 1918.
30. FO 371/3298, Lindley to Foreign Office, 25 January 1918.
31. For a detailed discussion of this extraordinary episode, see Kettle, *The Allies and the Russian Collapse*, pp. 176–219.
32. FO 371/2999, Buchanan to Foreign Office, 19 November 1917 (attached minutes).
33. CAB 27/189–18, Britsup-Rusplycom, 11 February 1918.

34. Captain George A. Hill, *Go Spy the Land*, pp. 94ff.
35. For a dated but still valuable discussion of the Brest-Litovsk Treaty, see J. W. Wheeler-Bennett, *Brest-Litovsk: The Forgotten Peace, March 1918*. For the impact of the treaty on British policy, see Richard Ullman, *Intervention and the War*, pp. 58–81; Kettle, *The Allies and the Russian Collapse*, pp. 250–69. For a discussion of the importance of Brest-Litovsk in the wider context of changes in the character of European diplomacy, see Mayer, *Political Origins of the New Diplomacy*, esp. pp. 293–312.
36. Lockhart, *Memoirs of a British Agent*, pp. 191–92.
37. Lockhart, *Memoirs of a British Agent*, p. 206.
38. FO 371/3298, 'Memorandum on the Status of Mr Lockhart's Mission to Russia'. Note also FO 371/3298, Foreign Office to Lindley, 14 January 1918, in which the Lockhart Mission is described as having 'a political character but with a commercial façade'.
39. FO 371/3298, Lindley to Foreign Office, 13 January 1918.
40. FO 371/3298, Report by Lockhart in Lindley to Foreign Office, 2 February 1918.
41. FO 371/3285, Lockhart to Foreign Office, 18 March 1918.
42. FO 371/3285, Lockhart to Foreign Office, 18 March 1918. A few weeks earlier, Lindley had informed London that agents had found definite evidence of links between the Bolsheviks and the Germans; FO 371/3299, Lindley to Foreign Office, 7 February 1918.
43. See, for example, Lockhart's comments contained in FO 371/3299, Lindley to Foreign Office, 16 February 1918.
44. FO 371/3285, Lockhart to Foreign Office 18 March 1918.
45. FO 371/3285, Lockhart to Foreign Office, 8 March 1918.
46. Ullman, *Intervention and the War*, p. 132.
47. On Lindley's journey out of Russia, see Lindley Papers, MS 1372/2, pp. 46–51.
48. FO 371/3285, Wardrop to Foreign Office, 24 March 1918.
49. FO 371/3285, Lockhart to Foreign Office, 8 March 1918.
50. Sadoul's letters covering his time in Russia are contained in Jacques Sadoul, *Notes sur la révolution Bolchevique*.
51. FO 371/3285, Lockhart to Foreign Office, 21 March 1918.
52. FO 371/3286, Lockhart to Foreign Office, 21 April 1918.
53. FO 371/3286, Lockhart to Foreign Office, 6 June 1918.
54. FO 371/3286, Balfour to Lockhart, 10 June 1918.
55. FO 371/3286, Lockhart to Foreign Office, 26 May 1918; FO 371/3286, Woodhouse to Foreign Office, 29 May 1918.
56. FO 371/3298, Report by Lockhart in Lindley to Foreign Office, 2 February 1918.
57. FO 371/3286, Lockhart to Foreign Office, 23 May 1918.
58. FO 371/3286, Lockhart to Foreign Office, 12 June 1918.
59. Swain, *Origins of the Russian Civil War*, p. 148.
60. For Lockhart's links with the 'National Centre', see the reports in FO 371/3287, Lockhart to Foreign Office, 6 July 1918; 16 July 1918; 20 July 1918; 21 July 1918; 23 July 1918. See also the 'Memorandum on the Internal Situation of Russia' which Lockhart wrote on his return to Britain in the autumn of 1918, contained in *British Documents on Foreign Affairs*, part 2, series A, The Soviet

Union, 1919–1939 (henceforth *BDFA*, 2A), vol. 1. On the allies' links with the URR, see Swain, *Origins of the Russian Civil War*, pp. 164–67, 172ff. Lockhart himself was inclined, at least with the benefit of hindsight, to be dismissive of Savinkov's abilities; see Lockhart, *Memoirs of a British Agent*, p. 181.

61. Hill, *Go Spy the Land*, passim.
62. Phillimore Papers, *Letters on Russian Affairs*, Letter from Cromie to Hall, 16 April 1918.
63. Phillimore Papers, *Letters on Russian Affairs*, Letter from Cromie to Hall, 26 July 1918.
64. On Reilly, see Robin Bruce Lockhart, *Reilly: Ace of Spies*; Michael Kettle, *Sidney Reilly: The True Story*.
65. FO 175/6, Reilly to Lindley, 23 July 1918.
66. FO 371/3336, Wardrop to Balfour, 19 August 1918; Lockhart, *Memoirs of a British Agent*, pp. 260–61.
67. FO 371/3285, Wardrop to Foreign Office, 24 March 1918.
68. FO 371/3286, Wardrop to Foreign Office, 10 June 1918.
69. FO 371/3336, Wardrop to Balfour, 18 August 1918.
70. FO 371/3337, Wardrop to Foreign Secretary, 7 September 1918.
71. FO 371/3337, Wardrop to Foreign Secretary, 30 August 1918.
72. Lockhart, *Memoirs of a British Agent*, p. 309.
73. 'Appeal From the Council of Peoples' Commissars to the Toiling Masses of England, America, France, Italy and Japan on Allied Intervention in Russia, 1 August 1918', in Degras (ed.), *Soviet Documents on Foreign Policy*, vol. 1, pp. 88–92.
74. Phillimore Papers, *Letters on Russian Affairs*, Letter from Cromie to Hall, 14 August 1918.
75. An eyewitness account of the invasion of the Embassy by Nathalie Bucknell, the wife of one of Cromie's staff, can be found in FO 371/3337, enclosed with Wardrop to Foreign Office, 7 September 1918.
76. FO 371/3336, Report (by Dutch Minister) in Findlay (Christiana) to Foreign Office, 17 September 1918.
77. 'Soviet Government Statement on Allied Responsibility for the Anti-Soviet Conspiracy', in Degras (ed.), *Soviet Documents on Foreign Policy*, vol. 1, pp. 98–99.
78. Valuable information about the whole episode can be found in Richard K. Debo, 'Lockhart Plot or Dzerzhinskii Plot?', *Journal of Modern History*, 43 (1971), pp. 413–39. A review of the literature on the affair is contained in John W. Long, 'Plot and Counter-Plot in Revolutionary Russia: Chronicling the Bruce Lockhart Conspiracy, 1918', *Intelligence and National Security*, 10 (1995), pp. 122–43.
79. Phillimore Papers, *Letters on Russian Affairs*, Letter from Cromie to Hall, 26 July 1918.
80. Although the details are unclear, it is clear that American information passed to the British cast doubt on Reilly's activities. See FO 175/6, Letter, dated 5 October 1918, (apparently from Lindley to Foreign Office).
81. William J. Oudenyk, *Ways and By-Ways in Diplomacy*, pp. 276–312.
82. FO 371/3336 Report (by Dutch Minister), in Findlay (Christiana) to Foreign Office, 17 September 1918.

83. The text of the letter can be found in FO 371/3336, along with the Report (by Dutch Minister), in Findlay to Foreign Office, 17 September 1918.
84. FO 371/3336, Report by Danish Minister at Petrograd, in Paget (Copenhagen) to Foreign Office, 20 September 1918.
85. FO 371/3336, Findlay to Foreign Office, 20 September 1918.
86. FO 371/3336, Clive (Stockholm) to Foreign Office, 20 September 1918.
87. The following details are all taken from material contained in FO 371/3337.
88. FO 371/3337, Lockhart to Balfour, 7 November 1918.
89. FO 371/3337, Memorandum by Bosanquet, dated 5 November 1918.
90. On Churchill's reaction to Cromie's murder, see Martin Gilbert, *Winston S. Churchill*, vol. 4, p. 225.
91. Frank Lindley noted that Cromie's activities had 'brought him into contact with Russians hostile to [the] Bolshevik regime', and acknowledged that this had eventually cost the Naval Attaché his life; FO 371/3336, Lindley to Foreign Office, 6 September 1918.

Notes to Chapter 6: The Worst Horrors in History

1. For a valuable examination of how Wilson's commitment to 'New Diplomacy' influenced his policy towards the Bolsheviks, see Betty Miller Unterberger, 'Woodrow Wilson and the Bolsheviks: The "Acid Test" of Soviet-American Relations', *Diplomatic History*, 11 (1987), pp. 71–90.
2. A useful discussion of the outlook of the various White Generals is contained in Richard Luckett, *The White Generals: An Account of the White Movement in the Russian Civil War*.
3. Peter Fleming, *The Fate of Admiral Kolchak*, p. xii.
4. FO 371/3313, 'Instructions for General Poole', 18 May 1918.
5. FO 371/3299, Balfour to Lindley, 7 June 1918.
6. FO 371/3299, Lockhart to Foreign Office, 6 June 1918.
7. FO 371/3313, Foreign Office to Lockhart, 1 June 1918.
8. Lindley Papers, MS 1372/2, p. 59.
9. For contemporary accounts of the Ambassador's time in Vologda, see Joseph Noulens, *Mon ambassade en Russe soviétique*, vol. 2, pp. 38–159; Lindley Papers, MS 1372/2, pp. 68–73.
10. There were of course a number of other British officials based in Russia during the summer of 1918, most notably the various agents engaged in Secret Service activities, as well as the members of an ill-fated Commercial Mission that was, for some inexplicable reason, sent to the country in the early summer of 1918 to identify opportunities for promoting trade.
11. FO 371/3339, Lindley to Foreign Office, 23 October 1918. Poole had clearly been considering the possibility of engineering a coup from the moment he appeared in North Russia; see FO 371/3313, Poole to DMI, 26 May 1918.
12. Young Papers, British Library Add. MS 61851, *Russian Realities*, p. 59.
13. A useful, if not wholly reliable, account of the British presence in the town at this time can be found in FO 371/3339, Douglas Young, Memorandum on 'The Relations of the British Military Command at Archangel with (i) the Provisional Government of North Russia and (ii) the Allied Diplomatic Corps'.
14. However, there was some contradiction between Poole's instructions and those of Lindley. The former was told when he left Britain that he would be 'under the general authority of the co-ordinating diplomatic official in Russia' (the role performed by Lindley); Lindley, by contrast, was told that he was required to 'superintend and co-ordinate the work of the various British missions, apart from General Poole's mission in Russia'. The potential for confusion was obvious.
15. FO 371/3339, Lindley to Foreign Office, 12 August 1918.
16. FO 371/3339, Lindley to Foreign Office, 12 August 1918; Lindley Papers, MS 1372/2, p. 77. Chaikovsky had been in contact with British officials more or less from the moment of the Bolshevik Revolution in November 1917.
17. For details, see Ullman, *Intervention and the War*, pp. 246–49; Swain, *Origins of the Russian Civil War*, pp. 212–14.
18. FO 371/3339, Lindley to Foreign Office, 6 September 1918. Lindley continued to fear that a further coup was likely throughout the final months of 1918; see FO 371/3341, Lindley to Foreign Office, 1 December 1918.
19. FO 371/3339, Foreign Office to Lindley, 11 September 1918.

20. On disagreements within the Cabinet over policy towards Russia, see Gilbert, *Winston S. Churchill*, vol. 4, passim; on disagreements over north Russia in particular, see Gilbert, *Winston S. Churchill*, vol. 4, pp. 257–79.

21. For a detailed discussion of the impact of Russia on the deliberations at Paris, see John M. Thompson, *Russia, Bolshevism and the Versailles Peace*.

22. *BDFA*, 2A, vol. 1, 'Report on the Work of the British Mission to North Russia from June 1918 to 31st March 1919'. The relevant section of the report was written by Lindley himself.

23. Papers of Major A. E. Sturdy, 73/9/1; 'October 1919 Report' (report by Ironside).

24. *BDFA*, 2A, vol. 1, 'Report on the Work of the British Mission to North Russia from June 1918 to 31st March 1919'.

25. Sir Charles Maynard, *The Murmansk Venture*, p. 17.

26. Maynard, *Murmansk Venture*, p. 79.

27. For a useful discussion of the role of American forces in north Russia, along with the views of the US Government towards its allies' operations in the region, see John W. Long, 'American Intervention in Russia: The North Russian Expedition, 1918–19', *Diplomatic History*, 6 (1982), pp. 45–67.

28. Maynard, *Murmansk Venture*, pp. 318–89.

29. Papers of A. E. Thompson, 80/28/1, Diary entry for 1 February 1919.

30. Even before the intervention at Archangel took place in August 1918, General Poole recognised that the prevailing attitude towards the allies was one of indifference; see FO 371/3313, Poole to DMI, 26 May 1918.

31. Sturdy Papers, 'Report on Intelligence Branch' (by Thornhill dated 30 September 1919).

32. Thompson Papers, Diary entry for 23 December 1918.

33. Ullman, *Intervention and the War*, pp. 202–6.

34. Arno W.F.Kolz, 'British Economic Interests in Siberia during the Russian Civil War, 1918–1920', *Journal of Modern History*, 48 (1976), pp. 483–91.

35. Papers of Colonel Josiah Wedgwood, PP/MCR/104, 'Confidential Instructions to Colonel Josiah Wedgwood. British Mission to Siberia'; Wedgwood's own brief account of the trip is contained in his *Memoirs of a Fighting Man*, pp. 139–42.

36. Wedgwood Papers, Undated and untitled report by Wedgwood on his mission to Siberia.

37. *BDFA*, 2A, vol. 2, 'Narrative of Events in Siberia, 1918–1920' (Appendix A, 'Instructions to General Knox').

38. Useful details can be found in David Footman, *Civil War in Russia*, pp. 85–134; J. F. N. Bradley, *Civil War in Russia, 1917–1920*, pp. 82–97.

39. Footman, *Civil War*, p. 90. For discussion of the role of the Czechoslovak Legion in the civil war, see Michael Kettle, *The Road to Intervention*, pp. 49ff; John Bradley, *Allied Intervention in Russia*, pp. 65–105. Useful documents relating to the role of the Legion are contained in James Bunyan, *Intervention, Civil War and Communism in Russia, April-December 1918*, pp. 60–111.

40. John Ward, *With the Die-Hards in Siberia*, pp. 9, 60, 64.

41. FO 371/3341, Eliot to Foreign Office, 19 November 1918.

42. M. Janin, *Ma mission en Sibérie*, p. 31.

43. Details of Nielson and Steveni's role are given in Fleming, *The Fate of Admiral*

Kolchak, pp. 113–16. Michael Kettle paints a rather different portrait in his treatment of the events in Omsk, suggesting that the two men may have played a more active role in the plot than suggested by Fleming.

44. Ward, *With the Die-Hards*, p. 127.
45. Fleming, *The Fate of Admiral Kolchak*, p. 95; for a somewhat different interpretation of Knox's views than the one presented here, see Swain, *Origins of the Russian Civil War*, p. 246.
46. Fleming, *The Fate of Admiral Kolchak*, p. 143.
47. This concern was comparatively widespread among the allied governments; see, *BDFA*, 2A, vol. 2, Balfour to Curzon, 25 May 1919.
48. Ward, *With the Die-Hards*, p. 165.
49. WO 95/5433, 'Diary of British Military Mission Siberia (May-October 1919)', 25 May 1919.
50. *DBFP*, first series, vol. 3, Eliot to Curzon, 29 July 1919.
51. *DBFP*, first series, vol. 3, O'Reilly to Curzon, 24 September 1919.
52. *DBFP*, first series, vol. 3, O'Reilly to Curzon, 16 August 1919.
53. *DBFP*, first series, vol. 3, O'Brien-Butler to Curzon, 3 November 1919.
54. Documents relating to Preston's investigations (including the cases cited in this paragraph) are located in FO 538/1.
55. *British Parliamentary Papers 1919*, 53 (cd 8), 'A Collection of Reports on Bolshevism in Russia'.
56. *BDFA*, 2A, vol. 4, Thomas Preston, 'A Brief and Impartial Retrospect of Events Which Took Place in the Urals and Siberia during the Years 1917–1920'.
57. FO 538/1, Eliot to Foreign Office, 6 October 1918.
58. Thomas Preston, *Before the Curtain*, p. 105.
59. FO 538/2, Jordon (Omsk) to Consul (Vladivostok), 12 July 1918.
60. FO 538/3, Nash (Irkutsk), 'Situation in Siberia, August 1918'.
61. For a description of life at the Mission, see William Gerhardi, *Memoirs of a Polyglot*, pp. 139–50.
62. Quoted in Davies, *William Gerhardie*, p. 80.
63. Gerhardi, *Memoirs of a Polyglot*, p. 153.
64. A useful account of outside intervention in south Russia can be found in George A. Brinkley, *Allied Intervention in South Russia*.
65. A useful first-hand account of life at Denikin's headquarters can be found in John Ernest Hodgson, *With Denikin's Armies*. Denikin's memoirs say surprisingly little about the British officers attached to his Headquarters.
66. FO 371/3978, 'Report on British Military Mission to Volunteer Army, November-December 1918' (by Lieutenant-Colonel Blackwood).
67. FO 371/3978, 'Instructions to General Briggs, appointed Chief of British Military Mission Attached to Denikin HQ', 31 January 1919.
68. Gilbert, *Winston S. Churchill*, vol. 4, p. 264.
69. FO 371/3978, Bagge to Foreign Office, 3 March 1919.
70. FO 371/3979, 'Report on the British Military Mission, South Russia' (by Holman), 8 October 1919.
71. FO 371/3978, 'Report on a Visit to the Headquarters of the Volunteer Army in South Russia' (by Poole); on the politics of the Volunteer Army, emphasising in particular the subordination of the civilian politicians to the White Generals, see Peter Kenez, *Civil War in South Russia, 1918*, pp. 191–218.

72. FO 371/3978, 'Report on a Visit to the Headquarters of the Volunteer Army'. While Poole was a good deal more impressed by the Don Army, the Volunteer Army and Denikin had by this time established their supremacy in guiding operations in south Russia.

73. FO 371/3979, Report by Major Torin, dated 15 September 1919.

74. Papers of Captain J. W. C. Lancaster, 88/65/1, 'Report by Captain J. W. C. Lancaster on the Evacuation of Odessa'.

75. Gilbert, *Churchill*, vol. 4, p. 264.

76. FO 371/3978, Bagge to Foreign Office, 3 March 1919.

77. FO 371/3979, Memorandum by Bagge (apparently written following Bagge's return to London), dated 30 September 1919.

78. FO 371/3979, 'The Political Questions Reacting on the Military Situation in South Russia' (Memorandum by Holman).

79. Papers of Major-General A. Wade, PP/MCR/238, 'The Memoirs of General A. Wade', p. 71.

80. Hodgson, *With Denikin's Armies*, pp. 141–42.

81. Hodgson, *With Denikin's Armies*, p. 10.

82. For a useful description of the intelligence operations run from Constantinople, see the papers of Major-General S. S. Butler, PP/MCR/107, 'The Memoirs of Major General S. S. Butler', passim.

83. For details see Michael Kettle, *Sidney Reilly*, pp. 68–91.

84. Keyes Papers, MSS Eur. F. 131/17, Memorandum by Bagge on 'Anglo-Russian Commercial Relations', dated May 1919.

85. *BDFA*, 2A, vol. 1, Report enclosed with Hill to Curzon, 22 June 1919.

86. Keyes Papers, MS Eur. F. 131/34, 'An Old Burberry: Russia 1919'.

87. Paul Dukes, *The Story of ST 25*, p. 41.

88. Details of the operation of this unit can be found in Augustus Agar, *Baltic Episode*.

89. Dukes, *ST 25*, p. 374.

90. On Bailey's career, see Peter Hopkirk, *Setting the East Ablaze*, passim.

91. For a vivid description of the flood of refugees, see Preston, *Before the Curtain*, p. 137.

92. FO 371/3981, Keyes to Foreign Office, 2 April 1920.

93. *BDFA*, 2A, vol. 2, Lowdon to Curzon, 21 February 1920.

94. FO 371/3981, Robeck to Foreign Office, 2 April 1920.

95. *BDFA*, 2A, vol. 1, Curzon to MacKinder, 6 December 1919.

96. FO 800/251, MacKinder to Curzon, 21 November 1919.

97. *BDFA*, 2A, vol. 2, 'Report on the Situation in South Russia by Sir H. MacKinder MP'.

98. FO 800/251, 'Notes on Points, Supplementary to his Memorandum of January 21 1920, Made by Sir H. J. MacKinder to Questions put to him at the Cabinet of Thursday, January 29, 1920'.

99. *BDFA*, 2A, vol. 2, 'Report on the Situation in South Russia by Sir H. MacKinder MP'.

100. *BDFA*, 2A, vol. 3, Memorandum by Keyes on 'The Anti-Bolshevik Movement in South Russia', enclosed with Keyes to Curzon, 26 April 1920.

101. For a lucid description of the theory and practice of War Communism, see Pipes, *The Russian Revolution, 1899–1919*, pp. 671–713; on the role of Trotsky

in organising the Red Army, see Isaac Deutscher, *The Prophet Armed: Trotsky 1879–1921*, pp. 405–47.

102. *BDFA*, 2A, vol. 4, 'Memorandum by Mr Lockhart on a Conversation with Mr Marakujef'.
103. *BDFA*, 2A, vol. 4, 'Secret Report', 10 February 1921.
104. *BDFA*, 2A, vol. 4, 'Secret Report', 10 March 1921.
105. *BDFA*, 2A, vol. 4, 'ST 28's Account of the Situation in Krondstadt from February 25 to March 11', Appendix to 'Secret Report', 24 March 1921.
106. *BDFA*, 2A, vol. 4, Kidston to Curzon, 14 March 1921.

Notes to Chapter 7: A Very Ordinary Bureaucracy

1. Leon Trotsky, *My Life*, p. 355.
2. See Gordon A. Craig, 'The British Foreign Office from Grey to Austen Chamberlain', in Gordon A. Craig and Felix Gilbert, eds, *The Diplomats, 1919–1939*, vol. 1, pp. 15–48. For a useful general description of the Foreign Office in the interwar years see David Dilks, 'The British Foreign Office between the Wars', in B. J. C. McKercher and D. J. Moss, eds, *Shadow and Substance in British Foreign Policy, 1895–1939*, pp. 181–202.
3. Craig, *The British Foreign Office*, p. 28. For Lloyd George's views on the failings of the 'Old Diplomacy', see *The War Memoirs of David Lloyd George*, vol. 1, pp. 46–47.
4. On the merger of the Foreign Office and the Diplomatic Service, see Christina Larner, 'The Amalgamation of the Diplomatic Service with the Foreign Office', *Journal of Contemporary History*, 7 (1972), pp. 107–26.
5. A useful account of Labour Party attitudes towards Russia, including the attitude of senior politicians towards their professional advisers, can be found in Andrew J. Williams, *Labour and Russia: The Attitude of the Labour Party to the USSR, 1924–34*.
6. For a somewhat different view of Curzon's concerns about the eclipse of the Foreign Office, see Alan J. Sharp, 'The Foreign Office in Eclipse, 1919–22', *History*, 61 (1976), pp. 198–218.
7. Sir Charles Petrie, *The Life and Letters of the Right Hon. Sir Austen Chamberlain*, vol. 2, p. 246.
8. On the origins of the Trade Agreement, see M. V. Glenny, 'The Anglo-Soviet Trade Agreement, March 1921', *Journal of Contemporary History*, 5 (1970), pp. 63–82.
9. Harold Nicolson, *Curzon: The Last Phase*, pp. 208–9; Earl of Ronaldshay, *The Life of Lord Curzon*, vol. 3, p. 354.
10. Stephen White, *Britain and the Bolshevik Revolution*, pp. 51–4.
11. *BDFA*, 2A, vol. 5, SIS Memorandum on 'Relations between the Soviet Government and Sinn Feiners', dated 20 April 1921; *DBFP*, first series, vol. 20, Memorandum by Roberts on 'Bolshevik Propaganda and the Trade Agreement', 22 June 1921.
12. See, for example, *BDFA* 2A, vol. 5, Secret Report of 21 April 1921, 'Bolshevik Aid to Indian Revolutionaries'; *BDFA* 2A, vol. 5, Secret Report of April 21 1921, 'Bolshevik Propaganda in the East'. See also Hopkirk, *Setting the East Ablaze*, pp. 95–122; White, *Britain and the Bolshevik Revolution*, pp. 110–40.
13. Quoted in White, *Britain and the Bolshevik Revolution*, p. 3. For evidence that this position was supported by Foreign Office officials, see the memorandum by Rex Leeper dated 12 September 1921 on 'Political Aspects of the Russian Famine Question', contained in FO 371/6851.
14. *DBFP*, first series, vol. 20, Curzon to Hodgson, 22 June 1921.
15. Papers of G. E. Cormack, 92/21/1, 'War Times in Russia', p. 15.
16. See, for example, *DBFP*, first series, vol. 20, Curzon to Hodgson, 26 September 1921.
17. For Hodgson's positive attitude towards his staff see FO 371/12605, Hodgson to Chamberlain, 8 August 1927.

18. For details of the Bolshevik leadership's attitude to the Commissariat of Foreign Affairs, see Theodore H. Von Laue, 'Soviet Diplomacy: Chicherin', in Gordon A. Craig and Felix Gilbert (eds), *The Diplomats, 1919–1939*, vol. 1, pp. 241–46.

19. On the low status of the Commissariat for Foreign Affairs, see Grigory Bessedovsky, *Revelations of a Soviet Diplomat*, p. 12.

20. On Chicherin, see Craig and Gilbert, *The Diplomats, 1919–1939*, vol. 1, pp. 234–81; on Litvinov, see Craig and Gilbert, *The Diplomats, 1919–1939*, vol. 2, pp. 344–77.

21. *BDFA*, 2A, vol. 6, Hodgson to Gregory, 29 September 1921.

22. Bessedovsky, *Revelations of a Soviet Diplomat*, p. 95.

23. See, for example, FO 371/11775, Hodgson to Chamberlain, 20 October 1926.

24. Preston, *Before the Curtain*, p. 180.

25. FO 371/10495, Hodgson to MacDonald, 11 March 1924.

26. *BDFA* 2A, vol. 6, Preston to Hodgson, 6 April 1923.

27. *DBFP*, first series, vol. 20, 'Note by Mr Peters of a Conversation on May 5, 1921, with Mr Karakhan'.

28. *BDFA*, 2A, vol. 5, 'Situation Report for the Period July 17 to August 7, 1921'.

29. *BDFA*, 2A, vol. 6, Hodgson to Gregory, 29 September 1921.

30. FO 371/10495, Hodgson to Litvinov, 31 May 1924.

31. Various documents relating to this affair are located in FO 371/12593.

32. FO 371/11797, Memorandum by Paton dated 4 March 1926 (enclosed with Hodgson to Chamberlain, 21 April 1926); FO 371/11797, Hodgson to Chamberlain, 2 July 1926.

33. FO 371/10495, Hodgson to Litvinov, 31 May 1924.

34. *DBFP*, first series, vol. 20, Hodgson to Curzon, 24 October 1921.

35. FO 371/11021, Memorandum by Hodgson on 'Suggested Investigation into Outlying Districts of Soviet Union', dated 3 February 1925.

36. FO 371/11021, Minute by Gregory dated 25 July 1925 on O'Malley, 'Account of a Journey to Russia, April to June 1925'.

37. *BDFA*, 2A, vol. 8, O'Malley, 'Account of a Journey to Russia'; O'Malley later published his impressions in his book *The Phantom Caravan*, pp. 66–87.

38. Preston, *Before the Curtain*, p. 173.

39. *BDFA*, 2A, vol. 8, O'Malley, 'Account of a Journey to Russia'.

40. Preston, *Before the Curtain*, p. 153.

41. See for example *BDFA* 2A, vol. 5, Rennie (Helsingfors) to Curzon, 29 June 1921; *BDFA* 2A, vol. 5, Wilton (Riga) to Curzon, 15 August 1921.

42. See for example *BDFA*, 2A, vol. 5, Etherton (Kashgar) to Curzon, 26 August 1921.

43. Some details of Etherton's time at the Kashgar Consulate can be found in P. T. Etherton, *In the Heart of Asia*, pp. 250ff. Further material is provided in Hopkirk, *Setting the East Ablaze*, passim.

44. *BDFA*, 2A, vol. 5, Secret Report, dated 8 June 1921, on 'The Insurgent Movement in the Ukraine'.

45. FO 371/9337, Secret Report, dated 16 April 1923, on 'General Conditions in the Interior: Secret Bulletin by the State Political Administration'.

46. *BDFA*, 2A, vol. 5, Secret Report, dated 19 August 1921, 'A Soviet Report on the Insurrectionary Movement in the Northern Commune'.

47. FO 371/9337, SIS Memorandum on the 'Reorganization of the Soviet State Political Department', dated 4 April 1923.
48. *DBFP*, first series, vol. 20, Hodgson to Curzon, 24 October 1921.
49. *BDFA*, 2A, vol. 5, 'Situation Report for the Period from July 17 to August 7, 1921'.
50. *BDFA*, 2A, vol. 5, Hodgson to Curzon, 10 August 1921.
51. Preston, *Before the Curtain*, p. 153.
52. Preston, *Before the Curtain*, p. 168.
53. Preston, *Before the Curtain*, pp. 175–76. However, Preston gave a rather brighter picture of Petrograd in his letters written at the time of his arrival; see *DBFP*, first series, vol. 20, Preston to Leeper, 19 November 1922.
54. FO 371/6850, 'Situation Report for Week Ending August 14 [1921]'.
55. *BDFA*, 2A, vol. 5, 'Memorandum Respecting Attitude of Soviet Government towards the Resumption of Trade with Western Europe', enclosed with Peters to Department of Overseas Trade, 26 May 1921.
56. *BDFA*, 2A, vol. 5, Hodgson to Curzon, 20 August 1921.
57. FO 371/6850, 'Situation Report for Week Ending August 14 [1921]'.
58. *BDFA*, 2A, vol. 6, 'Situation Report for the Month Ending November 30, 1921'.
59. *BDFA*, 2A, vol. 6, 'Situation Report, January 1 to 18, 1922'.
60. Preston, *Before the Curtain*, pp. 177–79.
61. *BDFA*, 2A, vol. 6, 'Review of the Present Situation in Russia', dated 3 February 1922.
62. The Cheka was in fact replaced in 1922 by the GPU (State Political Administration), which was in turn reorganised the following year. Hodgson and his staff persisted, however, in referring to the organisation as the Cheka throughout their time in Russia, a pattern that is therefore followed in the text.
63. *BDFA*, 2A, vol. 5, 'Situation Report for the Ten Days Ending September 21, 1921'; for other cases of persecution in the same month see also *BDFA*, 2A, vol. 5, 'Situation Report for the Fortnight Ending September 11, 1921'.
64. *BDFA*, 2A, vol. 6, Hodgson to Curzon, 22 May 1922; Hodgson to Curzon, 21 August 1922.
65. *BDFA*, 2A, vol. 6, Preston to Curzon, 13 January 1923; see also Preston, *Before the Curtain*, chapter 15.
66. *BDFA*, 2A, vol. 6, Hodgson to Curzon, 21 August 1922.
67. *BDFA*, 2A, vol. 6, Curzon to Hodgson, 10 April 1923.
68. *BDFA*, 2A, vol. 6, Hodgson to Curzon, 13 April 1923.
69. White, *Britain and the Bolshevik Revolution*, pp. 165–66; also see Lubov Krassin, *Leonid Krassin: His Life and Work*, p. 212.
70. *BDFA*, 2A, vol. 6, Hodgson to Curzon, 11 April 1922.
71. *BDFA*, 2A, vol. 6, Hodgson to Curzon, 4 July 1922.
72. *BDFA*, 2A, vol. 6, Peters to Curzon, 5 December 1922.
73. *BDFA*, 2A, vol. 7, Hodgson to Curzon, 5 October 1923.
74. *BDFA*, 2A, vol. 7, Preston to Hodgson, 26 October 1923.
75. *BDFA*, 2A, vol. 7, Hodgson to Curzon, 22 November 1923.
76. *BDFA*, 2A, vol. 7, Hodgson to Curzon, 28 December 1923.
77. *BDFA*, 2A, vol. 7, Hodgson to Curzon, 18 January 1924.
78. White, *Britain and the Bolshevik Revolution*, pp. 175–203.

79. The relevant documents are published in *DBFP*, second series, vol. 7, pp. 1–70; also see Gabriel Gorodetsky, *The Precarious Truce*, pp. 13–35.

80. *BDFA*, 2A, vol. 7, Hodgson to MacDonald, 25 January 1924.

81. *BDFA*, 2A, vol. 7, Hodgson to MacDonald, 10 April 1924.

82. *BDFA*, 2A, vol. 7, 'Memorandum Respecting the Political Situation in Leningrad', 15 April 1924.

83. *BDFA*, 2A, vol. 7, Preston to Hodgson, 28 June 1924.

84. *BDFA*, 2A, vol. 7, Hodgson to Macdonald, 1 May 1924.

85. *BDFA*, 2A, vol. 7, Hodgson to MacDonald, 7 July 1924.

86. Christopher Andrew, *Secret Service*, pp. 298–338.

87. Martin Gilbert, *Winston S. Churchill*, vol. 5 (Companion No. 1), pp. 244–46.

88. FO 371/11017, Hodgson to Gregory, 30 January 1925.

89. FO 371/11017, Minute by Maxe on Peters to Chamberlain, 4 December 1925.

90. Gabriel Gorodetsky, *The Precarious Truce*, pp. 84–5.

91. Lord D'Abernon, *An Ambassador of Peace*, vol. 3, p. 191.

92. FO 371/11786, Hodgson to Chamberlain, 6 May 1926.

93. CAB 23/53, Cabinet 41, 16 June 1926.

94. *Parliamentary Debates*, House of Commons, 197 (1926), cols 772, 776.

95. *DBFP*, series 1A, vol. 2, 'Memorandum Respecting Anglo-Soviet Relations' (by Orde), dated 16 June 1926.

96. See, for example, Hodgson's criticism of the 'diehards' in FO 371/11787, Hodgson to Chamberlain, 21 October 1926.

97. *BDFA*, 2A, vol. 8, Hodgson to Chamberlain, 20 May 1926.

98. *BDFA*, 2A, vol. 8, Preston to Hodgson, 13 April 1926.

99. FO 371/11798, Preston to Hodgson, 29 July 1926.

100. *BDFA*, 2A, vol. 8, Hodgson to Chamberlain, 30 July 1926.

101. FO 371/11787, Hodgson to Chamberlain, 21 October 1926.

102. *DBFP*, series IA, vol. 2, Memorandum by Tyrrell on 'Foreign Policy in Relation to Russia and Japan', dated 26 July 1926.

103. FO 371/11787, Memorandum by Tyrell, 4 December 1926.

104. FO 371/11787, Memorandum by Gregory, 10 December 1926.

105. FO 371/12589, Chamberlain to Hodgson, 18 January 1927 (on a recent meeting between Gregory and Rosengoltz).

106. Robert D. Warth, 'The Arcos Raid and the Anglo-Soviet "Cold War" of the 1920s', *World Affairs Quarterly*, 29 (1958), p. 123.

107. FO 371/12589, Extracts from Cabinet Minutes of meeting held on 17 January 1927.

108. CAB 23/54, Cabinet 13, 23 February 1927.

109. Christopher Andrew, 'British Intelligence and the Breach with Russia in 1927', *Historical Journal*, 25 (1982), p. 961. A further discussion about events leading up to the break can be found in Harriette Flory, 'The Arcos Raid and the Rupture of Anglo-Soviet Relations, 1927', *Journal of Contemporary History*, 12 (1977), pp. 707–23.

110. FO 371/12602, 'Report on Documentary Evidence Implicating Officials of the Russian Trade Delegation and Arcos in Revolutionary Propaganda and Espionage'.

111. FO 371/12602, Note by Palairet on the findings of the Arcos raid.

112. Jane Degras (ed.), *Soviet Documents on Foreign Policy*, vol. 2, 'Reply to the British Note Breaking Relations with the USSR', pp. 212–14.
113. FO 371/12593, Preston to Chamberlain, 8 June 1927.
114. The various documents relating to the charges of espionage are contained in FO 371/12593.
115. FO 371/12605, Chamberlain to Hodgson, 13 July 1927.

Notes to Chapter 8: *A Grotesque Vision of Life*

1. F. S. Northedge, *The Troubled Giant*, pp. 320–21.
2. For an account of the restoration of diplomatic relations, see Donald N. Lammers, 'The Second Labour Government and the Restoration of Relations with Russia, 1929', *Bulletin of the Institute of Historical Research*, 37 (1964), pp. 60–72.
3. For a useful discussion of British attitudes towards the Soviet Union during the 1930s, see F. S. Northedge and Audrey Wells, *Britain and Soviet Communism*, pp. 49–75. On the gradual decline of the crusading anti-Communist spirit among at least some Conservative politicians, see Sir Curtis Keble, *Britain and the Soviet Union, 1917–1989*, p. 120.
4. On Litvinov, see the chapter by Henry L. Roberts in Craig and Gilbert (eds), *The Diplomats*, vol. 2, pp. 344–77. On the problem of assessing Litvinov's relative importance in the Soviet hierarchy, see *DBFP*, second series, vol. 7, Ovey to Henderson, 15 December 1929; *DBFP*, second series, vol. 7, Ovey to Henderson, 28 July 1930.
5. See the comments by Malcolm Muggeridge on Ovey in *The Green Stick*, p. 282. For a rather less complimentary description of Ovey, see Crocker Papers MS 1387/20, Tatiana Crocker, 'Memoirs of an Adopted Child', p. 259.
6. FO 371/14052, Crowe to Oliphant, 14 November 1929.
7. FO 371/14052, Ovey to Henderson, 12 December 1929.
8. *BDFA*, 2A, vol. 9, Ovey to Henderson, 4 January 1930. Ovey was, however, certain during his first few weeks in the city that none of the local population was facing actual starvation; see RA GV P284a/29, Ovey to George V, 31 January 1930.
9. British Consuls who served in Russia during the early 1930s were on the whole linguistically more privileged than members of the Diplomatic Service. Both Reader Bullard, who served as Consul-General at Moscow and Leningrad, and Leslie Pott, a young Vice-Consul, apparently spoke good Russian when they took up their posts, even though neither man had previously been posted to the country.
10. Joseph E. Davies, *Mission to Moscow*, p. 22; for the French Ambassador's positive assessment of Chilston during the latter part of the 1930s, see Robert Coulondre, *De Staline à Hitler*, p. 112.
11. Fitzroy Maclean, *Eastern Approaches*, p. 17.
12. Earl of Avon, *The Eden Memoirs: Facing the Dictators*, p. 145. The American Ambassador in the Soviet Union from 1936, Joseph Davies, was more favourably struck by the building, describing it as 'a handsome old palace'.
13. FO 371/15625, Memorandum on 'Expenses of His Majesty's Embassy at Moscow', dated 3 December 1931.
14. Details about the lease and the building are contained in FO 369/2166.
15. FO 371/15624, William Strang, 'Report on Local Conditions in Moscow'.
16. FO 369/2166, Potts to Sherwood, 1 June 1930.
17. FO 369/2216, Bullard to Crowe, 6 November 1931.
18. FO 371/15624, Memorandum by Seymour on 'Expenses of His Majesty's Embassy at Moscow'; FO 371/15624, Strang to Foreign Office (Collier), 28 September 1931.

19. FO 371/16340 (Various dispatches and memoranda).
20. FO 369/2425, Chilston to Simon, 31 December 1934.
21. The details and quotations in this and the following paragraph are taken from various letters and memoranda in WORK 10/189; from FO 371/15624, William Strang, 'Report on Local Conditions in Moscow'; and from Crocker Papers, Tatiana Crocker, 'Memoirs of an Adopted Child'.
22. William Hayter, *The Kremlin and the Embassy*, p. 17.
23. *BDFP*, second series, vol. 7, Ovey to Henderson, 28 April 1930.
24. Crocker Papers, Tatiana Crocker, 'Memoirs of an Adopted Child', p. 232.
25. Davies, *Mission to Moscow*, p. 23.
26. FO 418/76, 'Report on Heads of Mission/Ambassadors', contained in Ovey to Simon, 4 January 1932.
27. Maclean, *Eastern Approaches*, p. 26.
28. George F. Kennan, *Memoirs, 1925–1950*, pp. 58–86; Charles E. Bohlen, *Witness to History, 1929–1969*, pp. 14–55.
29. FO 418/84, 'Report on Heads of Foreign Missions in Moscow', enclosed with Chilston to Eden, 10 January 1938; Hayter, *The Kremlin and the Embassy*, pp. 21–26.
30. For a first-hand account of preparation for a Russian posting in the American diplomatic service, see Kennan, *Memoirs, 1925–1950*, pp. 24–57.
31. *DBFP*, second series, vol. 7, Ovey to Henderson, 15 December 1929.
32. *BDFA*, 2A, vol. 9, Ovey to Henderson, 13 December 1929.
33. FO 371/16322, Ovey to Simon, 29 February 1932.
34. *BDFA*, 2A, vol. 10, Strang to Henderson, 19 August 1930.
35. FO 371/16322, Memorandum by Mr Vincent, dated 9 July 1932.
36. FO 371/17253, Strang to Collier, 6 October 1933.
37. FO 418/77, Ovey to Simon, 18 July 1932.
38. FO 371/15624, Strang, 'Report on Local Conditions in Moscow'.
39. Crocker Papers, Tatiana Crocker, 'Memoirs of an Adopted Child', pp. 272–77.
40. *BDFA*, 2A, vol. 15, 'Memorandum by Mr Maclean Respecting a Journey to Afghanistan by Way of Bokhara and the Oxus Back to Moscow through Iran and the Caucasus', 31 December 1938.
41. FO 371/22301, Vereker to Litvinov, 24 November 1938.
42. See, for example, details of the cases discussed in FO 371/21108, MacKillop to Foreign Office, 19 September 1937; FO 371/21108, Chilston to Eden, 20 December 1937.
43. The Secret Police were for some reason more determined in their attempts to penetrate the US Embassy, blackmailing officials there on several occasions. For details, see Loy Henderson, *A Question of Trust*, pp. 390–91.
44. A trip to the region by William Strang had been planned in 1931, to be partly funded by the India Office, but was abandoned when he could not be spared from his regular duties at the Embassy; for details, see FO 371/15624, Collier to Walton, 2 October 1931.
45. FO 371/16339, 'Report on a Week's Tour in the Crimea and Ukraine' (by Vyvyan), enclosed with Strang to Ovey, 1 August 1932.
46. FO 371/19457, Memorandum by Hayter, enclosed with Chilston to Hoare, 30 July 1935.
47. See, for example, *BDFA*, 2A, vol. 10, Paton, 'Three Weeks in the Volga Region

and South Russia'; FO 371/16339, 'Report on a Week's Tour in the Crimea and Ukraine' (by Vyvyan).

48. See, for example, FO 371/21105, George Vincent, 'Notes on a Car Journey from Moscow to Odessa'; FO 371/21105, 'Notes on Leaving Moscow' (by Simmons), enclosed with Chancery to Foreign Office, 8 September 1938.

49. FO 369/2425, Chilston to Howard-Smith, 4 March 1935.

50. FO 369/2425, Chilston to Simon, 31 December 1934.

51. Muggeridge, *The Green Stick*, p. 248.

52. FO 371/17253, Strang to Simon, 26 September 1933. On Duranty, see S. J. Taylor, *Stalin's Apologist: Walter Duranty, the New York Times's Man in Moscow*.

53. FO 371/17253, Strang to Collier, 6 October 1933; FO 371/17253, Collier to Coote (Moscow), 27 October 1933.

54. For details, see William Strang, *Home and Abroad*, pp. 78–120; Allan Monkhouse, *Moscow, 1911–1933*, pp. 281–325; the voluminous files of correspondence relating to the Vickers affair can be found in FO 371/17265–74.

55. Lord Vansittart, *The Mist Procession*, p. 461; Ovey set down his views in a blunt telegram to the Foreign Office, located in FO 371/17265, Ovey to Foreign Office, 16 March 1933. Ironically, Robert Hodgson was privately sharply critical of his successor for not being forceful enough when standing up to the Soviet authorities in defence of the interests of British citizens.

56. See, for example, details of the arrest and deportation of Robert Bell, contained in FO 371/21108 (various memoranda and dispatches).

57. On the life of Lady Paget, see Wilfrid Blunt, *Lady Muriel*. Various papers relating to Lady Paget's work in Russia are contained in the Leeds Russian Archive.

58. FO 369/2283, Bullard to Strang, 26 September 1932.

59. FO 369/2475, Galliene to Collier, 20 December 1937.

60. Among the huge literature on the origins of the planning system, useful sources include Alec Nove, *An Economic History of the USSR*, pp. 96–102; Edward Hallett Carr, *Foundations of a Planned Economy, 1926–1929*, vol. 1, part 2, pp. 787–915.

61. *DBFP*, second series, vol. 7, Strang to Henderson, 7 October 1930.

62. FO 371/15602, J. D. Greenway, 'Notes of a Journey in Russia', dated 27 June 1931.

63. See, for example, the comments by Ovey in RA GV P284a/29, Ovey to George V, 31 January 1930.

64. *BDFA*, 2A, vol. 9, Ovey to Henderson, 6 January 1930. Also see Ovey's comments in RA GV P284a/31, Ovey to George V, 3 March 1931.

65. *BDFA*, 2A, vol. 9, Ovey to Henderson 4 January 1929.

66. *BDFA*, 2A, vol. 9, Ovey to Henderson, 11 March 1930.

67. See, for example, FO 371/17251, Ovey to Foreign Office, 5 March 1933, a report based on accounts given to the Embassy by journalists and other non-diplomatic observers.

68. *BDFA*, 2A, vol. 9, Ovey to Henderson, 8 April 1930.

69. For an interpretation of the collectivisation process along these lines, see Lynne Viola, *The Best Sons of the Fatherland: Workers in the Vanguard of Soviet Collectivisation*.

70. *BDFA*, 2A, vol. 9, Ovey to Henderson, 14 March 1930.
71. *DBFP*, second series, vol. 7, Memorandum by Hardy enclosed with Ovey to Henderson, 21 April 1930.
72. For details, see Robert Conquest, *Harvest of Sorrow: Soviet Collectivisation and the Terror-Famine*, passim.
73. *BDFA*, 2A, vol. 9, Ovey to Henderson, March 14 1930.
74. FO 371/17251, Chancery to Northern Department, 19 June 1933.
75. *BDFA*, 2A, vol. 11, Strang to Simon, 9 April 1933.
76. FO 371/17251, Chancery to Northern Department, 19 June 1933.
77. *BDFA*, 2A, vol. 11, Strang to Simon, 17 July 1933.
78. FO 371/17251, Ovey to Foreign Office, 5 March 1933.
79. Marco Carynnyk, Lubomyr Y. Luciuk and Bohdan S. Kordan (eds), *The Foreign Office and the Famine: British Documents on Ukraine and the Great Famine of 1932–1933*, pp. xvii–lxi.
80. See, for example, *BDFA*, 2A, vol. 10, 'Leningrad and District, August 1930', enclosed with Keane to Strang, 8 August 1930.
81. FO 418/76, 'Report by Consul-General Bullard on Conditions in the Northern Part of his District', enclosed with Bullard to Strang, 6 August 1932.
82. *BDFA*, 2A, vol. 11, Strang to Simon, 8 May 1933 (summary of various letters).
83. FO 371/17251, 'Memorandum on White Sea Canal Works', enclosed with Strang to Simon, 24 July 1933.
84. *BDFA*, 2A, vol. 10, Paton Memorandum on 'Three Weeks in the Volga Region and South Russia', dated 13 August 1930.
85. *BDFA*, 2A, vol. 11, Ovey to Simon, 3 January 1933.
86. FO 418/77, Strang to Simon, 14 August 1932.
87. A detailed analysis of the social and economic significance of the Stakhanovite movement is contained in Lewis H. Siegelbaum, *Stakhanovism and the Politics of Productivity in the USSR, 1935–1941*.
88. *BDFA*, 2A, vol. 13, Charles to Hoare, 21 October 1935.
89. *BDFA*, 2A, vol. 13, Chilston to Hoare, 28 November 1935.
90. *BDFA*, 2A, vol. 13, Chilston to Eden, 7 September 1936.
91. FO 418/77, George Paton, 'Memorandum Respecting the Prospects of Completion of the Five Year Plan in Four Years', dated 13 July 1932.
92. *BDFA*, 2A, vol. 9, Ovey to Henderson, 18 February 1930.
93. *BDFA*, 2A, vol. 10, 'Leningrad and District, August 1930', enclosed with Keane to Strang, 8 August 1930.
94. FO 418/76, 'Notes on Conditions in the Leningrad District', enclosed with Bullard to Ovey, 8 February 1932.
95. *BDFA*, 2A, vol. 10, Strang to the Secretary of State for Foreign Affairs, 25 August 1931.
96. FO 418/83, Chilston to Halifax, 20 August 1938.
97. *BDFA*, 2A, vol. 14, Fitzroy Maclean, 'Account of a Journey through Siberia and Kazakhstan to Tashkent and Samarkand', enclosed with Chilston to Eden, 24 December 1937.
98. FO 371/19457, Memorandum by Hayter, enclosed with Chilston to Hoare, 30 July 1935.
99. FO 371/21105, Vincent, 'Notes on a Car Journey from Moscow to Odessa'.
100. *BDFA*, 2A, vol. 10, Strang to Reading, 3 November 1931.

101. *DBFP*, second series, vol. 7, Strang to Simon, 14 August 1932.
102. *BDFA*, 2A, vol. 13, Gilliat-Smith, 'Report on the Conditions in the Leningrad District: January 1936'.
103. *BDFA*, 2A, vol. 13, Chilston to Eden, 20 February 1936.
104. FO 371/20349, Minute on 'Report on the Conditions in Leningrad District, January 1936'.
105. FO 371/20350, Mackillop to Eden, 29 May 1936.
106. For an entertaining account of some of the more radical ideas articulated by Bolshevik intellectuals in the years after 1917, see Richard Stites, *Revolutionary Dreams: Utopian Visions and Experimental Life in the Russian Revolution*.
107. *BDFA*, 2A, vol. 13, Chilston to Hoare, 30 June 1935; *BDFA*, 2A, vol. 13, Chilston to Hoare, 9 July 1935.
108. *BDFA*, 2A, vol. 13, Chilston to Eden, 29 June 1936.
109. On the opposition to Stalin in 1932, see Leonard Schapiro, *The Communist Party of the Soviet Union*, p. 396.
110. The standard text presenting such an 'orthodox' view remains Robert Conquest's *The Great Terror*.
111. The classic 'revisionist' text which treats the Terror in this way is J. Arch Getty, *Origins of the Great Purges: The Soviet Communist Party Reconsidered, 1933–38*. A very valuable collection of articles on the whole question of the Terror can be found in *Russian Review*, 45 (1986), pp. 357–413; and *Russian Review*, 46 (1987), pp. 379–432.
112. *BDFA*, 2A, vol. 10, Ovey to Henderson, 2 December 1930; Ovey to Henderson, 2 June 1931.
113. *DBFP*, second series, vol. 7, Strang to Henderson, 27 October 1930; for a somewhat different view, see FO 371/15602, J. D. Greenway, 'Notes on a Journey to Russia', dated 30 June 1931.
114. *DBFP*, second series, vol. 7, Strang to Henderson, 30 September 1930.
115. *BDFA*, 2A, vol. 9, Ovey to Henderson, 11 February 1930.
116. FO 418/77, Ovey to Simon, 18 July 1932. Also see Ovey's comments in RA GV P284a/34, Ovey to George V, 26 June 1930.
117. FO 418/77, Ovey to Simon, 12 December 1932.
118. *BDFA*, 2A, vol. 10, 'Who's Who in Soviet Russia'.
119. *BDFA*, 2A, vol. 9, Ovey to Henderson, 11 Febrary 1930.
120. Earl of Avon, *Facing the Dictators*, p. 153.
121. FO 371/17251, Bullard to Strang, 19 July 1933.
122. *BDFA*, 2A, vol. 11, Ovey to Simon, 14 January 1933.
123. For further details about Stalin's complicity in the Kirov affair, see Robert Conquest, *Stalin and the Kirov Murder*.
124. *BDFA*, 2A, vol. 12, Chilston to Simon, 4 December 1934.
125. *BDFA*, 2A, vol. 12, Chilston to Simon, 18 December 1934.
126. The Embassy was, in any case, generally confident throughout the 1930s that the military was firmly subordinate to the civilian authorities. See, for example, FO 418/83, Chilston to Eden, 9 March 1937.
127. *BDFA*, 2A, vol. 12, Chilston to Simon, 22 February 1935.
128. *BDFA*, 2A, vol. 12, Charles to Simon, 3 June 1935.
129. *BDFA*, 2A, vol. 13, Gilliat-Smith, 'Report on Conditions in the Leningrad District, January 1936'.

130. For a useful account of popular attitudes during the Terror, see Robert Thurston, 'Fear and Belief in the USSR's "Great Terror": Responses to Arrest, 1935–1939; *Slavic Review*, 45 (1986), pp. 213–34.

131. *BDFA*, 2A, vol. 13, Chilston to Eden, 19 August 1936.

132. *BDFA*, 2A, vol. 13, Chilston to Eden, 24 August 1936.

133. *BDFA*, 2A, vol. 13, Chilston to Eden, 24 August 1936.

134. *BDFA*, 2A, vol. 13, MacKillop to Eden, 1 October 1936.

135. *BDFA*, 2A, vol. 14, Chilston to Eden, 6 February 1937.

136. *BDFA*, 2A, vol. 14, Chilston to Eden, 6 February 1937.

137. *BDFA*, 2A, vol. 14, Gilliat-Smith, 'Report on Conditions in the Leningrad Consular District for the Period January 1, 1936, to February 1, 1937'.

138. *BDFA*, 2A, vol. 14, Mackillop to Eden, 4 April 1937.

139. See, for example, *BDFA*, 2A, vol. 14, Mackillop to Eden, 6 July 1937; Mackillop to Eden, 18 September 1937.

140. See, for example, *BDFA*, 2A, vol. 14, Chilston to Eden, 11 January 1938.

141. *BDFA*, 2A, vol. 14, Chilston to Eden, 23 February 1937.

142. *BDFA*, 2A, vol. 14, Mackillop to Eden, 15 June 1937.

143. *BDFA*, 2A, vol. 14, Firebrace to MacKillop, 14 June 1937; FO 418/83, Firebrace to Chilston, 6 September 1937.

144. *BDFA*, 2A, vol. 15, 'The Red Army, by Colonel Firebrace', enclosed with Seeds to Halifax, 6 March 1939.

145. Maclean, *Eastern Approaches*, p. 84.

146. Maclean, *Eastern Approaches*, p. 86.

147. Maclean, *Eastern Approaches*, p. 88.

148. For Davies' views, see *Mission to Moscow*, pp. 172–84; for the views of the French Ambassador, see Robert Coulandre, *De Staline à Hitler*, pp. 88–92.

149. *BDFA*, 2A, vol. 14, Chilston to Halifax, 21 March 1938.

150. Maclean, *Eastern Approaches*, p. 114.

151. *BDFA*, 2A, vol. 14, Chilston to Halifax, 21 March 1938.

152. *BDFA*, 2A, vol. 14, Vereker to Halifax, 3 May 1938.

153. FO 371/22285, Chilston to Eden, 8 February 1938.

154. *BDFA*, 2A, vol. 15, Seeds to Halifax, 6 March 1939.

155. *BDFA*, 2A, vol. 15, 'The Political Stability of the Soviet Union by Mr Maclean', Memorandum dated 6 March 1939.

156. *BDFA*, 2A, vol. 15, 'The Red Army, by Colonel Firebrace', enclosed with Seeds to Halifax, 6 March 1939.

157. *BDFA*, 2A, vol. 15, Seeds to Halifax, 21 February 1939.

Notes to Chapter 9: Conclusion

1. For an eyewitness account of these talks, see Lord Strang, *Home and Abroad*, pp. 156–98.
2. Curtis Keeble, *Britain and the Soviet Union, 1917–1989*, p. 108.

Bibliography

A full bibliography of the sources relevant to this study would be longer than the main text. The sources listed below therefore consist of those cited in the notes, along with a small number of other items that have been of particular value in the preparation of this book. I have not listed many of the vast number of memoirs, books and articles specifically concerned with the narration and analysis of events in Russia. Nor have I listed many of the works on the history of the British Diplomatic Service and Anglo-Russian relations, except where they are of particular relevance. The date of publication is that of the edition consulted, not necessarily the date of first publication. In cases where publication took place simultaneously in the United Kingdom and overseas, only the place of publication in the United Kingdom is listed.

Unpublished Sources

Official Papers

All the following official papers are held in the Public Record Office at Kew.

CAB 23	Cabinet Minutes to 1939
CAB 24	Cabinet Memoranda to 1939
FO 65	General Correspondence before 1906 Russia
FO 175	Archives of the Archangel Allied High Commission Correspondence
FO 366	Foreign Office and Diplomatic Service Administrative Office: Chief Clerk's Department and successors
FO 369	Foreign Office Consular Department: General Correspondence from 1906
FO 371	Foreign Office Political Department: General Correspondence from 1906
FO 418	Confidential Print: Russia and the Soviet Union

FO 447	Embassy and Consular Archives Russia: Moscow Correspondence 1857–1950
FO 538	Archives of the Vladivostok High Commission
HD 3	Permanent Under Secretary's Department: Correspondence and Papers
WO 95	War Diaries, 1914–18
WORK 10	Public Buildings Overseas

Private Papers

For the sake of clarity, private papers are listed under the name by which individuals are most frequently referred to in the text and notes.

British Museum, London (Manuscripts Section)
Scott, Sir Charles
Balfour, Earl of
Young, Douglas

British Museum, London (Oriental and Indian Division)
Curzon, Marquess of Kedleston
Keyes, Brigadier-General Terence

Brotherton Library, Leeds University (Brotherton Collection)
Gosse, Edward (containing letters by Sir George Buchanan)

Brotherton Library, Leeds University (Manuscript Department)
Glenesk-Bathurst Papers (containing letters by Lady Georgina Buchanan)

Cambridge University Library
Hardinge, Sir Charles
Hoare, Sir Samuel
Wallace, Sir Donald Mackenzie

Churchill College Archives Centre, Cambridge
Spring Rice, Sir Cecil Arthur

Guildford Muniment Room, Guildford
Onslow Family Papers

House of Lords Record Office, London
Lloyd George, David

Imperial War Museum, London (Department of Documents)
Beaumont, Sir Henry
Butler, Major-General S. S.
Cormack, G. E.
Lancaster, Captain J. W. C.
Parsons, Lieutenant J. R.
Phillimore, Admiral Sir Richard
Sturdy, Major A. E.

Thompson, A. E.
Wade, Major-General A.
Wedgwood, J. C.

Leeds Russian Archive, Leeds University
Lindley, Sir Francis
Young, Douglas
Paget, Lady Muriel
Crocker, Tatiana

Public Record Office, Kew, London (FO 800 series)
Balfour, Earl of
Bertie, Sir Francis
Curzon, Marquess of Kedleston
Grey, Sir Edward
Lansdowne, Marquess of
Mackinder, Sir Halford
Nicolson, Sir Arthur
Spring Rice, Sir Cecil Arthur

In Private Ownership
Bosanquet, Vivian
Smith, Admiral Sir Aubrey

Doctoral Theses

Corp, Edward, 'The Transformation of the Foreign Office, 1900–1907'
(University of Kent, 1977)
McDonald, David Maclaren, 'Autocracy, Bureaucracy and Change in the
Formulation of Russian Foreign Policy, 1895–1914' (Columbia University,
1988)

Published Sources

Official Papers and Documents

The Bolshevik Revolution, 1917–1918: Documents and Materials, ed. James Bunyan and H. H. Fisher (Stanford, 1965)

British Documents on Foreign Affairs, part 1, series A, Russia 1859–1914; part 2, series A, The Soviet Union 1919–1939, ed. Dominic Lieven, series eds Kenneth Bourne and D. Cameron Watt (London, 1983–86)

British Documents on the Origins of the War, ed. G. P. Gooch and Harold William Vazeille Temperley (London, 1926–38)

British Parliamentary Papers

Documents on British Foreign Policy 1919–1939, first series, series 1A, second series, ed. W. N. Medlicott et al (London, 1947–84)

Hansard

Intervention, Civil War and Communism in Russia: Documents and Materials, ed. James Bunyan (Stanford, 1936)

The Russian Provisional Government, 1917: Documents, 3 vols, ed. Robert Paul Browder and Alexander Kerensky (Stanford, 1961)

Soviet Documents on Foreign Policy, 3 vols, ed. Jane Degras (London, 1951–53)

Memoirs, Diaries, Correspondence and Contemporary Writings

Agar, Augustus, *Baltic Episode: A Classic of Secret Service in Russian Waters* (London, 1963)

Alexandra, Empress, *The Letters of the Tsaritsa to the Tsar* (London, 1923)

Avon, Earl of, *The Eden Memoirs: Facing the Dictators* (London 1962)

Baring, Maurice, *The Puppet Show of Memory* (London, 1987)

Benckendorff, Count Constantine, *Half a Life: Reminiscences of a Russian Gentleman* (London, 1954)

Beresford, Colonel C. E. De La Poer, 'Kundschaftsdientse', *National Review*, vol. 56 (1910–11), pp. 954–64.

Bessedovsky, Grigory, *Revelations of a Soviet Diplomat*, trans. Matthew Norgate (London, 1931)

Bohlen, Charles E., *Witness to History, 1929–1969* (London, 1973)

Bruce, H.J., *Silken Dalliance* (London, 1947)

Buchanan, Sir George, *My Mission to Russia and Other Diplomatic Memoirs*, 2 vols (London, 1923)

Buchanan, Meriel, *Ambassador's Daughter* (London, 1958)

Buchanan, Meriel, *Petrograd: The City of Trouble, 1914–1918* (London, 1918)

Callwell, Major-General Sir C. E. (ed.), *Field-Marshall Sir Henry Wilson, Bart, GCB, DSO: His Life and Diaries*, 2 vols (London, 1927)

Chamberlain, Sir Austen, *Down the Years* (London, 1935)

Curzon, George N., *Russia in Central Asia in 1889, and the Anglo-Russian Question* (London, 1967)

Coulondre, Robert, *De Staline à Hitler: souvenirs de deux ambassades* (Paris, 1950)

D'Abernon, Viscount, *An Ambassador of Peace*, 3 vols (London, 1929–30)

Davies, Joseph E., *Mission to Moscow* (London, 1942)

Disbrowe, C. A. A., *Old Days in Diplomacy* (London, 1903)

Disbrowe, C. A. A., *Original Letters from Russia, 1825–1828* (London, 1878)

Dukes, Paul, *Red Dusk and the Morrow* (London, 1922)

Dukes, Paul, *The Story of 'ST 25'* (London, 1938)

Etherton, Lieutenant-Colonel P. T., *In the Heart of Asia* (London, 1925)

Fletcher, Giles, *Of the Russe Commonwealth*, in *Russia at the Close of the Sixteenth Century* (London, 1856)

Gerhardi, William, *Memoirs of a Polyglot* (London, 1931)

Gregory, J. D., *On the Edge of Diplomacy: Rambles and Reflections* (London, 1928)

Grey of Fallodon, Viscount, *Twenty Five Years, 1892–1916* (London, 1925)

Grove, H. M., *Moscow* (London, 1912)

Hanbury-Williams, Sir John, *The Emperor Nicholas II as I Knew Him* (London, 1922)

Hardinge, Sir Arthur, *A Diplomatist in Europe* (London, 1927)

Hardinge of Penshurst, *Old Diplomacy* (London, 1947)

Harris, James (First Earl of Malmesbury), *Diaries and Correspondence*, 2 vols (London, 1844)

Hayter, William, *The Kremlin and the Embassy* (London, 1966)

Henderson, Loy W., *A Question of Trust: The Origins of US-Soviet Diplomatic Relations*, ed. George W. Baer, (Stanford, 1986)

Henderson, Nevile, *Water under the Bridges* (London, 1945)

Henningsen, G. J., *Revelations of Russia*, 2 vols (London, 1844)

Hill, Captain George A., *Go Spy the Land* (London, 1932)

Hoare, S. J. G., *The Fourth Seal: End of the Russian Chapter* (London, 1930)

Hodges, Phelps, *Britmis: A Great Adventure of the War* (London, 1931)

Hodgson, John Ernest, *With Denikin's Armies* (London, 1932)

Hodgson, Robert, 'Memoirs of an Official Agent', *History Today*, vol. 4 (1954), pp. 522–28; pp. 613–17

Imperatorskoe Russkoe Istoricheskoe Obshchestvo: Sbornik, vol. 91

Izvolsky, Alexander, *The Memoirs of Alexander Iswolsky*, trans. Charles Louis Seeger (London, 1920)

Janin, General M. *Ma mission en Sibérie, 1918–1920 (Paris, 1933)*

Jesse, W., *Notes of a Half-Pay in Search of Health: or Russia, Circasia and the Crimea in 1839–40*, 2 vols (London, 1841)

Kennan, George F., Memoirs, 1925–1950 (London, 1968)

Kerensky, Alexander, *History and Russia's Turning Point* (New York, 1969)

Kerensky, Alexander, *The Catastrophe: Kerensky's Own Story of the Russian Revolution* (London, 1927)

Knox, Sir Alfred, *With the Russian Army, 1914–1917*, 2 vols (London, 1921)

Kokovtsov, Count V. N., *Out of My Past*, trans. Laura Matveev (Stanford, 1935)

Lensen, George Alexander (ed.), *Dmitri I. Abrikossow: Revelations of a Russian Diplomat* (Seattle, 1964)

Lichnowsky, Prince C. M., *Heading for the Abyss* (London, 1928)

Lloyd George, David, *War Memoirs*, 5 vols (London, 1933–36)

Lockhart, R. H. Bruce, *Memoirs of a British Agent* (London, 1937)

Maynard, Major-General Sir Charles, *The Murmansk Venture* (London, 1928)

Macartney, George, *An Account of Russia, 1767* (London, 1768)

Maclean, Fitzroy, *Eastern Approaches* (London, 1949)

Michell, Thomas, 'Constitutional Government in Russia', *Quarterly Review*, January 1863, pp. 60–95

Miège, Guy de: *A Relation of Three Embassies from the Sacred Majestie Charles II to the Great Duke of Muscovie, the King of Sweden and the King of Denmark in the Years 1663 and 1664* (London, 1669)

Monkhouse, Allan, *Moscow, 1911–1933* (London, 1933)

Muggeridge, Malcolm, *The Green Stick* (London, 1981)

Nabokoff, Constantin, *The Ordeal of a Diplomat* (London, 1921)

Nicholas II, *Letters of the Tsar to the Tsaritsa, 1914–1917*, ed. C. E. Vulliamy (New York, 1929)

Noulens, Joseph, *Mon ambassade en Russie soviétique, 1917–1919*, 2 vols (Paris, 1933)

O'Malley, Sir Owen, *The Phantom Caravan* (London, 1954)

Onslow, The Earl of, *Sixty Three Years* (London, 1944)

Oudenyk, William J., *Ways and By-Ways in Diplomacy* (London, 1939)

Paléologue, Maurice, *An Ambassador's Memoirs*, 3 vols., trans. F. A. Holt (London, 1923–25)

Pares, Bernard, *A Wandering Student* (Syracuse, New York, 1948)

Pares, Bernard, *My Russian Memoirs* (London 1931)

Petrie, Sir Charles, *The Life and Letters of the Right Hon. Sir Austen Chamberlain*, 2 vols (London, 1939–40)

Preston, Thomas, *Before the Curtain* (London, 1950)

Probyn-Nevins, W, *Apologia for Russia* (London, 1895)

Purchas, Samuel, *Haklyutus Posthumous or Purchas and his Pilgrimes*, 20 vols (London, 1905–7)

Rodd, Sir James Rennell, *Social and Diplomatic Memoirs*, 3 vols (London, 1922–25)

Rumbold, Sir Horace, *Recollections of a Diplomatist*, 2 vols (London, 1903)

Sadoul, Jacques, *Notes sur la révolution bolchevique* (Paris, 1919)

Spring Rice, Cecil, *The Letters and Friendships of Sir Cecil Spring Rice*, ed. Stephen Gwynn, 2 vols (London, 1929)

Strang, Lord, *Home and Abroad* (London, 1956)

Thompson, Sir Geoffrey, *Front-Line Diplomat* (London, 1959)

Trotsky, Leon, *My Life* (London, 1984)

Tyrkova-Williams, Ariadna, *Cheerful Giver: The Life of Harold Williams* (London, 1935)

Vansittart, Lord, *The Mist Procession* (London, 1958)

Vigilans, *The Dualism of England and Russia in the Far East and its Consequences upon the General Political Situation of Europe* (London, 1875)

Walters, W. H. H., *Secret and Confidential* (London, 1926)

Ward, Colonel John, *With the Die-Hards in Siberia* (London, 1920)

Wedgwood, Josiah C., *Memoirs of a Fighting Man* (London, 1940)

Wellesley, Colonel F. A., *With the Russians in Peace and War* (London, 1905)

Whitworth, Lord Charles, *An Account of Russia as it was in the Year 1710* (London, 1758)

Books and Articles

Abraham, Richard, *Alexander Kerensky: The First Love of the Revolution* (New York, 1987)

Anderson, M. S., *Britain's Discovery of Russia, 1553–1815* (London, 1958)

Andrew, Christopher, 'British Intelligence and the Breach with Russia in 1927', *Historical Journal*, vol. 25, no. 4 (1982), pp. 957–64.

Andrew, Christopher, *Secret Service: The Making of the British Intelligence Community* (London, 1985)

Beloff, Max, Lucien Wolf and the Anglo-Russian Entente, 1907–1914 (London, 1951)

Bradley, J. F. N., *Allied Intervention in Russia* (London, 1968)

Bradley, J. F. N., *Civil War in Russia, 1917–1920* (London, 1975)

Brinkley, George A., *The Volunteer Army and Allied Intervention in South Russia, 1917–1921* (Notre Dame, Indiana, 1966)

Brook-Shepherd, Gordon, *Uncle of Europe: The Social and Diplomatic Life of Edward VII* (London, 1975)

Busch, Briton Cooper, *Hardinge of Penshurst: A Study in the Old Diplomacy* (Hamden, Connecticut, 1980)

Carynnyk, Marco, Luciuk, Lubomyr Y., and Kordan, Bohdan S., eds, *The Foreign Office and the Famine: British Documents on Ukraine and the Great Famine of 1932–1933* (Kingston, Ontario, 1988)

Carr, Edward Hallett, *A History of Soviet Russia*, 14 vols (London, 1950–1978)

Cecil, Lamar, *The German Diplomatic Service, 1871–1914* (Princeton, 1976)

Cline, Catherine Ann, E.D.Morel, 1873–1924: The Strategies of Protest (Belfast, 1980)

Conquest, Robert, *Stalin and the Kirov Murder* (London, 1988)

Conquest, Robert, *The Great Terror* (London, 1968)

Conquest, Robert, *The Harvest of Sorrow: Soviet Collectivisation and the Terror-Famine* (London, 1986)

Conroy, M. S., *Peter Arkad'evich Stolypin: Practical Politics in Late Tsarist Russia* (Boulder, Colorado, 1976)

Craig, Gordon A. and Gilbert, Felix (eds), *The Diplomats, 1919–1939*, 2 vols (New York, 1971)

Cross, Anthony, *Russia under Western Eyes, 1517–1825* (London, 1971)

Crowe, Sibyl and Corp, Edward, *Our Ablest Public Servant: Sir Eyre Crowe, 1864–1925* (Braunton, 1993)

Davies, Dido, *William Gerhardie: A Biography* (Oxford, 1990)

Debo, Richard, 'Lockhart Plot or Dzerzhinskii Plot?', *Journal of Modern History*, vol. 43, no. 3 (1971), pp. 413–439

Deutscher, Isaac, *The Prophet Armed: Trotsky, 1879–1921* (London, 1954)

Deutscher, Isaac, *The Prophet Unarmed: Trotsky, 1921–1929* (London, 1959)

Dickie, John, *Inside the Foreign Office* (London, 1992)

Feldman, Eliyahu, 'British Diplomats and British Diplomacy and the 1905 Pogroms in Russia', *Slavonic and East European Review*, vol. 65, no. 4 (1987), pp. 579–608

Fallows, Thomas, 'Politics and the War Effort in Russia: The Union of Zemstvos and the Organization of Food Supplies', *Slavic Review*, vol. 37, no. 1 (1978), pp. 70–90

Fischer, George, *Russian Liberalism: From Gentry to Intelligentsia* (Cambridge, Massachusetts, 1958)

Fleming, Peter, *The Fate of Admiral Kolchak* (London, 1963)

Flory, Hariette, 'The Arcos Raid and the Rupture of Anglo-Soviet Relations, 1927', *Journal of Contemporary History*, vol. 12, no. 4 (1977), pp. 707–23

Footman, David, *Civil War in Russia* (London, 1961)

Galai, Shmuel, *The Liberation Movement in Russia, 1900–1905* (Cambridge, 1973)

Getty, J. Arch, *Origins of the Great Purges: The Soviet Communist Party Reconsidered. 1933–38* (Cambridge, 1985)

Gilbert, Martin, *Winston S. Churchill, 1916–1922* (London, 1975)

Gleason, John Howes, *The Genesis of Russophobia in Great Britain* (Cambridge, Massachusetts, 1950)

Gleason, W. E., 'The All-Russian Union of Towns and the Politics of Urban Reform in Tsarist Russia, *Russian Review*, vol. 35, no. 3 (1977), pp. 290–302

Glenny, M. V., 'The Anglo-Soviet Trade Agreement, March 1921', *Journal of Contemporary History*, vol. 5, no. 2 (1970), pp. 63–82

Gorodetsky, Gabriel, *The Precarious Truce: Anglo-Soviet Relations 1924–27* (Cambridge, 1977)

Grainger, J. H., *Patriotisms: Britain, 1900–1939* (London, 1986)

Hamilton, Keith and Langhorne, Richard, *The Practice of Diplomacy* (London, 1995)

Hamilton, Mary Agnes, *Arthur Henderson: A Biography* (London, 1938)

Hamm, Michael F., 'Liberal Politics in Wartime Russia: An Analysis of the Progressive Block', *Slavic Review*, vol. 33, no. 3 (1974), pp. 453–68

Harris, Jose, *Private Lives, Public Spirit: A Social History of Britain, 1870–1914* (Oxford, 1993)

Hart Davis, Rupert, *Hugh Walpole: A Biography* (London, 1952)

Hinsley, F. H. (ed.), *British Foreign Policy under Sir Edward Grey* (Cambridge, 1977)

Hopkirk, Peter, *Setting the East Ablaze* (Oxford, 1984)

Hopkirk, Peter, *The Great Game* (Oxford, 1990)

Horn, D. B., *Great Britain and Europe in the Eighteenth Century* (Oxford, 1967)

Hosking, Geoffrey, *The Russian Constitutional Experiment: Government and Duma, 1907–1914* (London, 1973)

Howard, Christopher, *Splendid Isolation* (London, 1967)

Hughes, Michael, 'British Diplomats in Russia during the First World War', *Journal of Contemporary History*, vol. 31, no. 1 (1996), pp. 75–97

Hughes, Michael, 'British Diplomats in Russia on the Eve of War and Revolution', *European History Quarterly*, vol. 24, no. 3 (1994), pp. 341–66

Hughes, Michael, 'Diplomacy or Drudgery?: British Consuls in Russia in the Early Twentieth Century', *Diplomacy and Statecraft*, vol. 6, no. 1 (1995), pp. 176–95

Hughes, Michael, 'In Praise of Folly?: Traditional Diplomacy in a Modern World', *Paradigms*, vol. 9, no. 1 (1995), pp. 1–16

Jones, Raymond A., *The British Diplomatic Service, 1815–1914* (Gerrards Cross, 1983)

Jones, Raymond A., *The Nineteenth Century Foreign Office: An Administrative History* (London, 1971)

Judge, Edward H., *Plehve: Repression and Reform in Imperial Russia, 1902–1904* (Syracuse, New York, 1983)

Katkov, George, *The Kornilov Affair: Kerensky and the Break Up of the Russian Army* (London, 1980)

Keeble, Sir Curtis, *Britain and the Soviet Union, 1917–1989* (London, 1990)

Kenez, Peter, *Civil War in South Russia, 1918* (Berkeley, 1971)

Kennedy, Paul, *The Realities behind Diplomacy: Background Influences on British External Policy, 1865–1980* (London, 1985)

Kennan, George F., *Russia Leaves the War* (London, 1953)

Kennan, George F., *The Decision to Intervene* (London, 1958)

Kettle, Michael, *Churchill and the Archangel Fiasco: November 1918-July 1919* (London, 1992)

Kettle, Michael, *Sidney Reilly* (London, 1983)

Kettle, Michael, *The Allies and the Russian Collapse: March 1917-March 1918* (London, 1981)

Kettle, Michael, *The Road to Intervention: March-November 1918* (London, 1988)

Kolz, Arno W. F., 'British Economic Interests in Siberia during the Russian Civil War, 1918–1920', *Journal of Modern History*, vol. 48, no. 3 (1976), pp. 483–91

Krassin, Lubov, *Leonid Krassin: His Life and Work* (London, 1929)

Lammers, Donald, 'The Second Labour Government and the Restoration of Relations with Russia, 1929', *Institute of Historical Research Bulletin*, vol. 37, no. 95 (1964), pp. 60–72

Larner, Christina, 'The Amalgamation of the Diplomatic Service with the Foreign Office', *Journal of Contemporary History*, vol. 7, nos. 1–2 (1972), pp. 107–26

Lee, Sir Sidney, *King Edward VII: A Biography*, 2 vols (London, 1925–27)

Letley, Emma, *Maurice Baring* (London, 1991)

Lauren, Paul Gordon, *Diplomats and Bureaucrats: The First Institutional Responses to Twentieth-Century Diplomacy in France and Germany* (Stanford, 1976)

Liddell Hart, Basil, *History of the First World War* (London, 1970)

Lieven, Dominic, *Nicholas II: Emperor of all the Russias* (London, 1993)

Lieven, Dominic, *Russia and the Origins of the First World War* (London, 1983)

Lockhart, Robin Bruce, *Reilly: Ace of Spies* (London, 1983)

Long, John W., 'Plot and Counter-Plot in Revolutionary Russia: Chronicling the Bruce Lockhart Conspiracy, 1918', *Intelligence and National Security*, vol. 10, no. 1 (1995), pp. 122–43

Luckett, Richard, *The White Generals: An Account of the White Movement and the Russian Civil War* (London, 1971)

Maugham, Somerset, *Collected Short Stories*, vol. 3 (London, 1976)

Mayer, Arno, *Political Origins of the New Diplomacy* (New Haven, Connecticut, 1959)

McKercher,B. J. C. and Moss, D. J. (eds), *Shadow and Substance in British Foreign Policy, 1895–1939* (Edmonton, Alberta, 1984)

Middleton, K. W. B., *Britain and Russia: An Historical Essay* (London, 1947)

Miller, J. D. B., *Norman Angell and the Futility of War* (London, 1986)

Monger, George, *The End of Isolation: Britain's Foreign Policy, 1900–1907* (London, 1963)

Morgan, Ted, *Somerset Maugham* (London, 1986)

Morris, A. J. Anthony, *Radicalism against the War, 1906–1914* (Totowa, New Jersey, 1972)

Neilson, Keith, 'Joyrides? Intelligence and Propaganda in Russia, 1914–1917', *Historical Journal*, vol. 24, no. 4 (1981), pp. 885–906

Neilson, Keith, *Strategy and Supply: The Anglo-Russian Alliance, 1914–1917* (London, 1984)

Nicolson, Harold, *Curzon: The Last Phase* (London, 1934)

Nicolson, Harold, *Sir Arthur Nicolson, Bart, First Lord Carnock: A Study in the Old Diplomacy* (London, 1930)

Nicolson, Harold, *The Evolution of Diplomatic Method* (London, 1954)

Nish, Ian, *The Anglo-Japanese Alliance: The Diplomacy of Two Island Empires* (London, 1966)

Nish, Ian, *The Origins of the Russian-Japanese War* (London, 1985)

Northedge, F. S., *The Troubled Giant* (London, 1966)

Nove, Alec, *An Economic History of the USSR* (London, 1969)

Pipes, Richard, *The Russian Revolution, 1899–1919* (London, 1992)

Platt, D. C. M., *The Cinderella Service: British Consuls since 1825* (London, 1971)

Pomper, Philip, *Sergei Nechaev* (New Bruswick, New Jersey, 1979)

Ramm, Agatha, *Sir Robert Morier: Envoy and Ambassador in an Age of Imperialism, 1876–1893* (Oxford, 1973)

Robbins, Keith, *Sir Edward Grey: A Biography of Lord Grey of Fallodon* (London, 1971)

Ronaldshay, Earl of, *The Life of Lord Curzon*, 3 vols (London, 1928)

Rothstein, Andrew, *When Britain Invaded Soviet Russia: The Consul Who Rebelled* (London, 1979)

Schapiro, Leonard, *The Communist Party of the Soviet Union* (London, 1970)

Searle, G. R., *The Quest for National Efficiency* (Oxford, 1971)

Sharp, Alan J., 'The Foreign Office in Eclipse', *History*, vol. 61, no. 2 (1976), pp. 198–218

Siegelbaum, Lewis H., *Stakhanovism and the Politics of Productivity in the USSR, 1935–1941* (Cambridge, 1988)

Simms, James Y., 'The Crisis in Russian Agriculture at the End of the Nineteenth Century: A Different View', *Slavic Review*, vol. 36, no. 3 (1977), pp. 377–98

Steiner, Zara, *The Foreign Office and Foreign Policy, 1898–1914* (Cambridge, 1969)

Steiner, Zara, 'The Last Years of the Old Foreign Office, 1898–1905', *Historical Journal*, vol. 6, no. 1 (1963), pp. 59–90

Stites, Richard, *Revolutionary Dreams: Utopian Vision and Experimental Life in the Russian Revolution* (New York, 1989)

Stone, Norman, *The Eastern Front, 1914–1917* (London, 1975)

Swain, Geoffrey, *The Origins of the Russian Civil War* (London, 1996)

Szamuely, Tibor, *The Russian Tradition*, ed. Robert Conquest (London, 1974)

Szeftel, Marc, *The Russian Constitution of April 23 1906* (Brussels, 1976)

Taylor, A. J. P., *The Struggle for Mastery in Europe, 1848–1918* (Oxford, 1957)

Taylor, S. J., *Stalin's Apologist: Walter Duranty, the New York Times's Man in Moscow* (New York, 1994)

Thompson, John, *Russia, Bolshevism and the Versailles Peace* (London, 1966)

Thurston, Robert, 'Fear and Belief in the USSR's "Great Terror": Responses to Arrest, 1935–1939', *Slavic Review*, vol. 45, no. 2 (1986), pp. 213–34

Tillee, Sir John and Gaselee, Stephen, *The Foreign Office* (London, 1933)

Tokmakoff, George, *P. A. Stolypin and the Third Duma: An Appraisal of Three Major Issues* (Washington, DC, 1981)

Ullman, Richard, *Britain and the Russian Civil War* (Princeton, 1968)

Ullman, Richard, *Intervention and the War* (Princeton, 1961)

Ullman, Richard, *The Anglo-Soviet Accord* (Princeton, 1972)

Unterberger, Betty Miller, 'Woodrow Wilson and the Bolsheviks: The "Acid Test" of Soviet-American Relations', *Diplomatic History*, vol. 11, no. 2 (1987), pp. 71–90

Viola, Lynne, *The Best Sons of the Fatherland: Workers in the Vanguard of Soviet Collectivization* (New York, 1987)

Volin, Lazar, *A Century of Russian Agriculture: From Alexander II to Khrushchev* (Cambridge, Massachusetts, 1970)

Walkin, Jacob, *The Rise of Democracy in Pre-Revolutionary Russia* (New York, 1962)

Warth, Robert D., *The Allies and the Russian Revolution* (Durham, North Carolina, 1954)

Warth, Robert D., 'The Arcos Raid and the Anglo-Soviet "Cold War" of the 1920s', *World Affairs Quarterly*, vol. 29, no. 2 (1958), pp. 115–51

Wheeler-Benett, J. W., *Brest-Litovsk: The Forgotten Peace, March 1918* (London, 1938)

White, Stephen, *Britain and the Bolshevik Revolution: A Study in the Politics of Diplomacy, 1920–1924* (London 1979)

Williams, Andrew J., *Labour and Russia: The Attitude of the Labour Party to the USSR, 1924–1934* (Manchester, 1989)

Wilson, Francesca, *Muscovy: Russia through Foreign Eyes, 1753–1900* (London, 1970)

Zelnik, Reginald E, 'Russian Bebels: An Introduction to the Memoirs of the Russian Workers Semen Kanatchikov and Matvei Fisher', *Russian Review*, vol. 35, no. 3 (1977), pp. 377–98

Zeman, Z. A. B., *Germany and the Revolution in Rusia, 1915–1918* (London, 1958)

Zenkovsky, Alexander V., *Stolypin: Russia's Last Great Reformer*, trans. Margaret Pataski (Princeton, 1986)

Index